Goethe and His Publishers

Siegfried Unseld

Goethe

and His Publishers

Translated by Kenneth J. Northcott

THE UNIVERSITY OF CHICAGO PRESS

Chicago and London

SIEGFRIED UNSELD, the publisher of Suhrkamp Verlag in Germany, is the author of *The Author and His Publisher,* also published by the University of Chicago Press.

The University of Chicago Press, Chicago 60637
The University of Chicago Press, Ltd., London
© 1996 by The University of Chicago
All rights reserved. Published 1996
Printed in the United States of America
05 04 03 02 01 00 99 98 97 96   1 2 3 4 5
ISBN: 0-226-84190-1
The publication of this work has been supported
with funds of Inter Nationes, Bonn.
This is an abridged version of the 1993 second, revised edition of *Goethe und seine Verleger,*
© Insel Verlag Frankfurt am Main und Leipzig, 1991.

Library of Congress Cataloging-in-Publication Data

Unseld, Siegfried.
    [Goethe und seine Verleger.   English]
    Goethe and his publishers / Siegfried Unseld ; translated by
Kenneth J. Northcott.
        p.   cm.
    Includes bibliographical references and index.
    ISBN 0-226-84190-1 (alk. paper)
    1. Goethe, Johann Wolfgang von, 1749–1832—Publishers.
2. Publishers and publishing—Germany—History—18th century.
3. Publishers and publishing—Germany—History—19th century.
I. Title.
PT2155.A1U5713   1996
831'.6—dc20
[B]   96-17077

∞ The paper used in this publication meets the
minimum requirements of the American National Standard
for Information Sciences—Permanence of Paper for
Printed Library Materials, ANSI Z39.48-1984.

FOR BURGEL ZEEH
and thus for all those who made
this possible for me

Contents

Preface

IN 1979, THE PLAN matured, analogous to the essays in my book, *The Author and His Publisher,* of working on Goethe and his publishers. At first it was only intended as an essay, which was then expanded into a ceremonial address on the occasion of my receiving an honorary doctorate at the Johann-Wolfgang-Goethe University in Frankfurt. It was only gradually that the studies expanded.

Thus for twelve years I was able to devote my limited, so-called spare, time to this work, mainly during my sojourns in the Buchinger reducing clinic in Überlingen; the euphoria of fasting probably did no harm to the playful seriousness of the book. Admittedly, if I had foreseen or even suspected the difficulties, I would never have embarked on such a bold undertaking as this. Anyone who works *on* Goethe has first to wrestle with him. He will experience two things. The first is that you come upon a detail and want to clarify it, and this opens up a dimension that is worth investigating. My advice to myself was to read Goethe, his poems, his writings, and his letters and not the secondary literature, for this is intimidating and often distorts one's view of the subject. But it would have been presumptuous not to take note of what Goethe experts had studied and revealed, often in a lifetime of work; I have mentioned these works with gratitude and, with their famous example before me, felt myself, like Isaac Newton, to be a dwarf on the shoulders of giants. The second thing you learn is that no one can express the processes and facts, the studies and results, of Goethe's thought and creative processes as well as he himself can. It is senseless to paraphrase him, to explain him in half sentences and sum up his thought processes in one's own concepts. In the introduction to his *Theory of Color* he makes a "special observation": "It is extremely difficult to report on other people's ideas, especially when they approach each other as neighbors, cross and overlay each other. If the reporter goes into great detail he makes people impatient and bored, if he tries to condense he runs the risk of presenting his own ideas as the other person's, if he avoids giving a judgment, the reader is at a loss; if he follows certain maxims, then his presentation is one-sided and leads to contradictions and the whole thing just spontaneously creates something else. Besides this the opinions and views of an important writer are not easily expressed. All theories to which originality can be ascribed are not that easily comprehended, are not that quickly epitomized and systematized.'' It is well then to take Goethe at his word and quote him in his own words even if in so doing we run the risk of excessive quotation.

It was never my intention to write a strictly scholarly work, but nevertheless this one will satisfy sound standards. My whole concern was to present a subjective perspective: A present-day publisher familiar with today's problems of the author-publisher relationship, and thus with experiences that he tries to realize in his work, is here paying attention to Goethe's special dealings with the publishers of his day. Certainly every piece of research on Goethe has to start with the reliable, exegetical reading of the texts. Anyone who works on Goethe will pose questions about his work and his life, about his inner and outer world, and these questions are of necessity linked to the person who poses them and who interprets them from his own point of view. The relationship of an author to his publisher, just like that of a publisher to an author, is complex and complicated and seldom restricted to the manuscript. Studies of such relationships also aim to interpret organically the existence of the writer, his world, his fellow men, the time in which he lives and which reflects his work. This study too must beg for indulgence for many apparent digressions and occasional unavoidable repetitions.

Apart from individual Insel Verlag editions, I mainly used the Artemis edition for my work; later on I included the Hamburg and Berlin editions. The attempt to unify Goethe's textual fabric was based on the Weimar edition. Letters, diaries, and the notes of his amanuensis, Johann Peter Eckermann, are alluded to only by the date. I wish the notes to the text to be, in their independence, like bottles of good wine in the cellar of the book.

"Born to Be a Writer"

ALL HIS LIFE Goethe was skeptical of, and critical towards, the "gloominess of the German book trade." Why was Goethe's relationship to publishers so problematical? Horace assigned the writer to the *genus irritable vatum* ("the easily provoked genus of prophets") and this classification holds good till the present day. But perhaps publishers, too, are problematical natures. They attempt to make the impossible possible, to create and sell that—as Brecht put it in an oxymoron—"consecrated . . . commodity," a book.[1] They attempt to combine spirit and money, soul and commodity, in other words to combine things that are in the general view, on principle, mutually exclusive; what they achieve is, in Theodor Adorno's words, "the paradoxical": "They sell what is unsellable, find success for him who does not seek it, change the alien into the familiar."

Can, must not, people of this sort fall prey to a *déformation professionelle?* It was the writer Friedrich Hebbel who said that it would be easier to walk on the water with Jesus than to walk through life with a publisher.

Is it therefore in the nature of things that Goethe should proclaim his trust in his publisher Johann Friedrich Cotta and then in the thirty-first year of their relationship express the wish that publishers might have their own particular hell? Those publishers! Goethe was always critical of them, skeptical, often unjust and also mistrustful. When Schiller wrote to Goethe in 1802 that it was "really beastly" that these gentlemen "can still demand of us that we promote their works ourselves," Goethe answered, angry at the "whole bunch of riff-raff" to whom he "devoted and swore greater and greater hatred."

Whatever Goethe did he was a writer. He was born to be a writer and he died writing. This was the way in which Thomas Mann interpreted Goethe's last movements—his hand tracing signs in the air—as the expression of a state "in the final blurred dreams" of his consciousness. Goethe had this consciousness of being a writer from the beginning. "Actually I was born to be a writer. Nothing affords me a more pure pleasure than thinking I have written something well." True the "more pure pleasure" was soon joined by resignation, doubt, despair and—at every point in his life—the feeling that he was a slave to the need to write. It was not only the Goethe of the year 1820 who knew "that writing is an incurable disease, and for that reason it is a good idea to resign yourself to it."[2] And this is especially true of the German writer. "A German writer, a German martyr!"[3]

Goethe is the writer pure and simple. He could not exist except by writing. Was he also what we call a successful writer? Could he manage to earn his living by writing?

At the beginning of his career there were two great successes, *Götz von Berlichingen* (1773) and *The Sorrows of Young Werther* (1774). In *Götz* he "had in my own way mirrored forth the symbol of one of the world's important epochs," and he writes about the success of this mirroring later on: "A strange satisfaction is generally felt when a writer felicitously recalls a nation's history for it: men rejoice in the virtues of their ancestors while smiling at their failings which they believe they themselves have long since got rid of. Such a portrayal never fails to meet with sympathy and applause, and in this respect I enjoyed a varied influence."[4] It is scarcely possible to describe the effect of this piece more modestly than with the words "strange satisfaction." The effect of *The Sorrows of Young Werther* was more like a storm. The epidemic frenzy of death that was caused by this youthful work was not without consequences for the author himself. In his autobiography he says: "The effect of this little book was great, nay, immense, and chiefly because it exactly hit the temper of the times. For just as it only requires a small match to blow up an immense mine, so the explosion which followed my publication was mighty because the youthful world had already undermined itself; and the shock was great, because everyone burst forth with all their exravagant demands, unsatisfied passions, and imaginary wrongs."[5] After the two initial successes there was a pause in his literary activity that lasted for the ten years following his entrance into the service of the court in Weimar, years that he sacrificed to "serious things." And it was a long time before he could offer and receive the "final fruits" of his life and his work—his *Works* in the "Complete Edition, supervised by the author himself" (referred to from now on as the "final authorized edition"), sometimes that Cotta, his publisher, from 1802 onwards, would characterize as "a national monument."

Throughout his life Goethe was not a wealthy man, but he was also not poor. What was the financial background of Goethe's life? His relative independence in financial matters came from the estate that Goethe's grandfather, who had lived in Frankfurt from 1687, had accumulated by his mercantile skill. When he died in 1730 he left behind him seventeen sacks of gold and goods to a total value of 89,000 guilders. His son, Johann Caspar, Goethe's father, who had been to the university, was an honorary Imperial Councillor in Frankfurt, but throughout his life he never practiced any profession that brought him in any money. Nevertheless he managed the estate so well that he and his family could not only live decently on the 2,700 guilders in interest and annuities (the city sheriff of the day earned 1,800 guilders a year) but also managed to reduce the capital by only 20,000 guilders to 69,000, an estate that permitted him and after his death his widow to support their son Johann Wolfgang in high style. I know of no other important author who had so firm a financial foundation on which to base his career. Kafka, Brecht, Hesse, Thomas Mann all had to make their own way. In Wetzlar, Johann Christian Kestner, the fiancé and later husband of Charlotte Buff, regarded Goethe as the son of a "rich" man, and another acquaintance referred to Goethe as the only son of a "very rich man, who bore the title of Imperial Councillor and lived on his annuities. His father insisted that he take up a profession, and for that reason he became a Doctor of Laws, and from time to time he plays the advocate—willingly or unwillingly—at which he performs excellently."

At the age of twenty-six, in November 1775, Goethe arrived in Weimar, invited there by Duke Carl August, who expected him to be a friend and adviser, a court official, and a court poet. Things were difficult at the beginning, as we learn from Goethe's letter of 22 January 1776 to his friend Johann Heinrich Merck: "I am now involved in all the business of the court and of politics and shall almost never be able to get away again. My situation is advantageous enough, and the duchies of Weimar and Eisenach are always a scene upon which one can see how suited one is to a world class role. So I am not in a hurry on that account and freedom and sufficiency will be the chief conditions of the new arrangement, even if I am ever in the position to recognize the utter shittiness of this temporal magnificence." But his situation was not as advantageous as all that. To begin with he had to live on the 400 guilders that his father, Johann Caspar, allowed him, grumbling the while, since as a patrician of a Free Imperial City, the friendship of princes and all the courtly sycophancy were anathema to him. The first gift that the duke made to Goethe was in April 1776, six months after his arrival in Weimar, when he put a little garden house on the Ilm at his disposal. In the same month he received Weimar citizenship. In June he entered the service of the state when he joined the duke's council as a privy legation councillor. His annual income as a civil servant rose from 1,200 thalers to 1,400 in 1780, to 1,600 in 1799, and to 1,800 in 1814. As the Saxon thaler was at this time worth about two Frankfurt guilders, his income gradually rose to the equivalent of his father's 2700 guilders per year from interest. From 1815 onwards he received, as the oldest Weimar minister of state, 3,000 guilders a year, a sum that was not increased, as far as we now know, for the rest of his life.[6] Philipp Friedrich Seidel's bookkeeping is the source of our information about Goethe's finances. Seidel was originally in the service of the father, Johann Caspar Goethe. He accompanied the son to Weimar in 1775 and worked there as his servant and secretary until 1788. From him we know that people earned little in Weimar at the time. Charlotte von Stein's husband, Stallmeister (keeper of the stables) von Stein, drew 1,600 thalers; the chamberlains, 1,000; ladies-in-waiting, 300. Herder, as general superintendent and consistory councillor, received 1,100 thalers; the actress Corona Schröter, who was employed by Goethe, received 400 thalers. So Goethe's income was quite respectable but still insufficient for his "somewhat ample way of life." Seidel noted that in 1776 when Goethe was earning 1,200 thalers, his expenditures were 1,411 thalers, and against his income of 1,400 thalers in the years 1780 and 1782 he had expenditures of 2,249 and 2,605 thalers, respectively. Seidel had to warn him repeatedly to make substantial economies. Once, in 1781, he energetically exhorted his master to save, to buy less wine, to acquire fewer books, and above all to save money on postage and use the "travelling post" rather than the more expensive individual messengers, but the warning bore little fruit.

Goethe's financial means were therefore limited, but throughout his whole life he was generous in money matters, although never extravagant. Martin Walser explains the truly minimal payments to his amanuensis, Eckermann, by that young man's attitude as a haut bourgeois; it was not so much that he was paid but rather that he was taken care of.

Introduction

In 1795 Goethe said—on the occasion of a valuation for the payment of a war tax—that he had no possessions. In 1807 his assets were—on his own admission—4,600 thalers, this after thirty-two years of civil service in Weimar.[7] When his mother died in 1808, the estate, although by then it had shrunk, brought him 22,000 guilders or 12,750 thalers in inheritance. The fifty-nine-year-old was not transformed into a wealthy man by this but he could go on living his life in the same way, and no servant now needed to reproach him for drinking too much wine or for excessive use of the post.

All in all, then, Goethe was well-situated materially. From the start he could be relaxed as he negotiated with his publisher, could express his wishes, or make demands that were commensurate with his reputation. And yet: why were his relationships with publishers so problematical, so intricate, complicated, and confusing—and why did they remain so? I shall try to approach this question both from Goethe's angle and from the angle of his publishers. Schiller knew Goethe's attitude: "Liberality towards his publishers is not his cup of tea."

There is also enough testimony to the fact that Goethe could be friendly and objective towards the task confronting publishers, towards booksellers and publishers. He praises his chief publishers, Johann Unger, Georg Joachim Göschen, and Cotta. In his twelfth book of *Poetry and Truth* he writes of a "balance" between the author and his publisher. "Both appeared, depending on how you take it, as patrons and clients. The authors who, irrespective of their talents, were generally respected and revered by the public as highly moral men, had an intellectual rank, and felt themselves rewarded by the success of their labors; the publishers were well satisfied to take second place and enjoyed a considerable profit."[8] But is that really the last word to be said about the relationship of author and publisher? Were the authors sufficiently rewarded by the success of their labors? And is the publisher satisfied just with enjoying a considerable profit? He told Schiller (on 28 April 1798): "what benefits the bookseller also benefits the writer in every sense, anyone who is well paid is read a lot and those are two commendable things." But does this exhaust the relationship of writer and publisher? In order to answer this question, we have to enter into the world of Goethe's relationships with his publishers. True, we do not want to lose ourselves in all the details for, strictly speaking, this would mean examining the publishing history of about seventy individual works and eighteen collected works (including thirteen "original" pirated versions). What were Goethe's relationships to the publishers of his day, what led him to particular publishing houses, what happened in each individual relationship, and why did Goethe change his publishers so frequently, until he finally found *his* publisher in Cotta? Who were these publishers, and how did they view their duties given the conditions of their day? Is the developmental process of Goethe's work and the effect of that work reflected in his communications with publishers? As a publisher who is himself bound up in relationships with authors, I shall look for answers to these questions—from the first anonymous publication to the final edition supervised by the author himself.

Note: The German expression *Ausgabe letzter Hand* is cumbersome to translate into English. It refers to the last edition of an author's works over which he exercised supervision before the edition was sent to the press. This is the sense in which, in the following work, the expression "final authorized edition" is used.—Trans.

First Publications

⚬ℑℭ⚬

"I do not like IN HIS AUTOBIOGRAPHY, *Poetry and Truth,* Goethe
any fuss." tells how a friend of his youth, Ernst Wolfgang
Behrisch, received his poetic productions indulgently
but warned him about the public: "he let me do as I liked," writes Goethe,
"but only on condition that I did not have anything published." As a twenty-
four-year-old, Goethe wrote the words that expressed both a creative credo
and a very early expression of a professional writer's skepticism vis-à-vis the
public: "In fact the beginning and end of all writing is the reproduction of the
world around me by that inner world that lays hold of everything, combines,
re-creates, kneads, and restores it in its own manner, and remains for all
eternity a secret, thank God, that I too will not reveal to the idle onlookers
and windbags. . . . But who creates children for the public. . . . But I beg
you to leave me the people I have put my stamp on, and Mercury and Iris
will not regenerate them."[1]

I do not wish to interpret more fully within the present context this most
important statement on the theme of the creative secret. Goethe's statement
that he is recreating the outer world through the inner one in his own manner
proclaims, even in these early years, the attitude of a writer unconcerned
with effect, who designs his own world in the face of orthodox attitudes,
fixed opinions, fashion, and direction. The young Goethe distanced himself
from "idle onlookers and windbags," the older Goethe from "the riff-raff"
and time and again from his "dear Germans," among whom "the vulgar has
a much greater opportunity of gaining the upper hand than in other nations":
the greatest of Germans always talked about his fellow-countrymen in terms
of a polarity of criticism and contradiction. True, everything was different

when it was a question of genuine readers. As early as January 1773, he could praise "friend public":

The Author

> What would I be
> Without you
> Friend public!
> All my feelings, a monologue,
> All my joy, dumb.

But from the outset, Goethe distanced himself from the anonymous public. On 11 May 1767, he wrote from Leipzig to his sister Cornelia in connection with a drama he had planned about Pharaoh's successors: "I would send it to you, if it were written legibly enough for you to decipher it, or for Horn to copy, but instead I'm sending you a few other productions, but I would prefer them not to be made public, you can show them to good friends but do not give anyone a copy." The fear of there being a copy can only be understood at that time as stemming from Goethe's fear of publicity. So a little while later, on 12 October 1767, he complained to Cornelia that friends had published copies "in cursed . . . weekly periodicals and even used the initials J.W.G. I could have gotten really mad about it," and he goes on, "I would gladly send you 'Annette' [poems addressed to one of his many inamoratas], if I was not afraid that you would copy it. For I did not even want to let anyone see the little book that I have done so much to polish and correct. Up to the present it has had twelve male and two female readers, and that's the end of my public. I do not like any fuss."

"The Accomplices."
Goethe's First
Offering to a
Publisher, Rejected

Only Ian C. Loram out of all the Goethe scholars records the following event. On Monday, 30 September 1765, Goethe left for Leipzig: leaving Frankfurt "with delight," and "I left behind me with indifference the worthy city in which I had been born and bred, as though I wished never to set foot in it again." Although during his three years in Leipzig Goethe studied life more than man—twelve love affairs besides Anna Katherina Schönkopf (the "Annette" of his poems and songs) are mentioned in the biographies, so that *Sturm und Drang* were experienced before it became a literary epoch—he did succeed in writing out *The Accomplices*. He finished a final version in Frankfurt and he offered this in 1769 to the publisher and bookseller Johann Georg Fleischer, who however rejected it out of hand. Doubtless the rejection was a shock for Goethe: "As my dread of the press gradually vanished, I had wished to see my comedy *The Accomplices*—upon which I set some value—published; but I found no publisher inclined in my favor,"[2] he writes in *Poetry and Truth*. Goethe never forgot Fleischer's rejection. Later on, when his essay *An Attempt to Explain the Metamorphosis of Plants* was rejected by the publisher Georg Joachim Göschen, he still remembered the event. Both versions only appeared posthumously. Only the "more decent" version prepared between 1780 and 1783 was accepted by Göschen for inclusion in the second volume of the *Writings* (1787–90). The pastoral play that he had written shortly before—*The Beloved's Mood*—did not appear until 1806 in the first Cotta edition.

In the winter of 1766–67, Goethe prepared "single sheets for theater lovers." They contained, anonymously, his poems to the actresses Corona Schröter and Caroline Schulze. Not a single copy of these prints is preserved.

At this time, Goethe was extremely productive. If all the manuscripts had been preserved, they would have filled several volumes of letters, dramas, and poems. But Goethe destroyed practically everything. Hundreds of poems were lost, he told Eckermann later. When a professor of literature once criticized poems that Goethe had read aloud, he did not write another poem for six months, so easily was the young poet influenced.

Behrisch, his confidant, knew of Goethe's relationships with the "girls," especially with Kätchen Schönkopf, the landlord's daughter whom Goethe met in April 1766 and on whom he now showered poems and songs. These poems and songs to "Annette" were collected by Goethe and arranged in order but Behrisch advised against publishing them; but since it was his (Behrisch's) great pleasure to occupy himself seriously with farcical things and to follow one particular crazy idea to the bitter end—as Goethe tells us in *Poetry and Truth*—Goethe agreed that Behrisch should copy the poems and make them into a single volume; this happened very gradually and this "enterprise provided an opportunity for the greatest possible amusement." Goethe had already sent his sister a little foretaste with six poems (also copied by Behrisch in May 1767). Before the work went to the press on 13 February 1769, he wrote, "It is my misfortune to be so reckless and look at everything from its good side. The fact that you looked at my poems from the bad side is my fault. Throw them into the fire and don't even glance at them when they're published, but do remain favorably disposed towards me. Between ourselves, I am one of those patient poets, if you don't like the poem then we'll write another."[3]

There is here already a hint of Goethe's fundamental aesthetic outlook; "to change what pleased me or tormented me, or occupied me in some other way, into a picture or a poem and so come to terms with myself" was how he characterized his lyrical impulse in *Poetry and Truth.* He constantly discovered minor as well as "significant" opportunities for turning the "general, the inner, the higher" that "the poet has in mind" into an image or a symbol. Goethe's whole lyric oeuvre exists in a tensional relationship between "occasion" and "significance," between the simple occasional poem and its artful arrangement. "All my poems are occasional poems," Goethe said to Eckermann in 1823, "they are inspired by reality and that is their basis. I set no store by poems that are conjured out of thin air." Goethe only included three of his early poems (pre-1769) in the eighth volume of the Göschen edition in 1789. That was how strict the forty-year-old Goethe was! Even the "First Weimar Collection of Poems" of 1778, collected for Charlotte von Stein, only circulated as a quarto volume with twenty-eight poems copied out in Goethe's own hand. It was not until 1812, when Goethe was sixty-three, that a separate volume of poems—not part of a collected works—appeared and this only as the title edition of volume 1 of the first Cotta edition. In Leipzig, Goethe got to know Bernhard Christoph Breitkopf, who was already celebrated as a music publisher, whose home was famous for its hospitality, and who had a personal library of 20,000 volumes. Breitkopf founded the publishing dynasty that bore his name. He had arrived in Leipzig as a poor printer's journeyman and laid the foundations of the music publishing company that his son Johann Gottlob Immanuel developed into worldwide significance. Goethe struck up a deep friendship with Breitkopf's eldest son, Bernhard Theodor, who knew the poems that Goethe wrote at this time and set them to music. They were performed in the Breitkopf home, often by the "beautiful Corona" (Schröter). Bernhard Breitkopf pressed Goethe to publish the songs that had been set to music. We owe him a debt of gratitude for without this pressure many a song—like the ones that were not set to music—would certainly have been lost. But Goethe was not mentioned as the author—he still seemed to want to avoid publicity. *New Songs Set to Melodies by Bernhard Theodor Breitkopf,* Leipzig, published by Bernhard

Christoph Breitkopf and Son, 1770 (the so-called Leipzig Songbook), was to be found at the Michaelmas fair in 1769. The volume contains 43 pages, and on the main title page there is a vignette of a rose with blossoms and leaves. No author was mentioned and yet how Goethe clung to this, his first, publication! In October 1769 he sent the book to the friend of his youth, Ernst Theodor Langer: "Here then are my songs . . . the story of my heart in little paintings. If ever poems were not written according to Batteux's principle,[4] then these are they, not a spot of imitation, everything Nature. And for this reason they will always be a monument to my own youth and to that of my friends." Everything Nature. The story of the heart. If the Annette poems still seemed a little artificial and narrow (Behrisch's delicate hand suited them well) then these were songs "without art or effort" ("let him sing them who wants to") although they still owed much to the formal treasures of the rococo, they were freer in tone, with greater feeling. Scholars claim to have recognized two themes, the theme of death and the loss of naiveté. From my point of view these poems are more the expression of the praise of "fickleness"; they exist in a tension between freedom and commitment, between pleasure and duty. It is tenderness, not duty, that should bind. "You young man / you young woman, Do not live too faithfully, too exactly / In narrow marriage." First play the "old game of youth" and don't fall too early into the "trap," going to the "fireside of marriage." "The loyal fox without the tail." (Aesop's fable: The fox who lost his tail in a trap wants to conceal the shame of his loss by persuading all the other foxes to cut off the troublesome thing.) "That's a warning about the trap." The turn towards nature contrasts with social convention; Goethe hated all pressure. We can recognize a clear attack upon the dominant poetics of the day in this first published work that must have appeared in a very small edition. The next thing to be published was the work he wrote, in Latin, for his licentiate, *Positiones juris,* printed by Johann Heinrich Heitz in Strassburg in 1771.[5] The law faculty in Strassburg had rejected his dissertation, *De Legislatoribus,* "ex capite religionis et prudentiae" and had forbidden its publication because it dissented from Christian doctrine. He was, however, allowed to discuss his fifty-six theses in public so as to gain his licentiate in law. In Frankfurt, where he returned in August 1771, he took the title of "Dr. jur." but he was only allowed to use this title officially when the University of Jena gave him an honorary doctorate in all faculties in 1825 (by then at the latest Goethe had received the honors of all honorary doctorates for all times!).

Three further writings appeared, also anonymously, in November 1772: *On German Architecture* (published privately by his Darmstadt friend Johann Heinrich Merck and printed by the Eichenberg booksellers in Frankfurt am Main whose owner was councillor Johann Konrad Deine—there were reprintings in 1773), and two theological pamphlets published by the firm of the Eichenberg heirs. The first pamphlet (January 1773), *The Letter of the Pastor at *** to the New Pastor at ****, contains the fictional note "from the French." The second, of March 1773, *Two Important and Till Now Undiscussed Biblical Questions, Answered Fundamentally for the First Time,* introduced a fictional Swabian country pastor as the author, and the place of publication was also fictional, "Lindau on Lake Constance" (both writings were also printed by Deinet in Frankfurt; *The Letter of the Pastor* in further individual printings till 1775).

Has ever an important author been launched so hesitatingly, so modestly, denying his identity and renouncing early fame? In his biography, Richard Friedenthal talks of Goethe's tendency to cloak himself in mystery and to disguise himself. Ian C. Loram sees inconsistencies and concludes, simplifying somewhat, "He simply did not know his own mind." I believe on the other hand that Goethe was acting quite consciously by waiting at first to see how his talent, his "calling," developed. He was not yet clear as to whether he should choose writing, painting, or the law as his profession. He did not yet know what would become of him, a stormy lover, a lawyer, an artist, a poet. He wanted to be free. He wanted to solve his life's problems playfully. What is absolutely clear is that he wanted to make no commitment, either to the idea of a career, or to women, that is, neither to Käthchen Schönkopf nor to Friederike Brion. On the other hand, he probably felt that he did not create his poetry, but rather that it created him, formed him, molded him. At that time he must have believed that his works were not worthy of bearing the name of an author—thus his flight into silence, into fiction, into anonymity. But there was something else that was essential to the young Goethe. He loved what he had written, loved the process of publication in which the text was objectified and transmitted to the readers who were of such importance to him. But he did not like the book as a chattel. In *Poetry and Truth* we read, "My earlier pleasure in communicating these things only through readings was renewed but to exchange them for money seemed hateful to me." The fact that he later revised his attitude does not change the fact that in his early years this was a determining factor in his life.

Certainly this attitude was also marked by some general—and known—facts concerned with the history of bookselling. It was only in the second half of the eighteenth century that authors changed their attitude towards the economic value of their products, because it was at this time that a decisive change in the market for books took place. The exchange trade—book for book—was replaced by the so-called net or cash trade (books in exchange for money).[6] This must also have played a role in Goethe's attitude towards his own intellectual products.

There is an established tradition of anonymous, or pseudonymous publishing: besides reasons of censorship—the writer could express himself more freely if he remained anonymous—there was above all the desire to document any *non*professional literary activity. Writing as a means of earning one's living was still looked upon as repellent to a man of standing and a man of the world—possibly even damaging to his profession: most authors saw themselves entirely as leisure and spare-time writers and Goethe, the lawyer, may at first have viewed his writing in this light.

Above and beyond this, middle-class writers were not viewed favorably by the nobility or the authorities: literary activity was often regarded as a hindrance to a career in the civil service. "The public placement of a name on title pages only became the rule towards the end of the eighteenth century, when the fame of German literature, promoted by the example of the German classics, had established itself on an international level."[7]

Goethe's First Larger Work, "Götz," Appears Anonymously as a Private Publishing Venture   In 1771, in Strassburg, Goethe got to know Wilhelm Friedrich Pistorius's *Lebens-Beschreibung Hernn Gözens von Berlichingen, Zugennant mit der Eisernen Hand* ("The Biography of Götz von Berlichingen, known as *Ironhand*") that had appeared forty years earlier in Nuremberg. The subject was of immediate interest to him. Looking back, he notes in *Poetry and Truth,* "If you consider exactly what was missing in German literature, then it was content, a national content; there was never a lack of talents." For his legal studies Goethe had read the handbook by Johann Phillip Datt that had appeared in 1698, *Volumen rerum Germanicarum novum sive de pace imperii publica libri V* ("A new collection of Germanic cases, relating to the public peace of the Empire, in five books"). Pistorius, whose 1731 biography of Götz was based on Datt, was Goethe's most important source. Herder had drawn Goethe's attention to an article by Justus Moser on the rule of force, which impressed Goethe. Moser characterizes the epoch of the rule of force as a period when "our nation had shown the greatest sense of honor, the greatest physical virtue and its own national greatness."[8] For Goethe this closed a circle of motifs, "the national," the juridical—that led into the arena of national honor—and a new concept by which history was to be understood apart from the essence of the immediate time. Herder was also able to fan Goethe's knowledge of Shakespeare's dramas into a passion. Goethe, who returned to Frankfurt in August 1771, made a speech on the occasion of Shakespeare's name day, October 14, that contains the program for the *Götz* drama he was now writing.

In *Poetry and Truth,* Goethe relates the stages of its genesis. Since these are so typical of all of his literary activity, I give them here in full. He had discussed the plan with his sister Cornelia, "in great detail . . . and I renewed this discussion so often without ever getting on with the work that she finally became impatient and with a benevolent urgency asked me not always to be indulging myself with words in thin air but finally to set down on paper what was so much on my mind. Spurred on thus to decisive action, I began writing one morning without having previously established a scheme or a plan. I wrote the first scenes and in the evening they were read to Cornelia. She approved highly of them, but only conditionally, as she doubted whether I would continue in the same fashion, indeed she expressed a disbelief in my persistence. This piqued me all the more, I continued the next day and similarly on the third; hope grew as each day's work was reported, and for me too everything grew step by step more lively as the material became more and more a part of me, and thus I was continuously engaged in the work I was pursuing without looking backwards, or to the right or the left, and in about six weeks I had the pleasure of seeing the manuscript bound."

Goethe developed a real passion in these weeks. In November 1771, he wrote, "You know me so well, and yet I will bet you cannot guess why I have not written. It is a passion, a completely unexpected passion: you know how something like this can throw me into such a whirl that I forget the sun, the moon and even the dear stars. . . . My whole genius lies in an undertaking where Homer, Shakespeare, and everything are forgotten. I am dramatizing the story of one of the noblest Germans, saving the memory of a good man, and the amount of work it costs me is really a true pastime for me."[9]

First Publications

The History of Gottfried von Berlichingen with the Iron Hand. Dramatized. There is one manuscript of this work and it is written with such care that it is a fair copy of the text; today it is in the Goethe-Schiller archives in Weimar. A copy of this first version was sent to Herder by Goethe at the beginning of 1772. Some of the original material was changed; whereas the historical Götz sits in his castle writing his report with his left hand, Goethe has him die a heroic death, his iron right hand pointing to the future: "Freedom! Freedom!" And those around him reply, "Noble, noble man. Woe to the century that rejected you. Woe to your successors who fail to recognize you." The story is unquestionably influenced by Shakespeare. The order of scenes in *Sturm und Drang* drama had a great influence on twentieth-century drama and was a strong influence on Brecht's theory of epic theater. When Goethe sent the manuscript to Herder, who was to give his critical reaction, he mentioned that it was only to be regarded as a sketch and not as a definitive text: "As the result of my hermit's existence here, you are getting a sketch that has been, it is true, drawn with a brush on canvas and is even somewhat fully realized in some places, but which still remains nothing more than a sketch." It is precisely his work on this play that makes it clear that Goethe regards the creative process as "work in progress," as a constant fashioning and refashioning, and this is in complete accord with his later theory of evolution.

During these weeks and months Goethe did not think that there was a possibility of the work's being published. Of course the manuscript attracted attention, and young people in Wetzlar with whom Goethe was acquainted through his work at the Imperial Supreme Court called him jokingly *Götz the Honorable.* It was certainly the mood in Wetzlar that inspired Goethe to rewrite the play. "I am now working on an imposing piece of work for publication."[10]

From November to December 1772 he was in Darmstadt visiting his friend Merck, now the minister of war at the court of the Hessian landgravine Caroline, and Merck became an important stimulus for him. Goethe's was a genius that strove to express artistic truth but it also consisted among other things in the fact that at every phase of his life he found the right person to make possible his life "as a work of art," whether teacher, beloved, patron, coworker, mediator—or publisher, and in this too Bertolt Brecht was not unlike him. Merck was born on 11 April 1741 in Darmstadt and committed suicide in 1791. An early visitor in the house of Goethe's parents, he was known there jokingly as "Mephistopheles." Goethe memorialized him in *Poetry and Truth* as "this strange man who had a great influence on my life." "There lay in his character a strange disparity; by nature a good, noble, reliable man, he had grown bitter towards the world and allowed this melancholy trait to dominate him to such an extent that he felt an insurmountable inclination to be a rascal and a rogue." There is no exhaustive account of Merck's relationship with Goethe. He never restrained his criticism; after reading Goethe's early tragedy *Clavigo* (1774), he said, "You mustn't write such piffle for me again, the others are also capable of that." Goethe quotes the statement in *Poetry and Truth* and adds that "Mephistopheles Merck" did do him some harm after all, because he could easily have written a dozen such plays at the time, of which three or four might have survived. Yet, as always, Merck, who suffered from the fact that he himself was not active creatively, recognized the creative quality in other people. He wrote to his wife, "I am really beginning to love Goethe. He is a person for whom, like few others, I have a place in my heart." He saw that in his *Götz* the twenty-four-year-old Goethe had his finger on the pulse of the time. People liked discoveries; Lessing had tried to rescue what had disappeared, and the Middle Ages, the late Middle Ages in particular, were very attractive. There was great lack of freedom at the time and thus the medieval rule of force had a special symbolic significance for the *Sturm und Drang*. In his article Justus Moser had remarked, "so every connoisseur has to admire the rule of force in the twelfth and thirteenth century as a work of art of the first order and it is right that our nation study this great period." Merck pushed for the completion of the rewriting. "The diapers dry if they are hung out in good time" was his motto, according to *Poetry and Truth*.

But Goethe, presumably thinking of his first rejection, was not to offer the text to a publisher; he wished to publish it anonymously. It was thus that the two friends hit upon the idea of private publication, and so in June (or July) 1773 Goethe's first longer work appeared, entitled *Götz von Berlichingen mit der eisernen Hand,* "A Play, 1773." Anonymous, without place of publication, and presumably in an edition of five hundred copies.

The printed text was the second version of the Götz material and no manuscript of it has been preserved. After this he only tried private publication once more. He handed over the second "rightful edition" of *Götz* to the bookseller Deinet in the publishing house of the Eichenberger Heirs.

Besides the certainly inadequate marketing strategy of the private press undertaking, another obstacle emerged as something that was far more restrictive; what many people have described as the greatest intellectual evil of the time appeared in the same year, a pirated printing, an unauthorized edition of *Götz*. One pirate and, immediately afterwards, a second seized hold of the originals and published two pirated versions without mentioning place of publication or author. In 1823 Goethe planned to publish the first version in the final authorized edition of his works. To get it ready for the press he had his servant Friedrich Krause make a copy of his manuscript of the *History of Gottfried* but this has not been preserved. The first version of the *History of Gottfried von Berlichingen* thus only appeared in 1832/33 in the final authorized edition (in volume 42, as volume 2 of the posthumous works).

Even if Goethe was, for the most part, protected from the censorship requirements of the eighteenth and nineteenth century that severely impaired the literary freedom of other authors, the effects of censorship can be seen in his work in subtle forms. The fact that he reworked the first version of *Götz* is presumably because of the censorship, in this case a form of self-censorship. The printing of 1773 represents a smoothing out of the 1771 manuscript. "Even the scenic device of the window that has to be smashed can be seen as a precautionary measure against the censor; the obscenity that Götz utters can thus be lost in the noise or swallowed behind the window."[11] In an epistolary poem to his friend F. W. Gotter, Goethe himself mentioned self-censorship and possible interventions by the censor.

The undertaking of private publication, whereby Goethe paid the costs of paper and Merck the costs of printing, was not a particular pleasure for either of them. Goethe was angry, Merck was staying in St. Petersburg and paid little attention to sales. On 10 July 1773, Goethe wrote to Heinrich Christian Boie, the publisher of the *Göttinger Musenalmanach,* a poetical annual, "I am put to the trouble of dealing with the thing, while Merck is away, what am I to do, I am afraid that if I don't do anything the whole enterprise will die of a stroke." Goethe set his friends in motion; they were asked to buy copies or to put them in the hands of booksellers. Goethe himself had to borrow money to pay back the debts that had accrued. He wrote to Kestner in the middle of July 1773, "I'm not suited to the trade of bookseller." As far as I am concerned this sums up Goethe's private publishing enterprise.

Goethe's attempt at private publication was, as is well known, not an isolated undertaking at that time. It rested—as was the case with other authors—on the fundamentally strained relationship that existed in the second half of the eighteenth century between author and publisher. The reproach made to the publisher was that the level of his profits was by no means proportionate to the small fees that the author received. The first result of this was the establishment of the profession of "independent writer," and this affected the authors of belles lettres especially, for it was precisely this group that had—for the most diverse reasons not the least of which was lack of self confidence—published their works without fee or in return for only a small sum of money. Goethe himself refers to these relationships when in *Poetry and Truth* he writes, "For the book trade in the previous period had more to do with important scientific books, from the different faculties with stock works for which a moderate remuneration was paid. But the production of poetical works was looked upon as something sacred and, in their case, the acceptance or increase of any remuneration would have been regarded almost as simony. Authors and publishers stood in the strangest reciprocal relationship. Both appeared, depending on how you take it, as patrons and clients. The authors who, irrespective of their talent, were generally respected and revered by the public as highly moral men, had an intellectual rank and felt themselves rewarded by the success of their labors: the publishers were well satisfied with second place and enjoyed a considerable profit. But now opulence again set the rich bookseller above the poor poet and thus everything was most perfectly balanced. Magnanimity and gratitude were not infrequent on either side. The publisher Breitkopf and the author Gottsched lived all their lives as in the same house. Stinginess and meanness, especially that of piracy, were not yet in vogue."

Nevertheless, a general commotion had arisen among the German authors. They compared their own very moderate, if not poor, condition with the wealth of the eminent booksellers: in what straitened domestic circumstances a universally esteemed German poet had to continue to struggle if he did not make his life comfortable by pursuing some other calling. Even the mediocre and lesser minds felt a strong desire to see their situation improved—to make themselves free of publishers.[12]

The authors' criticism of the established book trade became an all-embracing movement in the seventies and eighties of the eighteenth century. People took up the writer Friedrich Klopstock's idea of a republic of letters that—in a free exchange of thought and book—was to be free of the traditional book trade.

In principle it was a typical *Sturm und Drang* movement that was expressing itself here; it failed less because of the conditions of production than because of the logistics of distribution. It was only after a series of failed attempts to realize the idea that time taught them that something impossible was being attempted.

First of all it was a only a few friends who knew the text of the *History of Gottfried* through copies that had been sent them. Private publication also only reached a few readers. Goethe had not considered the possibility of a production of *Götz* either in the case of the first "dramatized" version or in the case of the second, "the play-version." He was therefore surprised that a year after the appearance of the play in his private publication two of the most important theaters in Germany dared to put on a production. The premiere took place on 14 April 1774 and the play was performed sixteen times.

On 22 September 1804 the most recent stage version was presented at the Weimar theater; the music was by Carl Friedrich Zelter and the premiere lasted for six hours. Later performances were cut, and Goethe produced it several times in the ensuing years.

The effect of *Götz von Berlichingen* was strange. On the one hand the manuscript—and the privately published—version had reached only a few readers; on the other hand the reaction of the intellectual public after the performances was absolutely tempestuous. The younger literary generation saw the realization of a new aesthetics in the novelty of the material and in the rejection of everything that had been canonized by classical and French drama. There were the critics, first and foremost Frederick the Great, who characterized the play in his work *De la littérature allemande* as "a detestable imitation of those bad English plays." Justus Moser in his treatise *On German Language and Literature* of 1781 stresses the play's national significance and rejects Frederick the Great's negative judgment.

Goethe had set the ball rolling with *Götz*. The *Sturm und Drang* had begun as an epoch. The most important successors were Schiller's *Robbers* in 1781 and a host of knightly dramas by a number of authors.

These numerous imitations can be explained by the growing interest in the Middle Ages which increased even more in the Romantic movement. Goethe writes in *Wilhelm Meister's Apprenticeship,* "The armored knights . . . were received with great applause . . . everyone was aroused by the fire of the noblest national spirit. How pleased German society was to find poetic delight on its own turf."

Chapter One

This interest was sustained until the end of the nineteenth century. Gerhart Hauptmann wrote *Florian Geyer,* a knight's tragedy, with the example of *Götz* in mind. Walter Scott translated *Götz von Berlichingen* into English in 1799, and was inspired by it to write his historical novels and epics.

Thus the effect of Goethe's drama was manifold. At first the book drew little attention, but after the productions it exerted a massive intellectual effect that once again confirmed the rank and reputation of the author, Goethe.

Clavigo, Werther   In *Poetry and Truth* Goethe tells us how, on his sister Cornelia's wedding day, 1 November 1773, he received a letter from a Leipzig bookseller, Christian Friedrich Weygand, who had just moved his business from Helmstedt, where it had been established in 1739, to Leipzig, where he hoped to establish its reputation by publishing the work of young and unknown authors. He asked Goethe for a manuscript. Goethe's memory plays him false when he writes that *Werther* had just been completed and that he sent the manuscript to Weygand; *Werther* was not begun until February 1774 and was completed in April of that year. In May 1774 he finished *Clavigo,* having committed it to paper in eight days. It was the first play of his that did justice to the stage—if you are not a dramatist when young, you are never one! Since he had had enough of private publishing he sent the manuscript, the first piece of writing that he put his name to, to Weygand. "If I mention my name, then I mention my whole self," was what he had written to Käthchen Schönkopf from Frankfurt on 23 January 1770. "*Clavigo,* a Tragedy by Göthe, Leipzig, the Weygand Bookshop, 1774" appeared in July 1774, to be followed by several pirated versions and subsequent editions. A short time after this he published, also with Weygand and listing both Leipzig and Frankfurt as places of publication, the *Newly Published Politico-Moral Puppet Play.* This too went through several reprintings.

We know little about Goethe's relationship to Weygand, his letters to him have disappeared. Yet his experiences with him cannot have been all that bad, for Goethe entrusted him with *Werther.* A rumor that *Werther* was first offered to a Frankfurt publisher and that he rejected it cannot be substantiated.

Weygand received the manuscript of *Werther* in May 1774. Goethe received the first three pre-publication copies on 19 September; he reacted enthusiastically to them and "circulated" them. The work appeared at the Michaelmas fair. "It's done, it has been published." *"The Sorrows of Young Werther.* Part One, Part Two, Part Three, Leipzig, published by Weygand, bookseller, 1774, 224 pages." A number of different reprints, some of which corrected the typographical errors of the first edition (though of course others then appeared) quickly appeared. This work, too, appeared anonymously, but in the storm that it loosed the name of the author broke through the anonymity. The whole world soon knew who the author was. The success was enormous—there had been nothing like it before—and on a number of different levels. In *Werther,* Goethe had created a work that had an effect on the whole of Europe, a work of world rank. The fact that the effect was immediate is very unusual, perhaps unique, in the whole history of the influence of great literary works. And we know too that there are few works that have been written in the last two hundred years that still move the reader today in the same way. It is still possible today to reconstruct the depths to which the author touched the nerve of his generation in this work. The poetic principle of the work, the particular epic perspective of the narrator, certainly contributes to this: Werther alone talks. There was already a tradition of the epistolary novel as a genre. Goethe made decisive changes in the model—and they were successful: he rejected multiple perspectives, he was less concerned with the authentication of the happening, with the description of facts, than with communicating to the reader the inner story of a soul in such a way that he, the reader, could sympathetically follow the same path as the hero. This purity of epic perspective (in our own century it is presented with the utmost clarity in the works of Kafka), the principle of seeing the external as the expression of the internal, understanding literary form as the cognitive parallel to the content: this is what determines the rank of a literary work.

"This book was probably the greatest literary success of all time," was Walter Benjamin's verdict in 1928 in the article on Goethe that he wrote for the Great Russian Encyclopedia. "It was here that Goethe perfected the model of the author of genius. If, that is to say, the great author from the very beginning makes a public event out of his inner world, makes the questions of his time totally into questions of his own world of thought and experience, in his youthful works Goethe represents this type of author to a state of perfection that had never before been achieved."[13] A Werther fashion grew up, a Werther fever, a Werther epidemic, a longing for suicide; there were porcelain figures of Werther and an *eau de Werther.* The appearance of the book gave rise to endless public pronouncements and reactions, an avalanche of secondary literature both for and against, pamphlets, parodies, imitations.[14] And the pirated versions, a sure indication of success, saw to it that the little volume reached the greatest possible number of readers. All at once, and to some extent overnight—and this was now clearly reminiscent of the case of *Götz*—Goethe had moved to the head of a new literary movement. He became the leader of the *Sturm und Drang,* a movement that Klopstock's religious epic *Messias* regarded as admirable, that Lessing as a critic valued very highly, that was praised by Herder with his interest in old Germanic things and that was even taken up enthusiastically in Christoph Martin Wieland's works. The movement bore on its shield slogans that called for a struggle for political freedom, for the freedom of the individual in society, for the removal of class barriers, and for the right to love. Shakespeare became the shining example, replacing the French. Goethe had revered him in his hymnic speech *For Shakespeare's Day* in 1771. The young authors, mostly twenty to thirty years old, now saw in Goethe *the* author of their generation; his language, his vital German, as powerful as it was full of feeling, became the expression of the longings of a whole intellectual generation. Many of those who sympathized with the *Sturm und Drang* movement were able to identify with the figure of Werther, the youth whose awe in the face of consciousness and whose fierceness of feeling foundered on the taboos of a "polished nation."

The inspired author was not afraid to make his private experiences public or to judge public events from the point of view of his private experiences. But beyond the interrelation of the individual and the general, does he provoke questions about his time, the movements of his day, the moods of his time? I am convinced that this did happen in the case of *Werther.* Unfortunately I find I cannot agree with those critics who assert that "It was not Werther who aroused sentimentality, he merely gave it form," and who conclude that "at the end of the decade we can state that no one any longer reads the work whose author everyone is talking about."[15] Writers and their relationship to the works of other contemporary authors are a special case, and the other distinctive feature is the unique situation of Weimar. It is possible that people in Weimar talked only about Goethe and less about his works, but what was the situation in Jena, in Frankfurt, and the other "Goethe places"? And probably the most important argument of all for the influence of *Werther:* the book started movements abroad as well—the large number of translations bear witness to this. The first French translation appeared as early as the beginning of 1775 and within three years there were five further translations into French. In 1779 it was translated into English and in 1781 into Italian; by 1788 there was a Russian edition. For more than half a century translations succeeded the German edition. I am convinced that in the case of *Werther* the author's personal worlds of thought and experience had an immediate effect upon their time.

This is also made clear by the intensity of the praise and censure meted out by contemporaries. On 30 January 1775, the horrified city councillors of Leipzig forbade the sale of the book on pain of a fine of 10 thalers; the ban was never lifted. The theological faculty of the University of Leipzig also forbade people to read it, the theologians seeing in the text an unauthorized recognition of suicide. One year later, the Copenhagen magistracy banned the Danish edition, its distribution was forbidden in Vienna, and the bishop of Milan made the, certainly, vain attempt to prevent people reading the Italian translation by buying up copies of the work. The Hamburg canon, Christian Ziegra, saw in *Werther* a "damnable piece of writing," a "Satanic bait." One further point of view seems important to me: Goethe had for the first time won over a large public. *Götz* did not have a very great effect on the public, but its author had been able to reach many individual readers. Now the public was there, and Goethe's friends and acquaintances recognized the significance of the work and declared their faith in it. Christian Garve, a moral philosopher and professor in Leipzig, asserted "I have read *Werther* . . . our fatherland will have to look for many more ripe and palatable fruits from such an author."[16] Wieland, too, proved to be "cured radically of all ill humor towards Goethe, this remarkable and great mortal." A remark by Heinrich Wilhelm von Gerstenberg—who was in the Danish army and was also himself a *Sturm und Drang* writer, an admirer of Shakespeare and one of Goethe's sporadic correspondents—is revealing in this context. Goethe had written to him on 18 October 1773, "My greatest wish has always been to be linked with the good people of my age, but this soon becomes so sour that one is glad to crawl back into oneself." Gerstenberg replied in January 1774 from Copenhagen, "Carry on, you German character you, as you have started. The praise you are getting from all sides gives me the courage to hope that you are the man to create in Germany a public that consists of Germans." Thanks to *Werther* Goethe had found a public that consisted of Germans, but they had to wait a long time until, in 1797,

Goethe published another work pregnant with a public—*Hermann und Dorothea.*

Against his will Goethe was for the whole of his life addressed as the author of *Werther.* Only later did he become the author of *Faust,* then the "Olympian" and then the "prince of the intellect." But that first label did bring him his own personal triumphs; Napoleon, who had read *Werther* several times, referred to the work in his conversation with Goethe. Small wonder that, with a success of this magnitude, edition followed upon edition. The publishing history of *Werther* is correspondingly complicated.

As early as 1775 Weygand had arranged for three further printings, a double printing of the original (which was followed by another double printing), two reprints with the fictitious place of publication as "Freystadt," then in 1777 one with the place name "Wahlheim." In spite of the ban by the Leipzig city council, the second "genuine edition" was published by Weygand at the beginning of 1775. Pirates took over the work within a year of its publication, and by 1787 there were *twenty* pirated versions! Probably because he was impressed by these unauthorized editions, Weygand did not reprint the original version for ten years. It was not until the year 1787 that he came out with a new edition and this was an amalgam of the first and second versions. This is incomprehensible since, with such rapid sales in the early years, the publisher must have recovered his costs. Fifty years later, on the occasion of the *Werther* jubilee in 1824, the then owner of the Weygand bookstore, Johann Christoph Jasper, came up with the idea of publishing a jubilee edition: he asked Goethe for additions or changes, or at least for a few words of introduction.

In a letter to Jasper on 22 May 1825 Goethe declared that he was prepared to write the introduction in exchange for an honorarium of "fifty full weight (Austrian) ducats" and twenty-four free copies (some bound); he demanded in addition that the copies should be "neatly and attractively bound, as they know how to do it in Leipzig." With this as a stimulus, Goethe read his "creation" once more and was shattered: what he had once written and recently experienced were concentrated for him in the poem "To Werther." "It is as though you were living in the early morning," but trouble and parting are unavoidable, and "parting is death." He placed this poem as a foreword to the jubilee edition and soon thereafter published it together with two other poems, "Elegy" and "Reconciliation," as the *Trilogy of Passion.* In the closing lines (that are also linked to the motto of "Elegy") he conjures up once more, as he had done in *Tasso,* the function of writing as a form of salvation: "Embroiled in such torments half indebted / May God give him strength to say what he is suffering."

The jubilee edition, postdated to 1825, appeared in 1824 as "*The Sorrows of Young Werther.* New edition, with an introduction by the author." Goethe liked the edition, which was embellished with an engraving on the title-page, a portrait of Goethe by Schule, and he liked giving it away as a gift. We are talking here of a new edition of the mixed edition put out by Weygand in 1787. From the time of the appearance of the 1825 edition the rights of the work belonged to Weygand and his legal successors, the firm of Gebhardt and Reisland; from 1838 onwards they regarded *Werther* as their property and always contrived to maintain this position in the face of opposition from later publishers of Goethe's works: even Cotta could not get hold of the rights to a separate edition; *Werther* was only published by Cotta in the final authorized edition.

We know scarcely anything about payments made for *Werther.* They were certainly not large. We can deduce this from two statements. Goethe wrote to a friend on 23 December 1774, two months after the appearance of *Werther,* "I simply cannot think what one gets for one's works. And yet the booksellers are probably also not at fault. My authorship has not yet put much fat into my soup and it will not and should not." Nevertheless the man who looks back in *Poetry and Truth* maintains that he is on the whole satisfied, because his royalty was not totally eaten up by the debts that he was forced to incur with *Götz.* Furthermore, in the weeks and months after the extraordinary attention that his book aroused, Goethe did not worry about his existence. He lived his success, he enjoyed the recognition of his genius. "I know of no one in the whole history of learning, who was so rounded and full of his native genius at such an early age as he was. There is no resisting: he carries everything along with him," observed a fellow author in 1774. Another German poet called him "The German Shakespeare."[17]

Old friends and new ones came to Frankfurt: Johann Caspar Lavater, with whom Goethe had made a trip on the Rhine, arranged for his portrait to be painted in Bad Ems. He went to Bensberg, to Darmstadt, he lived, wrote, painted "just like Rembrandt," and he also wrote the poems "An Schwager Kronos" and "Prometheus." He became engaged to Anna Elisabeth ("Lili") Schönemann—"new love, new life"—and traveled through Switzerland wearing a Werther costume. Then he again broke off his engagement, which was just one more stormy episode in his more than thirty-year self-defense against a permanent marriage bond. These were restless days, full of the vagaries of youth, as he fell from one "confusion" into another. He was afraid that he was wasting his "time and his talent." He confessed in October 1775 that the previous nine months had been "the most absent-minded, the most confused, the most complete, the fullest, emptiest, most powerful and the silliest" that he had ever spent in his whole life. He took the separation from Lili "very hard . . . and so I decided once more to run away."[18] He notes in *Poetry and Truth* that he wanted to go away, he had to go away, "away from suffocation" into "the free world."

For him the free world was Italy. It was for Italy that he set out, going by coach to Heidelberg, when the duke's coach, also en route to Italy, picked him up on 3 November 1775; he then turned round and went back to Weimar. He arrived in Weimar on 7 November and received an "enthusiastic reception." He struck up a friendship with the duke, Carl August, his wife Luise, the dowager duchess Anna Amalia, with Prince Constantine, the duke's brother, and began an intensive contact with Wieland and Karl Ludwig von Knebel. For fifty years Weimar was to remain the place where he lived and worked.

Goethe and the It has become clear, especially from the publishing
Pirates history of *Werther,* how insecure and problematic the circumstances of copyright and publishing were at that time. We have therefore to look at the history of the publication of Goethe's works and his relationships with publishers and booksellers against the background of the laws governing publishing and copyright, which had not yet been universally codified. The complete lack of laws in such a small area reflects, I believe, a general lawlessness in, and the collapse of, the Holy Roman Empire of the German Nation. Today we can scarcely imagine this, and the occasional pirated versions with which publishers have to grapple today bear no relationship to what was happening at that time. Today a pirated version is forbidden and its production can be actionable. At that time a pirated version could be forbidden and punitive action taken against its publication only in certain territories.

In the middle of the eighteenth century the book trade was at once flourishing and in the midst of a crisis. In the first comprehensive monograph on the history of the German book trade, Johann Goldfriedrich's *History of the German Book Trade*,[19] the second half of the eighteenth century is represented as the first epoch of modern literature, of the modern book trade, of modern writers and modern readers. What is modern is revealed above all in a tempestuously developing body of novels and in a new interest on the part of the public in the printed word: there was a real reading fever, a rage for reading. The lending library came into existence, and while authors, scholars, critics, and booksellers opposed this institution, because it carried less serious literature—trashy, dirty novels, knightly romances, adventure stories, and love stories—that promoted the stupefaction of the people, the public was enthusiastic and served as a spectacular and rapid impetus to the institution.

The then modern book trade was split apart, above all, by the problem of pirated versions—a decisive one for the trade. Imagine: a book appeared, carefully produced at the wish or behest of the author, the author had read the proofs and in the process had perhaps altered or expanded the book, he had put it into its final version and in the process incurred costs that the publisher had to take into account in his calculations. The author demanded his payment and his royalty. All of this was bound to have an impact on the selling price of the book. But there was no copyright, publishers had no rights, in other words each book that appeared was more or less beyond the reach of the law and could be pirated by anybody at all. The pirated version could be produced with worse and cheaper materials, was generally carelessly set, contained errors, and was moreover in every case cheaper than the original edition.

The struggle against the pirates and the struggle for the protection of the author dominated the media in the second half of the eighteenth century. The history of the *Göttinger Musenalmanach* of 1770 is a curious one and a good example of the problems that beset authors, printers, and publishers. Even before it was published, a Leipzig pirate had received advance sheets and reprinted them so rapidly that the Leipzig almanac appeared before the Göttingen one.

The struggle was carried on by both sides with energy, eloquence and a mass of pamphlets; there was not a journal, a magazine, not a popular almanac that did not take sides on the question. Even the theater was involved. A one-act play, *The Pirates,* appeared in Leipzig in 1804, and there was a production of a play in Prague entitled *This Is the Way a Writer Takes*

Revenge on Treacherous Pirates. The pirates themselves were not of the opinion that they were treacherous, however; their only intention was to promote literature. Pirating was at that time not forbidden by civil or by canon law. From the territorial and the judicial standpoints it was permissible. And it had great defenders in the philosopher Fichte and not least in the sovereign princes, who—adhering to the mercantile ideas of the age—were concerned in the first place with their own territory and made large profits from these versions. Imports were expensive and domestic production cheap. The landgrave of Hesse permitted the Darmstadt bookseller Wilhelm Krämer to reprint any foreign books that "were over-priced and that contributed the most to the enlightenment and education of the human heart and were engaged with the most necessary disciplines of learning." Since "foreign" could mean everything that was not Hessian, any book at all could for all practical purposes be reprinted.

There were many pirates in Berlin, Frankfurt, Hamburg, and in southern Germany, especially in Stuttgart, Karlsruhe, and Tübingen. The notorious pirate firm of Macklot in Karlsruhe was at their head: Frankfurt enjoyed the dubious reputation of being the main playground for pirates, after reliquishing to Leipzig in 1764 its position as the city that had, for almost two centuries, been the seat of the German book fair.

Johann Thomas Trattner of Vienna was regarded as the king of the pirates. He had a imperial privilege that allowed him to reprint "all books necessary for the promotion of study," and this, the most prominent and most public pirate actually received annual support from the court. Trattner founded a society to cull systematically the works of German authors and publishing houses, he even had the nerve to turn to famous scholars for suggestions for pirate versions. He was appointed to the post of court bookseller, court printer, and finally dubbed "Noble Knight von Trattner."

Of course the opponents of pirating were resolute and they defended themselves. They were led by the Leipzig bookseller and publisher Philipp Erasmus Reich and the Weimar publisher Friedrich Justin Bertuch, who characterized the pirates simply as "predators." Reich and Bartuch were also the first whom their colleagues called upon to obtain legal protection against reprintings in their territories.

However it was the authors who most clearly defended themselves against the pirates. Next to the publishers they were the people who were really affected. Lichtenberg was one of the pugnacious opponents and called the pirates "black printers" and the trade in their products a "black market," saying that the black printer was nothing more than a thief. Lessing (in *Live and Let Live, a Project for Writers and Booksellers*), Kant (*On the Illegality of Pirated Versions*), and Jean Paul (*Seven Last Words or Postscripts against Pirating*) fought side by side with Wieland against this fundamental evil in the book trade of the time.

Surprisingly enough, from time immemorial, from the very beginning until today, one institution—censorship—worked against the practice of piracy. However, in Goethe's time, this was an evil for authors as well. Manuscripts had to be submitted to the censor and the censor had to be paid by the publisher! Censorship affected the publisher more than it did the author and it affected the "political" author more than it did the literary one. Besides this, censorship was regional and had different effects in different states. What was permitted in some German states was forbidden in others. For a time the publication of Goethe's and Schiller's works was forbidden in Austria for moral reasons. All of these bans, together with the official reasons for them, naturally had to be observed by the pirates. Thus it was not so easy to pirate the works of subversive authors.

Goethe defended himself against the pirated versions of *Götz* in a relaxed and temperate fashion. He had previously experienced the enormous effect the two pirated printings of his *The Letter of the Pastor at *** to the New Pastor at **** had had. Lavater, who was probably the first to recognize Goethe's literary rank, reported that he had got to know the text in a pirated version. In the foreword to the "Second Edition" of *Götz* in 1774, published by the Eichenberg Heirs and Successors, the publisher wrote, probably in agreement with Goethe, "Scarcely had the play appeared than a pirated edition came out, something about which there would be no cause for complaint if it had not been done so cursorily." *Götz* had laid the foundation of Goethe's fame as a writer among the younger generation, and the pirates were hard on his heels as book succeeded book. Imagine if today an original edition and cheap pirated editions appeared at the same time and the book trade was allowed to distribute them. The original edition would be wiped out and this is what must have happened to Weygand, the publisher of *Werther*.

Goethe, who had moved to Weimar for "serious matters," remained resigned and reserved. Pirating seemed to him a national evil and it annoyed him because it meant that his works were distributed in a defective form and were received in the same manner, but he did not yet feel motivated to launch a counterattack. But the more massive the theft of his intellectual property became, the more he thought of possible reactions to it, and one such was his increasingly bad opinion of pirates who dubbed themselves publishers (he often included genuine publishers—but ones who opposed piracy with rather dubious methods—among this group as well).

The cunning with which the pirates operated is shown by the way that in his so very prominent case they represented themselves as the original publishers. In 1775/76 *Herr Goethe's Collected Works* was published by Heilmann in Biel in Switzerland. The edition consisted of three volumes and they contained all that had so far appeared: *Götz; Clavigo; Werther; Stella; Gods, Heroes, and Wieland; Erwin and Elmire.* You can imagine Goethe's surprise: the first complete edition of his works was a pirated version! And he was to be even more surprised, for in the succeeding years no fewer than twelve further pirated versions appeared, thirteen pirated versions of his *Complete Works* in all. Goethe could not remain indifferent, especially in view of the economic consequences. He himself received no royalties, while the pirates who produced these editions and the booksellers who distributed them realized turnover and profit. This is the root of his mistrust of the book trade as a whole, and however much understanding might have been expected of him, in his disgust and condemnation he no longer distinguished between the illegal pirates and the legal publishers. The publisher was for him the one who exploited the lack of the author's legal rights and made his profits from the lack of protection of intellectual property. An especially characteristic example in the case of *Werther* may be quoted here. The notorious Berlin publisher, Christian Friedrich Himburg, produced three successive editions of an unauthorized edition of *Goethe's Writings,* the first in 1775/76 and the second in 1777. Himburg sent a few "complimentary copies" of the third edition, in four volumes (1779), to Goethe, adding in the accompanying letter that he really regarded this edition, this collection of the works that was so beautifully printed, as a boon for Goethe. In fact it is impossible to credit Himburg with the consciousness of doing something illegal. Later in the same year, Himburg published an etching: *Works of Darkness or a Contribution to the History of the Book Trade in Germany. Allegorically Presented and as a Warning to All Honest Booksellers, to be had at C.F.Himburg's in Berlin.* Bandits from a robbers' cave are seen attacking people traveling along the road; just as they steal travelers' clothes, pirates steal the property of honest publishers—and Justice hides her head!

But the really infuriating thing about all the succeeding Himburg editions was that on the one hand they were especially well-produced, on wood-free paper, and like the previous editions they contained title vignettes and etchings in the text; on the other hand, the texts themselves were slipshod and grew worse from one edition to the next. It was these Himburg editions that were reprinted in a number of places (with increasingly bad paper and an increasing number of errors) and this in its turn had such a sensitive effect upon Himburg's market that the cunning man even produced copies of his own pirated versions with the imprint "Frankfurt and Leipzig." This was too much even for Goethe. We know his reaction from *Poetry and Truth:*

> When the demand for my works had increased and a collected edition was much called for, these feelings held me back from preparing it myself: Himburg however took advantage of my hesitation, and I unexpectedly received one day several copies of my collected works in print. With cool audacity this unauthorized publisher even boasted of having done me a public service and offered to send me, if I wished, some Berlin porcelain by way of compensation. His offer served to remind me of the law which compelled the Jews of Berlin when they married to purchase a certain quantity of porcelain, in order to keep up the sale of the Royal manufacture. The contempt which I felt which was shown for the shameless pirate that grew out of this led me to suppress the indignation which I could not but feel at such a robbery. I gave him no reply; and while he was making himself very comfortable with my property, I revenged myself in silence with the following verses:

> > Take your china back, your gingerbread!
> > For all Himburgs living I am dead.[20]

Was this reaction on Goethe's part—his revenge in secret—warranted by the case? He criticizes Himburg as an uncalled-for publisher and accuses him of "robbery." Given his position in Weimar could Goethe not have done more? In England from 1709 onwards there had been a sort of copyright and publishing law that had established a clear protection for intellectual property for a term of twenty-one years. In Saxony there existed a famous mandate of 18 December 1773 that forbade the pirating of books that had been exhibited at the Leipzig Fair, but no one took any notice of it. When, later, Göschen vigorously pursued the enforcement of the mandate he did not even have the support of the government of Saxony. Goethe's attitude towards pirates remained reserved until he got into difficulties with his later, legal, publishers Göschen and Cotta because of their illegal pirated versions, and the whole business of pirating was affecting his own income.

Later on he was personally to take a successful step against pirating, at the time when he succeeded in obtaining a privilege for the final authorized edition that made pirated versions impossible.

Goethe Makes Demands   The first person on whom such a demand was made was the Berlin bookseller Christlob August Mylius, Lessing's brother-in-law. In 1775 Goethe had written the play *Stella* as quickly as he could, and, almost concurrently, the singspiel *Claudine of Villa Bella.* The theme of infidelity, or the theme of fidelity to oneself against the conventions of society, was in the forefront of both plays. "There resides in every artist a seed of daring," he was to write in *Maxims and Reflections,* "without which no talent is conceivable." In the singspiel *Claudine,* the Bohemian, Crugantino, is thrown into prison after all sorts of machinations. He rebels against the reproaches of a friend of his father's (just as Goethe himself will rebel against Superintendent Herder when the latter reproaches him for his mode of life in Weimar). Crugantino: "Do you know the needs of a young heart like mine? A young hothead? Where is there a theater of life for me to play in? I find your bourgeois society insupportable!" He wants to break the framework of bourgeois convention, and there are two forces particularly to which he knows himself to be allied as a revolutionary, the intellect and Eros. "For life is love / and the life of life the intellect." Goethe had planned to write a novel, *The Sultan against His Will,* in which four different women are all interested in one man who loves them all equally. Like his idea for two earlier works, *Pharaoh's Successor* and *Caesar and Mahomet,* this was yet another plan that was not carried out. Ludwig Wittgenstein says with great insight, "I wanted to write and say that my works consist of two parts: of what is here in front of us and of all that I have not written. And it is precisely the second part that is the most important." This insight may have been attractive to the philosopher; for Goethe the artist and the man, the important thing was certainty of choice and of what he could repudiate.

In *Stella* Goethe departs from the framework of bourgeois life. Here is a man who like himself was incapable of being tied to one woman, who always loved two at the same time or admired some "person on the side." He is a man between two women, has left both, and will return to neither.

This is, in terms of the moral conventions of the time, a revolution in sensuality and morally audacious. The "We are yours" uttered by the two women at the end of the play smacks of a liberating act even in our own day. No contemporary dramatist of any standing has written such an "audacity"! And in this sense I also regret that Goethe rewrote the play for the complete edition of his works in 1816, giving it a tragic ending—a gesture of devotion to the court—with the thought that this would make the chance of a production more likely.

Goethe corresponded with his friend Merck on the question of the play's publication and asked him to serve as an intermediary. This too was to be characteristic of him from now on. He tried not to be directly involved in the business of publishing: through an intermediary he could set more stringent terms and make harsher demands. Merck had introduced him to Mylius and passed on Goethe's demand for twenty thalers from Mylius before the latter had seen the manuscript. One can understand Mylius's cool reaction; any publisher would refuse to accept what he had not read.

Mylius's letter to Merck of 17 October 1775 is an important document for assessing Goethe's attitude towards publishers. "It is perhaps wilfulness on the part of Herr *Goethe* to want to sell his manuscript in this way, for between ourselves it is rather odd to buy what you have not yet seen, a pig in a poke. Besides which there is not much to be done with such a small pièce. Incidentally, I am surprised that Herr *Goethe* is so anxious to torment booksellers in this way, since—as I have always heard—he has no need to do so for economic reasons. Is it perhaps his fame that has fetched such a high price for his manuscripts. I would have preferred Dr. *Faust* at a proportionate price."

And so its seems that Goethe had begun to assess his economic worth, and booksellers, while gnashing their teeth, allowed themselves to be tormented by him, just so that they might acquire and retain this "unusual genius," this "prolific writer." But what is a "proportionate price" for this? In January 1776 Mylius published *Stella, A Play for Lovers in Five Acts by J. W. von Goethe* in Berlin. Because Goethe was afraid that *Claudine* could be pirated—the manuscripts that he had sent out had not been returned to him—he asked Mylius to publish this play as well without more ado. It too appeared in 1776 (*Claudine of Villa Bella, a Play with Music by J. W. Goethe*) there was a second edition in the same year and after this his connection with Mylius ceased. Göschen was to bring out an "authentic edition" in 1788.

T W O

Goethe and Göschen

"The Stream of Life" "NOT LONG AFTER the meeting at which my grandfather had taken the patriarch of literature by storm, but had only extracted a hopeful promise, he achieved a much larger and more immediate triumph. He was charged with the publication of a collection of the great Goethe's entire works—an unparalleled honour for so young a firm." This is the way Viscount Goschen begins the sixth chapter—entitled, "Goethe, June 1786—Easter 1787"—of his grandfather's biography, *The Life and Times of Georg Joachim Göschen, Publisher and Printer of Leipzig 1752–1828.*[1] The patriarch in question was Christoph Martin Wieland, the most successful author of his time, who had been tutor to the crown prince, Carl August, in Weimar since 1772. Schiller, who was introduced to Göschen by his admirer Christian Gottfried Körner, an attorney in Dresden and the son-in-law of a close acquaintance of Goethe's, in his turn introduced Wieland to Göschen. Wieland and Göschen became friends, and from that moment on they both had but one aim—to win Goethe over to the publisher. They began to forge vigorous plans to establish a connection with him.

For the time being Göschen showed "a more enthusiastic affection for Wieland than for any of his other friends and authors . . . they had many tastes in common . . . both did obeisance to the surpassing genius of Schiller and Goethe—a genius that shone more brightly than any other—and both admired these literary giants even while they were smashing up much that was dear to both Wieland and Göschen."[2] Thus Wieland played a part in Goethe's joining the house but Wieland was probably also the indirect reason for Schiller's and Goethe's leaving the firm, one after the other, and going over to Cotta.

34

However, ten years were to pass before Göschen could become Goethe's publisher, for 1775 marked the beginning of the decade of "serious matters." Goethe arrived in Weimar on 7 November 1775 "at five in the morning." At first he was not sure whether he would stay for long. Weimar with its 6,000 inhabitants, its burned-out castle, its dirty roads filled with chickens and cows was not all that attractive. Again and again in the following decades Goethe was to interrupt his life in his main residence at Weimar by going on journeys. He was absent from Weimar for thirteen years or, to be absolutely precise, 4,765 days.

"From the first moment I saw him, how completely was this a man after my own heart," wrote Wieland to a friend on 10 November 1775; "how much I loved him as I sat, on that first day, next to that magnificent youth!"[3] A new dimension had been added to the court. "Filled with Goethe as a dewdrop is with morning sunshine," is what Wieland—who had for a long time been treated badly by the court—called the triumphal entry of a "true intellectual king" with "magical eyes full of divine glances."

Goethe embarked upon a decade of service as a civil servant and, as far as his activity as a writer is concerned, a decade of fragments, court plays, singspiels, masquerades, dramatic speeches, and, among other things, official writings. But we must not overlook the fact that this was the period in which he also drafted and planned the classical dramas. After Mylius had published *Stella* and *Claudine* in 1776 (there were a lot of pirated and partial printings as well) and in 1778 two versions of the monodrama *Proserpine* (first as a privately published edition printed in Weimar, then in the *Berlin Literary and Theater Journal of 28 February*) with several reprints, there was for a whole decade (1777–87) not one work of considerable size apart from poems and a few essays. Dodsley & Co., another pirate, allegedly published a work of nineteen pages in 1779, "*Secret News. The final hours of Waldemar a notorious freethinker. And how Satan half crushed him, and then in the presence of his beloved took him to hell as she stood by whimpering,*" a parody by Goethe of Friedrich Heinrich Jacobi's *Woldemar,* which was printed without Goethe's knowledge. The fairy-tale play *Lila,* smaller plays for the theater, songs, arias, and dedications had preceded it in 1777–78. Works for the court, *The Feminine Virtues of the Ruling Duchess of Weimar, Celebration of the Birth of Carl Friedrich,* and *The Speech at the Opening of the New Mountain Lodge in Ilmenau* followed. The court made more and more demands upon Goethe, and his literary production often had to be pressed into its service. He also had to play an active part in social events, as in the case of the so-called Venetian carnival that was organized in honor of the young duchess after the birth of the crown prince and which was led by the duke himself. Among those participating in the pageant (in which 139 people and 100 horses took part) was Goethe himself in old German costume—a white satin coat and breeches with a purple cloak and a feathered biretta on his head—riding a white horse covered with gaily colored cloths and surrounded by boys carrying torches. He could scarcely have been happy about that!

On 11 June 1776 Goethe was made a member of the privy council; he took part in 500 meetings of this body during his term of office. He was made responsible for the Committees on War and on Roads and all this at a time of unrest both outside and inside the state: Czar Alexander I of Russia died, leaving unstable conditions behind him; Bavaria was fighting Austria, France and Spain were conducting an unsuccessful siege of Gibraltar; Washington defeated the British and England recognized the independence of the United States, and Frederick William II became king of Prussia. Though the ideas of the Enlightenment and tolerance were making more and more headway internally, they were once more limited in nature after 1790. Goethe read Lessing's *Nathan the Wise* and his writings on *The Education of Mankind* written in 1780; he read Diderot and Rousseau; in Kant's essay *What Is Enlightenment?* he found the famous statement in which Kant defined the Enlightenment as "The exit of mankind from the dependence for which it is itself responsible."

Goethe's office gave him the power to punish and to praise, to degrade and to promote. Wherever he could, however, he gave his liberal ideas free rein. He intervened energetically in a hotly disputed internal matter: "The ban on marriage before the age of twenty four . . . (from the point of view of the Commission on War) is at present no longer necessary."[4] Deserters posed a massive problem. In Weimar, running the gauntlet for cases of desertion had not been abolished and the delinquents often bled to death in great misery. Goethe had, above all, to deal with deserters from the Prussian army who repeatedly fled to Weimar, and from there Frederick II demanded their extradition. Frederick also sent recruiters for his army into the Weimar area. Goethe was confronted over and over again with questions as to whether such recruitment should be permitted and whether he should extradite his own people, "an unpleasant, hateful and shameful trade" as he calls it in his submission to the duke.

Was it not to be feared that Weimar's own soldiers would be disloyal? The hussars of the Weimar corps d'élite were of course needed as protection, and sometimes as the carriers of the privy councillor's love-letters. In order, at least in part, to put the strained finances of the duchy in order he halved the military force.

Goethe's sympathies for American independence are well known.[5] The year 1782 became the high point of his career as statesman and politician. Up to that point his climb had been a steep one; from member of the privy council with the title of Grand Privy Legation Councillor in 1776, he was elevated in August 1779 to Privy Councillor. "It seems strange to me," he writes on 7 September 1779 to Charlotte von Stein, "that, at the age of thirty, I should, as if in a dream, aspire to the highest honor that a citizen can achieve in Germany." On 3 June 1782 he received the brevet of nobility from the Emperor Joseph II. Though he scarcely mentions this, it was more than a superficial mark of favor. Herr von Goethe was no longer a simple citizen; he could now be presented at court and was permitted to dine at the duke's table. In 1782 he took over the office of a chamberlain of the Weimar state. After having had to dismiss the previous holder of this office because he had incurred debts while administering the court treasury, the duke expressed the wish that "you make yourself more familiar with the affairs of the Chamber and thus try to make yourself suited to be its director." Goethe accepted; the chamberlain was a sort of finance minister. The new minister expressed the hope that "the new change in, and the extension of, my duties will be of value both to myself and to others." However there could really be no talk of its being "of value to others" because the promotion took place only in the face of opposition from other members of the council and the duke had to calm ruffled feathers on all sides; the courtiers continued to grumble for a long time. But even many of Goethe's friends made critical remarks about the new career. Herder, for example, regarded him, sullenly and possibly a little enviously, as having become the "factotum of the state of Weimar." Goethe complained in 1782, "The stream of life sweeps me along ever more strongly and I scarcely have time to look round."[6]

It was a time of radical change, and Goethe took his political duties seriously. His literary production began to be official. He campaigned for the simplification of "Chancery Style," suggested measures for "weakening" patriotic ties; he supported the petition of the Frankfurt Jew, Elias Löb Reiz, for a ducal pardon; the lawyer in him took up arms in a case to decide whether a student who had been expelled should be handed over to the Prussian military in exchange for a native of Weimar who had been pressed into Prussian military service; and he explored such questions as whether ecclesiastical penance should be abolished and whether the death penalty should not be retained for infanticide. As finance minister he had to decide on actions to recoup outstanding taxes, to make observations on bankruptcy proceedings and to punish people who were behind in their payments. He was responsible for the building of waterways and for mining; he was constantly making "Reports on the state of mining in Ilmenau." His official contact with the mine in Ilmenau and with scientific institutes in Jena, his journeys, his interest in nature and his reliance on nature also gave rise to a new attitude towards the sciences. Ever since he had been involved in "mining affairs" he had devoted himself "heart and soul to mineralogy." He tried to find a scientific basis for "the noble and wonderful drama" that would at one and the same time make clear and vivid to him the "origin and development of the surface of our earth and the nourishment that people draw from it." He engaged in geological and anatomical studies in which he reflected on the natural development of all living things from the realm of stones to plants and animals and finally to man himself. A hymnic essay with the title *Granite* was to be a preliminary study for the geological "novel of the universe." Granite for Goethe becomes the stone that is the origin of all mountainous formations, and from now on the prefix *Ur* ("original") has the force of a noun for him. "Molded form that develops as it lives" he calls it.

In all his scientific efforts there is a playful pleasure in uncovering secrets; but for him they are never an end in themselves though they repeatedly led him to other paths and other goals.

We should mention one more "sideline" that arose from his official activity—also something truly playful. When the ducal castle burned down, the theater was also destroyed and an amateur theater grew up in which Goethe was involved. He played a part in Richard Cumberland's comedy *The West Indian,* and from 1 October 1776 he was handed the directorship of the Weimar theater. He, the author of *Werther* and *Götz,* was to produce his own plays, *Erwin und Elmire,* for which the duchess Anna had composed the music, *The Lover's Mood, The Accomplices,* and *The Annual Fair at Plundersweilen.* He wrote plays and singspiels for this theater (*The Siblings, The*

Triumph of Sensibility, The Birds, Jeri and Bätely, and *The Fisherwoman),* he directed and often played the lead himself. They were all occasional productions, as the court society wished them to be; he called them the result of "poetical leisure" and in his old age he played down their importance to Eckermann, maintaining that in the first ten years in Weimar he had produced "nothing of poetic significance." In his diary he noted in entries that relate to hunting, masquerades, committee meetings, official inspections, the enormous amount of work he had to do. But he always knew that beyond his official duties he was destined for something else: "Actually I was born to be a writer." As far as the public was concerned, this was not yet obvious, as there were no publications of any length in these years, if we ignore Himburg's "anthologized" pirate editions of 1775, 1777, and 1779.

People saw the statesman but did not recognize the writer. Even the court society of Weimar only found out gradually that these secondary and occasional productions were in part based on "significant" events. Many of these plays and singspiels were a homage to the woman who had the greatest influence on Goethe: Charlotte von Stein.

Charlotte von Stein   According to biographers, the relationship of Goethe to Frau von Stein has been researched down to the last detail. Can a relationship that functioned for more than ten years as "Law and Oracle," can the relationship to a loved one who was "transubstantiated into all objects," and through whom "nothing could enter or leave him without paying her tolls and excise tax" really be completely researched? Are the more than seventeen hundred letters, notes, and jottings that Goethe sent to Frau von Stein not documents that need to be reevaluated? Goethe locked his writings up in the strong room of the library in Weimar without ever looking at them again, while for her part Frau von Stein destroyed what Goethe had written to her. Of course they should be researched. Biographers agree that there was no sexual relationship between the two; what they enjoyed was high love without physical union. Even Karl Rudolf Eissler in his psychoanalytical study[7] in which he voyeuristically investigates every detail with this one thought in mind arrives at this conclusion. He believes that Goethe was incestuously involved with his sister Cornelia at the time he wrote *The Siblings* and was beginning to dictate *Iphigenia.*

In his thoroughgoing biography Karl Otto Konrady dispenses with a new character sketch of Frau von Stein. There is, he says, nothing new to report and anything that is reported as new is pure speculation. But is it not possible that speculation of this sort could indirectly suggest new knowledge. Let us therefore hazard a speculation in the double sense of the word. Goethe met Frau von Stein shortly after his arrival in Weimar; the duke had conducted him to her house personally. In fact during the whole decade no one was to have a greater, more active, more long-lasting influence upon him than this woman. The meeting was anything but a coincidence. On no fewer than two occasions before going to Weimar Goethe had held the silhouette of Frau von Stein in his hands, in Zurich, at Lavater's home, who developed the physiognomical method of "furthering the knowledge of mankind and love of humanity," and in the summer of 1775 in Strassburg when the Hanoverian physician-in-ordinary Johann Georg Zimmermann showed it to him among a hundred other silhouettes. Zimmermann must have expressly drawn Goethe's attention to this silhouette, because in Strassburg in 1775 Goethe wrote these evocative words under the picture, "It would be a wonderful drama to see how the world is reflected in this soul. It sees the world as it is, and yet sees it through the medium of love. Thus the overall impression is one of softness." This positive judgment is remarkable and what else is remarkable are the two statements about the drama, about *play* and reflection, about the *mirror:* play and mirror are for me keywords in Goethe's relationship to Frau von Stein. In June 1777, shortly before he received the news of the death of his sister Cornelia, to whom Goethe felt an ambivalent bond of guilt and happiness ("The gods, the infinite ones gave all / to their favorites totally / all the joys, the eternal ones / all pain, the eternal totally"), he had characterized his relationship with Frau von Stein as "the thread of love." However, as early as November (in the face of the second anniversary of his arrival in Weimar which he had forgotten and to which Frau von Stein had drawn his attention) he raised the question: "Do I really love her or is it that her proximity pleases me like the presence of a glass that is so clear that everything is perfectly mirrored in it." Once more we have the image of the mirror in which he sees himself! Goethe's capacity for self-observation is immense: love as the reflection of the person who loves; but he had an equally great capacity for play, for revealing the person in the mirror as the true lover. What Goethe could not have known in Strassburg was that Zimmermann had already set out to be an eager intermediary. The "marshal's wife" made use of his services; she wanted to get to know the author of

Werther. Zimmermann, incidentally, warned her, "Mais pauvre amie, vous n'y pensés pas, vous *désirés* de le *voir* et vous ne savés pas a quel point cet homme *aimable* et *charmant* pourroit vous devenir *dangereux!*" (But my poor friend, you are not thinking, you want to see him and you do not know at what point this lovable and charming man could become a danger to you.)

Charlotte Albertine Ernestine von Stein was thirty-three years old when Goethe, seven years her junior, met her. There were seven children from her marriage of convenience to Marshal Josias von Stein. Five of them died. She was an ailing, lonely woman, disappointed with life, who blossomed into new life in her relationship with Goethe. She was described by friends as "dear soft Stein with such beautiful eyes." Schiller remarked laconically, "She cannot have been beautiful," but he added, "nevertheless her face has a gentle seriousness and a totally peculiar openness. Common sense, feeling and truth make up her being." Every onlooker was able to understand why Goethe had "attached" himself to her.

At the time Goethe was introduced to her he had once again failed in love. He had become engaged to Anna Elisabeth Schönemann (Lili) at Easter 1775; four weeks later came his first flight from the relationship, to the St. Gotthard, but he returned. On 30 October 1775 he set out for the south, on 3 November the coach arrived that took him back to Weimar; he wrote in the notebook that he kept on the journey: "Lili, farewell Lili, for the second time! The first time I left full of hope that our fates were to be joined! The die has been cast, we must play our parts separately." Again, as the best possible analyst of himself, he expresses an attitude of play, of playing a part. This time the beloved, Lili, was not unattainable, on the contrary she was his fiancée and was waiting for the bourgeois bond of marriage. But it was precisely this that caused Goethe to break off the engagement and flee. Once more, marrying became for him—as in the *New Songs* of 1770—a *strange* word. In his *Proposal for Goodness* he joked, "Marrying, my angel, is a strange word;/I thought that I must leave again at once." And in *Clavigo,* written in 1774, "at the time when the pain I felt about Friderike's situation frightened me" and he by his "poetic confession" wished to be "worthy of an inner absolution by means of this self-tormenting penance," he has Carlos say, though without seeming to be frightened, "Strange . . . marry, marry just at the time when life is first beginning to take off, to settle down domestically, to limit oneself, at the time when half of your journey has not been completed, half of one's conquests have not yet been made." Later he gave a clearer warning: "*Love* is something ideal, *Marrying* is something real and no one ever confuses the ideal with the real without being punished for it." To me this passage seems so important because in the ten years that he spent in Weimar under the influence of Frau von Stein on the one hand and carrying out his political duties on the other—the statesman's "Govern!"—he found a way of joining the ideal and the real and of arriving in this way at his humanity, at his idea of a whole in a way that rejects the one-sided and unconditional and reconciles the opposites. "Always strive for the whole and if you cannot become a whole / join yourself to a whole as an ancillary limb."

For anyone concerned with Goethe, the phenomenon of the relationship between Goethe and Charlotte von Stein has to be of the essence. Here the highest demands are always made and here the height is never scaled. One thing is certain; just in his letters to her alone, Goethe reveals himself as a great writer, with them alone he would have earned every literary prize of every age. But what price did *she* pay?

From the beginning, his relationship to Frau von Stein was on the highest level; it is an exalted love that excludes the sexual but is constantly aiming at completeness in love *and* suffering, in bliss *and* despair, in fulfillment *and* renunciation. "Dear lady, it is sad that I love you so much. If I am able to love someone more I will tell you. Farewell my love! You do not understand *how* I love you," is the way one of his notes written on 28 January 1776 concludes.

Charlotte von Stein had an inkling from the beginning that the relationship would fail. "I feel that Goethe and I will never be friends. The way, too, in which he treats our sex does not please me. He is, actually, what is called coquettish." Over and over again Goethe conjured up that original relationship between two souls: "You too, in time long past / Were my sister or my wife." Sister and wife, "woman" as, for example, Corona Schröter never was to him. He could not avoid telling Charlotte, "Schröter is an angel—if God would only grant me such a woman, I could leave you in peace—but she is never sufficiently like you. Farewell." True there were other angels that fascinated Goethe: Caroline von Iltern, who later became the wife of Freiherr Frederick Charles von Moser and whom Goethe generally called Lingen, Carolingen, or Misel in his diary,[8] Countess Adelaide Waldner (Misel Laide in the diary) and Viktoria Streiber, the daughter of the mayor of Eisenach (called Misel Viktorgen in the diary). Why did Goethe use code names in his diary? Why these pseudonyms, this camouflage, why the abbreviations, why the concealment of intensely erotic situations? Is he anticipating those insights that Kafka wrote for Milena: "Written kisses . . . are drunk up by ghosts . . ."[9]

Frau von Stein sensed that there were rivals and Goethe fed this suspicion. Thus on 17 January 1776, he writes: "Dear Lady, tonight I was at first in a very bad mood. Both Louise and I were depressed at your absence. Neither Keller nor dear little Bertolsheim could get me going. Finally I began to flirt and then things began to get better. Flirting is really the most proven palliative in such situations." On 12 June 1777: "In the garden in the open air! Since you've been gone I feel for the first time that I own something and that I have an obligation. My other little passions, pastimes and flirtations were only attached to the thread of my love for you, the thread that helps me get through my present existence, and now your absence makes everything fall to pieces." Doubts and suspicions were a fixed part of the relationship: "Why did you give us the power to look deeply / To see our future full of foreboding?" The more violently the relationship was felt—"My soul has taken firm root in yours . . . I would that there were some oath or sacrament that would make you mine both visibly and legally"—the greater was the fear of the consequences of so definite a commitment. Goethe had never undertaken so many journeys, his winter journey to the Harz (1777), the single journey to Berlin (May 1778),[10] journeys to Switzerland, to Gotha and Eisenach, the second journey to the Harz (1783) and the third (1784): in 1785 he went to Jena several times, in 1786 he was in Carlsbad. He was in love with his demonstrations of love and he was equally afraid of them. Charlotte must have thought that she had gained everything and also lost everything when she received the following tidings, a short postscript to a letter of 8 July 1781: "We are, I suppose, married, that is joined by a bond in which the letter consists of love and joy and the envelope of a cross, grief and misery." This is followed quite abruptly by greetings to the garden, to her husband, the marshal, as though he wanted to ask his forgiveness for the misunderstanding: "Farewell, my greetings to Stein. Help me to believe and to hope."

Did something happen on those evenings before Goethe left for Carlsbad and was it perhaps this "happening" that definitely determined his journey, his flight, to Italy? These biographical speculations are only negated by the fact that at that very moment Goethe was negotiating with Göschen about the financial arrangements for his journey. "I have reached agreement with Göschen about my writings," he announced to Frau von Stein on 6 July 1786. On 10 July he wrote to her, as he took his farewell, "So farewell my dearest, my only one, to whom my whole soul would reveal and dedicate itself; I rejoice in your love and rely on it for all time to come." Then on 21 July, three days before he left with his secretary at five in the morning to go to Carlsbad, he wrote his final lines to Frau von Stein: "If what I am doing is the will of gods who have for some time been my most loving masters." On 3 September 1786 he completed his first sojourn in Weimar, this time with a really long journey but also to recognize himself again or, in his own words, "to experience rejuvenation and rebirth." Secretly—using the pseudonym, Johann Philipp Möller—he set out with his servant Vogel on a journey to Italy.

Since Goethe stole away from Carlsbad society on 3 September 1786, "secretly" and with every appearance of flight, to set out for Italy, people look on his intense and untenable relationship with Charlotte von Stein as a motive for this "extreme necessity." But if we look at all the documents, this view cannot be sustained. From his earliest youth Goethe had wanted to see Rome. "The main thing," he wrote to Charlotte von Stein from Vicenza, "is that all the objects that have worked upon my imagination *in absentia* for more than thirty years and have for that very reason grown all too exalted, have now been lowered in pitch to the normal household key of coexistence." Thus it was not a flight from Charlotte von Stein, in no way a journey into disillusion, but the attempt to find out the truth of his existence. He also wanted to keep the excitement of the journey at arm's length, "so that the objects will not find a soul that is already elevated but will elevate that soul." From the outset he had considered documenting the journey, the journey to truth and self-discovery, the "long lonely road." "The waters flow from here to Germany and to Italy, I hope to follow the latter tomorrow. . . . Think of me in this important epoch of my life." These are the words he wrote to Charlotte von Stein as he crossed the Brenner on 8 September 1786. He was documenting the journey for her sake as well. And the documents describing his journey as well as the many letters to his beloved show how much effort Goethe had put into the authentic and the true, the licit and the classic. Charlotte had been his guide in and for Weimar, she had introduced him into society, she had also bound him to her. But Goethe avoided a final commitment.

Though I live for ever for her
For whose sake I should not live.

And:

Oh, my fate presses so hard upon me
That I strive for what is impossible.

When Goethe began his journey he was not thinking of a separation, neither from Weimar nor from Charlotte. He renewed his offer to serve the duke—on a new basis—in a letter written from Rome on 17 March 1788. "All I can say is: Lord, here I am, do with thy servant as thou willst. I shall be glad of any post, any little post that you keep for me, I will gladly fetch and carry, sit down and stand up." He had written to Charlotte on 27 October 1786: "It is only now that I feel how spoilt I have been. Ten years living with you, being loved by you, and now in an alien world. I said to myself beforehand only the direst necessity could force to me to make this decision. Let us have no other thought but of ending our lives together." The statement was unambiguous, Goethe believed in the truth of it and Charlotte probably also saw it in the same light. Four months later, on 21 February 1787, she was to read in a letter from Rome: "I depend on you with every thread of my being. It is terrible how often memories tear me to pieces. Oh, my dear Lotte you do not know what violence I have done myself—and still do—and you do not know that, at bottom, the thought of not possessing you consumes me and wears me down however I look at it." This may have fed Charlotte's doubts, and what must she have thought of his view of Italy, "I have nothing to look for in the world but what I have found"? Goethe wrote in his diary every day and had thought from the beginning about publishing the texts, he had also thought that Charlotte should help him do this. He wrote to her on 18 September 1786 from Verona, "I send a sign of life to my beloved on a really tiny piece of paper, but without telling her where I am. . . . I have kept a diary faithfully and have made a record of the most carefully selected things that I have thought of or seen; according to my calculations you can have it by the middle of October. I am sure you will like it and distance will give you more than my presence has often done. . . . Do not tell anyone about what you receive. For the moment it is for you alone." And on 14 October from Venice: "If you copy it gradually on quarto, but with broken pages, change the *Du* into *Sie* and leave out what concerns you and anything else you think should be omitted, then on my return I should find a version that I can correct and I could then arrange the whole thing in order."

But when Goethe arrived back in Weimar on 18 June 1788, a year and three-quarters after he had left, there was no more thought of cooperating on a joint preparation of the text for publication. Charlotte von Stein had observed with a sharp eye—and an even sharper mind—the change that had taken place in Goethe, had felt the deep influence of the "Roman beloved." She later read with horror the *Roman Elegies* when they were published in Schiller's periodical. This was the beginning of what Goethe had written about his *dismissal:* "I was dismissed back to formless Germany out of an Italy rich in form and I had to exchange a joyful sky for a dark one. My friends instead of comforting me and coming back to me drove me to desperation. My delight in the most distant scarcely known objects, my sorrow, my laments over what had been lost seemed to insult them, I missed any sort of sympathy, no one understood my language."

Even Charlotte no longer understood him. When Goethe concealed his relationship with Christiane Vulpius from Charlotte von Stein for a whole year, the latter felt this to be an unacceptable insult. On 8 June 1789 the two broke off all relations; five years later, rather stiffly and formally, they resumed them but only socially. A poetic fragment written in 1795 sets a keystone:

Yes, I loved you once, as I have never loved anyone since,
But we did not find ourselves, and in all eternity we shall never find ourselves again.

Charlotte von Stein died on 6 January 1827. There were no messages from Goethe. A friend remarked: "His oldest friend, Frau von Stein, died a short while ago at the age of eighty-four: he was deeply affected even though he didn't say a word about it."[11]

In a love relationship it is freedom that creates bonds. Can we interpret the "strange but immense saying" in the twentieth and last book of *Poetry and Truth*—"nemo contra deum nisi deus ipse" (no one is against God unless it is God himself)[12]—as meaning that only the lover can also determine the boundaries of love? Goethe "always ascribed immense things to his partners as well as to his friends and collaborators. This is part of the economy of his life, an economy based on great consumption."[13] Is this "immensity" the sacrifice that people—in this case, as so often, women—have to make if they want to take part in the lives of geniuses? Bertolt Brecht at all stages of his life, including that of exile, demanded sacrifices of this sort. But for our topic it has to be of interest what influence Frau von Stein had upon the writer, and that influence was present not only in her function as a mirror for reflections and the object of projections.

Julius Petersen related the "divine woman" from the poem *Dedication,* "the transfigured image of an earthly woman," to Charlotte von Stein, "who, like no other, clarified and ennobled the poet's creations."[14] The connection is bold but not without validity. The stanzaic epic *Dedication* was written in 1784 as an introduction to the religious epic *The Secrets*[15] that he had written for "you"—for Frau von Stein and Herder—and which remained a fragment. Twice, in a first edition of the writings that Göschen published in 1787 and later in the large edition of the works put out by Cotta in 1806–1810, Goethe placed *Dedication*—without altering the text—at the beginning of the first volume as an introduction to the works. He thus placed the poem in a most prominent position. The *Deutscher Klassiker Verlag* edition of Goethe's works that prints all the poems in a "collective and occasional chronological order" also starts with *Dedication.* The editor, Karl Eibl, emphasized the special position of the poem: "Although the removal of *Dedication* from *The Secrets* to the beginning of *The Writings* was a sort of emergency measure, and although the allegorical manner of the representation is rather untypical of Goethe, this construction of a poetic dedication, at least in its central motif of the matutinal scenery of dawn with the gradually dissolving mists of the night, and the related theme of the relationship of Poetry and Truth, can act as representative of Goethe's conception of poetry." Goethe gives no indication that the matutinal phenomenon, the "divine woman" with the veil, is supposed to be Frau von Stein (there can be none, since Goethe always avoided revelations of this sort), but in the poem there are enough intimations of what Frau von Stein really meant to his life and work during the years in which he saw her "transubstantiated into every object." In the poem "the divine woman" hands him the "veil of poetry"—a woman of whom it is said, "You gave me peace when passion wormed its way restlessly through my young limbs." The poem shows that the paths of truth bring us happiness and unhappiness and can perhaps lead to a life that oscillates between the poles of solitude and partnership.

In the school of Frau von Stein Goethe experienced truth about himself and time and again the insight that he was actually "a . . . writer." Although encouraged by his friends, Goethe could not continue writing *Poetry and Truth;* later he was to say that he could only tell the true story of his first ten years in Weimar "in the cloak of a story or a fairy-tale; the world would never again believe that it was actual fact. . . . what I became and achieved the world may know; the actual details of it remain my secret." The religious epic *The Secrets,* whose humane religion was inspired by Frau von Stein, remained a fragment. The great dramatic works, *Iphigenia on Tauris* and *Torquato Tasso* could only have been written within the Weimar constellation in which the reconciliation of the ideal with the real appeared possible. "Iphigenia" is not Schiller's "beautiful soul," not the virgin who can absolve man, she is rather the woman matured in guilt and sacrifice who discovers that the divine does not reside "in heaven above" but is only actualized in man and his deeds. "I brood all day about Iphigenia," Goethe wrote to Frau von Stein on 14 February 1779 when he began writing it down, and he goes on to say that he is burdened with official duties and "has only one foot in the spurs of the poet's hippogriff." The five acts were completed on 6 March after six weeks of the most intimate liaison with Charlotte von Stein. The first performance took place on 6 April, Goethe played Orestes, Corona Schröter Iphigenia. In his diary we read, "*Iph* performed, very good effect especially upon chaste people." On 12 July *Iphigenia* was produced again with substantially the same cast. Frau von Stein, jealous of Caroline Schröter, attended neither of the two performances.

In the play *Torquato Tasso* the poet, Tasso, and the man of the world, Antonio, quarrel about the topics of poet and society, freedom and attachment, about Rousseau's ideal of nature and the ideal of the humane person. Princess Leonore wants to reconcile the two. Goethe's "day of invention" for *Tasso* was 30 March 1780; he began writing in October. The work began under the sign of his relationship to Frau von Stein. He confesses in a letter of 20 April 1781, "as soon as I began writing *Tasso* I prayed to you. My whole soul is with you." The revision that took place during and after his Italian journey reflects a relationship in the process of dissolution and the final breach between them. The poet Tasso violates the social mores of the court before the forum of courtly society, and twice in the course of his passion for the princess he wounds the moderation of the courtly community. The princess admonishes him:

> No further Tasso! There are many things
> That should be vehemently grasped:
> But there are others that can be achieved
> Only by moderation and renunciation.
> This is what men say of virtue and of the love
> Related to it. Think well on this!

At the end Tasso is reconciled with the man of the world, Antonio, who stands so "firm" while he, Tasso, is only "the storm-tossed wave." However:

"Mighty Nature / that formed these rocks also / gave the wave its motion." Tasso founders on the rock of "the disproportion of talent with life." True, a God still permitted him to say what he suffered and his suffering changes the man of the world into a friend; true, Tasso will produce new poetic creations, but Goethe here bids farewell to the picture that he had painted up to this time of the poet as a genius hopelessly alienated from the world. Here too we see the effect of the constellation of Weimar: the poet as the man who despises the world, and the man of the world who strives for totality—Goethe later emphasized the fact that the conditions of the court, of life, and of love in Weimar were the same as those in *Tasso,* and thus he could "with justification say of his portrayal, *It is bone of my bone and flesh of my flesh,*" as he said to Eckermann in 1827.

Goethe had learned from Charlotte the "power of love" and the "spirit of purity" that motivated his writing of *Iphigenia,* "and yet my inmost soul is dedicated ever and solely to the divine love that gradually expels what is alien by the spirit of purity that is itself thus finally becoming pure as spun gold." Frau von Stein's school became for Goethe a school of self-education. His diary entries in which Frau von Stein figures with the expressive sign of the sun—0— were little more than keywords. In the course of time however they took on more and more the nature of reports, minutes of a "private education" (to Charlotte von Stein 4 November 1782): "it occurred to me that my inner being has become firmer in the course of a year" (2 September 1777), and "every day I gain more insight into and skill in active life" (end of April 1780). "Walking early in the Stern I pondered where and in what places I still lacked something . . . tried to make certain things as clear as possible to myself" (28 August 1780). What he "became and achieved" is to be ascribed to Charlotte von Stein, she pointed him towards that "hard work of self-observation" and to the ethical goal that Goethe, seeking purity, mentions ever more frequently in his diary. On 5 June 1776 Goethe had already written in his diary the first words of the Horatian Ode, "*Aequam memento (rebus in arduis servare mentem)*" (Remember in the face of the most difficult things, to keep an even mind), a call for moderation. On 30 November 1777 at the beginning of his secret journey to the Harz he wrote: "Spent the whole day in equal purity." On 12 February 1778: "continuing pure alienation from people. Peace and certainty in life and action. A great deal of happy and lively imagination in myself." At the beginning of the year 1779 there is again a remark about "striving for purity." In the middle of February a brief note that he is beginning to write *Iphigenia.* "Totally unsullied it is only the heart that enjoys it"—is what he writes about his play *Iphigenia*. In November 1777 we read in the diary, "Divine Fate . . . let me now also enjoy purity fresh and at one with myself."

"Wanderer's Nightsong," sent to Frau von Stein, describes the longing for "sweet [soul] peace." And a few weeks later a further essential statement followed: the poem "Why didst thou give us deep insights?" The poem links the experience of the present with thoughts of primeval relationships and the transmigration of souls. Goethe himself interpreted it: in a fragment of a letter to Wieland, we read, "I cannot explain the significance—the power—this woman has over me in any other way than by the transmigration of souls—were we indeed once man and wife?—Now we know of ourselves—veiled in spiritual fragrance—I have no name for us—the past—the future—the all." Goethe wrote this poem down on paper in his own hand and dated it 14 April 1776.

> Oh thou wast in times gone by
> My wife or my sister,
> You knew every trait of my being,
> Discovered how the purest nerve resounded
> Could read me with a glance,
> He who is hard for mortal eye to penetrate.
> You dripped moderation into my hot blood,
> Directed the wild crazy course,
> In your angel's arms the
> Shattered breast revived itself.

Here Goethe, as far as he was able to, clings to Charlotte von Stein's influence on him. Yet in the following verses those "hours of bliss" were already consigned to the past, to "memory," and the new state is now "pain." However there remains for him the old truth, and once more he conjures up a playful happiness.

> How fortunate that the same fate that tormented us
> Is powerless to change us.

Goethe published three poems at this time in which the name "Lida" appears: "To Lida," "The Goblet," and "Distance." In 1820 he wrote a poem in connection with these three poems, "Between Both Worlds." When Viktor Hehn gave his lectures on Goethe in 1848 he said, "It is not yet possible to say who this Lida was. She belonged to the highest realm, that much is certain. Goethe himself did not dare to raise the veil that covered this love. . . . Lida aided the inner purification of the poet . . . her influence, her love contributed to the development of the artist in him, to making him happy and wise, and to fixing a lovely human morality in his whole being and character." In 1848–51 Adolf Schöll published Goethe's letters to Frau von Stein in three volumes,[16] and from that time on Lida has been identified with Charlotte. There is an indication in the first version of the poem "To Lida." In this version the first line runs "The only one, Lotte, whom you can love" while in the version of 1789 the line runs, "the only one, Lida, whom you can love." The lines *Why didst Thou give us deep insights* are reckoned among Goethe's best-known. In all there are seventeen poems in the complex "To Lida." They have connecting themes, the moderation of hot blood, the clarity of love, the conflict between love and non-love, the problems of freedom and bondage, of proximity and distance. They show how much this relationship continued to affect Goethe and that he was still affected even after the relationship broke up. There was no place in Goethe's nature, characterized as it was by change and alteration and always ready to be subject to and to assimilate new experiences, for a "sloughed off snake's skin," only the "Shaped form that develops as it lives." Once again, in the two versions of the poem "To the Moon," Goethe casts up the sum of his relationship with Charlotte von Stein. The first version is the song of a restless person, of the Sturm und Drang man, who sees himself for the first time tied to a specific place; the second, more extensive version, already shows evidence of moderation and of someone looking back at a happiness, a person hoping to be healed.

A variant from her own pen was found among Charlotte von Stein's papers. Goethe's final version of the last strophe runs

> What is unknown to men,
> Or not considered,
> Wanders in the night
> Through the labyrinth of the breast.

Frau von Stein changed it to:

> Or else despised,
> Shines through the night
> In divine garb.

Goethe conjures up the individual in whose breast lie the stars of fate; Charlotte von Stein makes the stars shine as the sign of a higher, more pure, world that is "unknown or else despised" by many people. Charlotte's adaptation is the settlement of her account with Goethe.

In his old age, on 2 April 1818, Goethe wrote to Karl Ernst Schubarth, the philologist and aesthete—who had asked for an elucidation of Goethe's relationship to Frau von Stein in his work *On Making a Judgment about Goethe with Reference to Related Literature and Art*—that he would "gladly confess that he had learned a lot from persons who liked to reflect kindly upon me and that he had for that reason venerated and admired them. In this way Delbrück drew my attention to the fact that my few little poems to *Lida* were the most tender of all. I would never have thought this and would have even been much less aware of it and it is true! It gives me pleasure to think of it now and to recognize it."

In 1820 two poems, "For Ever" and "Between Two Worlds," appeared in the journal *On Art and Antiquity* edited by Goethe. "For Ever" was written in 1784 and was planned as part of the epic *The Secrets:*

> The light . . .
> That burns only to give poets beautiful images
> That I had discovered in her
> In all my finest hours and found it for myself.

Once more Goethe's self-observation and his school of auto-didacticism! In the poem of 1820, "Between Both Worlds," Lida/Charlotte von Stein and Shakespeare are mentioned in the same breath as those to whom he owed his "venerable total profit":

> To belong to one alone,
> To venerate one alone,
> How this unites heart and sense!
> Lida! Joy of closest nearness,
> William! Stars of the most beauteous heights,
> What I am I owe to you.
> Days and years have passed away,
> And yet upon those hours together,
> Rest my venerable total profit.

Goethe published his observations "Shakespeare without End" in Cotta's *Morgenblatt* on 12 May 1815. What did Shakespeare mean to him at this time? The observations begin with his insight into man's capacity for reflection: "The highest goal that man can achieve is the consciousness of his own convictions and thoughts, the understanding of himself that introduces him to the recognition of alien convictions." Shakespeare, he said, communicated this to him in his "play form," in his attempt by means of his plays—that contain less "sensual action" and more "spiritual word"—to establish a balance between should and would. Such "benefit flows into him both from Shakespeare's works and from Frau von Stein's nature."

In his early years in Weimar Goethe often spoke of the "fate" that guided him, of the "gods" that favored it. He tried to maintain a sort of balance in his life between his existence as statesman, civil servant, writer, scientist, socialite, and lover, a balance that he himself could acknowledge. There was, and this is how he sums up his existence in a diary entry in the year 1778, "a lot of work in me." But over and over again there was play as well.

This juxtaposition of seriousness and playfulness, a fluctuation between "peace and war" was what he had experienced in the course of the year. He accompanied Duke Carl August on a journey to Berlin from 10 May to 1 June 1778 at a time of political unrest. On 1 May, Goethe had sent "To the Moon" ("Blessed is he who shuts himself off from the world without hatred") to his "dearest Frau," as he often addressed Charlotte in letters. On the way there they stopped with the prince in Dessau; Goethe was—as he wrote to Frau von Stein on 14 May 1778—"very moved at the way the gods have allowed the prince to create a dream around himself. It is, as one goes through it, like a fairy-tale that is being read aloud and has the complete character of the Elysian fields, one thing melts into another in the softest possible diversity." Then three days later in Berlin, "It is a beautiful feeling to sit at the source of war at the moment when it begins to overflow. And the magnificence of the royal city and life and order and excess would be as nothing without the thousands and thousands of people ready to be sacrificed for it. People, horses, carriages, ordnance, armament, the place is swarming with it all." In this juxtaposition of "the most pure sweetness" on the one hand and the "preparations for war on the other" Goethe is not reacting as a man of action but as an observer; he will talk later of his "quiet and cold path of observation" (letter to Schiller, 16 August 1797). He sees himself as a chronicler, he has the feeling that he is getting closer and closer to "the goal of dramatic being," the feeling that he is enduring the movement of "war and peace." He feels this because "what affects me more closely is how great men play with people and the gods play with great men" (in a letter to Frau von Stein). Goethe the observer sees the events of his day as a double game.

Work and Play. Goethe expressed it at the beginning of the year in a special manner. On the occasion of Duchess Luise's birthday he wrote the "dramatic fancy *The Triumph of Sentimentality*," his "latest madness," in which the "devil of parody" was still in the saddle. The leading characters, Andrason, "a humorous king," and Mandandante, his wife, were played by none other than Goethe himself and Caroline Schröter. King Andrason is embarrassed, he does not know how his play is to go on; a lady-in-waiting says to him, "You are a German, and in the German theater anything goes." But King Andrason does not want to disappoint his audience. He calls upon the gods for help for he has himself noticed that "of course we are actually playing ourselves."

This thought about plays and playing is something that Goethe will not let go of; later he was to dedicate the last piece in the *Xenien* (a poetic collaboration with Schiller) to this view. He had picked up Homer again and had drawn inspiration from his judgment on Xenion's suitors: "Everything was only a game! / You suitors are indeed all still alive / here is the bow and here the place for the wrestling." In Homer the suitors are killed, in the *Xenien* they are challenged to a playful defense.

Numerous self-interpretations by the still youthful privy councillor—he was only thirty-seven when he fled from Weimar—aim at this time at gaining experience and making light of disappointments, seeing them as a plus in the formation of his own personality and using them as such. "Renunciation" became a keyword for him from 1782 on: "in the midst of happiness," he wrote, "he was living in a constant state of renunciation." This is the origin of the renouncers in the *Journeyman Years*.

Goethe now recognizes that the Weimar years are, up to this point, reflections. "The existences of strangers are the best mirrors in which to recognize our own existence," he writes to Charlotte von Stein in September 1783, and he knows that reflections in the moral sphere are essential to education. Later in 1823, he will maintain in his writings on literature "that repeated moral reflections not only keep the past alive but intensify it into a higher life." As a "form of play" and as play and reflection Shakespeare and

Frau von Stein were essential to Goethe. Andrason's insight, "actually we are playing ourselves," characterizes Goethe's creative process, but his attitude towards publishers also results from this.

The Mediator   Paris was to be a school for Goethe, but Rome was to be the university. It is as though all the years of his life before the Italian journey were merely preparation for it. He took nothing from Carlsbad but a "saddle bag and a badger-skin satchel"; his "papers" were the manuscripts of *Iphigenia, Tasso, Egmont,* and *Faust,* and en route he bought a small suitcase.

Goethe gave his journey the air of a flight, traveling incognito as a painter, Johann Philipp Möller, "Early in the morning at 5 a.m., I stole away from Carlsbad, otherwise they would not have let me go," he wrote in his *Diary of the Italian Journey for Frau von Stein* (1786), sketches of the journey that were intended for her alone; indeed they were written for her. In December, he confided to her, "The fact that you were sick, and that it was my fault that you were sick weighs so heavily on my heart that I am unable to express it. Forgive me! I myself was engaged in a life and death struggle and no tongue can express what was taking place inside me; this plunge has brought me to myself. My love! My love!"

Yet Goethe had put a lot of things in order by 2 September. In a long letter to the duke he asked for "an indefinite leave of absence." His servant, the court auditor Seidel, was to take care of his house and keep an eye on "Fritzgen," Charlotte von Stein's fourteen-year-old son who was living in the house on the Frauenplan. His second servant, Johann Georg Paul Götze, was loaned to Knebel. He asked Herder to "give my greetings to those who are left behind and if possible say something sensible to them on my behalf, so that they will forgive me for leaving clandestinely." Seidel was the only one to find out where the first stopping place was—it was Rome: "To M. Joseph Cioja, for delivery to M. Jean Philippe Möller in Rome." And "at eleven o'clock at night," he wrote once more to Frau von Stein, "Finally, finally I am ready, actually I could do another eight days work here but I want to be off and once more I say adieu to you as well. Farewell my sweetheart, I am yours." "He left his friends a bit rudely" was Charlotte von Stein's comment.

But the most important directions he gave on this busy 2 September

were about the preparation of the edition of his *Writings* for Georg Joachim
Göschen. "The first four volumes," he wrote to Duke Carl August, "are
finally in order, Herder stood by me faithfully and indefatigably; as for the
last four . . . I'll first see what has to be done if it isn't to be a complete
mess. . . . I am leaving all on my own under an assumed name and I hope
that this whole rather strange-seeming enterprise will turn out for the best."
He told Göschen, "I intend taking a little journey—I have told court auditor
Seidel everything. The one thing missing in the first volume is the dedication
to the readers. . . . I am enclosing a number of different comments that refer
to the publication, make what use you like of them. . . . should a case arise
where no one knows what decision to make, I would ask you to ask Herr
Superintendent General Herder in Weimar." He then signed the contract
with Göschen. "Attested to on 2 September 1786, J. W. von Goethe," and
he asked Seidel to take care of it.

Goethe's journey was a calculated undertaking. It had to be because it
had to be financed. What was more important than to learn something about
the pirates? Should he not seek out a publisher who would publish a decent
edition of the *Works,* edited by himself, and pay him a royalty?

The suggestion that Goethe was negotiating with the prestigious Berlin
publisher Johann Friedrich Gottlieb Unger at this time is a legend that was
created by Göschen's grandson Viscount Goschen—on the basis of a mis-
reading of a letter—although Unger, who was later to publish the works of
the Romantics, had already made a name for himself. He ran a printing firm
in Berlin, a publishing house, and a type-casting works.

An item in the Jena *Allgemeine Literaturzeitung* (31 May 1786) reported
that Goethe was, for the first time, working on an edition of his *Collected
Works* that would finally contain what had previously been published against
his will and apparently in false form.

Goethe now established a method that had been proven by his friend
Merck, an employee of the bookseller Christlob August Mylius, and he was
to use it for the whole of his life. He used an intermediary to take care of
the negotiations, while he settled the business details. However Goethe still
had a precise notion of how negotiations should be carried on: "Business
and generosity are a gift from heaven, a substitute for unhappiness in love,"
is what he says in *Stella.* He observes in his diary, "The pressure of business
is very good for the soul, for when it is freed from it, it plays more freely
and enjoys life." In *The Elective Affinities* he would later maintain, "Only

one thing lets us establish ourselves and settle down; to separate everything that is actually business from life. Business calls for gravity and rigidity, life calls for arbitrariness; business demands pure order, in life there is often a need for inconsequentiality, it is pleasant and amusing." In 1817 he wrote in the *Museums of Jena,* "Every piece of business conducted by men is actually set in motion by ethical levers. Everything depends on personality." This point of view—so important for me—was expressed by Goethe in a conversation with Friedrich von Müller: "Matters of business must be carried on abstractly, *non-humanely,* with affection or dislike, passion, favor, then you can achieve more and achieve it more quickly. Laconic, imperative, succinct." Laconic, imperative, succinct—once more we can learn something from Goethe. The separation of business and life, the separation of his negotiations with publishers from his own attitude to life, this was something that he carried out quite systematically. His contemporaries were very clear about this: Schiller wrote to Körner, "Herder admires him just as much, or even more, as a businessman as he does as a poet."

The intermediary for the first legitimate edition of his collected works was Friedrich Justin Bertuch (1747–1822). He must have appeared brilliant to Goethe and he looked like one whose qualities were as valuable to him as they were suspect; in all his business dealings with him he always kept his distance. Bertuch, a civil servant at the court, and also a private entrepreneur, was one of the richest men in Weimar and a respected citizen. At court he held the office of private secretary and keeper of the purse. He was a successful manufacturer and knew how to combine the common and the public good with his own private use. In 1782 he published anonymously *How does a private state best serve the poor and control beggary?* and in 1791 he proposed to the duke that a "State-Industry Account" be established, "a charitable, public or private, institution that would make it its only business in part to seek out the natural resources of the province and to further their cultivation and in part to enliven the artistic activity of its inhabitants, to guide and perfect it. "Bertuch is an enlightener and a businessman, philanthropist and exploiter, all of that."[17]

Bertuch was not only successful as an entrepreneur, he was also a successful writer of plays for the amateur theater at the court and he acted in the productions; he was a translator—his translation of *Don Quixote* is supposed to have been the best of his day—and he published Goethe's *Contributions to the Science of Optics.* In 1774 he had planned, together with Wieland, to found a publishing business, in order that "the best writers in Germany will be tied to us by their works for which they will receive a higher price . . . to balance out the great mob of booksellers, and consequently to force them to treat worthy academics more justly and fairly: at the moment they treat them as though they were working for them by the day and pay them accordingly." The plan never came to fruition; in its place Bertuch and Wieland published the periodicals *Teutsche Merkur* and the *Allgemeine Literaturzeitung,* among whose contributors were Goethe, Schiller, Kant, Fichte, and Wilhelm von Humboldt.

Bertuch was an unusual, if irritating, phenomenon. In a conversation in 1821, Goethe called him, "The greatest of virtuosi in the acquisition of borrowed plumes." Schiller denied having contacts with Bertuch and commented (letter to Körner on 29 August 1787) that Bertuch and Herder "hate one another like the serpent and the Son of Man."

Goethe, who had derided and mystified Bertuch in his first years in Weimar, kept his distance; he invented the verb "to bertuch." Goethe's remark about the acquisition of borrowed plumes is especially pointed, for Bertuch had imported another idea from Paris—the manufacture of artificial flowers.

Christiane Vulpius, later Goethe's wife, then twenty-nine years old, worked in Bertuch's factory as a binder: that "uneducated factory girl," as Frau von Stein was to say later. Goethe's meeting with Christiane took place in the park in Weimar on 12 June 1788.

Bertuch had suggested that Goethe negotiate with Göschen. Bertuch's suggestions must have seemed strange to Goethe, for Georg Joachim Göschen was an unknown quantity as a publisher when Bertuch first recommended him in the first half of 1786, and somehow this is what he remained. "There's something not quite right about him," Goethe was to remark later.

Georg Joachim Göschen was born on 22 April in Bremen (the exact date is not documented). His mother died when he was young, his father, a merchant, soon got into economic difficulties from which he escaped by running away. The thirteen-year-old orphan then lived with relatives, was apprenticed to Kramer, the Bremen bookseller, and later gained a position with one of the largest booksellers in Leipzig, Siegfried Leberecht Crusius. Soon he had contacts with the Leipzig literary scene.

There were in Leipzig at that time about twenty-three publishers and twelve printing works. In 1785 Göschen decided—he was now thirty-three years old—to found his own publishing house. He borrowed the start-up capital, a sum of 3,000 thalers, from Christian Gottfried Körner, a Leipzig acquaintance and friend of Schiller. At the Easter Fair he exhibited his first six titles, among them Zacharias Becker's vademecum, *Emergency and Aid Book for Farmers*—one of the greatest bookselling successes of the time in Germany.

The second number of *Thalia,* the journal that was published and mainly written by Schiller, made its appearance in the second list of the new publishing house. This identified Göschen as a publisher of the most important contemporary literature.

Through Schiller, Göschen met the author Christoph Martin Wieland and they became friends; Wieland's biographer describes how taken Wieland was with Göschen. Göschen was "a man of intellect and all-round knowledge" who "was conscious of the worthiness of his profession" and who carried on his business "for his own profit but also at all times for the honor of our literature, for the writer's greatest advantage and, from the point of view of typography, for the honor of Germany." Wieland himself could not yet become one of Göschen's authors, he was bound by contract to another publishing house; nevertheless in 1789 Göschen published Wieland's *Thoughts on the Freedom of Thinking about the Subjects of Faith.* Göschen had an outstanding circle of advisers in Körner, Schiller, and Wieland, and another member of it was the man whom Goethe had chosen to be his intermediary and who recommended him so urgently to the new house, Friedrich Justus Bertuch. Goethe was not aware of Bertuch's ties to Göschen and what he also did not know was the substantial interest that lay behind Bertuch's recommendation. Larger capital sums than Göschen had up till then at his disposal were needed to make Goethe commit himself to such a new publisher. Aware of Göschen's limited resources, Bertuch had made an arrangement between himself and Göschen "that they were mutually committed to the joint publication of Goethe's works and would share the profit and loss equally." Göschen and his partner (Körner) were to be responsible for two-thirds and Bertuch for one-third of any loss sustained.

In June 1786 the first negotiations between Bertuch and Göschen took place and once again Goethe launched his idea of an eight-volume edition of his complete works with a demand for a payment of three louis d'or per signature. Göschen asked Bertuch to seek a reduction from Goethe. Bertuch intervened and was successful because reckoning up the number of signatures printed was also another burden for Goethe. However, in the process, Goethe raised his demand to a lump-sum payment of 2,000 Imperial thalers.

Göschen, who wanted to have Goethe as an author at all costs, was ready to meet the demand. In Goethe's letter to Charlotte von Stein on 6 July 1786 he sounds a note of satisfaction: "I have reached agreement with Göschen about my writings. I gave way on one point [about the fixing of a price per signature for the second edition], as for the rest he agreed with everything." The contract was signed on 2 September 1786. This contract contains some remarkable provisions. In paragraph 1 the author promises, "conditionally," that "if he has the time he will do his best to give the last four volumes a more complete form than would appear from the announcement." It was further calculated that Himburg's pirated version should be declared the model for the design and layout, and finally "the author leaves the typography and the embellishment of the work entirely in the publisher's hands." A royal octavo edition was supposed to be "stipulated" later. Such imprecise conditions are often the seeds of misunderstanding and contention. Paragraph 10 contains an option clause: "The author will offer his succeeding works to the publisher, Herr Göschen, before offering them to others, but reserves the right to impose other conditions according to the circumstances." With what caution or even mistrust did Goethe the lawyer approach this contract! The collaboration lasted for five years. Goethe kept to the letter of the contract. The relationship between author and publisher was always only indirect, but it was an intensive one both by letter and through intermediaries; they never met in person.

"The dignity of the printed book" Göschen's pride in his significant acquisition is reflected in two actions. In mid-July 1786 he announced the edition in the *Journal von und zu Deutschland:*

The Collected Works of the Privy Councillor von Göthe [sic]
in eight volumes, published by Georg Joachim Göschen in Leipzig.

Without doubt the public will be glad to learn that Privy Councillor von Göthe in Weimar has decided to publish a complete edition of his collected works with my publishing house. His friends and the admirers of his muse both inside and outside Germany have long wished for this decision, and the public longed for several works of the author, whom it has placed among its favorite poets from the very beginning . . . .

As support for his advertisement, Göschen published in it a letter from Goethe as a "statement by the author":

> You know the reasons that finally encourage me to publish a collection of all my writings, both those that have already appeared and those still to be published. . . . You will receive for this purpose my complete works divided into eight volumes.

VOLUME ONE

Dedication to the German public.

The Sorrows of Young Werther.

VOLUME TWO

Götz von Berlichingen. The Accomplices.

VOLUME THREE

Iphigenia. Clavigo. The Siblings.

VOLUME FOUR

Stella. The Triumph of Sentimentality. The Birds.

VOLUME FIVE

Claudine. Erwin and Elmire. Lila. Jeri and Bätely.

The Fisherwoman.

VOLUME SIX

Egmont, incomplete. Elpenor, two acts.

VOLUME SEVEN

Tasso, two acts. Faust, A Fragment.

A moral and political puppet play.

VOLUME EIGHT

Miscellaneous writings and poems.

In the letter Goethe goes on: "I can say with certainty that the first four volumes will contain the pieces announced above; how I wish that I had the tranquillity and the opportunity to give you, at least in part, those works that are just begun and which are placed in the sixth and seventh volumes in their complete form; then the form of the last four volumes would be completely different."

The division of the works in volumes five to eight was in fact changed later on; the division of volumes one to four, on the other hand, is in accordance with the announcement.

Göschen could not have been very happy about announcing things that were fragments and incomplete and the expression of a hope that perhaps much could be finished which would give the volumes a different form. He always mentioned this announcement in his later complaints about Goethe. At first however Göschen saw in this "declaration of the author" "the most secure certification of *authenticity* and of my *legal ownership of this edition.*"

It is typical of Göschen to address an admonition and a warning to pirates, for it was clear to him that they were the people who were lying in wait for such a prey. Thus the advertisement finishes with a proclamation:

> *To the Pirates.* I can certainly imagine very easily that the works announced here will be seen by you as a very nice speculation; but allow me, gentlemen, to assure you before you get to work that I have taken some very pretty measures against you, and have enough courage to dash all your hopes—even if I have to sacrifice all my profit—if you think by your illicit activity to interfere with my legal earnings. Whatever reputation you still enjoy will certainly be forfeit by such an undertaking. You will be so shamed, that your own wife, your own child will look at you with disgust and no honest man will wish to share a glass with you.

Göschen's appeal seems to have had an effect; at least there is no mention of a pirated version of his edition.

Yet Göschen had little luck at first. He did not enroll the 1,000 subscribers he had hoped for and he ascribed that to the announcement of writings that were as yet incomplete, as he wrote to Bertuch on 29 October 1786: "Göthe played a nasty trick on me by announcing that he was sending the writings in incomplete form. It has done a lot of harm to the subscription list." Göschen had at first been optimistic about the sales of the edition. When he accused the "German spirit" (in letters to Bertuch, 12 July 1786 and 18 March 1787) of not being steadfast "in purchasing its great writers," he still reckoned on getting subscriptions for a thousand copies. As to the remaining thousand copies, he said that "he was also not afraid of their not meeting their costs and making a profit even without a subscription." But the response to the subscription offer was not good. At the Easter Fair in

1787, 692 copies had been sold to subscribers. After the publication of volumes 5 to 8 there was a continuous drop in sales.

Things were complicated for the young publisher by Goethe's leaving for his Italian journey and only communicating with him infrequently. He complained to Bertuch time and again, "I don't know where Goethe is." The Weimar edition makes no mention of any communication from Goethe to Göschen between 20 February and 15 August 1787. In the face of intervals of this length and the difficulty of communicating with Rome there was no question of production proceeding normally. Goethe, mistrustful and absent, now engaged his intermediaries, who could only act according to the terms of the contract. Seidel, in fact, left in charge of financial matters, came up with the individual parts of the manuscript only after he had received an advance. This must have angered and displeased Göschen. "Do your business with Göschen and make sure you get money for the last part of the manuscript at once. Do not hand it over before then—you only need refer to your contract," was what Goethe wrote to Seidel from Rome on 9 February 1788. He also informed Göschen on 27 October 1787, "I am sending an open copy of this letter to Seidel, so that he will know what is happening between us." Seidel received the following instruction: "Copy the letter to Göschen or at least make excerpts from it so that you will at least be *au courant* and will remember what has been negotiated with him." And then follows the statement that applied both to Göschen *and* his fellow publishers: "It's not just him but all of them." The letter ends with the warning, "The rest of volume five with the copperplate is to pass through your hands and you will not hand it over without receiving cash. The contract stipulates that and there's no need to make any excuses." Thus Göschen was involved with two intermediaries and gradually felt the mistrust that underlay the stipulation about advances.

However, as difficult as the relationship with Goethe was, Göschen had the main points of the contract in mind and he did not stint his personal attention; he chose the paper, the binding, and was not ready to leave proofreading to the proofreaders but read the proofs himself as well. He sent the printed sheets to Herder, who had been given that responsibility by Goethe, and Herder told Göschen that Goethe was not interested in the way the printing turned out—that proved to be a mistake. The first four volumes came out in May 1787 and on the title page of some copies there appeared: "*Goethe's Writings:* Parts I–IV."

The public's reaction does not seem to have been very positive. "Book-sellers who took copies from the fair for speculative purposes want to return them. People do not understand *Iphigenia,* and *The Siblings* is boring. *The Triumph of Sentimentality* is out of date and comes too late, *The Birds* is too dark. The devil knows what people want," Göschen complained to Herder and Bertuch. What is more, Göschen forgot to send Goethe complimentary copies! Goethe is annoyed. When he finally receives the volumes, he writes at once, "what is to be said in this connection?" and tells Göschen on 27 October 1787, "I cannot say that the sight of the first three volumes of my writings . . . gives me great pleasure. The paper seems to be good printing paper rather than writing paper, the format is too small after the pages have been cut, the letters appear dulled, the color like the paper is uneven, so that these volumes look more like an ephemeral journal than a book that should last for a time. There happened to be a copy of the Himburg edition here—it looks like a dedication copy compared with yours. But still it's done now and cannot be undone. I also find in some pieces that I have leafed through that there are typographical errors and omissions, but I cannot decide whether the manuscript or the proofreader is to blame." Goethe now de-mands that the "better edition be produced on Dutch paper, as was stipu-lated in the contract." Goethe had sent Seidel a letter from Rome asking him at the same time to tell Bertuch of its transmission to Göschen. Bertuch comments, in a letter of 19 November 1787, that Goethe's complaint about the printing is simply "an echo of the jaundiced Herder," but as to the demand for a "better" edition, Göschen should disabuse Goethe of "this false illusion." "I must confess that I would not have thought Goethe capable of such a trick."

Göschen was downcast. He had taken every possible care, whereas Goethe had taken no interest in the printing nor had he himself read the proofs. He complains to Bertuch (on 22 November 1787), "A letter like Goethe's can ruin your good nature. There has not been a line printed in this type before and it's supposed to be dulled! The paper that is white but not thick so as to keep the volumes to a reasonable size is supposed to be printing paper—I wish it were. Herder ought to compare the edition of his own works with it. . . . I can assure you on the Bible that had I known Herder and Goethe from the angle from which I now know them, I would not have been happy about publishing their works. Are 2,000 Reichsthalers child's play?"

Göschen simply did not get over Goethe's criticism. In his letter of 19 November, Bertuch spreads the word that "Seidel himself supposes that the manuscript itself was responsible for the typographical errors and the omissions." Göschen wanted to have "satisfaction from Herder and damn him." There is no evidence that Herder was involved in an intrigue, all we know is that he and Bertuch were bitter enemies.

Schiller writes to Körner on 29 August 1787: "Things have got to such a pitch with Herder that his whole expression changes when Bertuch's name is mentioned. But even the pliant Bertuch is vulnerable on this one point and feels something extremely unusual for him—passion." Goethe's relationship with Bertuch also begins to cool; Bertuch's business manners obviously annoy him, the *Du* becomes a *Sie* again, and finally they break off the relationship altogether. It may be that this annoyance spilled over onto Goethe's attitude to Göschen.

Goethe simply had special standards and his own criteria for the printing, as well as for the aesthetic beauty, of a book. In his speech at the opening of the Friday Society on 9 September 1791 in Weimar, he said, "Therefore letterpress printing and its freedom puts us immeasurably in its debt and bestows an enormous benefit." "The art of printing is a factor," he wrote in 1820, "from which the second part of world history dates." Again and again he talked of the "dignity of the printed book" and wished to have "beautiful type and wide margins" as the true ornament of every book. The critics of the time however had different standards. They liked Göschen's edition, and the influential journals praised the production.

Goethe's mother shared her son's criticism; in a letter written on 9 March 1789 she observed, "As far as I am concerned Göschen is a s[coundre]l, there he is sending the eighth volume bound in paper like the four first parts—whoever fooled him into binding the fifth volume so magnificently? But he'll get his comeuppance, I sent him a letter complaining about this unexemplary behavior."

The critics did not, however, know that the first volume contained a text that Goethe had carefully worked over but that has caused all editors since the greatest difficulty: the famous second version of *Werther,* with the title *The Sorrows of Young Werther.* Göschen published this, too, in 1787 side by side with volume 1 of the *Writings*—probably as a protection against pirated versions. It was in this separate edition that the name of the author—Goethe—first appeared.

The origin and constitution of the text of this second version are not without a certain editorial piquancy. On Sunday 30 December 1781, Goethe had invited Christian Joseph Jagemann—the dowager duchess's librarian since 1775—to a midday meal; he was a connoisseur of the Italian language and Goethe wanted to discuss the Italian translation of *Werther* with him. But the first edition was missing from his library. He sent a note to Charlotte von Stein: "My soul longs for you once again. To keep myself in check I have invited Jagemann to a meal. Send me Werther's Italian letters and your German copy." Unbelievable as it seems, neither Goethe nor Frau von Stein had a copy of Weygand's first edition. Frau von Stein sent him a pirated version by Himburg. Six months later, on 19 June 1782, he again asked Frau von Stein to "send me my printed works, I have a strange idea and want to see whether I can carry it out." Julius Petersen remarks of this "idea" that it was probably the reworking of *Werther.*

But the privy councillor of the Weimar decade was no longer the Sturm and Drang figure of the years in Wetzlar and Leipzig. Goethe, since having once more to busy himself with *Werther,* was thinking of changes, insertions, explanations, tonings-down, all of which were to make the background more understandable. In November 1782 he wrote to his friend Knebel: "I have gone through my Werther and will write it out again in manuscript, he is returning to his mother's womb and you shall see him after his rebirth. As I am very composed, I feel that I have skill enough to undertake such a delicate and dangerous task." And to another in May 1783, "I have taken up Werther again in my quiet moments and I think, without harming what caused such a sensation, that I can screw it a few notches higher. In the process it was my intention to place Albert in such a light that he will, it is true, be mistaken by the passionate youth but not by the reader. This will have the desired and the best effect. I hope you will be satisfied." In June he writes to Frau von Stein, "I am making corrections to Werther and I am constantly finding that the author did a very bad thing in not shooting himself after he had completed it." In June 1786 Goethe offered Göschen, through the agency of Bertuch, a "revised" *Werther.* He himself was, however, working on changes. Herder and Wieland were working with him. On 6 July he writes to Frau von Stein; "Herder has the right sense for Werther and has discovered what is not quite right with the composition. . . . Wieland is also going through things with great care and so it will be easy for me to put some order at least into the first four volumes." On 1 September he also writes to her, "We have come to a decision about the end of *Werther*. After Herder had carried it round with him for a few days, we gave preference to the new version. I hope the change will please you and that the public will not scold me." As far as Goethe was concerned, the revision was finished on 2 September. He told Göschen that Seidel would be handing over the manuscript and left it to Göschen, as we have already mentioned, "to make what use he wanted" of his remarks about the printing. This was to prove a mistake.

The changes consist mainly of a stylistic polishing of the first version, the deletion of swearwords, and the avoidance of dialect turns of phrase. Goethe maintains a regular word order and divides the long periods up into parts. But he also changed a lot of the content. He dispenses with the passage in which Werther's encounter with high society is characterized as the underlying conflict. Albert is made into a more sympathetic character; now he is even more worthy of Lotte's love and thus the conflict becomes more manifest, the suffering greater, the climax more insistent. The scene of Lotte with the canary is inserted. The most important addition is Werther's meeting with the farm lad who becomes a murderer, a meeting that points to the inexorable approach of the tragedy. Goethe expands the editor's report, and it is at this point that the greatest changes are undertaken.

The striking thing about the edition of the second version is that Goethe, although he had been working on the revision of the content for years, had neglected the external form, that he himself read none of the proofs and entrusted proofreading to others.[18]

As we have already mentioned in connection with the history of the printing of *Werther*, Goethe by refusing to read proof did not control the "use of it as you see fit" that Göschen's printers had made of it. There is one thing that is totally inexcusable, however: in the course of revising the text he did not use the first edition but the text of Himburg's pirated version that Frau von Stein had loaned him, "J. W. Goethe's Writings. First Volume, Third Edition, Berlin 1779. Christian Himburg, Publisher." There is a copy of Goethe's handwritten corrections in the Weimar archives. Goethe overlooked the fact that Himburg was not only a pirate but also an "improver": Himburg or his assistants had changed Goethe's style, shortened it, and, in the terms of the day, "modernized" it. A few of the stylistic changes were along the lines that Goethe was now working on. Himburg's text also contained mistakes and omissions. Had he not noticed? Or did he approve? Goethe had instructed Seidel to copy out the text of the Himburg edition again, and the manuscript that resulted does contain all of Himburg's changes and errors. It contains, further, idiosyncrasies of Seidel's orthography and punctuation. This manuscript is also in the Weimar archives and could have been referred to by Bernhard Seuffert, the editor of the nineteenth volume of the Weimar edition in 1899. To this day it is impossible to decide which forms of the text and which characteristics were really authorized by Goethe and which he had not seen. The copyists and proofreaders changed a lot of things of their own accord. Seuffert determined that there were "five proofreaders" and he did not succeed in completely distinguishing among them "in spite of the good advice and the explanations of the experienced gentlemen in the archives."[19] The relationship between Göschen and Goethe continued, more sensitive on both sides, more angry, more impatient. When Goethe delivered the texts for the fifth volume, he asked Göschen to "pay the royalty to Seidel." As always, Goethe kept strictly to the contract: laconic, imperative, succinct. This was not easy for Göschen, as he always approached all his writers trustingly, without calculation. For Göschen the material result of Goethe's writings must have been disappointing. Up to September 1789 he had spent 7,087 Thalers and taken in only 5,367.

It was not only the actual loss and the declining sales that affected the publisher; the continuation of the edition itself was constantly interrupted even after Goethe had returned to Weimar from his Italian journey on 18 June 1788. Goethe insisted that production continue and this was also Göschen's firm intention, as the subscribers were allegedly "demanding" the volumes that the publisher had agreed to produce. In July Goethe made excuses for the fact that his *Tasso* had not yet reached the desired state of completion. Finally Göschen suggested that Goethe produce the eighth volume of miscellanea first. Goethe agreed and thus in October 1789, two and a half years after the contract had been signed in Carlsbad, the eighth volume was produced.

But then there began for Göschen the "tale of woe" connected with the publication of *Tasso*. On 12 March 1780 Goethe had, as we have already mentioned, his "day of invention" and began to write and dictate. The first act was finished on 12 November 1780 and a year later, on 14 November 1781, the second act was done. As far as Goethe was concerned, the whole play was finished on 20 February 1785. In the "Avertissement" of 15 July 1786 Göschen announced the new work, "Tasso, in Two Acts." But he did not receive the manuscript before Goethe left. Goethe took the so-called *Urtasso* with him on his Italian journey. This *Urtasso* has been lost. We know of Goethe's statements from Italy, from Venice: "This evening I ordered for myself the famous song of the boatmen, who sing Tasso and Ariosto to their melodies." He wrote to Knebel on 19 February 1787, "Now I'm at work on *Tasso,* and it has to be finished." And in his *Italian Journey* on 21 February 1787, "I have to destroy completely what I have here, it's been lying around too long and neither the character, the plan, nor the tone bear the least relationship to my present intentions." This was all a sort of self-fulfilling prophecy, for Goethe had hardly worked on *Tasso* at all in Italy. Even after his return to Weimar the work progressed only haltingly and with great difficulties. In October 1788 he wrote to Knebel, "*Tasso* is only progressing slowly," and to Herder in December, "*Tasso* is still not finished."

It is easier to trace the genesis of the text than it is in the case of *Werther* as there are two manuscripts preserved from this period of writing. The first fair copy was prepared from dictation. A second fair copy was made on the basis of this one, and this was to serve as the printer's copy. As Goethe and Göschen were pressing, the third act of this second copy was given over to a second copyist, Johann Paul Götze. Goethe, who traveled a lot with Götze, promoted him to the position of Inspector of Roads and later appointed him Commissioner for Roads. Götze, however, was not au fait with the refinements of spelling and accuracy; he introduced errors into the manuscript. Later on, the first copyist, Christian Georg Vogel, was instructed to produce a fair copy for the printer according to the codified orthography in a manual he had been given.[20] Goethe, who was constantly making alterations and felt himself unequal to the task of proofreading, now asked Wieland to supervise the orthography and punctuation for the printer's copy. Wieland's corrections can be recognized in the second fair copy.

Goethe apparently had kept the fair copy and the printer's copy in his own hands until the very last minute. He could also either approve or change both Vogel's orthography and Wieland's corrections—the latter were mainly concerned with punctuation.[21] Whereas in the case of *Werther* and *Iphigenia* Herder had been solely responsible for giving the approval to print, Goethe himself "actively authorized" the printer's manuscript that was to go to Göschen.

He wrote to Göschen from Weimar on 22 June 1789:

I am enclosing the scenes of a play that I had reckoned would only involve a year's work in the writing. What has come of it is up to the public to decide. I now recommend taking the greatest care in making corrections. The previous volumes are decent, but not without faults; in the case of this play I would ask you to correct even the most minute error by substituting a new page. In view of the great care that I have lavished on this play, it is also my wish that it should come into the hands of the public in pristine form. If you want to start off the text with Roman letters, I have no objection.

. . . The manuscript of *Tasso* will follow piecemeal. Please send me immediately three copies of the printed signatures.

But the manuscript of *Tasso* did not follow piecemeal. A week later Göschen received news from Goethe that he could not yet tear himself away from a "continuation of the manuscript." Goethe continued working, as what he wanted was to present the manuscript to the public with "unheard of care," "perfectly free" from any errors. He was able to write to Herder on 2 August 1789, "You can imagine how happy I shall be if you like *Tasso,* for I have spent more time and energy on this play than I should have. For two days now I have been able to say that it is finished." On 10 August he wrote to Herder, "How happy I am that you like *Tasso.* I hope the last two acts belong with the first. Your applause is a rich reward to me for the tremendous care with which I have worked on this play. Now we are free of all passion for undertaking such a logical composition. The fragmentary form of erotic fun [that is, the *Roman Elegies*] pleases me better."

The printer's copy now went in batches to Göschen in Leipzig and the signatures came back to Weimar in batches. In August Goethe insisted that the sixth volume of the writings, containing *Tasso* and *Lila,* was to be ready for the Michaelmas Fair, in other words it had to appear at the end of September. This was not possible, the publisher would have had to be a magician, and Goethe was in the wrong when he complained about the "dilatoriness" of his publisher. But there was something else too. Göschen's concern was to get his young publishing firm going—publicity and reconstruction were called for. He had discussed a "Historical Calendar for Ladies" with Wieland, in the second volume of which (1791) Schiller's *History of the Thirty Years War* was to appear. This undertaking must have been important to him and he certainly did not want it to take second place after the sixth volume of Goethe's *Writings.* "Meanwhile Goethe has certainly held us up long enough," he wrote to Bertuch on 16 December 1789, "and it is only fair that he should be patient." Göschen was not mistaken; the calendar, with a sale of 6,000 copies, was a great success and attracted a great deal of journalistic attention, whereas when Goethe's sixth volume finally appeared in January 1790 *Tasso* hardly secured the plaudits of the public. The seventh volume, containing the Faust fragment, *Jeri and Bätely* and *Fun, Cunning and Revenge,* was to be published at once. Goethe had had the opportunity during his Italian journey of "thinking over the *Faust* plan."[22] He sent Göschen the printer's copy of *Faust* in January 1790. The volume appeared in May—the eight-volume undertaking was now completed.

The Breach with Göschen   Goethe was satisfied with the quality of the text in the edition, but he was annoyed at the poor sales and blamed their lack—in this he is no different from today's authors—on his publisher. During this period Goethe's critical statements about publishers and his "brave publisher" increased. Göschen was annoyed; he felt that Goethe no longer trusted him.

But another unpleasantness was added; there was in the contract a proposal for a new "Edition, in royal octavo, for connoisseurs of beautiful editions"; this was to include all eight volumes, but Göschen gave up the idea. What he did was to print only 500 copies of the edition, from volume 5 onwards, on Dutch paper; and there was a plan to reprint the first four volumes. This reprinting never took place. The signatures that were completed on Dutch paper were used for the production of individual editions. One thing that was completely at odds with the contract was the fact that Göschen brought out a second four-volume "inferior" edition at a cheaper price for the less affluent "lovers of Goethe's writings"—a move directed, of course, against the pirates. Bertuch had suggested to him that this edition should appear without the Göschen imprint, but he omitted either to tell Goethe about the edition or get his permission for it. In this way a perfectly law-abiding publisher produced a pirated version for Goethe! Naturally, when Goethe learned of this he was disappointed and lacked motivation for any further collaboration.

Before the "Collected Works" were complete, Goethe offered the firm, in accordance with his contract with Göschen, his new work, *An Essay to Explain the Metamorphosis of Plants.* Göschen made the mistake of asking a botanist for an evaluation, in other words he asked one of the very experts that Goethe makes direct fun of in the work. The verdict was negative, and Göschen refused the manuscript. Goethe describes the process in his report on the "Fate of the Manuscript" of his essay:

> I told him therefore that I had a work ready, scientific in content, that I wished to have published. I am not interested in pursuing the question as to whether he no longer expected a great deal from my works or whether, in this case—as I can guess—he sought information from experts, something to be expected in the case of a venture into a new field. It is enough to say that I found it hard to understand why he refused to publish my monograph, since, in the worst case, by the small sacrifice of six signatures of waste paper he would have kept for himself a productive, reliable, modest [*sic!*] author, now reappearing.
>
> Again I found myself in the same situation as the one I was in when I offered Fleischer the bookseller my *Accomplices,* but this time I did not at once take fright. Ettinger in Gotha, seeing the possibility of a connection with me, offered to take it over and so these few signatures, beautifully printed in Roman type, took their chance in the world.

We know how controversially the *Metamorphosis* essay was received; even Goethe's friends were skeptical about his botanical theories. But Göschen was deeply affected, he could not get over his own decision to turn the work down. In spite of this, in 1791, he once more offered to publish another work by Goethe. Goethe answered him on 4 July 1791:

> My thanks for the books which you sent me and for the views you express in your letter. . . . I was sorry that you rejected my little essay on metamorphoses and I had to look round for another publisher and enter into relationships that I cannot immediately break off. . . . I shall risk publishing a new theory of colors at Michaelmas. I can assure you quite honestly that I would very much have wished to see everything in one person's hands.
>
> I am working on quite a long novel and I shall have more cause to work for the theater than I have up till now. I have not yet got everything back from my Italian journey. A little book of elegies that I wrote in Rome, and a similar one of epigrams from Venice are also ready and waiting for the right moment to appear. Since, as you yourself say, my works are not so current as others that are more to the taste of a larger

public I am bound, in view of the circumstances, to get to work and I can, regrettably, foresee that the firm that publishes my future writings will be completely distracted. . . . I wish you a sincere farewell and ask you to remember me.

Göschen still did not see his mistake. He wrote to Carl August Böttiger, who was later to take over the function of an intermediary: "A peddler cannot be a patron." That is an astonishing sentence for the person who was later to say that the publisher was "in the first rank" among businessmen. When things do not pan out, the author is bound to hold the publisher guilty for not having done enough for his work, to have done too little in the way of publicity, to have undertaken too little to win readers. It is not the work, it is not the market, it is the publisher who is guilty. Göschen's whole temperament was opposed to such an attitude and he must have felt humiliated. He was not one to give in and when he did, he did not do it generously and with understanding but meanly, protesting both outwardly and inwardly and complaining of Goethe's "harassment." The two could not work together for long in such circumstances; their characters and temperaments were too different. Göschen could find no way to counter Goethe's prejudice against the position of the publisher ("it's the same thing with him as it is with the whole bunch").

True, the Goethe of 1791 was not the Goethe of 1786, when his relationship with Göschen had begun. Between these two dates Goethe's "italianità" took place and there was an immediate precipitate of this in the first volume of a new complete edition that appeared under a different imprint and contained *The Family Tree of Joseph Balsamo, called Cagliostro; The Roman Carnival;* and the epigrams and elegies from Venice and Rome.

Goethe's Italian experiences were intertwined with his experiences of the French Revolution. And when he reported to Duke Carl August from Rome that he wanted "to close off his first (or actually my second) existence as a writer and begin a new one whatever happens," this points to a deep change that was bound to have an effect on his relationships with publishers. He became more and more conscious of the material value of his works, he now demanded honoraria for poems and epigrams that appeared in the *German Monthly* and in Schiller's *Musenalmanach*. Göschen, who was involved with the results of Goethe's first spell as an author, could not see that he had begun a second one in Italy. And yet it is incomprehensible that Göschen invested so little patience, intelligence, and later even interest in the author whom he had previously wooed with all the means at his command. When he was offered *Herrmann and Dorothea,* he replied to Böttiger, who was acting as intermediary: "I would certainly like to publish Goethe's poems, primarily so that people could see that Goethe has not broken with me for good. See if the matter can be arranged. But my friend I have no money to spare until Easter of next year. But then I am at your command." The publisher Friedrich Vieweg reacted differently and won.

After Goethe, Ascent No matter, the years after the separation from
into Fame with Goethe, that is after 1791, were high points in
Wieland Göschen's publishing career. He realized his "great undertaking," the publication of Christoph Martin Wieland's collected works in four separately set and printed editions, with similar bindings and texts, each edition consisting of thirty volumes. To this day, no literary publisher has ever put such an undertaking in motion for a single author. Göschen, it is true, did consider Wieland the greatest poet of the time and he was careless enough to express this superlative publicly. But he also backed this view up by creating four editions that were outstanding both as to their typographical form and their content. But in the truest sense of the word this undertaking was to cost him dearly.

It was eight years after the initial discussion between author and publisher before Wieland and Göschen could sign and seal—on 14 April 1792—the contract for the *Collected Works,* supervised by the author himself. As Wieland was later to characterize and define it in the preface to the edition: "The concept of an edition supervised by the author includes within it the duty on the part of the author to accord his works—however important or insignificant each individual one may appear in itself—the greatest inner worth, the most perfect polish, in short the highest degree of perfection that it is possible for him to achieve." Wieland is here formulating essential principles for an edition supervised by the author. However, the edition that was announced rested upon a shaky base. The rights to seventeen of Wieland's significant works (*Musarion, The Graces, The New Amadis, Agathon, The Story of the Abderites* among others) had belonged since 1768 to the publishing house of Weidmann's Heirs & Reich in Leipzig. The firm had always paid Wieland generous royalties and had kept his books in print. Now it was defending itself by every possible means against the competitor whose firm had just been founded and was not yet fully established. A significant problem of authors' and publishers' rights arose here for the first time: May a publisher produce a complete edition, if the rights of a considerable portion of the author's oeuvre are held by another firm? And, was Wieland entitled to "improve" the works that he had handed over to Weidmann, and not to offer them to the firm to which he was bound by contract? A legal battle developed that Göschen fought through three courts, and it was watched with great interest by the public. Wieland had made his promise to and had entered into an agreement with Göschen, "because, as long as you wish to be my publisher, I prefer you on personal grounds." But he warned him time and again, "The mere thought that this accord could be the *grave of our friendship* is insupportable to me." Göschen argued against Weidmann; he wanted the whole, not just parts, and of course he would not sell the books that Weidmann had published as individual editions with his own imprint on them. Under pressure from Göschen, Wieland himself intervened in the legal battle. He presented a set of "principles" in November 1791 that were to "determine the mercantile relationship between writer and publisher."

The verdict of the Leipzig court two years later (November 1793) was in Göschen's favor. The path to the edition seemed to have been cleared. However, scarcely had this difficulty been overcome than new ones arose. The greatest difficulty of all was Göschen's ambition to create something unique. He was not satisfied with the quality or capacity of the Leipzig printers and wanted to use the "new" Roman letters.

An innovation that Göschen introduced was a machine for calendering paper. But this innovation proved to be a problem during the printing process; in the extraordinarily hot summer of 1794 the "calendered vellum papers" were spoiled and the whole process had to be started over again in November.

Repeatedly, as soon as one problem was solved, the next one arose, economic, financial, political. The country was at war, French troops occupied Frankfurt and other cities; there was no longer any question of normal trade and traffic. Göschen risked everything, his existence, his own and his relatives' estate, his connections; even Wieland was constantly forced to "warn rather than encourage." The risk of failure and with it the ruin of the publishing house was great. But Göschen would not be sidetracked. He goes on to say that to a certain degree he wants to act both aristocratically and democratically: "Every shop assistant, every poor student, every country parson, every moderately well-paid officer should be able to buy your works. They should be read by the whole of Germany and have an effect on the whole of Germany. I want to complete the undertaking in four years." The first four volumes of the four separate editions appeared from the 1794 Easter Fair onwards.

No question, a masterpiece! Göschen must have known that he had attained his goal, that by producing this edition he had become a publisher. He had fought for the rights of, and had created a representative monument to, the author and to himself, and he had the sensitivity to present the outstanding undertaking to the author in a special setting.

Göschen did three great things with his edition of Wieland.

1. He "made" an author by the unusual undertaking of producing four editions, and had made him the premier German-language author of the day. The son of the Würtemberg author Christian Friedrich Daniel Schubart characterized the edition as "the greatest bookselling enterprise in Germany." Bertuch reacted enthusiastically in a letter to Göschen dated 6 November 1793: "I will do still more and in the very next number of my journal I shall publish a short essay on the advantages of Roman type over German type, and I shall set up your edition of Wieland as a specimen and an example. I hope that your enterprise will be successful, as Wieland is without doubt the nation's leading classical poet; people will always buy him and every German who collects only a few dozen books and only lays claim to a wisp of literature and taste will have to have his Wieland just as much as a Frenchman must have his Voltaire or an Englishman his Milton and Pope."

Goethe, however, cocooned himself in silence. Schiller, who took a critical view of Wieland, turned down the invitation to write a review with the words: "He did not [know] . . . what he could praise in it beyond the contribution made by the publisher." Nevertheless the public was impressed by the undertaking.

Today editors of Wieland's works still recognize the great service Göschen performed. "The Wieland edition prepared by the author himself is a monument erected by Göschen to the author and to himself."[23]

2. He established himself as a significant publisher. In the course of the production of the four editions he demonstrated a responsibility unusual for a publisher at that time. He staked his whole existence and that of his publish-

ing house on the realization of the great undertaking, "the great wager." He carried on his legal battle, and the result was a pioneering one for the development of authors' and publishers' rights in Germany. Authors' rights have precedence over publishers' rights: this is the principle which every publisher, right down to our own day, must observe. The fundamental discussion at the time was also important for the development of the "independent writer."

3. He set new standards for book production. By his careful selection of paper, by his introduction of the calendering of paper, by the improvement of printing and printing colors, by the typography that he supervised down to the very last detail (he personally read the proofs of the "royal octavo Edition"), what he achieved was exemplary. He was justifiably called the "German Bodoni." The next works that he published, the writings of Klopstock, Schiller's *Don Carlos,* the New Testament, and his edition of Homer, were masterpieces of the art of printing and they were national monuments. It was said in German bookselling circles that he had regained an international reputation for German printing.

Wieland too recognized Göschen's achievement. "None of my friends has deserved as much of me as you do," he wrote on 27 October 1797, "and you continue to make ever greater contributions to the fame of our nation which we hope will not always be indifferent, but will finally recognize your skill, so that the nation that invented typography will not steal from you the fame of having brought it to perfection and will not deny the thanks that the man who had the courage to persevere and the consummate skill to create this fame for it deserves."

The thanks that he deserves? Göschen, it is true, did escape the ruin of his enterprise, but he certainly made very little profit, yet he was still in a position to continue his undertaking. While the books were still in production Wieland now expressed his admiration for Roman type: "I cannot take enough delight at the pure beauty of the letters. Each one of them is in its way a Venus di Milo."

Göschen was recognized by the public as an important publisher. Showered with praise, he now entered the lists publicly in the interests of authors' and publishers' rights. He fought for a new order in bookselling and against the "thefts" of the pirates. In 1802 he collected his thoughts on the subject in a work: *My Thoughts on the Book Trade and Its Defects, My Few Experiences and My Inconsequential Suggestions for Improving the Same.* His central idea is set forth in paragraph 4: "The book trade is a trade with books . . .

but if books are the intellectual products of the most excellent men of the age who are competent to instruct and improve people, or to embellish life, then the bookseller is a merchant who is trading with the noblest of goods and if he carries on his trade with dignity he is worthy of being in the first rank of businessmen."

People did pay attention to Göschen's suggestions, but they also opposed them. Booksellers had been meeting since 1797 in the Booksellers Exchange. Göschen demanded that this exchange be given "backing, dignity and duration." The meeting of deputies was on the point of establishing an association of this sort, but everything collapsed as a result of the Napoleonic Wars. The association finally came into being in 1825 when the Börsenverein (Exchange Association) was established. Göschen could be called the initiator of the association.

Göschen continued to run his business with "dignity" and success for two more decades.

Goethe and Göschen came to terms once more after the parting of the ways in 1791, again when they signed a contract. With Schiller acting as intermediary, Göschen accepted the publication of Goethe's translation of *"Rameau's Nephew. A Dialogue of Diderot's.* Translated from the Manuscript and Accompanied by Notes by Goethe. Leipzig, G. J. Göschen, 1805."

Goethe later forgot the quarrels with Göschen and only remembered his achievements. In 1817 he wrote, "I had every reason to be content with Herr Göschen, the publisher of my collected works." On Göschen's death, Goethe himself said, "I had done my utmost in those last volumes that Göschen published, for example, in my *Tasso* I had perhaps transfused more of my heart's blood than was proper, and yet this brave publisher, whose word I have to honor, told me that this edition did not sell especially well." And later on he also recognized that Göschen was not so wrong when he complained "people are not very interested in Goethe's writings." Goethe himself saw that the first collection of his works had appeared at an unfavorable point in his life. The fame of the early years had faded and interest in the new quality of his artistic work had not yet been aroused: "unfortunately the edition of the same [the first complete edition] fell at a moment when Germany knew nothing more about me and did not want to know, and I thought I noticed that my publisher was not completely satisfied with the sales."

But Viscount Goschen found it hard to explain the "fateful breach": "This is the way a publisher's decision is explained, a decision which to us—judging it *post facto*— appears to be the greatest mistake in my grandfather's life as a publisher." And at the end of the chapter, "and thus Goethe's prophecy was realized. His writings were divided among different publishers and the fame of being the main publisher of the greatest poet of his time was lost to my grandfather for ever."

THREE

Between Göschen and Cotta

❧⁂❧

1789 and the Roman Carnival   IN JANUARY 1789, six months before the outbreak of the French Revolution, Goethe wrote that "freedom and equality can only be enjoyed in the fever of insanity." The statement is not a piece of dramatic prose, it is not put into the mouth of a character in one of the so-called revolutionary dramas. It is found in a series of carefully worked out studies with the title *Roman Carnival*, printed by Johann Friedrich Unger, with the place of publication listed as "Weimar and Gotha," and goes on "Commissioned by Carl Wilhelm Ettinger." The luxury edition of three hundred copies appeared for the Easter Fair at the end of May 1779. The title page did not reveal the name of the author, but the name of the writer might have been guessed by the place of publication, Weimar, and by the engraving on the title page by Johann Heinrich Lipps, the Swiss painter and engraver whom Goethe had met in Italy and who was professor of drawing in Weimar from 1789 to 1794. The book contains twenty copperplate engravings, colored and etched—on the basis of sketches made by Goethe's housemate in Rome, the painter Christian Georg Schütz—by Georg Melchior Kraus. The painter and graphic artist Kraus came from Frankfurt. He taught Goethe portrait painting in 1775 and in 1780, at Goethe's wish, became director of the newly founded school of graphic art in Weimar. Though Unger was to publish the work, he shrank from taking the risk, and Ettinger in Gotha was commissioned to publish it.

It was the most luxurious edition of a single work produced during Goethe's lifetime. The three hundred copies were sold out in no time; "they made themselves"—as Goethe remarks in his *Second Italian Sojourn*—"into rarities." When he had to give the copy from his own library to the castle library at Wilhelmshöhe because its copy had been stolen by the French, he was left without a copy. At an auction where he was bidding for a copy, he was outbid.

Goethe was not only dissatisfied with the production of the book, he was irritated and angry. He sent a copy to his friend Johann Friedrich Reichardt on 29 June 1789 with an expression of his deepest displeasure: "Here is the *Carnival:* I am most dissatisfied with the way it is printed. I lavished the greatest care on this little piece of writing and sent a very beautifully written copy to the printers, and now there are the most frightful typographical errors in these few pages and I cannot bear to look at them any more. Herr Unger should restrict himself to printing *Eulenspiegel* on blotting paper and not have the temerity to misuse beautiful type and beautiful paper."

With regard to the *Roman Carnival* people spoke of the "miracle of its existence." There was a scholarly dispute as to why Goethe should have expressly chosen to describe the Roman carnival. He had seen it twice in Rome and he had disapproved of, even detested, it. Why then should he have produced the study after his return to Weimar where he was overburdened with responsibilities and where he was totally overworked? We might also question why Goethe waited another quarter of a century to select, edit, and publish his Italian notes, and why he gave preference to his description of the carnival, which was the only individual work he published in the year 1789.[1]

Goethe saw the Roman carnival for the first time on 10 February 1787, reporting to Duke Carl August the fact that the "festivities took place beneath our windows." A week later he wrote to Frau von Stein of "the deadly boredom" of the great balls in the Teatro Aliberti, and on the same day he noted something about "faded carnival foolery," actually using this as a title. The sharpest criticism follows on 20 February, on Ash Wednesday. "Now there's an end to foolery. The innumerable lights were a wild spectacle last night. One has to have seen the carnival in Rome in order to be completely rid of the wish ever to see it again. There is nothing to write about it, it might at best be entertaining if it were described orally. What one feels is unpleasant about it is that people lack any inner happiness and that they lack the money to express the little bit of fun that they still like to have. The wealthy people are economical and restrained, the bourgeois is without means, the people poor. There was an incredible noise on the last day but no really heartfelt joy. The sky, so interminably pure and beautiful, looked down on this foolery with such a noble and innocent air." A passionate entry but actually it is aimed less at the events of the carnival than at the onlookers, who lack "inner happiness." The remark he makes in a letter of 17 April 1789 to Duchess Anna—staying in Rome at the time—is arcane: "I hear that you are less pleased with the Carnival, I hope you will be more pleased with the *Description of the Roman Carnival* that is coming out at the Easter Fair this year. If, as I hope to, I succeed by means of this little essay in making something that is not enjoyable, enjoyable then I shall be pleased." Why did he wish so urgently to make the unenjoyable enjoyable?

What was it that led to such a detailed description and such a carefully planned publication? Friedrich Justin Bertuch, who with his "office for industry" had become more and more of a publisher and entrepreneur, had asked Goethe for figurines of new fashion- and mask-models for his "Journal of Luxury and Fashion." In a letter to Frau von Stein on 19 January 1788, Goethe says, "Please tell Bertuch that I will get him some drawings and descriptions of masks."

There are two further motives of a quite different sort that may have been important to Goethe. He loved children and wanted to bring presents from Italy for Fritz von Stein and for Herder's children. Goethe designed masks for them himself. "For the children's pleasure, carnival masks and a few pieces of Roman dress are also described more than drawn and then washed over with color like an Orbis pictus," he tells Herder.

A second motive could have been Goethe's inclination to describe festivals. His life partnership with Christiane Vulpius began on 12 July 1788 and she loved celebrating festivals. How often did Goethe describe festivals, the Imperial coronation, the Rochus festival in Bingen, the carnival in Cologne: he organized masquerades for the court and wrote the great fancy-dress ball at the Imperial court for the first act of *Faust,* Part II.

Another, inner, process also motivated Goethe. As Isabella Kuhn rightly assumes, "the second look" was a decisive factor in his relationship to things.[2] Goethe once observed:[3] "Yet one must in any case see things again and again if one is to acquire a pure impression of the present. It is a strange thing about the first impression, it is always to the highest degree a mixture of truth and falsehood." We know that Goethe saw the Roman carnival for a second time in 1786, the following year: "It was the second time I saw the carnival and it soon occurred to me that this public festival, like any other repeated and lively activity, took its decisive course," is what we read in the "report" for February 1788 in the "Second Sojourn in Rome" that first appeared in the final authorized edition of 1829, something in other words written or rather edited decades afterwards. Goethe also mentions in this passage that he made notes of the individual events as they took place and that this was the "preliminary work" he was to use later for the *Carnival*. In a letter of 24 July 1788 to Christian Gottlieb Heyne, the most famous classical scholar of his day, Goethe writes that at the time only "simple things interested him. For example to what extent the material that is being used determines whether the skilful artist forms his work in one way and not another."[4] Isabella Kuhn makes a connection between the *Roman Carnival* and the essays that Goethe offered Wieland in September 1788 for publication in the *Teutsche Merkur*. In fact these essays do reveal a form of art historical reflection that we come across many times in the late eighteenth century. The "material" of art became—according to Lessing's *Laocoon*—an object of consideration. In his scientific reflections Goethe establishes a connection in which material is the "original form" and art a sort of metamorphosis.

This art theoretical connection however does not explain unambiguously enough why Goethe worked on the description of the Roman carnival more intensively than on the other works, for example, on the Italians, on Naples, on the imitations of Raphael's *Christ and the Twelve Apostles.*

In talking about the Italian journey Goethe once remarked that in the long run everything is ethical. The first two parts of the great work on the journey appeared in 1816–17, still under the collected title "From My Life," with the subtitle "I too in Arcadia." Only later, in the final edition, were the volumes entitled *Italian Journey.*[5]

The texts then have an expressly autobiographical character. The description of the Roman carnival also bears the stamp of Goethe's experiences after his return home. On 18 June 1788 Goethe returned to Weimar. The very next day he visited the duke, who monopolized him throughout the following days, weeks, even months: court duties and official service make up Goethe's daily life. He travels, visits societies, and everywhere he is made to report on his impressions. He shows his sketches and pictures (he produced 450 landscape drawings and more than 350 drawings of art and architecture in Italy). He tries to reproduce his first impressions of Italy. He had earlier wanted Paris to be his school and Rome his university. "Although I am still the same, I believe in the very marrow of my bones that I have changed." "The soul swells, the individual feels a sort of transfiguration of itself, the sense of a free life, a higher existence, lightness and grace." "I am starting a new epoch," he observes in his diary (27 October 1787) and he goes on to say that his spirit has been so enlarged by all that he has seen and learned "that I must confine myself to some one work." "The individuality of a human being is a strange thing. I have only just learned to know mine, since this year I have on the one hand relied entirely on myself, and on the other have had to consort with completely strange people."

The first—and only—book of this new epoch is *The Roman Carnival.* But when Goethe wrote it out in January 1789 he was far removed from the euphoria of October 1787.

As early as 19 June 1788 he made a note of Frau von Stein's "strange mood . . . which was very painful to me." He does not want to give her the diary of his journey though he had written it for her: he would rather throw it into the fire. That summer he writes, "I stayed [in Weimar] for the sake of my friends, just as I came there for their sakes. At the same time I had to repeat obstinately to myself that I could have stayed away, I want no part of people." In his second sketch for *Poetry and Truth* he says, "Indifference to everything after the loss of my Roman happiness. Isolation." In the retrospective view of *The Fate of the Manuscript of the Essay to Explain the Metamorphosis of Plants* that we have already quoted, we read the following statements: "I was dismissed back to formless Germany out of an Italy rich in form, and I had to exchange a joyful sky for a dark one." "My friends, instead of consoling me and taking me back to their bosoms, drove me to desperation. My delight in the most distant, scarcely known objects, my sorrow, my laments over what had been lost seemed to insult them. I missed any sort of sympathy, no one understood my language." Wieland asked him at the end of August for some contributions to his *Teutsche Merkur,* and this was why he asked Frau von Stein to give him back his letters so that he could gradually "concoct something out of them." There was no way that he could look through the old papers without such a purpose in mind. He promised Wieland a series of short essays and was prepared to be involved every month, "so that I can make some sort of division, connect one essay with another. . . . Science, art, morals, everything is amalgamated in my work." He made Schiller's acquaintance on 7 September. The latter, it is true, was at once doubtful "whether we shall ever become very close to one another . . . his world is not mine, our ways of looking at things seem to be fundamentally different." The first essays in Wieland's *Teutsche Merkur* appear anonymously in October. Since "nothing seemed to want to get moving properly," he starts putting his sketches in order. On 27 December, in a letter to Herder, he sums up the half year that has passed since his return: "I feel only too keenly what I have lost."

At the beginning of January 1789 he reminds Bertuch of *The Roman Carnival.* "If it is to be published by Easter, then it is time to start thinking about it. I'm in the process of doing something for the *Merkur* and could take this opportunity to write a few pages to accompany the etchings."

There was one more experience that was important for him. In the wake of Laurence Sterne's *A Sentimental Journey,* travel descriptions had been almost entirely devoted to the feelings and perspectives of the traveler. "I on the other hand had seized upon the principle of effacing myself as far as possible and of assuming the object for myself as purely as I could. I kept faithfully to this principle when I attended the Roman Carnival, I set up in great detail a schema of all that took place. . . . It was on this preparatory work that I based my *Roman Carnival.*" Goethe is in fact still adhering to these principles since he describes the Roman carnival not from the perspective of the traveler but from that of an objective observer; this too was only to be achieved by his "second look."

In the opening lines he is struggling with the objection that a mass of living sensual objects cannot perhaps be described but can only be seen, but "as it was neither especially enthralling to the eye, nor satisfying to the disposition . . . the movement . . . monotonous, the noise deafening, the end of the days unsatisfactory," the description itself has to legitimize the undertaking, the description of the inner reality of the festival. As a scientist he wanted to establish the nature of the festival; as a great formal epic poet he wanted to describe the form of the happenings. But the inquiring poet is concerned with the story from within. That is how the introductory statement is to be interpreted: "The Roman carnival is a festival that is *not actually given to the people, but which the people give to themselves.*" The festival is not commanded by, nor presented by, the state. The circle "of friends moves of its own accord," the festival becomes the expression of the people's conception of itself, it becomes a "national event" as well as a "natural event."

Nothing is forbidden on carnival days but blows and knifings. This reminds the Romans of another festival, the "Festival of the Saturnalia." Under Saturn's rule people re-experienced the felicitous Golden Age free from guilt and sorrows; in memory of this, people in ancient Rome celebrated the Saturnalia from 17 December to 19 December in a boisterous series of festivities, when all businesses were closed and social distinctions seemed to be erased. Masters allowed their slaves every sort of freedom; indeed, on 19 December, masters and slaves changed roles and clothes, the slaves sat at table and were served by their masters. Here too freedom and equality could be achieved only under the rowdy conditions of a festival.

The carnival's "long and narrow" street "cannot be encompassed." But the person who is describing it here has an overall view. The tumult is scarcely to "be distinguished" but he sees the distinctions, a "first degree of the crowd." The person describing puts order into disorder, into what is happening, with the hand of the artist. The "Corso," the street leading from the obelisk of the Piazza del Popolo to the Venezia, limits the festivities, the describer opens them up; for him the carnival is nothing new and strange "but simply attaches itself quite naturally to the Roman way of life." The describer reports what "people either do not experience or else take no notice of." There is no place, no point of view for the describer. There is no first-person in the narrative, the more neutral "we" is seldom used, and the whole is dominated by the impersonal "one." The author leads us very calmly through the confusion, through the pell-mell "of all ages and classes." A masterly stroke leads to the climax. But the climax is not that of the Roman carnival; it is not the horse races of the final day toward which the description moves. It moves on to the candlelight festivities of the final night, the *Moccoli* (candle stumps): one person calls to another, as he tries to blow out the other's candle, "Sia ammazzato chi non porta moccolo!" ("Let him be killed who does not carry a candle stump!"). The blowing out and relighting, together with an unbridled shouting, bring "mutual interest into the huge crowd." The freedom of murder among the conditions of the carnival! The describer fixes one particular scene: a boy extinguishes his father's candlelight and does not stop shouting "Sia ammazzato il Signore padre!" In vain the father chides him for this indecency. The boy asserts the freedom of the evening and only curses his father more strongly. In this way the old Saturnalia, the equality of slave and master, of old and young, is reborn in the madness of this candlelit night. The boy's statement must have shaken Goethe, he must have seen in it a symptom, even a signal. There was no "brilliant procession taking place," he says, "but rather it is a sign that is being given here." What sign? What he can only mean is "signs of the times," the original title of the revolutionary drama *The Excited Ones*.

Goethe was deeply shocked in 1785, as he writes in the *Campaign,* by events in France in those turbulent prerevolutionary years. His "frightful premonitions" were alas all too quickly confirmed. "I took them with me to Italy and brought them back again in even more acute form." What are these signs, what are these premonitions? In my opinion Goethe indicated them in the final chapter of *The Roman Carnival,* which he entitled "Ash Wednesday."

"Life as a *whole* cannot be encompassed, it is unbearable, even alarming"—that is Goethe's experience after his return from Rome: he knew that "in every great separation . . . there is a seed of madness, one must avoid incubating it and nourishing it." Life in detail and the personal can be enjoyable just for the moment; we learn that "the liveliest and highest pleasures . . . appear to us only for a moment." We also learn that the saturnalian ideas of equality, the ideals of the candlelight festival, can in reality be achieved only by force. For this reason the ideals of freedom and equality can "only be enjoyed temporarily in the giddiness of madness."

We cannot assume, given the careful composition of this description, that it is a coincidence. The fact that it was described in this manner six months before the outbreak of the French Revolution shows that it was more concerned with the happenings of the time than is generally assumed. Goethe's vision was the vision of Lynceus the watchman, whose name derived from the Greek Lynx and whose sharpness of vision on his tower was proverbial.

On the day Goethe saw the carnival in Rome, he writes in his journal, "for one aspires more to the general when one views the objects more closely and more sharply." That is Goethe's vision, a vision of things and not a vision brought about by things. He is "at and with things." The achievement of freedom and equality through force are not consistent with his view. All force is "repugnant to him in the depths of his soul *because it is not in accord with nature,*" and it is only from what is natural that existence, that greatness can develop; it is Mephisto who reflects, "Everything can be achieved by force." Goethe's message runs differently. Preserve yourself in defiance of every force! He reworked the singspiel *Lili* in Rome, and this now includes the lines:

> Preserve yourself
> In defiance of every force,
> Never bow down,
> Show yourself powerful,
> Summon up
> The arms of the Gods.

Here we see Goethe the individualist and the outsider defying the force and horror of the approaching revolution with the help of the Gods. This was his attitude: "It is better for injustices to occur than for them to be removed in an unjust fashion."[6] This characterizes Goethe's attitude both to the French Revolution and as the observer of the waning *ancien régime*. Eckermann records Goethe's statement, "It is true that I could not be a friend of the French Revolution, because its horrors were too close to me and angered me every day and every hour, and at that time its beneficent results were not yet apparent. I could also not be indifferent to the fact that at the same time people in Germany tried to produce *artificially* scenes similar to those that were, in France, the result of a great necessity."

How was it that Goethe had a premonition of the outbreak of the French Revolution, which came as a surprise to most of his contemporaries? "I was hardly reestablished in Weimar life and in the circumstances there with regard to business, studies, and literary works, when the French Revolution developed and drew the attention of the whole world to itself. In the immoral abyss of city, court, and state that was opened up by an episode that epitomized the corruption of the court—the so-called 'Affair of the Diamond Necklace'—the most horrible consequences appeared like ghosts to me, and for a while I could not rid myself of their appearance; as this was happening I behaved so strangely that some friends in the country with whom I was staying at the time admitted to me that when the first news of it came through to us I had for the moment given the appearance of being mad. I followed the process with the greatest attention, and tried while in Sicily to obtain news of Cagliostro (involved in the Affair of the Diamond Necklace) and his family."

I would like to assume that Goethe found it important in January 1789 to fix his judgment and disseminate it—under the cloak of anonymity it is true, but of course in the form of an outstanding book. He originally thought of publishing it in Bertuch's *Journal of Luxury and Fashion,* but that publication may have appeared too small, not important and serious enough, for Goethe's message. Out of this arose the idea of a separate book that would print these "signs" in large characters. To Goethe's regret it appeared in an edition of only 300 copies. "The carnival," he wrote in December 1789, "also found some admirers in Germany. The pusillanimity of the entrepreneurs, Bertuch and Krause, counseled them to print only a small edition—that is now completely out of print—and no one has the courage to print a second edition." *The Roman Carnival* still appeared in Bertuch's journal in 1790, and after this a number of pirated versions appeared in a "Pocket Book of Old and New Masks," in a *Carnival Book for Young and Old*. In 1792 the book was reprinted legally in the first volume of *New Writings*.

When the *Italian Journey* appeared in 1817 it was not greeted exclusively with enthusiasm. Goethe had repeatedly made crtical statements about Christian-Roman art and had not attempted to conceal his dislike of Christianity. Goethe the "heathen" was indicted. There was another offense on top of his heathenism. Goethe's periodical *On Art and Antiquity* appeared at the same time as *The Italian Journey*. In this periodical he polemicized violently against "neo-German religious patriotic art." In the efforts of the Romantics to revive old German art, Goethe saw "an affectedly pious non-art" against which he now programmatically pitted his Italian confessions. Criticism and rejection of Goethe's work was twofold in origin. His critics claimed that Goethe had praised only the mediocre and had shown no sense of the admirable. He was castigated for having viewed the procession of the doge in Venice, for example, simply as a superficial spectacle, and for not being affected by the picture of ancient grandeur. It was wrong to look at Italy only from the point of view of the North, the traveler should actually enter it from the South in order to get to know it properly.

However, Goethe had had something else in mind. He was not looking for Italian art, he was looking for the great art of antiquity; he had left Gothic behind him, the "Gothic method of decoration," for example, of the Strassburg minster. Palladio, who produced nothing arbitrary or conceited, had opened up for him the path to "the whole of life and of art"—and the path to himself. He too was in Arcadia, "at the place." He called his condition in Rome a quiet, attentive happiness. To be awake was for him "a sharper vision." "I am now beginning to see the best things for the second time when the initial astonishment dissolves into a coexistence and a closer feeling for the value of things." Striving after objectivity and form, liveliness and clarity, this is what constitutes the Roman, the classical, for Goethe. In face of the sea animals at the Lido, he exclaims, "How delightful, how magnificent a *living* thing is. How suited to its condition, how true, how *existent!*" In front of the temple in Assisi he voices his impression in two words, "So *whole!*"

Understandably enough, the impressions of his Italian journey were manifold. It is interesting that he constantly repeated them in his letters to his duke. There were of course reasons for this: the duke had always shown him great understanding; during the whole time he was in Italy he received his full salary and he remained a privy councillor, but now he was relieved from carrying out the duties of his chancery office. He could return with a mind at ease. But he had a hard time saying farewell to Rome—to Italy—and his return journey lasted almost two months. What he saw in the process was determined by impressions garnered in Italy, above all from Palladio. He had learned from Palladio that perfect art is perfect objectivity. Goethe had acquired a new striving for form and clarity. He had painted more than he had written in Italy (if we disregard the clerical work, the journal, reports, diaries, and letters). He wrote morphological studies, little that was new, but he revised and edited. The old Frankfurt singspiels *Erwin und Elmire* and *Claudine of Villa Bella* were rewritten, *Iphigenia* was given a new form, the free rhythm of his poetic prose works was replaced by the definite rhythm of verse; *Tasso,* too, was looked at in this way. He learned from the "being" of the old artists "that like nature they were at home everywhere, but they also knew how to produce something true, something living." They remained "great in what was natural": this was the sum total of his view of Palladio.

His actual experience was that of a rebirth. "I consider the day that I set foot in Rome a second birthday, a true rebirth," he says at the beginning of his sojourn and he is forever wishing to be "reborn and educated"; shortly before his return he writes to Duke Carl August, "In this year and a half's solitude I have found myself again, but as what?—as an artist."

Johann Friedrich   When Goethe first made contact with Johann Fried-
Unger's Bitter Fruit   rich Unger, the latter was, in contrast to Göschen,
already an established publisher. Both were roughly the same age, Unger thirty-five, Goethe thirty-nine. Even beyond the borders of Germany Unger enjoyed an equal reputation as printer, publisher, and typographical artist. We know little of his life, not even his exact date of birth. We do have an entry in the baptismal register of the church in Dorotheenstadt in Berlin (in the churchyard of which Hegel and Fichte, Brecht and Johannes R. Becher are buried): "Johann Friedrich Unger was baptized on 26 August 1753." It is the first document in Unger's life and one of the few that have been preserved. In November 1779 he applied for the privilege of founding a printing press, to which the owners of the printing

houses that already existed in Berlin raised the objection that there was no need, that the existing capacity was sufficient, and that in any case they did not earn enough. Unger was enough of a live wire so that in spite of the objection he received his privilege. In 1791 he set up a type foundry in which one of his students, Johann Christoph Gubitz, created, on Unger's orders, the famous Fraktur. Goethe thought highly of the Unger Fraktur. "German script is comparable, in its decoration, to gothic buildings that turn our gaze skywards and fill us with astonishment and admiration. The gothic style in architecture and in our letters should be considered the revelation of the German spirit." Unger was an active man, engaged in many areas of his profession. His stylish printing of books and the sort of ornamentation he used for them soon made him famous. In 1800, the Prussian king, Friedrich Wilhelm II, decided to establish a teaching post for xylography at the Academy of Fine Arts in Berlin and to appoint Unger the professor. His wife, Friederike Helen von Rothenburg, the daughter of a Prussian general, presided over a pleasant social life in their household. One of their frequent guests was the Berlin musician and writer, Johann Friedrich Reichardt, who was in touch with Goethe and had set some of his poems to music.

We can deduce from booksellers' advertisements what Unger's activities were as a publisher of literature, the sciences, calendars, and periodicals. At the end of the fourth book of Goethe's *Wilhelm Meister's Apprenticeship,* for example, there is the notice: "Johann Friedrich Unger announces the following new works for the Michaelmas Fair of 1796," and this is followed by four pages of advertisements for fourteen works, among them: "An examination (in detail) of the operational plans ascribed to Freiherr von Mack for the 1794 campaign in the Franco-Austrian War"; "Handbook of Political Economy for use in academic lectures. Prepared on Adam Smith's principles by Georg Sartorius"; Wackenroder and Tieck's "The Heartfelt Outpourings of an Art-loving Monk"; "Cookbook (the most modern from Berlin), or directions for the tasty preparation of meals, sauces, and baked goods"; "Wittstock (Levin Martus), one thousand and sixty-two tables for specie and the exchange of friedrichs d'or, ducats, sovereigns. Carefully worked out for the greater convenience of the trading public"; and "Woltmann's History of the European States." In addition, there was the sixth volume of Goethe's *New Writings* and a separate edition of the *Apprenticeship.* A motley program; today such an announcement would render a publisher implausible. Goethe was probably displeased too; in any case, there are scarcely any advertisements for other works in the first editions of his writings that were published by Unger's successor, Cotta. But in all fairness, it was not until a hundred years later that publishers began to specialize, and up till that time every publisher offered a wide-ranging program.

The documents of Goethe's relationship to Unger were published in 1926.[7] The book contains eighty letters from Goethe to Unger as well as verbal statements by Goethe about Unger, or ones that he made in letters to third parties or wrote down in his diaries. Unger was friends with Karl Philipp Moritz, whose works he published, and Carl Friedrich Zelter, both of whom were also friends of Goethe. Moritz had met Goethe in Rome and had engaged in a lively exchange of ideas with him during his whole stay in Italy. He stayed with Goethe in Weimar from December 1788 till February 1789. Goethe influenced his literary work and took advantage of Moritz's great knowledge of prosody; he also used him as a mediator with Unger. "I have Moritz to thank for the fact that you trust me and think me worthy to publish your sublime intellectual products. I shall always remember him with gratitude for this," the publisher to wrote Goethe after Moritz's death in 1793.

It is a publisher's duty not only to produce and distribute books but also to keep constant contact with an author, inform him and tell him of important occurrences. Carl Friedrich Zelter later cemented Goethe's relationship with Unger.

Zelter, who was born nine years after Goethe and died in the same year as he did, had been in contact with him from 1799. The former master mason became head of the Berlin Singing Academy and professor of music at the Academy of Arts in Berlin; he was probably Goethe's most intimate friend and—next to Knebel—the only one who kept up with him till his old age. Goethe preferred Zelter's settings of his poems and ballads to all others, even to Schubert's. When Unger's wife sent him some compositions by Zelter in 1796, he replied to her: "I cannot judge music, for I lack knowledge of the means it uses to achieve its ends; I can only talk of the effect that it has on me when I surrender myself wholly and repeatedly to it and this I can say of Herr Zelter's compositions of my songs; I would scarcely have believed music capable of such tones." The friendly relationship between the two was naturally good for Goethe's relationship to Unger.

These were important prerequisites, for from the beginning there was a shadow over the relationship. *The Roman Carnival* had been published by Ettinger in 1789, but it had been printed by Unger. Goethe was not happy with the way the printing had turned out. Yet the fact that, in spite of Goethe's annoyance, the relationship proceeded without friction was certainly the work of both parties. Unger's totally uncholeric disposition—in contrast to Goethe's—made him numerous friends, among them the important Berlin publisher and bookseller Friedrich Nicolai, and even his competitor Göschen spoke kindly of him: "He is wealthy, has no children and is glad to work for prestige." And it was without question an honor for Unger to be the publisher of the man whom he considered the most important writer of the age. He knew what he owed to Goethe, the "most admirable," the "most honorable Privy Councillor."

The great respect that he had for Goethe is clearly expressed in his letters. And Goethe really loved to be praised by Unger and his wife, to whom he wrote in June 1796, "I value the interest that good and cultivated souls show in me and my works, by which I am able to bring a part of myself to distant and unknown minds."

Thus the relationship—one that was certainly not without its snags— remained a friendly and objective one until Unger's death in 1804. Unger was to write to Schiller in 1800, "It was a piece of luck for me to get to know Goethe in Leipzig, I do not know of a more charming man."

The Roman Carnival had appeared at the end of May 1789. It was important to Goethe for the edition to come out at this time, just as the whole year of 1789 was important. Goethe looks back in the *Daily and Annual Volumes* (published between 1822 and 1825) and he mentions that his work on *The Roman Carnival* immediately after his return from Italy had brought him "a lot of pleasure." *The Great Cophta* was written gradually, conceived of first as an opera and then worked out as a play, later being called a "comedy." The central figure of the play is the alchemist, adventurer, and swindler Alessandro Count of Cagliostro, actually Giuseppe Balsamo. Cagliostro is interpreted by Goethe as the symptom of a crisis in the political order. He was involved in corrupt practices in France (the infamous Affair of the Diamond Necklace being the most conspicuous) that had shaken Goethe and that he had described in the final part of the *Campaign in France.*

Goethe had visited the Balsamo family in Palermo on his journey to Sicily in 1787 and had given them financial support. When he later heard that Cagliostro had been condemned to death as a heretic, a sentence commuted to life imprisonment, he sent the family, anonymously, all his royalties from *The Great Cophta.*

The Great Cophta had been inspired by the distress caused by the Affair of the Diamond Necklace. Goethe wanted to represent mercilessly the necessity of revolution in France; of course he did not approve of the results, but he opposed those Germans who denied the necessity. "I could never respect these people" is the complaint of the knight in the *Great Cophta* about the ruined nobility, "they are unworthy of any protection. It is a favor to humanity to have them punished according to their merits, if by this they are prevented from pursuing their arts."

The play was given two performances in Weimar at the beginning of 1792, but Goethe's recollection in the *Campaign in France* was that "no happy spirit reigned over the whole thing"; "because the play was performed very well it had a repugnant effect."

Goethe spent a "few very happy days" with Karl Philipp Moritz in the spring of 1791. He records that he discussed almost everything that he had written about art and about his "theory of Nature" with Moritz, and had benefited from him and from his remarks. In Goethe's record of letters written on 30 May 1791 we read, "Berlin Moritz Cagliostro . . . offered." There is also a letter as a supplement to the *Italian Journey,* most probably addressed to Unger, from which we learn how important this material is to Goethe even in the special way in which the publication is presented. He wants the play about *The Family Tree of Joseph von Balsamo, Called Cagliostro,* to be translated into French immediately and writes: "When I was searching for Cagliostro's family tree, I found at the same time letters from his family whom I got to know in Palermo, as well as other papers that were connected with this. It seems to me that one could make a small self-contained work out of this, which would be interesting at the present moment and at the same time very important for the completion of the files. When printed it would only take up about two or three sheets. But since I would like a simultaneous translation into French, the question would be whether it might not be printed with the translation in adjacent columns, or on facing pages and then the whole thing could be bound and sold. I wouldn't care about the format, except that it would have to be quarto if the family tree is to be added to it as a title engraving. If octavo were chosen then the family tree could be prepared in small folio and inserted, but in the case of such an important document as this that puts the seal on the whole Roman inquisition, this would be unseemly and niggardly. I await your opinion on this and enclose a rough outline, on another sheet, of what you might expect of this work." There was no other text for which Goethe had wanted a French translation included in the first edition. At this point he wanted to be heard in France as well. We can assume that the idea of a bilingual edition goes back to his conversations with Karl Philipp Moritz. There is no indication in the documents and sources as to which translator Goethe had in mind, in any case the translation was not made. On 17 November 1791, Goethe received his royalties, in February 1792 the text was published in Berlin, as Unger announced, and at the Easter Fair of 1792 there appeared *"The Great Cophta. A Comedy in Five Acts by Goethe,* Berlin. Johann Friedrich Unger. 1791. pp. 241" and at the same time the text appeared in [Göthe's] New writings. Volume One. "The Great Cophta. The Family Tree of Joseph Balsamo, called Cagliostro." The text includes an engraving: Cagliostro's family tree. Goethe was constantly returning to the connection between the Affair of the Necklace and the French Revolution, and he constantly emphasized the historical significance of his play. "Basically it is not only of moral but of historical significance; the fact immediately precedes the French Revolution and is to a certain extent the foundation of it. The Queen, Marie Antoinette, so closely involved in the Affair of the Necklace, lost her dignity, her respect, and thus in the popular opinion of the people had lost the point of view that made her unassailable. Hatred hurts no one, but contempt is a person's downfall." After *The Roman Carnival* this is the second piece of documentary evidence for Goethe's having seen an omen of the French Revolution in the Affair of the Diamond Necklace.

In his scientific writings there is another indication of how much "the long-time drift of my intellect towards the French Revolution" had occupied his mind. This preoccupation explains "the boundless efforts to master poetically this the most terrible of events both in its causes and its effects." This is why he made "A suggestion as to how to be good": "Everyone, no matter who, should test his authority and ask himself, what are you actually doing in your situation and what are you called upon to do?"

A year after *The Great Cophta,* Unger published *"The Bourgeois General. A comedy in one act. Second sequel to the Deux Billets."* The play, which was written in three days in April 1793, did not appear in the *New Writings* and no author was named. "Small productions have the advantage that they are written almost as quickly as they are invented," Goethe wrote to Herder on 7 June 1793, "from the moment I had the initial idea less than three days passed and it was completed." Goethe chose Germany as the scene of the play, in contrast to the setting of *The Great Cophta,* so that it should reflect

German politico-social conditions both polemically and comically. He was concerned with mirroring, in the consciousness of narrow-minded philistines, the enormous events that were taking place in the world. Just as later, in *Herrmann and Dorothea,* here too he expressed his conviction that it was not a question of a mass movement but of the improvement of social evils. "Let everyone begin with *himself,* and he will find plenty to do." All the legitimate editions and the pirated versions appeared anonymously; it was not until 1808 in volume 9 of the *Works,* published by Cotta, that the author's name was mentioned.

What could the motives have been? Certainly he did not want even a "small production" that was invented "so rapidly" to fall into oblivion. Goethe's inspiration for *The Bourgeois General* was two peasant plays that he had arranged for the theater in Weimar in the spring of 1793. The first of the two farces stems from the *Deux Billets* written by the French dramatist Jean-Pierre Calris de Florian in 1779 followed in 1782 by a pseudonymous German version. *The Bourgeois General* was first produced in Goethe's presence on 2 May 1793 in the Court Theater at Weimar; the production was repeated twice in the same year. From 1800 to 1805 the piece was produced under Goethe's direction once a year. Goethe set great store by meticulous attention to detail. Thus the main character, Schnaps, unpacks pieces of his uniform from a Jacobin valise—the valise was a genuine French piece. "I found it on my journey [autumn 1792] on the French border, where the emigres had fled and where someone either lost it or threw it away. The things as they appear in the play were all in it; after that I wrote the scene." This is how Goethe remembers it at leisure, decades afterwards (in 1828).

In 1805, after seeing a production, Schiller recommended some changes to his friend; he suggested "omitting the moral passages especially in the role of the nobleman. . . . This little play deserves to continue to find the favor that is accorded it, and . . . it would be a very good thing to speed it up." Goethe replied on the same day that a number of different things had been changed and that he was sending him the prompt copy from which he could see what alterations had been made; he himself had thought of cutting the figure of the nobleman completely, "because it's worth the trouble, for to have one play more in repertory is more important than one thinks." Everyone of our present-day dramatists would agree with this statement, even Bertolt Brecht, the only contemporary writer who, like Goethe, both wrote plays and was the head of a theater. But in the end there was no reworking of *The Bourgeois General*. We know that Schiller wanted to use the material later. In his unpublished works there is a sketch of a two-act comedy whose main character, as in Goethe, was to be called Schnaps.

Immediately after *The Bourgeois General* Goethe wrote two plays that remained fragments, *The Excited Ones* and *The Girl from Oberkirch*, again against a background of "the tremendous movements in the general political course of the world." The theme of *The Excited Ones* is the revolt of the French peasants against their squirearchy, a revolt that developed into open rebellion when events in France had "excited" the rural population. The revolt is not actually the central event of the play—that was to be presented in the fifth act, but that act was never written.

Eckermann noted Goethe's statement about *The Excited Ones* on 4 January 1824: "I wrote it at the time of the French Revolution and it can be regarded, to some extent, as my political creed at that time."

Goethe did not want to be a friend of the people. He maintained a distance from events in France. Thomas Mann thought that the French Revolution had tormented Goethe "like nothing else in his life." Hegel, Herder, and Hölderlin, even Schiller and Klopstock, were partisan. Goethe took up his own position. He was the observer, he was the onlooker. "If a poet wants to have political influence," he confided in Eckermann in March 1832, "he must declare himself for a party; and when he does this, he is lost as a poet, he must say farewell to his free spirit, his unbiased conspectus, and in its place he must draw over his ears the cap of bigotry and blind hatred." He had always known that he would attract enemies and polemics by this. "You know," he continued to Eckermann, "I am on the whole very little concerned about what is written about me"; he worried little that "certain people" despised him. "In order to do these people justice I would have had to become a member of a Jacobin club and preach murder and the spilling of blood!" Goethe had foreseen the French Revolution and the end of the *ancien régime*. He kept quiet after the outbreak of the French Revolution. The first mention of it does not appear until seven months later, on 3 March 1790. His situation "was as happy as anyone could desire." Then, "you can imagine that the French Revolution was also a revolution for me." However, he added immediately afterwards, "Incidentally I am studying the ancients and am following their example as well as one can in Thuringia." Why did Goethe remain silent for so long? He was certainly kept informed of the progress of the revolution, conversation at court was mainly about what was happening in Paris. As early as September 1789 Wieland had written in the *Teutscher Merkur* "On the legality of the Use That the French Nation Made of Force in Their Declaration." Klopstock rejoiced in verse that France had liberated itself. "The most noble deed of the century / it raised itself to Olympus." Goethe regarded this with some distaste. Every sort of "apostle for freedom" was repugnant to him, he had written as early as the *Venetian Epigrams* (1795): "Nail every visionary to the cross when he reaches the age of thirty." He was especially critical of the "new literary figures" who thought that politics was poetry.

It was only later, after the events at Valmy, where Prussia and Austria succumbed to the French revolutionary army in 1792, that he made the memorable statement that was chiseled into the war memorial at Valmy: "Here and now begins a new epoch in world history and you can say that you were present at that beginning."[8] He could not be a "friend of the French Revolution," a friend of "autocratic arbitrariness." He was convinced "that no revolution is ever the fault of the people, but of the government. As long as governments always remain just and are always alert, ready to meet the needs of the people by making appropriate improvements and do not resist to the point where what is necessary is forced on them from below revolutions become impossible." When Goethe drew up the balance sheet of his political ideas—in the famous conversation with Eckermann on 4 January 1824—Eckermann noted him as saying, "Because I hated revolutions, I was called *a friend of the status quo.* But that is a very ambiguous title and one I would refuse to stand for. If the *status quo* were completely admirable and just, I would have nothing against it; however, since besides much that is good, there is a lot that is bad, unjust, and imperfect, being a friend of the *status quo* means little more than being a friend of what is passé and bad."

"Time is however always in a process of progression and human affairs take a different turn every fifty years. . . . If however a people have a real need for massive reform, God is on their side and it will succeed." The revolution "in France resulting from a great necessity" and its later "beneficent results," and the view that there really was a "true need for massive reform," are important aspects of Goethe's political thought. Bertolt Brecht's statements about the uprising of 17 June 1953 are along the same lines as Goethe's. I know this is a rather bold suggestion, but in Brecht's poem "The Solution," written in 1953 "After the uprising of 17 June," after the Stalinist secretary of the Writers' Union had demanded that the people atone for the crime of the uprising by working twice as hard, come the ironic and satirical lines: "Would it not be / simpler for the government / to dissolve the people and / elect another?" Brecht saw, as Goethe did, the need for a reform, and he knew that it had to come from below.

Goethe's three "revolutionary dramas," *The Great Cophta, The Bourgeois General,* and *The Excited Ones,* together with *The Natural Daughter* and a whole number of smaller outlines of plays, writings, prose works, and the fragmentary satirical novel *The Journey of Megaprazon's Sons* have not received the scholarly attention they deserve. "No poet of the classical age of German literature paid more attention to the French Revolution in his works than Goethe did."[9]

The most important event for Unger at this time was probably the appearance of the seven-volume edition of Goethe's *New Writings* in the years between 1792 and 1800. There do not appear to have been any formal contracts, only agreements from one volume to the next, in the process of which a new clause was inserted by Goethe: in every case he granted rights for just one edition, but he did promise an option on future work, on conditions that were to be worked out in each case. Volume 1 (1792) contained *The Great Cophta* and *The Roman Carnival;* the second volume *Reynard the Fox* in twelve cantos (1794); volumes 3–6 *Wilhelm Meister's Apprenticeship* (1795 and 1796); volume 7 (1800) contained *Songs, Ballads and Romances, Elegies I/II, Epigrams, Venice 1790, Prophecies of Bakis, Four Seasons, Speeches on the Theater Given in Weimar.* This concluded the edition of the writings. "I can give you confidential information about my other commitments as an author," Goethe wrote to Johann Friedrich Cotta on 22 September 1799. "Herr Unger will print my short and scattered poems as a seventh volume, and there may be something similar for the eighth." But this did not happen.

Goethe wanted a special edition of the seventh volume of *New Writings.* He enquired of Unger on 2 April 1800,

> Might I ask you to print a special title for the copies you intend for me; it should run as follows:
>
> Goethe's
> Latest Poems
>
> In this way I could also do a favor to those persons who do not possess the first volumes.

This special and apparently small edition is one of the greatest bibliographical rarities in the whole of the Goethe literature. One of Unger's greatest achievements is certainly that he "demanded" *Wilhelm Meister's Apprenticeship* from Goethe. The work appeared not only in the framework of the seven-volume edition of the *New Writings* but simultaneously as a separate four-volume edition: "*Wilhelm Meister's Apprenticeship. A novel. Published by Goethe.*" The four volumes of the separate edition contained supplemental notes that were glued in (though because of numerous double printings and mixed copies these were not in all the copies of the first edition), poetic compositions, but not the engravings that were in the *New Writings* edition.

Altogether Goethe worked for half a century on the novel complex, *Wilhelm Meister*. The beginnings of the first version, with the title *Wilhelm Meister's Theatrical Mission,* go back to 1777.[10] He constantly returned to the work in the ensuing years; in November 1784 he thought that he had the sixth book completed and he went on working, but the seventh book was not completed. The journey to Italy, his participation in the French campaign, his work on *Reynard the Fox* and the revolutionary dramas, his optical and morphological studies forced the novel into the background. Nine years later the "Wilhelm Meister material" was again revived for him. "It forced him," as he wrote in October 1791, into "a calm activity that will compensate me for many a sad hour that I have spent in the last year and a half." He was in the best of moods, "friendly as a little earwig" was what Charlotte von Stein said to her son Fritz on 24 November 1793. It was in such a mood that he told Knebel, "Now I know in my mind and I have decided what to start next year with—you have to attach yourself forcefully to something. I think it will be my old novel."

In 1794 he began to write, fascinated now by the idea of opposing the "horrors" of the revolution and the wars with new ideals of culture and education. In his reworking of the novel, Goethe used the old manuscript of the *Theatrical Mission* as a basis, but this and other manuscripts have not been preserved. It was not until 1910 that a copy of a copy came to light— written in rather an adventurous orthography by his friend Barbara Schultheiss and her daughter in Zurich—and was first published in 1911. We do not know whether the copyists made errors and, if they did, what the errors are. But at least it was now possible to make a comparison with the version of the novel that was executed. The hero of the *Theatrical Mission* is a talented young writer. Art and the theater are elements in the education of the Wilhelm Meister of the *Apprenticeship;* Wilhelm's "innermost need" is "to develop his leanings more and more towards the good and the beautiful." In the course of its reworking the novel about the artist became a novel about the age. The narrated time lies between the American War of Independence and the French Revolution. The characters belong to the most varied social classes and represent tendencies towards the dissolution of the fundamental conflict between the nobility and the bourgeoisie, as Goethe saw it. Theater is no longer the goal but a station on the road of Wilhelm Meister's development: social conditions and the events of the time affect him. It is the goal of his apprenticeship to attempt to combine practical activity and intellectual creativity, as Goethe later expresses it in his essay on Winckelmann: "Human beings are able to do a lot by the appropriate use of individual forces, they can achieve extraordinary things by the combination of different abilities; but they achieve the single, unexpected thing only when all the characteristics are equally combined within them."

Goethe's letter to Unger agreeing to the publication of *Wilhelm Meister* has not been preserved. Did Unger have any notion of the work that had been announced? He wrote to Goethe on 15 April 1794: "I think myself infinitely fortunate that you, Most respected Herr Privy Councillor, are favorably disposed to the idea of my publishing the novel and I could have no greater joy than that which your letter brought me and on the document that I am enclosing I commit myself to the exact fulfilment of all the conditions it contains. The whole public will be endlessly grateful to their premier author for a work that is valued above all else and for which they have been hoping with the keenest longing. I am not capable of expressing my extraordinary pleasure at the goodness you have shown me, I cannot wait for the moment when I shall receive the manuscript." Unger constantly urged Goethe to go on writing *Wilhelm Meister* and to complete it. On 10 May 1794, he wrote, "the public is now completely in the mood for politics, but only a Goethe can change this mood and everyone will seize upon your novel greedily and put political works to one side."[11] It was probably this insistence that made Goethe decide to agree to entrust the definitive publication to Unger. The first volume was printed and published at a time when Goethe was still occupied in writing out the rest of the parts.

"The printing of the first volume of *Wilhelm Meister* had begun, the decision was finally taken to declare as complete, a work on which I had so much still to do," Goethe wrote in retrospect, "and I was happy to have the beginning out of my sight, even if the continuation and the prospect of completing it placed me under a great deal of pressure, but necessity is the best adviser."

However, something important happened in the summer of 1794 besides his being under pressure from his publisher and his contractual agreement with him. Goethe had gone to Jena in June. There he met Schiller, who invited him to collaborate with him on *Die Horen* along with others. To be sought were Herder, Fichte, Hölderlin, A. and W. von Humboldt, J. H. Voss and A. W. Schlegel. Goethe confirmed his collaboration in a letter: "but certainly a closer association with such splendid men as the participants will start up again in lively fashion much that has come to a standstill in my work."

Goethe had recognized that discussion with this circle could be advantageous to the progress of *Wilhelm Meister.* He had agreed to let Schiller participate in the process of writing, indeed to develop the whole work discursively with him. On 6 December he sent him advance sheets of the first book ("We finally have the first book of Wilhelm Schüler, who, I don't know how, has got hold of the name Meister"), asking for his criticism and assuring him that he would, from the third book on, give him the text "in a manuscript that was still flexible." Schiller read the book, "with really heartfelt pleasure." His letter of 9 December marks the beginning of a spirited correspondence on poetic theory and practice that is virtually unique in the history of literature. Goethe thanked Schiller for his letter on the very next day: "You have shown me great kindness in ranking the first book of my novel so highly. After the strange fates suffered by this work both internally and externally, it would be no wonder if I were to become completely confused about it. In the end I simply stuck to my idea, and I shall be happy if it leads me out of the labyrinth."

Under the pressure of "necessity" and Schiller's and Humboldt's enthusiastic prodding, work proceeded rapidly. Goethe had the manuscript of the third book ready to send to Unger towards the end of January 1795. On 11 February he finished the fourth book and sent it to Schiller. "How I hope that my fourth book will find you in good health and in a good mood and that it will keep you entertained for a few hours. May I ask you to mark what seems questionable to you. I also commend my hero and his society to Herr von Humboldt and the ladies." Availing himself of this license, Schiller was especially critical of the development of the "Hamlet" section: "this material [should] not be presented seriatim but . . . should be interrupted by some significant intervening circumstances." Goethe followed this advice. He went to see Schiller in Jena in mid-February 1795, was happy about the "good mood" that this conversation had put him into, and remarks gratefully in his letter of 18 February: "How much more advantageous it is to be reflected in others than in ourselves." Again the concept of the mirror, again a not unimportant observation that shows how much it is Goethe's poetic practice to mirror the work in progress in something else and in this way to bring himself closer to the text and make himself "newly acquainted with it." Goethe carries on the art-theoretical discussion with the aim of changing the text until the point is reached at which he considers it definitively fixed for him. After that, his involvement wanes, he even refuses to read galley proofs and, as we know, scarcely ever again picks up books that have already been published (unless friends and readers draw his attention to typographical errors).

The fifth book is the occasion for Goethe and Schiller to commit to paper the most essential art-theoretical views in their correspondence. Schiller writes to a colleague in June 1795 that "in the course of his revision of the manuscript of his continuation of W. Meister Goethe has put pen to some interesting material on the difference between the novel and the drama, the central idea of which I find very pleasing. The novel he says calls for opinions and events, the drama character and action—*coincidence* can be part of the action of a novel, but man has to try to give coincidence form. In the drama it is fate that must dominate and act against man." Schiller elevates himself to the role of the co-author, says he is full of admiration, makes more and more intense suggestions, but at the same time his criticism becomes all the more explicit. The difficulties that were to come with the eighth book can be found in Goethe's letter of 25 June 1796. "First read the manuscript and enjoy it as a friend and then examine it and acquit me if you can. Several passages need to be expanded, many call for it and yet I scarcely know what is to be done, for the claims that this book make on me are limitless and cannot in the nature of things be completely satisfied, although everything should to some extent be resolved." After receiving the manuscript of the last book, Schiller sends four long letters in July. On 2 July, "I cannot describe to you how much the truth, the beauty of the life, the simple richness of the work moved me." He assures Goethe that their discussion of this work will never dry up: "A worthy and truly aesthetic estimation of the whole work is a great undertaking. I shall devote the next four months to it and with pleasure . . . make it into a sort of religion for me to make your business mine, to develop everything that is real within me into the purest mirror of the spirit that lives in this shell and thus in a higher sense of the word show myself worthy of the name friend. What a lively experience it has been to participate in the process of learning that excellence is a power and that it can only act as a force on selfish natures, and also that in the face of excellence there is no freedom but love." Goethe was to use this last remark in slightly altered form in Ottilie's diary in the *Elective Affinities:* "In the face of the great advantages of another there is no means of salvation but love."

In Schiller's letters Goethe finds "voices from another world." On 5 July he writes to him, "Do not tire of telling me your true opinion and keep the book for a week." And on 7 July, "Go on making me acquainted with my own work." Schiller takes this at face value, but when in his letter of 8 July he talks of a "mistake"—Goethe should legitimize by a more meaningful and rational expression the theatrical processes that the reader may subordinate to the imagination as frivolous—Goethe answers in a pique, in a slightly wounded tone. "The mistake that you justly remark about emanates from my innermost nature, from a realistic tic that makes it a pleasure for me to remove my existence, my actions, my writings from the sight of others. And so I would always like to travel incognito. . . . be more reckless than I am and in this way—I would say—place myself between myself and my own appearance." Another revealing insight: where Schiller fails to see Goethe's reference to reason, Goethe sees his realistic side; where Schiller criticizes the frivolous and the insignificant, he touches on Goethe's nature to be "more reckless," which leads him, when in doubt, to choose the insignificant over the significant expression. Although Schiller would have liked to continue the discussion, Goethe now breaks off the conversation and does not grant Schiller his wish to be allowed to read the eighth book for a second time. Goethe talks of "the difference of our natures," and their correspondence on the topic is abruptly broken off.

From 10 August onwards Goethe is once more busy revising the end of the work and on 26 August he sends the manuscript to Unger. The fourth and last volume appeared in October 1796. As far as he was concerned, this was the completion of a work that he characterized to Unger in the following terms: "Of all the works that I have ever written this is the most obligatory and, in more senses than one, the most difficult." The most "obligatory" in that it is the one that most strictly obeys the demands of detailed poetic portrayal and is therefore the most difficult to accomplish.

Both author and publisher could well be satisfied. Unger had the satisfaction of seeing the text printed in the Fraktur that he had created. He had written to Goethe on 23 May: "It is you, most honored man, that I have to thank for the pleasure that the new German characters afford the public, because it was you that honored them with your approval and permitted such a magnificent product to be printed in them—without this permission it would have been a long time before they could have been used as frequently as they are now—must we not respect a public that is guided by the taste of a *Goethe?*" Not everyone was happy with the typeface. Schiller complained that it was much too small and that the reading public would be made blind by it. On 25 July 1796 he sent Goethe an epigram: "The following epigram is the latest thing to come out of Berlin, as you will see":

UNGER
On the two works published by him:
Wilhelm Meister and the Journal Germany.

To recommend the characters' new profile I had to choose the master's work for the *first* test, If it survives the second test, and even the bungler's work fails to bring it into disrepute, then everything is settled.

Goethe's mother thought differently. She wrote to her son Wolfgang on 15 June 1794: "Herr Unger also deserves praise and commendation for the magnificent paper and the unsurpassable characters—I am happy beyond all expression that your writings, both old and new, have not seen the light of day in Latin characters which I think are so awkward—it's not so bad for *The Roman Carnival*—but, for the rest, I beg you stay German in the characters as well."

Wilhelm Meister's Apprenticeship was taken up immediately by Goethe's contemporaries. It was greeted extravagantly by some, sharply attacked by others, while still others found the work "awkward and silly." Wieland pronounced it a "truly horrible work" and the outraged F. H. Jacobi thought it "offensive as a whole." Friedrich Schlegel stated: "The French Revolution, Fichte's scientific doctrine, and Goethe's 'Meister' are the most important trends of the age," although in the original version Schlegel added, "but all three are only trends without being thoroughly executed."[12] Jean Paul reacted differently: "Goethe's 'Meister' recalled with his magic wand the Romantic-epic form, or the spirit that is lodged in the Old French or Old Franconian romances, into new and fresh pleasure palaces, as though from ruins that had collapsed on top of each other."

What could not be foreseen was the influence of the *Apprenticeship* on the further development of the history of the *Bildungsroman* in the nineteenth century and, in our century, on Thomas Mann and Hermann Hesse.

Anyway, it was a great success for author and publisher. But the voices of criticism and growing discontent were also heard. The second volume of the *Writings,* with *Reynard the Fox,* contained a large number of typographical errors. When they were discovered, it was still possible to add a list of errata to the copies of the first printing that were still on hand, but to Goethe's surprise there were two duplicate printings of volume 2 in which the list of errata was missing, because the errors had already been partly corrected.

Goethe's relationship with Unger was also to some degree determined by the question of royalties. While he received 500 thalers each for volumes 1 and 2 of *New Writings,* he now demanded 600 thalers for each volume of *Wilhelm Meister*—volumes 3 and 4 of *New Writings.* Unger accepted the demand.

Goethe's contemporaries were critical of his demands for such high fees. In August 1795 Wilhelm von Humboldt wrote to Schiller: "I hear a lot of talk about his [Goethe's] behavior towards his publishers, people here say it is extremely harsh and unfair." Wieland was especially critical. He is supposed to have said, "At the end of the second volume of Wilhelm Meister, Goethe hoped to get by with four. Now he is already talking about five volumes. . . . Goethe simply has no manuscript."

It is possible that Goethe had thought, as the work proceeded, of publishing the *Apprenticeship* in five volumes. After the third volume had been set, he wrote to Unger: "I can imagine that you wish to have the manuscript of the last volume of the novel soon, and I can assure you that it will be a very happy moment for me when I send it off. . . . Your, and the public's, expectation is certainly no greater than my wish to make a good thing of it and to spare no effort to that end. It is . . . the hardest [piece of work] and yet it must, if it is to succeed, be done with the greatest freedom and lightness. To do this requires time and the right mood. . . . Several people, and even close friends and acquaintances, swear and bet that I shall not be able to complete the work, as it is structured, in *one* more volume." Unger did not reply to this letter: in any case Goethe finished the *Apprenticeship* with the fourth volume; but whereas the previous volumes had each contained roughly 300 or 400 pages, the size of the final volume is 507 pages. But Goethe had once more made an inexcusable mistake; he had not read a single proof! No one noticed that the printer had read Riemer's handwriting wrongly in a number of places. It is true that Goethe had received the manuscript back—which was not usual at that time—but he did not use it for the preparation of the next edition. Instead a duplicate printing had also fallen into his hands and he used it as a basis for the next edition, so that Goethe himself "damaged" the form of the text. A modern critic writes, "This carelessness in the choice of the drafts of his texts had considerable effect on the text of his works and presents us even today with very complicated editorial problems."[13]

The diaries tell us about Goethe's carelessness in philological questions connected with the text as far as his own works are concerned. He was to write to Knebel some years later, "Riemer is very good. We are reading Wilhelm Meister together in preparation for a new edition. Because I wrote this little work, as I did my other things, as a sleepwalker, his remarks about my style are extremely instructive and delightful. Incidentally nothing will be changed except what could count as an orthographical or typographical error in the strict sense." Actual practice was often at odds with such avowed caution.

The occasional mention of duplicate printings characterizes a phenomenon that irritated Goethe and other authors of the time probably much more than ordinary typographical errors. Unger's publishing firm had, like other publishers, a very ugly practice. Goethe always granted rights for only one printing, but he forgot or left it to the publisher, whose risk it was, to determine the size of the printing. The publisher did not want, on the one hand, to risk too much with too large an edition, yet on the other he wanted and had to carry on his business at a profit and simply had to sell as many copies as possible; thus the one legitimate first edition sometimes appeared in batches of different printings. This was the way in which the so-called duplicate printings came about, bearing—and this is totally reprehensible—the same date as the first printing. As Goethe usually received a flat rate of royalty for *one* edition, the process of issuing the first edition in batches was at the very least incorrect and, in every case, unfair to the author. The duplicate editions often contained mistakes and differed from the first printing. Copy was, at that time, handset, that is, lines were made up from individual characters and then were put into forms for printing. This standing type was not preserved but was distributed as soon as it had been printed. This meant that when there was a reprint the text had to be reset and in the process mistakes could easily be made; for the sake of profitability cheaper paper was often used in these reprints.

A scholar who has written on the duplicate printings of Goethe's works in a number of articles has recorded the discrepancies; they certainly reflect no credit on German publishers! He discovered that the Unger publishing firm printed Schiller's drama *The Maid of Orleans*—the rights to which were limited to the years 1802–04—eight (sic!) times, and even after 1804, but actually dated all of the printings "1802"!

It was also proven that there were numerous duplicate printings of Goethe's *New Writings;* duplicate printings of all but volume 7 exist—in some cases more than one additional printing. Unger's procedure was also obfuscated by the fact that, with Goethe's knowledge, he made individual editions of *Wilhelm Meister,* with a new title page, out of the copy of the first collected edition. The production of separate editions was practiced—as a sort of established right—by all the publishers of collected editions of Goethe's work and tolerated by the authors.

We can assume that Goethe saw through these practices. And he was warned. On 28 April 1801 August Wilhelm Schlegel wrote to him: "Unger has played some nasty tricks on me, reprinted the first part of Shakespeare behind my back and afterwards, when I spoke to him about it, refused my justified demand and behaved very badly, so that I really had to sue him. . . . I am telling you this because you are now connected with Unger as a publisher; I do not know what your contractual arrangements are with him, I can only say that I can state with certainty that he has reprinted the first part of your *New Writings* and the first part of *Wilhelm Meister.* A very honest man and an expert has assured me that he has seen this with his own eyes. Give Schiller a tip about this too."

We have to ask ourselves why Goethe did not complain to Unger, why he never protested. Now, we know that Goethe did not care for direct personal confrontation. Presumably he also did nothing because the procedure was in some way or another "customary," and because there were no formal contracts.

But after 1797 a certain estrangement grew up between Goethe and Unger. Unger eyed with suspicion the personal connection between Goethe and Cotta. He wrote to Carl Böttiger, Goethe's intermediary, "Is it possible that my Goethe has deserted me because another bookseller has entertained him for four weeks, well, I'll say no more about it." Perhaps he did have something to say about it and should have gone to Goethe in Weimar and talked with him. He must have known that Goethe, when once wounded, could hardly be won over for a further relationship. "As far as the Himburgs go, I'm dead," was the way he wanted to say farewell to the pirate publisher and this would soon be true of Unger. One more personal meeting took place, but it was more of a coincidence. Not that Unger had gone to Weimar. Goethe was at the Leipzig Fair with the duke from 28 April until 16 May 1800. In his journal (10 May) he wrote, "Met messieurs Unger and Woltmann." The meeting does not seem to have made a great impression on him. There is no mention of a conversation in the journal, nothing about the seventh volume of the *Writings*—no question about the sale of the edition, no accusation, no complaint. Cotta is accorded a different honor, however. The journal reads: "went walking with Herr Cotta and discussed various literary matters."

Goethe reacted in his own way. As early as 1798 he had rejected all thought of offering Unger his *Herrmann and Dorothea*. The more Unger pressed him for new manuscripts, the more hesitantly and the more negatively Goethe reacted. "Will Göthe publish an eighth volume of his *Writings?*" Unger asked Schiller in 1801. "I shall very shortly ask him for one, that is, if I hear from you that it would not be too importunate. In Leipzig he promised to come to Berlin. But he did not say when." Thus we know that the two had after all talked with one another on 10 May 1800! Schiller did not reply to Unger's letter; he knew that Unger's request would be too "importunate."

Goethe had another reason, and for him an essential one, to be angry with Unger. Unger published a journal, *Germany,* and Goethe was outraged by many of the articles in it. It would be the same later on with Cotta's *Morgenblatt.* House organs are a particular problem for publishers.

Goethe the cosmopolite did not like the Germans; he felt that he was revered by them, recognized as famous, but that in comparison with other authors he was read too little, his books did not sell well enough, and above all he did not feel that he was liked. His critical remarks about the Germans are legion: "Are you looking for enthusiasm among German readers? You poor thing. Happy if you could even hope for politeness." For Goethe, "German" was a point of self-tormenting debate. "Germany is nothing, but every individual German is a lot. But the latter imagines that it is the other way round."

He made his general judgments and condemnations but they were never absolute, he took them back, often questioned them ironically, knowing full well that the characteristics he praised in the Germans were also his own and that he also had to correct the very errors that he censured.[14]

Goethe countered the Romantics' demand for a "national literature" with his cry for a "world literature." "National literature does not say a lot, the epoch of world literature is now upon us and everyone must make every effort to hasten that epoch," he was to say retrospectively in a conversation with Eckermann (31 January 1827). Small wonder that the national-conservative attitude of Unger's periodical *Germany* did not please Goethe and that he made fun of it in the *Xenien*.

> Do not be seduced to Unger's old German oak,
> Its bitter fruit nourishes no clean animal.

That is to say: the nourishment of this periodical is bitter, astringent, and more or less only suited to hogs. On 6 March 1802 Unger told Schiller that "I am publishing a new journal *Irene* edited by Herr von Halem. I would like you and Herr Privy Councillor v. Göthe to contribute a small essay or an unpublished poem to it, so as to raise the level and bring glory to the periodical by the addition of your names." A major error on Unger's part! He was not concerned with the substance but with the names of the authors who would "raise the level and bring glory to" his journal. Schiller reacted with anger and told Goethe, "You have been politely invited, along with me, to make a few contributions to von Helm's *Irene*. It is really bestial the way these gentlemen, who do their utmost to annihilate us, still demand that we promote their works. However I am prepared for the sake of Unger, who made this request of me, to give him a truly heartfelt answer." Goethe reacted immediately, "I wish you a wonderfully good humor and a wonderfully harsh fist when you answer the irenic invitation. It would be really wonderful if you could manage to compose an epistle that would cover the whole mob to whom I devote and swear more and more hatred." One can, one must understand the authors. They were obliged to take the point of view that the publishers were only concerned to exploit them and not to disseminate literary works that by their form and their content would contribute to bringing about a change in the times.

Schiller wrote the letter, but it has not been preserved. (Did Unger suppress Schiller's reply? Did he not want to pass on to posterity this criticism from the pen of the great author?—a publisher may from time to time be led into such temptation.)

Goethe and Unger never discussed the matter; Goethe always tried to avoid such confrontations and Unger was perhaps totally unconscious of what he had done to Schiller and to Goethe. The correspondence became one-sided: "It would have given me the greatest pleasure," Unger wrote to Goethe, "if I had had the good luck to get even a hint of goodwill from you as proof that I have not been entirely effaced from your memory. I am not conscious on my side of having deserved such a punishment." He sent Goethe an edition of the works of Ewald von Kleist printed on the "best paper." Goethe reacted calmly, expressed thanks for Kleist's poems and letters that "take us back to a time that certainly appears very different from our own." This letter of 8 June 1803 is the last that Goethe sent to Unger. Unger died on 26 December 1804. His widow wrote to the Most Honorable Privy Councillor on 26 January 1805: "If your Excellency had some commissions to send to my deceased loved one, I am here ready to accept your commands concerning them." There were no more commands. Frau Unger tried to carry on the work of the publishing firm and the printing works that were heavily in debt. The widow Helene Friederike Unger died on 21 September 1813 and all the securities of the publishing house, the printing works, and the writings were scattered, as Zelter wrote to Goethe on 14 March 1831, "to the four winds."

Herrmann and Dorothea   The earliest piece of evidence for the plan of *Herrmann and Dorothea* dates from 7 July 1796. The last part was written in July 1797 and in October of that year *Herrmann and Dorothea* appeared as a "pocket book for 1798" in five different designs and layouts. But Unger was not the publisher. Goethe had not made a formal publishing contract with Unger and the Unger edition is a not a "complete works" in the sense of the Göschen or Cotta editions, where there is a firm plan of what the contents are. The Unger edition is a collection of individual editions under the title *New Writings.* All the evidence points to the fact that negotiations were taking place for the continuation of the Unger edition, in the course of which the plan was apparently made to extend it to eight volumes, analogous to the Göschen edition. The relationship with Unger was therefore a very loose one and could be broken off at any time. Thus Goethe felt under no obligation to offer *Herrmann and Dorothea* to Unger. Goethe indicated his new publishing strategy in two draft letters. On 3 March 1797 he wrote that, before going on with the *New Writings,* "he intended to bring a few minor things to the public's attention in another way." By indicating that they were minor things Goethe played the process down, but he had, nevertheless, reached an agreement with Vieweg about *Herrmann and Dorothea.*

Why did Vieweg and not Unger publish *Herrmann and Dorothea,* why did Goethe choose another approach to the publisher, why "another way"? Perhaps it was a sort of infidelity, because he let another publisher have the "greatest work" of the period, while the *New Writings* were being produced by Unger. Why this strange "business posture" that is "probably unique in the history of the book trade." Why this "strange . . . method of negotiation," Loram asks.[15] Why the unusually high demand for royalties, a thousand gold thalers for 2,000 hexameters, an "enormous royalty" in Caroline von Humboldt's opinion? Why play the game of buying a pig in a poke, when Goethe was certain that he had written a significant work? Goethe's coup made waves among his contemporaries and among people in the trade who were in the know. I am sure that it was not an unintentional infidelity, but a clearly calculated publishing strategy on his part. For this work—with its special importance for Goethe and his Germans—he wanted a different, a larger, circulation than the doubtless serious, but conservative, Unger could offer. Vieweg seized his chance, paid the royalty that was demanded—the highest of its time—and remained the only publisher to make a profit on an individual work by Goethe in his lifetime.

But what was so special about it?

First, contemporaries regarded *Herrmann and Dorothea* as a "supreme work" and Goethe regarded it in the same light. The history of its genesis is extraordinary. The epic was written according to the strictest principles of poetics on the one hand, and in intensive contact with future readers on the other. Goethe was in Jena from the middle of August 1796, where he spent almost every evening with Schiller. They discussed the progress of the poem, but mostly they discussed the main aesthetic problem, the hexameter form.

Wieland had criticized Johann Heinrich Voss's Homer translations in the December number of the *Teutsche Merkur* and August Wilhelm von Schlegel, in the *Allgemeine Literatur Zeitung,* found fault with the "artificiality" of the verses.[16] On the other hand, both Schiller and Goethe were taken with Voss's idyll *Luise.* "I had long felt inclined to try my hand in this field [epic poetry] and I was always frightened off by the elevated concept of the unity and indivisibility of the Homeric writings," he wrote to the classicist Friedrich August Wolf in 1796. "Now since you suggest that these writings all belong to one family, it is less temerarious to dare to appear in more elevated society and to follow the path [with *Herrmann and Dorothea*] that Voss has indicated so beautifully in his *Luise.*" In his famous letter to Körner, Schiller documented his part in the writing of *Herrmann and Dorothea* and recorded Goethe's great achievement and what he was accomplishing day by day. "Goethe is now working on a new poetic work that is also for the most part complete. It is a sort of bourgeois idyll, not it is true inspired by Voss's *Luise,* but recently aroused by it: incidentally its whole manner is opposed to Voss. The whole thing is structured with astonishing understanding and executed in a true epic tone. I have heard two-thirds of it, four cantos, that are excellent. The whole thing will occupy about twelve signatures. He has carried the idea around with him for several years, but its execution which has taken place under my own eyes was carried out with unbelievable ease and speed; for nine days on end he wrote more than a hundred and fifty hexameters a day."[17] This tempo was maintained in Jena, but Goethe had to go back to Weimar on 5 October and the work came to a standstill. The last two cantos, he tells Schiller on 15 October, "will have to stay in limbo for a time." He made no progress with the further cantos and began a constant revision of the ones he had already written. At the beginning of December he wrote the elegy *Herrmann and Dorothea,* that was designed as an introduction to the epic, but Schiller advised against publishing it quickly (the poem was first assigned to the *Elegies* in 1800 and published in a special edition in 1820 according to the original plan). Two-thirds of the text was finally completed on 5 December and Goethe hoped that in the new year he would be "in the mood for the rest." In the first half of March 1797 Goethe was again staying with Schiller in Jena and the last cantos were quickly written. There were to be nine cantos with nine headings, conforming to the nine muses: Mnemosyne spent nine nights in Thessalonian Pieiria in the arms of Zeus and bore him nine daughters who became the inspirational goddesses of literature, the arts, and the sciences. Poets appealed to them when they were starting great undertakings.

On 28 April 1797 Goethe could say: "My poem is finished. It consists of two thousand hexameters and is divided into nine cantos." On the same day he wrote to Heinrich Meyer, his closest adviser about matters relating to art, saying that he saw in the poem "the fulfillment of at least a part of my wishes."

Goethe found the material for his epic poem in an anecdote that tells of the expulsion of the Salzburg Protestants at the end of 1731. The anecdote provides the main points of the story: the young girl driven from her homeland, the young bourgeois till then frightened of women but suddenly inflamed at the sight of the foreign girl, his decision to marry, and finally the happy union. Goethe gives the story its unique poetic form, first under the influence of Voss's translations of Homer and encouraged by the insight of Friedrich August Wolf, who no longer ascribed the works of the Greek rhapsodist to a single author but to several. He creates something new, and what I find admirable is that he enters into his epic not only obsessively and completely subjectively, but at the same time he formulates new and objective standards for epic poetry. In his two letters to Schiller dated 19 and 22 April 1797 he makes his comments about the poetics of the poem. "I want to send you at once a thought about epic poetry. Since it should be listened to as peacefully and comfortably as possible *reason* probably makes more demands on it than on other forms of poetry. . . . One of the chief characteristics of the epic poem is that it is always moving backwards and forwards and so all retardations are epic. But there may not be any actual *hindrances,* these really belong in the drama." "I tried to subordinate the law of retardation to a higher one, and it seems to be governed by the one that states we may, indeed should, know the outcome of a good poem, that it is actually only the How that may arouse our interest. . . . In my Herrmann, the nature of the plan produces a special charm and everything appears complete and finished and yet at the same time the retrograde motion marks the beginning of a new poem." The effort of completing his poem intensifies, in his discussions with Schiller, into a joint effort to derive and determine the laws of modern poesy and the distinctions between genres from classical literature; the theoretical fruit of these efforts is, as we know, Goethe's and Schiller's essay *On Epic and Dramatic Poetry* published in December 1797. Is there anywhere in literature after Goethe another example of such creative energy, the writing of a poem that is completely original simultaneously with the determination and derivation of laws and standards for the literary genre; is there ever again such an objectivization of the subjective as that which Goethe ascribes to the achievement of the "artistically true," ever such a unity of the theory and practice of literature? In the literature of our own century we might think vaguely of Hugo von Hofmannsthal, of Thomas Mann who—in his reflections on the writing of his own novels—defines the "art form" novel; or of Bertolt Brecht whose most impressive achievement is "The Theory of the Epic Theater" that he went on developing and to which he gave a final condensed form in his *Small Organon for the Theater.*

The second special thing: As in scarcely any other poem Goethe was concerned in *Herrmann and Dorothea* with maintaining contact with his readers from the very beginning. Time and again he read passages to friends and acquaintances while he was composing the work. Thus Schiller's sister-in-law Caroline von Wolzogen reports in *Schiller's Life* on a reading on 17 September 1796: "as soon as it had been written Goethe read aloud, with great emotion and with tears streaming down his face, the canto that contains Herrmann's conversation with his mother under the pear tree." "That's the way you melt from the heat of your own coals, he said, drying his eyes." Goethe also read aloud to the duke and a small group of courtiers, and one listener remarked, "Wieland cried." Caroline von Humboldt records a further reading by Goethe: "He read us as much of his latest poem as he had completed. There is nothing to say about it, you have to hear it in order fully to enjoy the sense of inmost admiration for this divine man to whom it is given to express in words the deepest truth and the fullest humanity."[18]

And there is still a third special thing. The ceaselessly moving course of world history, the aftereffect of the French Revolution, plays a part in the writing of *Herrmann and Dorothea,* indeed it creates the actual background consciousness of all the larger works that he wrote in these years, *Wilhelm Meister's Apprenticeship,* as well as the epic *Herrmann and Dorothea.* The Terror of the French Assembly and all the events that accompanied it are registered by Goethe. This "head-rolling world history" is clearly to be heard in *Herrmann and Dorothea.* Carl August Böttiger already records this "constellation" at that first reading by Goethe.

It rests on a tremendous footing, on the French Revolution, and because of this it hurries along, a generation ahead of its time by depicting effects that were only truly assessed thirty or forty years later. Only this fearful and, in its own way, unique overthrow of so many nations could have made this poem possible. It is the *only Odyssey* that still seemed possible in our days. For, like the original, the mistakes of a single human being rest on the powerful background of the struggle between two parts of the world—of a Troy that has been destroyed and of the Greeks ruined on their return, so here the *rapid* wooing by an honest and honorable innkeeper's son of a noble bride fleeing in poverty rests on a flood of war and emigration that will perhaps never be seen again in any succeeding century.

Böttiger was wrong here, he had to be wrong, he could not foresee the horrors of the twentieth century. But the aftershocks and the aftereffects of the "international coup" were correctly recorded by Böttiger, as Hegel was to note twenty-five years later when in his Berlin lectures on aesthetics he expressed the opinion that "the great interests of the time, the struggles of the French Revolution, the defense of the fatherland, played a most worthy and significant part in this poem."

However critical Goethe was of the French Revolution, *Herrmann and Dorothea* is in the end a positive reaction to this cosmic event. In the poem Goethe sits in judgment on the limited view of life of the petite bourgeoisie, whose highest goods are money and possessions. Against these falling values he sets the values of assiduity, readiness to help, respect for the other person. Clear relationships of one person to another are dominant, the love of the son for the father, the love of the mother for her son, and Dorothea's inner decision—freely taken—in favor of Herrmann and the common stability of the "union." If in a time of "instability" the individual is "vacillating," "we want to hold fast and endure."

Once again: Goethe knew what he had given to his Germans in *Herrmann and Dorothea* and now he wanted it to be read, to be distributed and discussed; he wanted success, and to that end he wanted it published in an outstanding form. He quite consciously avoided Göschen, whose attention Böttiger—in spite of everything—had drawn to the work; *Herrmann and Dorothea,* Böttiger wrote to Göschen on 28 December 1796, "must become the first popular poem to present a younger generation." But it was no longer possible to establish a connection between Goethe and Göschen. The connection with Unger had also grown cooler and cooler. But then Böttiger had a new idea. He was associated with the bookseller Friedrich Vieweg, who had founded his publishing house in Berlin in 1786—under the influence of the Enlightenment philosophers—and had published theological and belletristic works. He was soon in a position to unite under his own roof the most important scholars and authors of the day. Lessing published his polemics against Pastor Götze with Vieweg, and Wieland, Herder, and Johann Heinrich Voss also submitted original contributions to his annual literary almanacs and calendars. Vieweg was especially anxious to find authors and contributions for his calendars. Was it this new calendar-form or the larger distribution that won Goethe over to accept Vieweg's offer? In any case he stressed the point to Heinrich Meyer (on 18 March 1797), after he had completed his negotiations with Vieweg: "and it will also appear in the form of a calendar with Vieweg. In this way it will be most widely read and it will bring in the most money. What more can an author ask for?"

Goethe suggested "a most odd procedure" to Vieweg. He formulated his conditions in a letter on 16 January 1797, and in the letter he speaks of Vieweg in the third person—"I want to hear what Vieweg thinks." "I am inclined to entrust an epic poem to Herr Vieweg in Berlin. *Herrmann and Dorothea* will be about two thousand hexameters strong. And it will be in such form as to constitute the contents of his almanac for 1798, and also to enable it after two years to be included in my works again. As far as the royalties are concerned I am giving Senior Consistory Councillor Böttiger a sealed letter which contains my demands and I wait to hear what Herr Vieweg thinks he can offer me for my work. If his offer is less than what I ask for, then I shall take back my sealed letter and the negotiations will be at an end; if it is higher I shall not ask for more than I do in the sealed letter entrusted to the Senior Consistory Councillor."

A demand of this sort, for something a publisher does not know, is impossible if the publisher is to make an offer: if a publisher goes along with such a demand his reputation will soon be ruined. But Vieweg was probably told about the poem by Böttiger so that he didn't have to buy a pig in a poke. For Goethe however the game was to assess the stake that the publisher wished to make on his own account.

In the letter that he had deposited with Böttiger, Goethe had written: "For the epic poem *Herrmann and Dorothea* I am asking One Thousand thalers in gold. Weimar 16 January 1797. Goethe." We do not know what Goethe had in mind and what had motivated him to follow this strange procedure. He tried something similar again later on and came out the loser; the procedure is intolerable to publishers who know their business; they would have refused then, just as they would today, to take part in auctions of this sort.

But how did Goethe arrive at the sum of 1,000 thalers of all things? The question has not yet been asked in the literature on the subject. We can only guess—1,000 hexameter couplets equals 1,000 thalers. That could have been just the model for Goethe, "the gambler," who did business laconically, imperatively, and succinctly. There is a wider aspect that we need to shed light on here. During the months that *Herrmann and Dorothea* was being written, Goethe and Schiller were in closer contact than ever before or than they ever were after. When the publisher Cotta could no longer afford to publish *Die Horan,* the hyperactive Schiller had already got something to put in its place; he had developed the idea of the *Musenalmanach* and had already found a publisher. In Jena he had made the acquaintance of Dr. Salomon Michaelis, an unusually cultivated and socially well-versed aesthete who had founded a bookstore and a publishing house. He made Schiller "the fabulous offer of 1,000 thalers for royalties" for the publication of such a *Musenalmanach.*[19] The documents—Schiller's contracts with Michaelis—were preserved and appear in the appendix to the Schiller *Nationalausgabe* but they do not mention 1,000 thalers, only 300 Imperial thalers. But be that as it may, given Schiller's financial situation, this sum must have been attractive to him. There is no doubt that he would have told Goethe about it, so why should Goethe not ask a similarly high sum for his *Herrmann and Dorothea?* Schiller's contact with Salomon Michaelis did, it is true, bring him money but it brought him no luck from the publishing point of view.

The collaboration of Goethe and Vieweg was quite a different story; the latter met Goethe's demand and offered exactly 1,000 thalers. People have assumed that Vieweg discovered the sum through an indiscretion on Böttiger's part: Böttiger's letter to Vieweg, in which he wrote, "you cannot offer less than 200 fr[iedrich's] d'or [= 1,000 thalers]," has been preserved. Whatever the truth, Vieweg met the demand and *Herrmann and Dorothea* was entrusted to him. It was certainly a large sum and an unusual one; Goethe wrote to Schiller on 29 January: "Furthermore, I have negotiated my epic poem, and a few charming events have taken place in the process." Schiller replied on 31 January, "as to the epic poem, I hope you have fallen into good hands. The work will sell brilliantly, and it is fair that the publisher should not try to make a profit on writings of this sort, but should be satisfied with the honor. He can grow rich on bad books."

I cannot agree with Schiller on a single point in this statement. A publisher who is forced to make a profit on "bad books" cannot also build up a program with good books, and it is more than an irony of history that the sale of this particular book proved how wrong Schiller was. *Herrmann and Dorothea* was a profitable undertaking for the publisher.

The poem appeared in October as "Paperback for the year 1798": "*Herrmann and Dorothea* by J.W. von Göthe, Berlin, Vieweg the Elder. 174 pp." There was a title engraving that represented the Prussian royal family and further landscape engravings after Chodowiecki. The text was set in Fraktur. The paperback appeared in five different editions, and the finest copies were bound in morocco or embroidered silk. Purchasers received a knife and a pair of scissors as a free gift, so that the target group of buyers, society ladies, would also get something practical and enjoy having sewing implements as well as the poem. Schiller comments on this in his letter to Böttiger of 18 October 1797: "the highest and the lowest needs of mortals are seen to be satisfied." At first author and publisher seemed very satisfied, sales flourished, and the epic became one of the favorite poems of the day. Within a short time the poem had captivated its readers, and Goethe existed once more as a writer. Side by side with the author of *Götz* and *Werther,* now the author of *Herrmann and Dorothea* became a favorite with the public. No other book by Goethe was adopted so rapidly by the literary, critical, and academic public.

Even the most important aesthetes devoted long laudatory articles to the poem. August Wilhelm Schlegel observed: "the chief impression is emotion . . . one that rouses us to salutary activity. *Herrmann and Dorothea* is a complete work of art in high style and at the same time comprehensible, heartfelt, patriotic, and popular." Wilhelm von Humboldt wrote: "We recognize the faithful and complete picture of the world and of humanity in the bare depiction of the simple action of the poem."

Perhaps it was this great resonance that made Vieweg overstep the mark. As was expressly provided, he had been granted the rights for only two years, from 1798 to 1800. In 1799 he had yet another strange idea. He came out with a new edition that included ten etchings and gave it the title of *Goethe's New Writings.* Goethe who had in the meantime already been in touch with Cotta, wrote to the latter on 22 September 1799: "That Herr Vieweg is also publishing *Herrmann and Dorothea* as the first volume of my latest writings is a bad thing, nothing was agreed about this between us." In 1806 and again in 1825, Vieweg produced illegal editions. Goethe continued to protest. "It is sheer piracy. He has absolutely no right to do this, and he hasn't even bothered to send me so much as a greeting; which is of course quite natural[!]."[20]

Though Goethe finally limited himself to verbal protests, Vieweg was finished as far as he was concerned. Once again he had had bad experiences with a publisher!

It is true that he was not mistaken in his own evaluation of his "favorite poem." While *Werther* had addressed only an educated stratum of the public, the whole public felt itself addressed by *Herrmann and Dorothea,* "Tailors, seamstresses, maids—everyone is reading it." Even in old age Goethe was to say that *Herrmann and Dorothea* was the only one of his great poems that still pleased him.

He wrote to Schiller on 3 January 1798, "As far as the subject matter is concerned I have, in *Herrmann and Dorothea,* granted the Germans their wish and now they are extremely satisfied." Are they still satisfied today? Ernst Beutler, the editor of the Artemis edition of Goethe's works, found *Herrmann and Dorothea* "homogeneous, without dross" and "pure"; on the other hand Oskar Seidlin, writing in the seventies, was of the opinion that there wasn't a single dog, "especially not a young dog," that could be enticed from its lair by *Herrmann and Dorothea.* Now, whether that is the task of literature is another matter. I confess that I had my difficulties in the course of reading and re-reading the poem several times—the author often neglects to find the right expression, there are whole sections of the poem where the versification lacks power, the overall idyllic tone is truly no longer timely. And yet I am able to admire the work, I can understand Goethe's intention, which was to contrast the old values with the collapse of values in his own day, and to confront the collapse of social order with the higher order of poetry. We admire the intention, but we can no longer heed the message. The familial role that Goethe assigns to woman in *Herrmann and Dorothea* is obsolete. Dorothea's maxims can only be accepted as historically conditioned. It may also be true that the claim to the highest aesthetic form, so often made by critics, does make it more difficult to approach the poem.

Another point of view also comes to mind: the perspective of the "alien," the refugee, the asylum seeker. A hundred and fifty years after Goethe, Bertolt Brecht, like many others, had to accept the fate of exile, and in his *Conversations with Refugees* he presented the exiles' situation. I still think that Goethe, who could not have foreseen the streams of refugees of the twentieth century, does give us an example of how one should treat "foreigners."

Goethe wrote that he had given the Germans what they wanted as far as the subject matter was concerned. What does he mean by "subject matter"? Is it the narrow world of the small town, the German petite bourgeoisie with its stereotypes, or perhaps the "prosodic organization," that is, the form given to the poem by the hexameter? Or was it his hope that the "power" of the individual would be able to assert itself "against the power" of the universal? Perhaps the painter of humanity saw here the "true, the genuine human proportions."

Be that as it may, a publisher, Vieweg, with his 1,000 thalers did what Goethe wanted—he took a risk. But did he have to produce illegal editions? And should we be surprised if Goethe regarded publishers with skepticism?

FOUR

Approaches to Cotta

Johann Cotta and His Beginnings — GREATNESS IN PUBLISHING is not the greatness of an individual. Great publishers are also not born great but become great through the literary-intellectual constellation into which they have entered and which they were able to create as publishers. The duty of the publisher is service. Service to others. Service to the author. Anyone seeing how a publisher treats his authors, sees what sort of a firm it is.

Johann Friedrich Cotta, who was born on 27 April 1764 and raised to the nobility and made a hereditary Freiherr in 1822, never thought that he would become a publisher, that he would become the greatest publisher of his day, "the Napoleon among booksellers." He did not want to take over his father's publishing firm or the store known as "J. G. Cotta's Bookstore, Tübingen."

We can understand Cotta's hesitation, his refusal to take over the bookstore; he heard from his father, Christoph Friedrich Cotta, more about the difficulties than the fascination of the publishing profession.

Cotta had fourteen siblings; he was the fifth child, his parents' third son. His mother, Rosalie Pyrker, was a singer at the court opera in Stuttgart who was imprisoned for "insubordination" by Duke Charles Eugene for no less than eight years. His godfather, Johann Friedrich Cotta, the chancellor of the university, wanted him to study theology, but his first professional goal was different; he wanted to become an officer in the so-called corps of engineers and therefore studied physics and mathematics.

Cotta later took up the study of law. His studies were interrupted by a journey to Paris in 1785 which not only afforded him a knowledge of the

French language but also brought him into touch with some highly individual, cultured, and important personalities with whom he was to maintain ties for the rest of his life.

A decisive event determined his life. His teacher had recommended him as a tutor to a Polish prince, but then conditions changed there; he was refused the post, but received 1,500 guilders as compensation. This gave him the opportunity to discuss the purchase of the bookstore with his father. Meanwhile he completed his studies in Tübingen and became a doctor of law. He seldom used the title (in contrast to his future author who used the title but did not hold it). Though Cotta registered as an advocate in the ducal court in Tübingen, he asked Philipp Erasmus Reich, the most celebrated bookseller of the day, for advice concerning the financing and the profitability of a publishing house and a bookstore. His letter stated, "I would accept nothing but good books for publication and I would always see to it that the paper and the printing were handsome." For him it was not a question of fashions and trends, but of publishing things that were both internally and externally good and of creating a public for them. Cotta remained true to his credo. Encouraged by Reich and after a conscientious examination of the prospects of the publishing trade, he and his father agreed on the sum of 17,000 guilders for the purchase of the firm. His settlement money from the Polish prince covered the first interim payment. Cotta moved to Tübingen into the two cramped Cotta houses that stood next door to each other and took over the business on 1 December 1787. His fellow student Christian Jakob Zahn joined the firm in March 1789 as a partner and stayed with Cotta until 1798.

Cotta had to recognize the fact that there was very little writing going on in the Tübingen and Stuttgart area at that time. The position of Stuttgart, which had no attraction as the literary capital of the state, was later summed up in these words: "When we think about the intellectual history of Swabia we suddenly discover that Stuttgart did not exactly assume the central position that it otherwise enjoys," but the exceptions to this were "the tradition of the press, the theater, and Cotta."[1]

The firm began to flourish. Cotta took regular trips through the German states and was a regular visitor to the Leipzig fairs. He made his first journey on foot so as to economize. The firm had only a few employees at the time. Cotta himself took care of the extensive correspondence, kept the account books, and gave orders to the printers. He wrote a graceful hand that was hard to decipher, that not only causes difficulties for us but caused them for his contemporaries as well. Schiller sometimes laughed at the cursoriness of Cotta's letters, Cotta's closing greeting—"hurriedly"—was for him simply "Cotta's formula." But how much Cotta had to supervise and coordinate! It is no wonder that his way of working was described as a mixture of "varied activity and burdensome business confusion." But the hardworking, dynamic man managed to restore the "shattered business" and so was able to part company with his partner, Zahn, in 1798 and buy him out.

There was no stopping Cotta's ambition as a publisher after this parting. He had in the meanwhile acquired the crucial mentor for this new perspective on his publishing activity—a man of genius, Schiller.

How did Schiller come to Cotta? He was first of all an adviser, editor, and initiator, someone who attracted the brilliant people of his time to Cotta. But how did he come to Cotta as an author, when he was in any case partly de jure and partly by promise tied to Göschen and had entered into a contract with the Leipzig publisher Siegfried Leberecht Crusius, for his collected prose works and poems, a contract that empowered Crusius to claim these rights even after Schiller's death?

Schiller and Cotta: In publishing, "normal" business procedures can
Mutual Respect turn out to be mistakes. This was absolutely true of
Göschen. From his point of view he conducted nego-
tiations in a "normal" manner, and yet on three occasions this had proved to be an error vis-à-vis Schiller. Three mistakes that a publisher simply should not make; the first was unforgivable, the second understandable, and the third explicable on the basis of the author's psyche. A publisher may never answer the question as to who the firm's most important author is. (I had the good fortune never to have to answer it, perhaps because the lodestar, Brecht, was not challenged, because the effect of Hermann Hesse was bound-less, because Max Frisch's work was not yet completed, and because Samuel Beckett was honored and beloved by all and held in high esteem even by those who in 1969 declared literature dead.)

Göschen was careless: as far as he was concerned the most important author of the time was not Schiller but Christoph Martin Wieland; it is unforgivable for a publisher to say such a thing, it was bound to be insulting to Schiller, and it called into question the whole basis of Schiller's connection with Göschen.

The second, understandable, error arose out of the first: Göschen published Wieland's collected works in four editions, each separately set, printed on different paper, and bound in different materials, each edition consisting of thirty volumes. The investment in this enterprise pushed the publisher—who was always working on the brink of financial difficulties—considerably over the brink. Göschen had to pay for his ambition to produce the most aesthetically pleasing editions and for using foreign fonts and paper from selected paper mills. Even when his undertaking was successfully completed, Goethe and Schiller were not exactly happy to hear what Bertuch said to Göschen on 6 November 1793: "Wieland is now incontestably the leading classical author in the nation."

Into the bargain, the irony of this author-publisher relationship was that Schiller had suggested Wieland to Göschen and advised him to publish Wieland's collected works. In October 1792, Göschen discussed the edition of his calendar with Schiller. "I advised him against the whole calendar enterprise," wrote Schiller (to Körner on 15 October 1792). And he continues, "If, instead of his calendar, military journals, devotional books etc., Göschen were to take on *nothing* but *Wieland's writings and our Deutscher Merkur* he could, in five years, become the most respectable of booksellers and a wealthy man." How could Schiller give this advice at a point in time when the little firm of Göschen was putting out Goethe's works under the most difficult conditions and selling few of them, and when Göschen—as Schiller knew—had acquired the publishing rights to Lessing's works. Was not Göschen, on the basis of Goethe's works, the "most respectable" bookseller? If anyone were aware of this it must have been Schiller. Schiller's role in the literary politics that were at the time being engaged in intensively by the most powerful authors of the day—with the exception of Goethe—is very ambiguous.

Göschen's third mistake: a publisher can put an author under an obligation by paying him advances but he cannot make an author be morally obligated in this way; financial dependence does not create moral ties. Göschen was deeply in debt, but as tardy as he was toward his creditors, the printers and the paper merchants, his authors were served well and meticulously by him. The payment of advances was normal practice and every author wanted what Wieland mentioned to Göschen in a letter in November 1788—for his publishers always to "multiply the half dozen by two." At the same time, the year 1788 was one of the worst years ever for the book trade as a whole: two booksellers had offered Frederick the Great's works for "ready money" at the Michaelmas Fair, compelling other booksellers to concentrate all their financial resources on those exclusively and not to buy any other works. Frederick the Great, the publishers insinuated at the time, was once again ruining the German lands!

Throughout his years in Jena Schiller was himself always in the gravest financial difficulties. True, Goethe had intervened with the duke and obtained a chair for him at the university, but it was an honorary chair. Certainly, Schiller had many irons in the fire, his journalistic works were sought after, his publications with Göschen and Crusius were not unsuccessful, but his royalties were by no means sufficient to secure his existence. He was deeply in debt to Göschen, he was often unable to meet the agreed deadlines for his manuscripts, and, especially in the case of the *Thalia,* which was very close to Göschen's heart, there was always a delay. It was his "chest complaint" that kept him from any sort of work for days, weeks, even months. His marriage to Charlotte von Lengenfeld did, it is true, make him happy and give him a boost, but now that there were two people to care for, his living expenses rose. Above all he had no domicile; he wanted an "Établissement that will lift me above my worries and assure me a happy and peaceful existence," he wrote to Göschen on 8 March 1789, and Göschen immediately helped him. Schiller promised in return a work that "could be started at the latest in two years and will not end before my life does and will, as I believe, become and remain a lucrative article for my friend Göschen, combining the advantages of a new journal with the lasting value of an individual work." How was Göschen to react to this? Certainly a publisher knows that authors need such projections, that the only one who achieves the possible is the one who keeps the impossible as a goal. We do not know what "lucrative" plan Schiller had in mind at that time, presumably it was what was later realized as *Die Horen.* But one thing is certain, Göschen must have had the impression that Schiller would feel a lifelong obligation to him. A little later, Schiller sent him the manuscript for the *Thalia* with the promise that there would be no more delays with manuscripts and that Göschen, when Schiller "has wielded his historic pen in a few more essays," should be the publisher of the work "that I shall produce with the greatest maturity and at my leisure." In the correspondence between Göschen and Schiller we can follow the way in which both erected an ideal edifice for common projects at this time, and neither of them, least of all the publisher, had any idea that this would shortly collapse like a house of cards. What Schiller expected of his publisher at this time is certainly inconceivable and unbelievable.

Charlotte von Lengenfeld wanted to give Schiller an English Bible; Göschen had to procure it. After Schiller's marriage Göschen invited the couple to stay with him while they were visiting Leipzig. Schiller, however, had a guilty conscience because he feared that Göschen "would preach the duties of an author to him in an awful voice"; his letter written on 30 July 1789 conjured up ill-temperedly the "duties of an author to his publisher," but closed, as did so many others, with the formula "ever yours." He finally sent the manuscripts for at least one issue of the *Thalia* to Göschen with his letter of 21 December and thanked the publisher for his patience and "continuing friendship."

In January 1790, Schiller once more got into serious financial difficulties. He had borrowed from a moneylender in Dresden, and the latter was demanding—with threats—repayment by the end of the year. Schiller writes to Göschen on 10 February, "I know you will do what you can to help relieve me of this unpleasant burden. I will gladly pay 6% interest if you could advance the whole sum of 200 thalers for a period of 3–4 months." Göschen gave it to him without interest, but we can see, in the light of the relatively small sum involved, how desperate Schiller's situation must have been or, at least, how desperate he felt it to be. He could now work uninterruptedly for a year; he was free of debts and received an advance of 400 thalers from Göschen for an essay on "The Thirty Years War" for the second number of Göschen's *Historical Calendar for Ladies*. On 27 October 1790 Schiller thanked him for sending him the first copies, "that have turned out simply brilliantly. . . . I can tell you, my friend, how impatiently I wait to hear of the success of our calendar, I am more anxious than over the outcome of a battle." That was the extent to which Schiller's judgment of a publication could change!

But in the new year he again had a debt to settle and this time he hit on an unusual idea. On 28 January 1791 he not only asked Göschen once more for the "same favor," he simply anticipated it. "Trusting in your goodness I have taken out a bill of exchange in your name which will be presented to you within the next few days . . . please be good enough to accept it and do not take offense at the liberty I have taken." Göschen cashed the bill of exchange—what must he have thought of the liberty his author had taken?—and this at a time when he himself did not know where he was to drum up the money to run his business. Schiller repeatedly promised contributions to the firm's calendar, he repeatedly drew advances, and again and again he was late and the publisher was constantly postponing the deadlines. In May 1791 Schiller had his third major illness and thought he was dying. As he once again needed money, he offered Göschen *Don Carlos* in a "new and improved form" and promised him the manuscript by the new year. Göschen responded by sending him another advance. Schiller acknowledged receipt: "from the account that you sent me in your last letter, I have recently seen, my dearest friend, what an obligation I am under to you, and how much your goodness turns into my *duty*, what my own heart would tell me without any other spur." Again Schiller mentions *duty*, underlining it. However the question always was, could Göschen take this declaration at its face value?

Schiller was seriously ill for nine months and his work came to a standstill. Crusius too was now reminding him about the delivery of his "History of the Netherlands." While convalescing, Schiller was able to complete the final part of his *History of the Thirty Years War* and send it to Göschen. He promised further manuscripts for the *Thalia* that was now appearing bimonthly. On 16 December 1791 he wrote to Göschen: "I received the 200 thalers in good order, my dear friend, and I send my best thanks for them. . . . In just a week's time I shall put my body and soul into continuing the work and I shall not stop until I am able to write: Finis." That was certainly his intention. By exerting himself to the utmost he managed to finish the work in September 1792. Meanwhile friends had successfully urged the duke of Augustenburg to give Schiller a pension of 1,000 thalers for three years— this meant release for him, release from his perpetual financial misery. In September 1792, when he had finished work on *The Thirty Years War*, he wrote to Körner: "now I am free and want to remain so forever. No more work that is imposed on me by someone else or that has any other mainspring but amusement or the pursuit of an inclination." This statement shows how Schiller suffered by always having to work on commissions and take advances, always earning royalties that were insufficient for his existence. At this point a great relationship was exhausted. Göschen simply could not understand it when on 4 May 1794 Schiller suggested to him that the *Thalia* should be buried; he did this on the same day that it was agreed between Cotta and Schiller to publish the *Horen*. This was the day that Schiller and Cotta met for a coach ride out to the environs of Stuttgart. The two Swabians, almost the same age, got on well together, and Schiller presented Cotta with his plan for the *Horen*. Cotta was enthusiastic and for his part told Schiller of his plans for an independent, nonpartisan daily European newspaper. That day they agreed to both of these undertakings.

In March 1794 Schiller was in Tübingen and met Cotta in person for the first time. What the two of them discussed is not known, but something strange happened. Schiller asked Cotta for a payment of 200 thalers against a bill of exchange that he had made out in the name of Göschen. But that was not the limit. That was to be kept for 4 May; on that evening Schiller wrote to Göschen: "I hope you received my last letter in which I asked you to accept a bill for 200 thalers payable in mid-June and which Herr Cotta of Tübingen will present to you. . . . I needed money and did not know where else to lay hands on it, if I was not to give Herr Cotta my *Callias*." This must have been a terrible blow to Göschen! *Callias*, which was to become Schiller's chief work on aesthetics, had been unequivocally promised to Göschen and here was Schiller suggesting that he might possibly change over to Cotta as his publisher. Göschen was wounded. He did not fight, but he showed his irritation and, in spite of everything, this was another mistake on his part. Of course, if we think of what Schiller had written to him five years before, and it is worth repeating it here, his attitude is understandable. "Rely on me therefore, my dearest friend, to do everything in my power always to link my own happiness with what is best for you and to think of them both as indivisible."

Cotta and Schiller each had a holographic contract for the other to sign a few days later: Cotta's contract, for the publication of a "General Newspaper for the European countries by Herr Court Councillor Schiller" and Schiller's for the literary monthly the *Horen*. Both contracts were signed in Jena on 28 May 1794, but Schiller recalled his signature on 14 June because, for reasons of health, he was unable to devote himself to the "risky undertaking" of editing a political daily newspaper. But it was certainly not for health reasons alone. "Inclination and inner vocation" were what was decisive. The *Horen* was now more important to him than a daily political newspaper. We also read in the program for the *Horen*: "At a time when the sounds of war nearby strike fear into the fatherland, when the clash of political opinions and interests renews this conflict in almost every circle and all too frequently scares off the muses and graces from them, when no salvation from this all-pursuing daemon of criticism of the state is to be found either in contemporary conversations or in the measures taken: it may be just as daring as it is commendable to invite the distracted reader to take part in a conversation totally contrastive in nature. . . . But the more the narrow interest of the present creates a tension in people's minds, confines and subjugates them, the more urgent is the need to liberate them by a general and higher interest in what is, from a purely human point of view, raised above all the influences of the day and to reunite the politically divided world under the flag of truth and beauty."

In a letter to Cotta in June, Schiller held out to him the prospect of fame: "As far as the publisher is concerned, I doubt whether a bookseller can undertake anything more creditable than a work of this sort that unites the leading minds of the nation, and if this were the only piece of writing that you published, this one work alone would make your name immortal among German booksellers." Here for the second time we come across Schiller's advertising jargon; after promoting Göschen to the rank of Germany's "most respectable bookseller" as a result of his publication of the edition of Wieland's works, now Cotta was to become "immortal among German booksellers" by his publication of the *Horen.* Schiller was, however, pursuing another goal with his literary politics; he wanted a "freer hand" so that he could in a foreseeable time give his own works to Cotta and also bring him new authors, first and foremost Goethe. This intention coincided with Cotta's own ambition: he, too, wanted to publish Goethe. By an option clause contained in the contract for the *Horen* (the publisher's prior claim to the author's next works) it was now possible for authors to change publishers and for new works to be transferred to Cotta. Schiller saw this as a back door both for himself and for Goethe. "As far as I am concerned," he wrote on 14 June 1794, "this is the only possible way for you to publish all my future writings, for as soon as I am writing for the journal all other ties will be broken." These words, "to publish all my future writings," were Cotta's signal.

Schiller and Cotta soon became friends. Cotta was not yet a very experienced publisher, but he was sensitive enough to suspect that one must talk, talk, talk with authors; and in numerous conversations with Schiller he had recognized the complexity of the latter's finances and the psychological situation that arose from it. From the very beginning, then, he saw the need to pay Schiller enough in royalties as adviser, editor, and author for him to go on writing without having to worry. "From this time on," writes Liselotte Lohrer in her history of the firm of Cotta, "the poet's material suffering was at an end. Cotta regarded it as a *nobile officium* to make it possible for his great friend to work in a carefree atmosphere."[2] The royalties received by the author were for Cotta an essential element in his conception of publishing. He loved both things, money and mind; he liked the book as a commodity in its double function, as something designed by the author as an intellectual product, changed by the publisher into a commodity under "the pressure of business" as Goethe put it, and changed back again into intellectual property in the hands of the reader. I do not believe that there can be reconciliation between money and mind, not even in the realm of publishing; on the contrary the whole business of publishing draws breath from this tension.

Be that as it may, Cotta paid fees for advising and royalties for written works that were unusual for the time. He knew the criticism that writers leveled at the low royalties paid to authors and countered it with his *nobile officium,* higher royalties. In retrospect he was able to say in 1826, "The higher royalty that is paid at once gives scholars more scope for the development of their powers; the public finds itself ready to believe in the possibility of the endurance of a new approach, one that the publishers themselves, through what they offer, believe to be justified. I believe that I am the one who first introduced higher honoraria for scholars. On the whole I have never found myself in a position to regret it. Literature can only improve if you respect it, if you really respect it, and the public's receptivity reciprocates it in direct proportion to the whole field that is opened up to scholars." Cotta could say this in 1826 with justification; he had not only paid an "honorarium" but fair recompense. Jean Paul's widow, Caroline Leopoldine Friederike Richter, wrote on 26 May 1826 to the Cotta bookstore, "If a history of German literature worthy of the subject should appear in the future, then booksellers—who have performed essential services to literature and thus to the progressive education of the German nation—should also be remembered as objects of fame. Among all of them the firm of Cotta, or rather its owner, Herr Freiherr von Cotta, must be singled out and praised, because it was he who was the first to pay authors a worthy royalty commensurate with their work and effort. . . . He it was who first hit upon the idea of making literary possession the common property of the German nation by making available cheaper editions of the collected works of famous writers." A verdict that would be music to any publisher's ears. Cotta could be assured that Goethe would agree. Goethe wrote to Schiller in April 1798, "what is good for the bookseller is, in every sense, good for the author; if you are well paid, you are widely read and those are two praiseworthy objects." Though we can certainly agree with Goethe about the first part, his conclusion, that if you are well paid you will be widely read, is very questionable.

Cotta, then, paid fair royalties but he did not regard himself as a patron. He was calculating and courageous enough to ask relatively high prices for his books. Of course this aroused envy. Cotta valued his authors' intellectual products, he valued the commodity, but he valued the business he did with them just as much. His other business activities were complex. He diversified his material risk, set up printing works and paper mills, took shares in a hotel in Baden-Baden, was involved in the modern pursuits of ballooning and steam navigation and was a landowner in the grand manner with extensive holdings and estates. None of this was kept concealed from his authors. They did not begrudge him these things simply because, on the score of royalties, they had nothing to complain about. They saw in Cotta the publisher who rewarded the "termination of authors' modesty," paid them fair royalties, and in this way created a basis for their work, assured it, and in all cases made it to some extent possible.

Schiller flourished in this new relationship. The fire of his productivity was rekindled, he was intensely active as Cotta's adviser, as the editor of the *Horen* and, at first covertly, as the author of "future writings" that Cotta was to publish. Because of Schiller's activity on behalf of the company, especially through the connections with authors that arose out of the *Horen,* the firm of Cotta was thrust more and more into the national, even the world, literary context. In the course of their conversations Cotta, like Schiller, even thought of moving the firm to Weimar. At this time Schiller was a sort of "refuge" for younger authors. Young and coming authors often orient themselves towards the particular style of a prominent colleague whom they regard as an example or whom they oppose in their writings with all their youthful, often aggressive, powers; there were, and are, authors who exercise such a positive or negative influence upon younger ones. Schiller was without doubt an author like this and he, quite differently from Goethe, also possessed the ability to recognize qualities in a manuscript that were opposed to his own way of writing; if he thought he recognized "poetic substance" in a manuscript, he did not hesitate to recommend it. On 9 March 1795 he wrote to

Cotta, "Hölderlin is writing a little novel, *Hyperion,* of which a part was included in the last issue but one of the *Thalia.* The first part—about twelve pages long—will be finished in a few months. I should be very glad if you would accept it for publication. It is quite brilliant and I also hope to have some influence on it. I set a great deal of store by Hölderlin as a contributor to the *Horen* in the future, for he is very hardworking and certainly not lacking in the talent to amount to something in the world of literature." The *Horen* had published the poems *The Wanderer* and *The Oak Trees,* and *Hyperion* then appeared in two small volumes in 1797 and 1799, published by Cotta; sales were poor and Cotta could not risk carrying out his original plan of publishing an edition of the poems.

It is true that Cotta had to wait longer for Schiller as an author than had been planned. This arose out of the slowness with which Schiller produced his works because of his illness, and also because of his existing, but ever more obscure and uncertain, ties to other publishing houses. *Wallenstein* was especially long in the writing. "You can look forward to Wallenstein," he wrote on 5 January 1798, "nothing in my whole life has ever been so successful and I hope, in this work, to have wedded the force and fire of youth with the peace and clarity of more mature age." *Wallenstein* finally appeared in 1800 and *Mary Stuart* a year later. On the other hand there were other things that Cotta probably had to bite the bullet on. The *Collected Poems* were published in 1799 by Crusius; Schiller gave Unger—incomprehensibly and without motivation—*The Maid of Orleans* as a *Pocketbook for the Year 1802.* In Schiller's case Cotta let such infidelities pass, but in the case of other authors, for example Jean Paul, he threatened to sever his connection with them. But after the Unger edition all the rest of Schiller's dramas were published by Cotta. They were collected in 1804, while Schiller was still alive to see the printed sheets, but he was dead by the time the complete twelve-volume edition of his works, edited by his friend Körner, was published between the years 1812 and 1815.

Schiller's relationship to Cotta may be regarded as an ideal author-publisher relationship, not only because Cotta was always standing by ready to be helpful in any situation, but because above and beyond this they both communicated with each other as equal partners. Both were thus able to discuss private matters with one another, tell tales about the family, in a more relaxed manner. Schiller produced a small epistolary work of art with his letter to Cotta telling him that he had finally received the patent of nobility that made him and his wife more or less acceptable at court, something which must therefore have been important to him, although he said that Cotta could "easily imagine, that as far as I personally am concerned, it is a matter of some indifference." Their common Swabian origin certainly played a part in their relationship, but what was essential was the satisfaction of material interests and the mutual recognition of each other's achievements. Schiller stated this early on in a letter dated 29 May 1798: "I hope and wish, my valued friend, that this letter will find you once more in the circle of your own people. I still remember with joy the day that you gave us here, and the new proof of your friendship and love for me and my family that you yourself gave me on your journey touched me to the heart. . . . I never doubt for a moment that our relationship came about through a common external interest, and in the course of our closer acquaintanceship took such a fine and noble turn that it will remain indestructible. We now know each other and each of us knows that our intentions to one another are heartfelt and honorable in a true Swabian manner and that our trust is based on mutual esteem: the greatest security that a human relationship needs." In contrast to Schiller's ties to Göschen, here were two partners of equal value who were secure in their relationship. It is characteristic that Schiller's letter went on, after an emotional statement of this sort, to say, "now to an urgent matter of business."

The Connecting Link: But author and publisher threw themselves most in-
The Horen tensively into the periodical *Die Horen.* Cotta proba-
bly suspected that this could not turn out to be a very profitable project. Schiller it is true knew why he wanted a periodical like this; it could become an instrument of his literary politics. He told his publisher, "This undertaking *suits* me, I am *recognized* in this field, I have *sufficient* material and even with my *low level of health* I can still be active in it, because I shall be doing it out of inclination and from an inner vocation." But it also "suited" Cotta and for a number of different reasons. There was the expectation of fame and honor from having in his firm a publication that would be the subject of discussion, that would function as a mirror of the consciousness of the period, and there was also the thought that he would acquire new and important authors to make the firm the home and the center of attraction for the great minds of his time.

Publishers in this century have regarded things no differently. The periodical *White Leaves* (*Weisse Blätter*) was designed in the firm of Rowohlt and Kurt Wolff and was critical of the *New Review* authors Thomas Mann and Gerhart Hauptmann.[3] After leaving the S. Fischer publishing house in 1950, Peter Suhrkamp repeatedly thought about having his own periodical published by his own newly established firm, taking as its model Cotta's *Morning Paper for the Educated Classes*. I too was ambitious enough to want a periodical; it was to be the enlightened focal point for the intellectual trends of the time and a forum for authors. I was sure that I had found the ideal editor and the first number appeared in 1965, produced with great intensity and with the collaboration of important authors. From number 15 on, contributors made "wreaths for literature" and proclaimed its death. I personally found this attitude, resulting from the student unrest of the time, irrational and laughable; understandably, the firm could not support it, and so the editor (Hans Magnus Enzensberger) and I parted company, precisely at a point that made it possible for him to operate outside the firm. Later on, none of the participants was interested in talking about the "death of literature" any more.

My experience with this periodical, *The Time Table,* is for me decisive for the question of whether a publishing house should publish a periodical. Either the periodical is from the very beginning supported purely by the interests of the firm and the contents determined by in-house editors, or it is independent of the firm and then runs the danger—if the editor cannot coordinate the firm's interests and independent editorial conditions—of no longer being a forum for authors and literature but of becoming a different concept that the firm's authors can no longer support.

Die Horen was Cotta's first undertaking of this sort. The very name given to it was ambitious: Horen. Horae are goddesses of Greek mythology responsible for agricultural fertility; Hesiod equated them with law and order, justice and peace, in a tradition that goes back to late antiquity, and still exerted an influence upon Schiller, who interpreted them as the incorporation of the four seasons.[4] The first issue of *Die Horen* appeared on 15 January 1795; by 1797 twelve (quarterly) volumes had been published, each with three parts, making a total of 1,400 pages and 77 contributions. It did not die as a result of ideological quarrels, or primarily because of a falling circulation, but because the authors lacked interest.

The start was, it is true, sensational; Schiller designed an "Invitation to collaborate" that was sent to the most important authors of the time, professional writers and academics. It is at the same time the prototypical reaction of German classicism to the events of the French Revolution.

Invitation To Collaborate
DIE HOREN

A periodical with this title will appear at the beginning of the year 1795, and a society of well-known scholars has been assembled for its production. It will deal with everything that can be treated tastefully and philosophically and will also be open to philosophical studies and historical and poetic statements. Everything that is either only of interest to the academic reader or that can only satisfy the non-learned reader will be excluded; but, in particular, it will unconditionally refuse anything relating to state religion and the political constitution. It will be dedicated to the *beau monde,* for education and culture, and to the *academic* world for a free investigation of truth and a fruitful exchange of ideas, and while its inner content will be concerned with the enrichment of learning itself, it is hoped that its form will at the same time enlarge the circle of readers.

It was established that all articles should be "historical, philosophical or aesthetic in content." What was not mentioned in the contract, but was expressly agreed between Cotta and Schiller, was that political discussions were not to be included in the periodical. Schiller wanted to turn his thoughts not to the present but to the future of mankind and to try, as he wrote in the announcement that appeared in several German periodicals, "to reunite under the flag of beauty and truth a world that is politically divided."

Payments for contributions were also determined in detail. They were to be variable, the lowest 3 louis d'or, the highest (then determined specially for Goethe) 8 louis d'or; the "median price" was to be 5 louis d'or.

An editorial committee with five members was nominated—under Schiller's supervision—to which Goethe, Fichte, Körner, Humboldt, and Karl Ludwig von Woltmann (historian, diplomat, professor of philosophy and history at Jena) were appointed. "The majority of the committee decides on the worthiness of the pieces submitted." This was a birth defect of the periodical. It is impossible for a committee to decide whether to accept or reject. The arrangement was a mistake insofar as all the work finally fell on Schiller and, however much Goethe cooperated at a later stage, Schiller's was the ultimate responsibility. When he resigned, the fate of the periodical was sealed.

There is still one particularly important point that must be mentioned. In the contract Schiller had—whether under Cotta's influence or not has not been determined—thought up a clause that can be regarded simply as referring to the naked recruitment of authors: "The publisher of *Die Horen* makes it a condition that he has the right of first refusal of the other writings of regular contributors to the extent that these are not subject to other contractual obligations before the appearance of *Die Horen*." This clause in the contract is unambiguous. What Schiller and Cotta had in mind is clear: it was the way for Schiller to leave Göschen definitively, and it had to be the bait with which to catch Goethe. No documents exist in the light of which Goethe could have had recourse to this clause, but we may assume that Schiller had told him about the background and that he would have explained to him the possibilities it afforded for changing publishers. It is not known whether authors acted in accordance with the clause; indirectly it had its effect, for a few *Horen* contributors became Cotta authors: not least among them Hölderlin and Jean Paul.

The first issue is impressive: contributions by Schiller, Goethe, Fichte, Herder, Schlegel, and many other eminent writers and thinkers. *Die Horen* was the standard intellectual forum of the time; it achieved a rank that could never again be achieved by a publisher's periodical. Literature, art, and philosophy were represented by their most important authors. Schiller sent his contribution for the first issue, *On the Aesthetic Education of Man in a Series of Letters,* to Cotta with the comment: "I have to state that these letters, which will cover the whole of the theory of art, are the best things that I have ever written and that I am capable of "; they were letters "with which I hope to achieve immortality." Goethe's reaction was revealing. He found the letters, he wrote to Schiller, "pleasant and beneficial" but saw in them only a confirmation and an acceptance of his own thinking: "I find what I have long recognized, what in part I have lived, and in part wish to live, expounded in such a coherent and noble manner. . . ." Fichte's contribution was entitled "On the Stimulation and Elevation of the Purest Interest in Truth"; Schiller rejected a second submission, "On Spirit and Letter in Philosophy," but he found Herder's contribution, "One's Own Fate," excellently suited to *Die Horen* because "though it has something mystical about it, it will be tied in with some universal truth by this article." The first numbers could not have been bettered. The format was generous, special fonts were chosen for the typesetting, the printing was adequate, papers and binding materials were also specially selected, and the dust jacket maintained classical typography. Royalties were very generous. The first edition consisted of 1,500 copies, but this was soon increased to 2,000 by a reprinting. Cotta was more than satisfied.

Goethe was quite ready to think for and contribute to the success of *Die Horen;* he put his advice at Schiller's disposal, helping out where he could. Their letters attest to this. After Schiller, he of all the authors made the most contributions; true they were not the "main works" that had been wished for—*Wilhelm Meister, Faust,* and *Herrmann and Dorothea*—but number by number they are significant contributions.

Goethe's *First Epistle* was published in the first number; it was written for Schiller in the form of a Horatian epistle. After this came the collection of novellas, *Entertainments of German Emigrés.* These prose stories were exciting; they made immediate reference to happenings of the time, something that did not really fit in with the consciously nonpolitical conception of *Die Horen.* Schiller intervened in the *Entertainments* that followed as a sequel in order to draw Goethe's attention to the lack of a point of balance. In the following "parts" a balance was achieved in the dispute. The high point of the *Entertainments* is without doubt the strangely puzzling text of Goethe's "Fairy Story," the enigmatic nature of which has occupied interpreters and authors down to the present. Peter Handke's "fairy story," "Absence," was inspired by it.

The fifth "part" in the fourth year was produced by Schiller in collaboration with Goethe, who contributed an essay on "Literary Sansculottisme." Goethe's *Roman Elegies* appeared in 1795, as part 5 of the first year. They had originally been intended for part 1 of *Die Horen;* when Schiller received the texts from Goethe in October 1794, he was surprised that Goethe did not want them to appear in the first "part." Goethe expected negative criticism; he knew the Weimar public and their moral conventions: "I would wish," he wrote to Schiller at that time, "that you not let them out of your hands, but that you read them to the people who have to judge as to their admissibility." We do not know whether Schiller did this; he reacted positively two days later: "We all thank you very much for the elegies. There is a warmth in them, a tenderness and a real poetic spirit that really makes one feel wonderfully good among the works our present poetic world gives birth to. It is a true vision of the good poetic genius." In fact the elegies were not received as being so "wonderfully good" after their appearance in *Die Horen.* Among Goethe's close circle of friends, Herder, Duke Carl August, and Frau von Stein took offense at the publication, while others reacted enthusiastically, expressing the opinion that the *Elegies* surpassed everything that Ovid, Propertius, and Catullus had written. Goethe translated the hymn ascribed to Homer—*To the Birth of Apollo*—in part 9 of volume 3 (1795), and his translation of *Benvenuto Cellini* was published in eleven installments starting with part 6, volume 6. Georg Christoph Lichtenberg, a fellow author commented: "You have given me and all the people I know a great gift in your Benvenuto Cellini."

Everything seemed to be optimal, but the misery that every periodical has to experience soon began. Works by authors who matter cannot be produced on command, and here they failed to materialize: this was a bitter experience for Schiller. Deadlines can have a stimulating, but very often paralyzing, effect. As early as 29 December 1794, Schiller complains, "We have very few good collaborators, in spite of all the display of magnificence that we are making to the public; and of the good ones we have, half of them cannot be counted on for this winter. . . . Göthe does not want his elegies put into the early parts, Herder wants to wait until a few parts have appeared, Fichte is snowed under with lectures, Garve is ill, Engel lazy, and I have not heard from the others. So I cry: 'Lord, help me or I shall sink!' All this was before the first number had appeared. Later on tensions arose among the authors; Schiller asked Goethe for a reprint of *Wilhelm Meister,* but Goethe would not give it to him because the novel had been promised to Unger and he was opposed to having it reprinted. Contributions promised by Kant and Jean Paul did not materialize. Schiller commissioned a contribution from Garve on "the relationship of the writer to the publisher," but Garve did not send it; Fichte was bitter because his second contribution was rejected; he ceased to be a collaborator and began to criticize the periodical's attitude.

Was the level too high? Many contributions were criticized for being too hard to read and for being too complex; booksellers returned copies, and Cotta reduced the circulation to 1,500, then to 1,000 copies.

In spite of all this, the periodical might perhaps have survived, but another circumstance raised the hackles of contemporaries who were already irritated by the authors' talk of "magnificence" and by the claim to monopoly. The initial criticisms, written perhaps by those authors who had not been invited to collaborate on *Die Horen,* sounded unfriendly. But there was then an extensive review in the *Allgemeine Literatur Zeitung* in Jena. This was striking, comparable in our own day to praise or damnation in the *New York Review of Books.* The author of the review was Christian Gottfried Schütz, professor of poetry and rhetoric in Jena and also the newspaper's publisher; the reviewer was enthusiastic and was of the opinion that *Die Horen* would soon put all other journals out of business. The whole thing blew up into a scandal when it was discovered—through an indiscretion—that Cotta had ordered the review and had paid the writer or, in the public view, bribed him. Everything appeared in all the gazettes and, with a certain amount of justification, the critics now jumped on the publisher, the newspaper, and above all the editor. Schiller's goal, "the aesthetic education of mankind," was unacceptable and was subjected to increasingly harsh criticism. The publisher Nicolai's verdict came when *Die Horen* had been in existence only six months. "It positively appears that these gentlemen believe that if they say the most trivial things in scholarly terms this constitutes philosophy. Whatever is said in these scholarly quiddities about beauty, about art, about male and female really shows that these gentlemen do not know what they want. People are complaining about this in almost every part of Germany. I am sorry that our German prose is once again being spoiled by really good minds. Did the ancients ever write thus? If you read an English book you enjoy it. I shall soon not read any more German."

Criticism of *Die Horen* became excessive; regular feuds between authors erupted in the newspapers. Wilhelm von Humboldt collected opinions in Berlin and sent them to Schiller; according to these the bookseller and pub-lisher Unger is supposed to have said that *Die Horen* should cease publication after the end of the year because everyone is dissatisfied with it. Schiller replied to Humboldt on 21 August: "I was very amused at your last letter with the news of *Die Horen;* in the meanwhile it cannot be denied that you and I have deserved to be disappointed in our expectations, because our expectations were not founded on a proper assessment of the public. I believe now that we were wrong to treat materials of this sort and in this form in *Die Horen* and, if the periodical lasts, I shall guard against this mistake. Opinions are too general and too much in agreement for us to dismiss them out of hand and ignore them." The crowd of critics grew and grew. Herder's essay, *Homer a Favorite of Time,* appeared in part 9; he was accused of plagiarism. Goethe kept a very careful ear open for these critical voices. In October he suggested to Schiller, "Shouldn't you now take a careful look around at everything and collect what has been said in particular and in general against *Die Horen* and make a short report about it at the end of the year?" Schiller knew what sort of real *ecclesia militans* had formed against *Die Horen*. In fact he had difficulty in countering these attacks. Contributions to *Die Horen* were anonymous, and for this reason many of the critics often misidentified the authors of contributions.

Schiller received a flood of letters of protest, letters from friends, letters from readers, anonymous letters. Finally he resigned. "If there are readers," he wrote to Cotta on 3 September 1795, "who would rather taste watery soup in other journals than a hearty meal in *Die Horen,* and find nothing more in the 56 numbers of ours that they have already read than in the journals that are coming out now, then this is really a bad thing, but I do not know what to do to help. It is difficult to write for such a public a journal that affords one any pleasure. . . . If in spite of all these efforts the voice of the public is against us, then the undertaking has to be abandoned. It is impossible for me to defend myself any longer against apathy and taste-lessness, for pleasure and confidence are the heart and soul of my activity." Schiller's letter to Cotta in October 1795 was a reaction to a large number of critical opinions: "It is utterly ridiculous to see philosophical neophytes and second-raters in Leipzig and Halle angry about my aesthetic letters, while Kant himself, the most competent judge of the thing speaks of them with admiration, even though I undertook to contradict him on a number of points."

The whole situation grew more somber. "The good is seldom pleasing." Schiller's statement is banal but it is on target and it is still true today. The answer he arrives at in the light of this judgment, "to let collaborators come on the scene who are pleasing to the public even if to me they are an embar-rassment," was not a solution. The decision to give up *Die Horen* had already been made in December 1795; the reason was not just the public, but the "irresistible tendency in my works to bow to no alien law and particularly to surrender myself primarily to poetic activity, and *secondly* the poor support on the part of those who collaborated on *Die Horen*." Early in 1796, Schiller tried once more to sum up the situation: "The demands of the scholars and the wishes of readers with good taste are too often at odds; the scholars demand depth and thoroughness and that easily produces aridity and obscurity, the latter demand simplicity and beauty and that can easily lead to superficiality. The great difficulty of steering a successful course between the two cliffs will to some extent serve as an excuse for the shortcomings of our work." And once again, he formulated his original intention: "to fight with all my strength against shallowness in reasoning and against the trivial, flabby taste in poetry and art that have etched themselves into our times and to cast out the ruling spirit of frivolity in favor of more manly principles. My undertaking may fail, but I can never regret having tried it."[5] This is clearly enough a swan song. Cotta advised him to carry on; he wanted to keep the periodical, even if the circulation should fall below 1,000.

On 24 August 1797, Goethe sent Schiller from Frankfurt a significant (at least in retrospect) suggestion: "I want to tell you of a work that I have started and that will be good for *Die Horen.* I have about two hundred satirical French etchings in front of me, I have just schematized them. . . . I am now beginning to describe them individually and it is going very well, since they generally have something thoughtful to say, are witty, symbolic, allegorical, they often offer themselves as well as, if not better, to the imagination as to the eye, and when you are able to survey a mass of this sort you can make some very useful comments about the French spirit and art in general and in the particular. As long as you do not aspire to, and have no wish to, *Lichtenbergize,* it can always be presented cheerfully and merrily enough, so that people will take pleasure in reading it. I shall certainly find some more and probably earlier ones in Switzerland. A very nice article can come out of this which will be a decent contribution for the October number."

It is remarkable that Schiller reacted in the same way as later students of Goethe did. He was hardly interested in the suggestion and yet he should have been, simply because of the painful editorial situation of *Die Horen.* However, Schiller was now busy with Goethe's criticism of his, Schiller's, ballad "The Cranes of Ibycus" and also with his account of Hölderlin's visit. Goethe had arrived in Frankfurt on 3 August and had seen his mother again for the first time after four years. The main excitement was the aftereffects of the occupation of Frankfurt by the French the previous year, from 14 July to 8 September. Both the public and Goethe were in a constant frenzy of getting and spending, and there was a "great inclination on the part of the reading public towards journals and novels," for the simple reason that these provided entertainment for the sake of entertainment. "Poetry," said Goethe, "is as unpleasant in the wide world as . . . a faithful mistress."

He wrote to his friend Böttiger:

> I have to send you a line from the lively city of Frankfurt. My stay here is at present very interesting. You can see the French Revolution and its effects much more closely and immediately here, because it has had such great and significant consequences for the city and because here you are involved in a multiplicity of relationships with that nation.
>
> At home we always see Paris as something distant, so that it looks like a blue mountain where the eye can discern little, but where imagination and passion can become that much more effective. Here you can distinguish the individual parts and the local colors.

"The French Revolution and its effects" is an astonishing turn of phrase for this moment in time. Goethe understands the revolution as change, he is concerned with understanding how conditions inside France have changed.

Whereabouts in Frankfurt Goethe saw the French etchings is not clear. He immediately made a selection and divided them up, using a special system he had devised; it was a division directed against foreigners, against natives, and among the latter especially against the enemies of art.

A few days before he wrote Böttiger, Goethe had visited the collection of paintings belonging to the Frankfurt banker Johann Friedrich Städel and, the day after, he described from memory eight paintings in Städel's possession. All this may have moved him to give that description of the French etchings.

One thing is certain: we have to take Goethe's critique of a number of French satirical etchings seriously with respect to his attitude to the French Revolution. He himself set great store by the satire project. The critique was written down by Goethe's secretary Geist from dictation; it appeared for the first time in 1896, in an unreliable text, in volume 47 of the Weimar edition of Goethe's works.

In January 1798 the decision to cease publishing *Die Horen* was finally taken. The subject of discussion was now *Die Xenien,* the "almanac of the muses," a joint effort by Goethe and Schiller of some 400 distichs in the style of the Latin satirist Martial which was now available in its third edition. But *Die Horen* remained silent and was allowed to "die in its sleep." Schiller was once more working intensively on *Wallenstein* and so he was able to write to Cotta, "I am very happy that *Die Horen* has ceased and I merely ask you to avoid all fuss and, when you dispatch the eleventh and twelfth parts, to notify the booksellers without making a public statement." Of course the *Xenien* almanac was now to be brought out again. "To console the public for the cessation of *Die Horen,* I would be particularly glad if in the next four weeks a second edition of the almanac of the muses could be announced on the news page of the literary newspaper."

Goethe was told by Schiller on 26 January 1798: "I have just formally signed the death warrant of the three goddesses Eunomia, Dike, and Irene. Please shed a friendly Christian tear for these noble corpses, condolences however are forbidden." Goethe replied the next day, "For my part your allowing our three friends to die was never entirely unexpected," and he continued, "What do you say to the idea that monthly journals should only be published for a year? . . . Great diversity would have to be the rule, interesting—and not too lengthy—articles, so that in the one year everything could be finished and at the end it could be sold as a complete work." But neither Schiller nor Cotta were to react to this idea. Now it was a question of getting good material for the final parts, something, it is true, they did not succeed in doing. Goethe could not be persuaded to offer anything new and attractive beyond the rather tiresome continuation of his *Cellini.* The final number of *Die Horen* appeared in Jena on 12 June 1798.

Schiller's dramatic works and the famous productions of them followed hard upon the decision to cease publication of *Die Horen.* These included the *Wallenstein* trilogy, *Mary Stuart, The Maid of Orleans, William Tell,* and *The Bride of Messina.* Goethe was able to publish *Herrmann and Dorothea* on 29 November 1797.

Goethe produced no great new literary work until the appearance of *The Elective Affinities* in 1809 (aside from *The Natural Daughter*), but he translated Benvenuto's biography, wrote some tragedies, poems, and elegies and had to attend to his "public offices," directorship of the theater, supervision of academic arrangements in Jena and Weimar, the remodeling of the theater buildings in Weimar and Lauchstädt. He became president of the Jena Mineralogical Society and he delved into the history of the theory of color. Finally in August 1796, he says, "Sent off eighth book of *Wilhelm Meister.*"

The last part of that novel appeared in October 1796 as the sixth volume of *New Writings,* Unger's edition of his works. The seventh volume of the

New Writings was delayed until 1802. Schiller recommended that he gather the poems, which had been published in a number of different places, into the seventh volume, that is, the *Ballads* and *Romances* as well as the *Elegies* and the *Venetian Epigrams*. However, even before Unger died in 1804, Goethe's relationship with Cotta had begun.

Goethe's and	Schiller wrote a letter to Goethe on 13 June 1794. It
Schiller's Relationship	is his first letter to him, the initial contact between
with Cotta	the two. The letters on both sides, intended from the

beginning for the public, were later to form an unusual book containing more than a thousand pages. It is also the documentation of the beginning of the epoch in which Goethe established a new relationship to a publisher. At the beginning of June he had received the author's copies of the second volume of his *New Writings*. The new work in these is *Reynard the Fox;* Goethe had worked on this during the campaign in France. It is a treatment of the old animal poem in which the fox with a cheeky élan and cunning slyness avoids every danger and is finally promoted to the rank of "Imperial Chancellor." Goethe omitted any topical references, but in spite of this the epic was a statement about the events of the day.

There were changes in his private life. On 8 June 1793 Goethe received from Frankfurt the books that he wanted from his father's library. In August on a visit to Frankfurt he discussed the sale of the house in the Hirschgraben, and his mother Aja moved.

The campaign in France lay behind him. Goethe had taken part in this campaign at Duke Carl August's request, but this was the end of his participation in the great political events of his time. He once more drew up a balance sheet of his political thinking—"I prefer to commit an injustice than suffer disorder." In my opinion the statement is an exact reflection of the way Goethe was thinking at the time. He wanted to create order at least in his personal sphere, in the world that he had designed, in the same way as he was to realize it poetically in *Herrmann and Dorothea*. Now, at the end of 1793, and in the following year he tried to achieve such an order and, at the time, he no longer allied himself with any one publisher.

At the end of December 1792 he had refused the post offered him in Frankfurt and so set the seal on Weimar as his permanent residence. The duke rewarded him on 17 June 1794; the valuable property on the Frauenplan that had been completely at Goethe's disposal since June 1792 and in which he lived securely, domestically, and tenderly with Christiane was now presented to him by the duke. He added 1,500 thalers to the deed for "the furnishing of the house in proper style"; the duke's treasury also paid the ground rent. Princely thanks.

Thus Schiller's letter encountered a changed Goethe. He had left world politics behind, refusing any further active participation; and Weimar was the place where he would live and write.

What were his thoughts when Schiller's letter arrived? Meetings between the two had previously been ill-starred, though Goethe had not recognized this. On their return from Switzerland in December 1779 the duke, accompanied by Goethe, had visited the "Hohe Karlsschule" in Stuttgart in which Schiller was a pupil. While Goethe's diary records in detail the other stops that they made, there is no mention of this one. Schiller saw in one and the same person the famous author of *Götz* and *Werther* and the privileged civil servant who had just recently been appointed privy councillor. One was a person who had in all respects arrived, the other was suffering under the duress of the duke of Würtemmberg, with *The Robbers* in his head and ready to rebel and to flee. When almost eight years later, in July 1787, Schiller arrived in Weimar, already the celebrated author of *The Robbers,* of *Fiesco,* and *Don Carlos,* he had every right to expect a friendly reception at the "Court of the Muses." But things turned out differently. Goethe, whom he primarily wished to meet, was in Italy at the time. Herder received Schiller kindly but made his indifference clear when he told Schiller that he had read nothing of his. Wieland most probably knew Schiller's dramas but they were not to his taste—too rough, too direct, not finely shaped, not delicate enough. Carl Ludwig von Knebel, Goethe's friend and the caretaker of his house on the Frauenplan, invited Schiller, while Goethe was still away, to visit him in the garden of Goethe's house. But Schiller was disappointed in Knebel. "A certain childlike simplicity of good sense characterizes Goethe and his whole sect here. People would rather look for herbs or do mineralogy," he wrote to Körner about his visit. Weimar society, in general, was not greatly to Schiller's taste.

He could with justice feel that he was superior. "I am really too much a man of the world among them, they are quite inexperienced." He took part in the celebration of Goethe's birthday, however, in Goethe's house while the latter was absent. "We stuffed ourselves heartily and I drank

Goethe's health in Rhine wine. He could hardly have imagined in Italy that I was among his house guests, but fate arranges things wonderfully." Goethe was back in Weimar on 18 June 1788; the "world" knew it and Schiller hoped that they would meet. Schiller reviewed *Egmont* on 20 September in the *Allgemeine Literatur Zeitung* and awaited a reaction from Goethe, but there was none. He lost all his composure when he confessed to his friend Körner on 2 February and 9 March 1789 that "to be around Goethe very much would make me unhappy. . . . In fact I believe he is an egoist of quite unusual rank. . . . I hate him because of this, even though I love his mind from the bottom of my heart and think a great deal of him." And, "This person, this Goethe is in my way, he reminds me so often that fate has treated me harshly. How easily *his* genius was borne by his fate, and how have *I* had to struggle to this very moment." Goethe himself kept his distance from such statements. He did not allow himself to be moved to make statements like Schiller's, even if he did not appreciate Schiller's dramas that were proclaimed by the youth of Germany and could not and might not agree with the theses of the philosophical essays. His praise caused the duke to offer Schiller a professorship in Jena, and Goethe was happy that Schiller moved to Jena. Schiller could not refuse the professorship though it was unpaid; to do so would have signified a breach. Schiller the diplomat, Schiller the literary politician, knew that when he wanted to set something in motion on the literary scene with *Die Horen* and with Cotta he could not do it without Goethe. "I look upon him as a proud prude on whom one has to sire a child." It cannot be said more clearly. And he did sire a child for the proud prude with his letter of 13 June 1794; the letter is a model of wooing, a model of his "moving eloquence":

> High-born Sir
> Honored Privy Councillor
> The enclosed letter contains the wish of a group that has boundless admiration for you, their wish is that you will honor the periodical of which we are talking with your contributions, the quality and value of which are unanimously respected among us. The decision on the part of your high-born self to support this undertaking by your participation will be decisive for the success of the same, and we subject ourselves with great readiness to all the conditions which you may want to impose if you should agree.

Here, in Jena, Messieurs Fichte, Woltmann, and von Humboldt have agreed to join me in the publication of the periodical, and since, in accordance with a necessary arrangement, judgments on all manuscripts that are received have to be culled from a small committee, then, high-born Sir, you would place us infinitely in your debt if you would allow us from time to time to send you for your criticism one of the manuscripts that are received. The greater and closer the cooperation you bestow upon our undertaking, the more the value of it will rise in the estimation of that public whose applause is the most important for us. I remain sincerely,

High-born Sir

Your most obedient servant and

most sincere Admirer

Jena, 13 June 1794   F. Schiller

The letter broke the spell. Its humble, even obsequious, unconditional and admiring attitude did not fail in its effect on Goethe. He replied, it is true, rather distantly, but soon started to talk about the productive things that were later to distinguish the correspondence.

High-Born Sir

   You open up to me a doubly pleasing perspective both as to the periodical that you propose to publish and the participation to which you invite me. I will join the society gladly and wholeheartedly.

   If there are some things of mine that have not yet been published that would be suitable for such a collection then I will gladly tell you: but certainly a closer relationship with such excellent men as the people undertaking this will set in motion again much that has come to a halt in my work.

   It would be interesting to discuss how to reach agreement on the principles for judging manuscripts that are submitted, how to keep an eye on form and content so as to distinguish this periodical from others and to maintain its advantages at least for a number of years.

   I hope that we can soon discuss this face to face, and I send my best wishes to you and your collaborators.

   W. 24 June 1794   Goethe

This is the beginning of a unique relationship between two great minds. Not a "male" friendship, not an intimate brotherly relationship, they bore themselves like diplomats, sometimes friendlier, sometimes more hostile, great powers who made alliances for common actions but who maintained their different points of view. Looking back, however, it was the common ground that was stressed. "For me it was a new spring in which everything was germinating in its appointed order and was sprouting from seeds and branches that had opened up," Goethe recalled later; his memorial essay for Schiller is entitled "Happy Event." The event resulted from a meeting on 20 July 1794; after a session of the Society for the Study of Nature in Jena they apparently got into conversation on the "Metamorphosis of Plants." Goethe says that he created, "with many characteristic strokes of the pen, a flower before his [Schiller's] own eyes. He listened and observed all this with great sympathy, with distinct powers of comprehension; but when I had finished, he shook his head and said, 'that is not an experience, that is an idea.' I stopped short, somewhat irked, because this marked most strongly the point that separated us." This is characteristic of the relationship between the two. There were always attempts at, and statements of, agreement, but that agreement scarcely came about, for, in spite of everything else, it is what separated and differentiated them that is stressed. The 1,000 letters written in the ten years that the correspondence lasted are, in the truest sense of the word, conversations; they do not reveal any poetic secrets, they clarify positions the differences in which are fascinating given the disparity in character of the two. Schiller's constant recollections motivate Goethe, fire him; he confesses more about himself than he had ever done. "They wanted me to talk about myself, and so I made use of this permission." And he asks, "I would like to know how you went to work in such cases." Schiller makes demands of the text that go beyond the subjective aspect. And in the course of this the different views of the two come to light. We have seen this in their cooperation during the writing of *Wilhelm Meister,* when Goethe replies to one of Schiller's objections: "The difference in our natures, means that it (the work) can never completely satisfy your demands."

At the beginning they were in each other's "way," they never used the familiar form of address, neither had any understanding for the life the other led. But they would often find themselves as a part of each other, often as the opposite pole. The correspondence is described as the high point of German classicism, as the meeting of life and consciousness, of maternal arrogance and patriarchal reason. It is considered "European property" and "the most lively document from their masons' lodge." Georg Lukács accords it, in 1947, the rank of "an historical document of the greatest importance for the artistic attitude of a great turning point in time" and of a "topically significant art historical heritage" that will continue to exert an influence. An example of such continued influence can be given from the same year, 1947. Bertolt Brecht was staying in Switzerland after his exile in America. He states in his working diary that he was reading Lukács' essay on the Goethe-Schiller correspondence and, inspired by it, read the letters themselves on 2 January 1948. Schiller interested him especially; he was amused by "Schiller's pleasure in tragic subjects," his emphasis on ideas, on the concept, and on theory, and he says that Schiller saw, with extraordinary clarity, the dialectic in the relationship of epic and drama while his, Brecht's, suggestions were often "misunderstood" because they were "critically oppositional" in nature. It is not surprising that Brecht sees himself in the tradition that emanates from Schiller, whereas Thomas Mann, and above all Hesse, lay stress on Goethe's experience of the subjective. Dürrenmatt too is closer to Schiller, just as Max Frisch is closer to Goethe when he says that it is not the time for first-person stories, yet human nature does not perfect itself "anywhere but in the individual ego."

A high point of the correspondence comes right at the beginning. In his letter of 23 August—was it a birthday greeting?—Schiller wrote a splendid description of their ways of thought, analyzed how Goethe "subsumes the whole of nature in order to throw light on the individual object, you seek the explanation of the individual in the totality of its phenomenal forms." Here too Goethe reacted favorably; he saw Schiller "drawing up a balance sheet of my existence" and of encouraging him "by your interest to make a livelier and more diligent use of my powers." It is this letter that inspired Goethe to start a collaboration "with pleasure." "For as I feel, in lively fashion, that my undertaking exceeds the measure of human powers and their earthly life, I would like to deposit several things with you and thus not only receive but also enliven." Goethe used his communication with Schiller for this "deposit," for this storage in the sense of putting things aside and using them later for higher purposes.

Schiller never ceased, in Cotta's name, to urge famous writers and above all Goethe to collaborate on Cotta's publications. "Cotta may be right," Goethe wrote to Schiller on 6 December 1794, "in demanding *names* he knows, he is aware that his public looks more at the stamp than at the contents." Goethe did not want to be used as such a "stamp." He kept his distance, he waited for the right opportunity; he did not want to rush, especially in the matter of royalties, for only then, he wrote to Schiller, who was putting pressure on him, "can one make one's calculations and one's conditions, for to measure our crops by any bushel that Cotta chooses would not serve us in the long run." The first contacts between Goethe and Cotta were thus few and far between. One meeting took place on 24 April 1795 in Jena, when Cotta stayed with Schiller on his way back from the book fair. Cotta wrote to a friend, "We spent a very pleasant day together in Goethe's company." No letters have been preserved from this time.

The decisive meeting took place in September 1797. Schiller had told Cotta of Goethe's journey and stopover in Stuttgart and had carefully prepared him in his letter of 21 July. "Goethe is going to Switzerland in a few days and will doubtless call in to talk to you [in Tübingen]. Receive him kindly and see to it that you introduce him to a few interesting people. Let the businessman Rapp also know that I have tentatively recommended his house to him; I think Rapp will be delighted to make his acquaintance." Goethe led a very social life in Stuttgart, and in the evenings he read aloud to Rapp from *Herrmann and Dorothea*. When Rapp wanted to send his five-year-old daughter away, so that she should not disturb the reading, Goethe appealed on the girl's behalf and she was then allowed to stay and listen to the reading sitting at her mother's feet. Goethe was very pleased when at the end of the reading the child asked that "the gentleman go on reading." On 7 September he arrived at Cotta's in Tübingen. He wrote to Schiller, "I have a pleasant room at Herr Cotta's and a pleasant, though narrow view of the Neckar valley between the old church and the academic building." Cotta treated him in more than friendly fashion. He arranged meetings with professors at the university, accompanied him on walks, showing him university institutes, and visited the Zoological Library with him. Goethe reported to Christiane, "I am being looked after well here at Herr Cotta's. The town itself is hideous, except that you only have to walk a few steps and you are in a beautiful spot."

Little as Goethe liked Tübingen, his relationship with Cotta grew ever better. He wrote to Schiller on 12 September: "The better I get to know Herr Cotta, the better I like him. For someone whose way of thinking is ambitious and who is an entrepreneur, there is so much that is moderate, soft, and calm about him, so much clarity and persistence, that I find him a real figure." The final days till 15 September were filled with walks, visits, and sightseeing. On the morning of 16 September Goethe left Tübingen with his secretary Geist and his coachman Kolb, by way of the Danube valley, to go towards Switzerland where, in Schaffhausen, he described in detail the Rhine Falls under the title "Excited Ideas" (when, as he was visiting the falls, a rainbow appeared above the force of the rushing waters he noted, "Safety cheek by jowl with terrible force"). He then went on to Zurich, whence, on 19 September he wrote to Cotta telling him of his safe arrival: "In memory of your kind reception and of such a diversity of pleasant and useful entertainment, not less than of the enjoyment of the care you exercised which extended to my whole journey." And a few days later Cotta received a letter from Schiller: "Goethe cannot say enough good things about his visit to you. He was very happy in your house, and talks to me about you yourself with real interest." Then he quoted from Goethe's letter and closed his own, "It is no small pleasure to me that you have entered into a closer relationship with G on this occasion. It can lead to something very important if you make use of it."

Cotta was quite ready to "use" this opportunity. In the letter he wrote to Schiller in reply he mentioned his "indescribable pleasure," for he would never have dreamed that "he was in Goethe's good books to that degree. This has to occasion double the pleasure in the case of so rare a man as he is. . . . I shall never forget the hours that I spent with him and will only regret that I cannot spend my life with you and with him, one becomes a totally different person in such company and you never feel the worthiness or unworthiness of a person more than when you see from such examples what a man can become and, from one's own examples, what one is not." Cotta also confessed to Schiller that he felt far too shy in this first meeting with Goethe to mention anything "in this respect"; he did not wish his concern to take on "the appearance of self-interest." But then Cotta expressed a wish that was, on the one hand, new and unusual for him, but which on the other was the position that Goethe had always wished to take towards his publishers: Cotta asked Schiller to play the role of intermediary with Goethe:

> I only once voiced the wish to enter into a literary relationship with him
> as well, and he did not seem totally opposed to the idea. If you would
> like to add to the many proofs of your goodwill towards me by acting
> as a middleman in this, you would put me under a real obligation to

you. I cherish, it is true, the proud wish that a relationship of this sort, once begun, would never be severed, I would therefore always do my utmost to preserve it and never let any of those who entered into such a relationship with me regret it.

If, therefore, you would use your influence with G., I would gladly accept any conditions, and I would as far as possible give proof of there being another interest beside the purely commercial one.

It was in this way that the basis of Goethe's relationship to Cotta was established. Because of the commitments Goethe had already entered into, Cotta did, it is true, have to wait a long time for the fulfillment of his ambitious wish to be Goethe's only publisher—it was not until 1802 that the first works by Goethe appeared with the Cotta imprint, but the path had been cleared. Schiller willingly functioned as a middleman in order to enhance the reputation of the firm of Cotta and to make it into the most important publishing house in Germany, but also probably with the view—as we can see from the correspondence—of enticing Goethe away from his scientific works into the field of poetry. Schiller repeatedly urged Goethe to "continue his poetic activity." Time and again he invoked "the development of your being"; he always saw a "necessary natural process." "You must have had a certain, not very short, epoch of what I would like to call your analytic period, in which by dividing and separating you sought to achieve a whole, when your nature had simultaneously been at odds with itself and had sought to restore itself through art and science. Now, it seems to me, you are returning to your youth fully developed and mature and you will combine the fruit with the blossom. This second youth is the youth of the gods and it is, like them, immortal." However, Schiller also assumed, with a certain satisfaction, the role of mediator who, as Goethe's agent, discussed royalties and sought to raise them. Schiller did not do this, in the final analysis, to relativize his own royalties, he acted entirely as Goethe thought fit. Goethe based his calculations on other offers but, for reasons of noblesse, he made these known not by himself but by his friend. Years after Schiller's death he regretted having lost this mediator and said how much he missed him.

It is clear in Schiller's and Goethe's relationship to Cotta that it was not Goethe who decided that Schiller should be the mediator, but Cotta. Schiller felt bound to make responsible suggestions, he advised for and against, he cautioned and he recommended the publisher to take action, even if no deal was to be expected. There was no one in Goethe's immediate circle who could estimate the success of his works on the market and their effect on the public as well as Schiller could. For me, an outstanding example is Schiller's magnificent letter to Cotta dated 18 May 1802. He says that "he had spoken with Goethe on your behalf . . . about the works to be published." He first passes on Goethe's idea of publishing an almanac of songs to appear at the same time as Cotta's *Pocket Book for the Year 1804,* "22 Songs for a social gathering," but Goethe did not only want to realize this beautiful and exceptionally successful project, he had others in mind. One was "The History of Art in the Last Century"; further, *Winckelmann and His Century* (1805) and the *Life of Benvenuto Cellini.* Schiller told Cotta frankly that he did not think that there would be any profit to be made on these works and yet—and now comes the statement that not only represents a summation of his assessment of Goethe but that also illuminates the relationship of an author to his publisher—"perhaps you could ignore all these risks in the hope that you would recoup all your losses with Goethe's *Faust.* But aside from the fact that it is doubtful whether he will ever finish this poem, you can rely on him not to sell it to you more cheaply than to another publisher, in spite of earlier circumstances and the sums that you have sacrificed, and he will make heavy demands. It is, not to mince words, impossible to find a bargain in G. because he knows his own value and has a high estimation of himself, and pays no attention to the fortunes of the book trade, of which in any case he only has a vague idea. No bookseller has maintained a relationship with him; he has up till now never been satisfied with a single one of them and many of them were probably not satisfied with him. Liberality towards his publisher is not his way."

This is absolutely true. Time and again Schiller encouraged Cotta to take over Goethe's smaller works as well and to make him "attractive offers": "A man like Goethe, who comes only once in the course of centuries, is too valuable an acquisition not to be bought no matter what the price." Cotta reacted, but these undertakings did not meet with success nor did they have an effect on contemporaries. It is remarkable that there were failures, at the beginning of Goethe's relationship with Cotta, but they did not place a burden on the relationship. Goethe distinguished himself from other authors by not blaming the publisher for these failures. The publisher for his part could feel that even when the books failed they did him honor and he could offset the deficit with the profits from his *Musenalmanach*s. Thus the beginning of Schiller's and Goethe's relationship with Cotta was, taken all in all, a "happy event."

"Brought about by the Mediation of Councillor Schiller" Schiller did it; Goethe came to Cotta. Let us set the date as 27 May 1798. Goethe was in Jena from 20 May. He left Weimar in a very happy frame of mind because the criticism of *Hermann and Dorothea* he had received was positive and so "I enter on the last stage of my poetic career in harmony with the critics." He spends a lot of time with Schiller, they take walks, talk about Humboldt's analysis of *Hermann and Dorothea,* and again discuss principles of the whole epic genre. The conversation is fruitful, "because it brought up the most important questions about things poetic." On 27 May he sends a detailed letter with materials for the *Propyläen* (Schiller's original suggestion was that they should be entitled "The Artist"). The conception of the *Propyläen* is characteristic of Goethe's publishing aims. It was not to be a so-called reader, but he did want a work that was readable and "welcome" to an educated public, that would endure and whose "extensive scope" would be beyond doubt; "the work will not be advertised until it appears." A short while later, another directive for Cotta as a rejection of "the trumpet tone" of *Die Horen:* "I wish only that you will not add another word of praise or recommendation."

Despite such muted advertisement, and in spite of proceeding carefully with its presentation, the undertaking was soon abandoned. The *Propyläen* was a business loss; of the 1,300 copies that were distributed only 450 were taken up. Cotta did not have the courage to tell Goethe this. He wrote to Schiller and he informed Goethe that the periodical could not be salvaged. "I dare not think about this matter," he wrote on 5 July 1799, "if it is not to make my blood boil, for I have never till now had such a vile opinion of the German public." Schiller it is true did not want to give up the periodical yet and wanted to try and see, having regard to the capital that Cotta had invested, "whether we cannot still flirt with the periodical," and so he suggested to Goethe, "if you were to put something out of *Faust* into it, there might be a lot of good consequences." But Goethe suspected that this was only the "case of a lost arrow that one shoots another one after." The *Propyläen* could not be saved.

The intensive relationship between Cotta and Goethe endured until

Goethe's death. Simply in terms of the time it lasted it is a unique relationship between an author and a publisher. It is not without emotion that we read the close of the penultimate letter from Goethe to Cotta on 16 June 1831: "But let it not end without courage! but rather with the assurance that I try to use every good moment to be true to the end to those who are a part of me." There can be no greater substance in a relationship, no attitude can be clearer, and this is true not only of the relationship of an author to his publisher but generally of a relationship between two human beings. Ever since 27 May 1798, Cotta had reached the goal of his desires; even if the first and second mutual projects proved to be failures, he could be sure that he would become the publisher of future writings by Goethe, the author who, unbeknownst to Cotta, would go down in history as the greatest German writer of all time; the obstinate pursuit by Cotta of his goal is a sign of his genius as a publisher.

But he did have to be patient. Goethe put him to a harsh test: first of all the two loss-making undertakings of *Die Horen* and *Die Propyläen,* then only minor works: *Mahomet* and *Tancred; After Voltaire* in 1802 and in the same year *What We Are Performing. Prologue on the Occasion of the Opening of the New Theater in Läuchstadt;* then *Benvenuto Cellini* (1803) and the collection of letters and essays, *Winckelmann and His Century* (1805).

There was a new work in 1803. The *Pocket Book for the Year 1804* contained *The Natural Daughter,* Goethe's last play (if we do not take the 1808 *Faust* into consideration), the culmination of a series of dramas that included *The Bourgeois General, The Excited Ones,* and *The Great Cophta. The Natural Daughter* again reflects the confusion of revolution; it was a play that had already been sketched out during the campaign in France eleven years earlier and planned as a trilogy. The play received its first performance on 2 April 1803; it was not a success either in the theater or in the reviews. Schiller (who had drawn Goethe's attention to the source of the play, *Mémoires historiques de Stéfanie-Louise de Bourbon-Conti, écrit par elle-même*) was one of the few—like Schelling and Fichte—who had a word of praise for it. Herder expressed himself judiciously in conversation but closed with the well-known *mot:* "I like your *Natural Daughter* far better than your natural son!" is what he is supposed to have written or said to Goethe who—and such was his capacity to be wounded—immediately severed all relationships with him. Critical opinion has changed in our own century. The critic Rudolf Alexander Schröder characterizes *The Natural Daughter* as the most "magnificent attempt to control the times that Goethe had ever undertaken." More recently Dolf Sternberger praised the play as a "Parable of Persecution."

Thus it was only much later that Cotta could harvest the fruits of his relationship with Goethe. These are the main mileposts: (A) the first edition of the works (1806–10), originally planned to contain twelve volumes but then numbering thirteen; (B) the twenty-volume edition of 1815–19; (C) the main undertaking, the forty-volume complete edition, supervised by the author, of 1827–30. Cotta could also bring out, in individual editions, the following works as "significant novelties": *Literature and Truth* (including the *Italian Journey*) (1811–17), *The West-East Divan* (1819), *Wilhelm Meister's Journeyman Years,* first version (1821). *Faust,* Part I, originally appeared as the eighth volume of edition A, from which—as was the case with other works—a separate individual edition was produced using the same type as the complete edition.

The relationship between Goethe, Schiller, and Cotta is documented in numerous letters; visits were relatively few, contact through a third party occasional. The correspondence between Schiller and Cotta was published for the first and only time in May 1876, edited by Wilhelm Vollmer; it was a reliable edition already prepared from original manuscripts and furnished with model notes, tables, and index—an exemplary work for the general history of the book trade.

After this edition, the idea of publishing the correspondence between Goethe and Cotta offered itself as a matter of course. But difficulty after difficulty arose, even in the separate publication of Goethe's letters to Cotta. Cotta's letters seemed to literary scholars to be more or less business correspondence, and they did not like to see Goethe in the lowlands of business. Dorothea Kuhn has painstakingly researched the history of the correspondence between Goethe and Cotta.[6] The scholarly contempt for Cotta's letters was mistaken, and to call the letters writen by both of them merely business correspondence was simply wrong. The letters preserve what is immediate in a fascinating human relationship with its high and low points; they witness to the experience of two men, their attitudes to life and work, and above all to their efforts to create something in common—the "work": to write the work, to publish the work. Goethe saw his partner as "pressured by business"—that was Cotta's position, not Goethe's. But Goethe also recognized that, by the process of book production, his intellectual property was changed into a commodity that had to survive in the marketplace; that it was, in other words, subject to commercial practices, principles, or even pressures. When he thought these factors were sensible, he accepted them; but if it seemed the right thing for his work, he resisted or changed them. Here, too Goethe set his customary standards for business dealings.

Goethe and Cotta did not give each other anything for nothing, and in reading these letters one has the impression that they both knew what they were getting into, as if each of them had a specific task, a specific role, and as though they were "playing" their roles. In any case, two statements from the beginning of the relationship are revealing. Goethe said soothingly to Cotta on 30 October 1805, "One comfort remains: those who learn early on to survey life's happenings in large terms find a certain balance in themselves even in the midst of the greatest evils." Cotta replied on 12 November 1805 in "utmost reverence": "The spirit always conquers what is otherwise merely dead force. Let us hope for the best and be ready for the worst! This is in fact not a mere slogan of mine at the moment but a norm for all my dealings."

Numerous works have investigated the great theme of this author-publisher relationship.[7] All of these works, however, treat their theme without the advantage that I had. As the basis for my considerations I was able to use Kuhn's edition of the correspondence between Goethe and Cotta.[8] Isaac Newton characterized the history of scientific progress in a few words: "If I was able to see farther it was because I was standing on the shoulders of giants."[9] I only hope that I can "see farther" with the aid of the materials produced by Kuhn. And I thank her in the way Bertolt Brecht once thanked Alfred Döblin. "I believe that I cannot play a more important role on your behalf than by exploiting you."[10] Thus I place myself on the shoulders of Kuhn's work and use her edition in which one's own discoveries are certainly still to be made.

A page from Goethe's handwritten statement of account
with Cotta (Schiller National Museum).

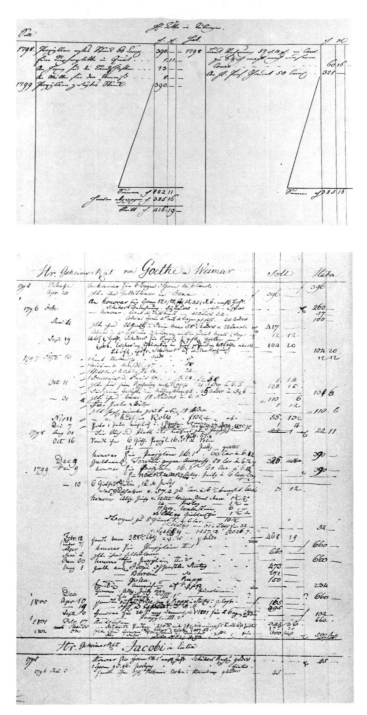

Extracts from Cotta's ledger with Goethe's debit and credit
(Schiller National Museum).

Goethe's letter to Cotta, 3 February 1826, after the completion of
the contract for the "final edition" (Schiller National Museum).

Austrian privilege (1825) for the "final edition" of Goethe's *Works*
(Stiftung Weimarer Klassik, Weimar).

Johann Peter Eckermann
(1792–1854). Crayon drawing by
J. J. Schmeller (ca. 1825) (Stiftung
Weimarer Klassik).

First edition of the *Journeyman Years*
(Stuttgart and Tübingen: Cotta, 1821) with a
portrait of Goethe (pencil drawing by Fräulein von
Foelkersahm), from the estate of Ulrike von
Letzekow (FreiesDeutschesHochstift/Goethe
Museum, Frankfurt am Main).

Faust, Part 2 (1831).
The fair copy that was sealed in August 1831
and reopened on 8 January 1832 for private
readings (Goethe und Schiller Archiv in
the Stiftung Weimarer Klassik).

FIVE

The First Complete Edition

Goethe and Cotta Schiller had moved to Weimar at the end of 1799
and he bought a house there in 1802. Cotta could rely
on him for advice and Schiller was always ready to collect intelligence from
Goethe and to "sound him out." "If I can get a poetic spark out of Goethe,
then I shall not fail," he wrote to Cotta on 8 June 1804, "but unfortunately
at the moment I see little sign of it, as he has other things on his mind."
The other things were scientific in nature. In June Goethe spent three days
unpacking a collection of minerals from Leipzig. In September he was appointed president of the Natural History Society. Goethe's reaction was typical; he expressed his thanks for the honor but, "Since this will cause an
increase in my obligations, I would like to be informed, before saying whether
I find myself in a position to take over this honorable duty, about the constitution and the present situation of the society as well as its future intentions."
In October he became president of the Mineralogical Society in Jena. He
then became active in the Weimar theater; he rehearsed Schiller's *William
Tell* and in November he produced Schiller's *Homage to the Arts,* in celebration of the marriage of the crown prince of Weimar, Carl Friedrich, to the
Grand Princess Maria Pavlovna. And there was something else occupying
his mind: on 13 September he had received his appointment as a real privy
councillor with the title of "Excellency." Cotta, by the way, had addressed
him from the beginning as "Gracious Herr Privy Councillor" and from 27
September 1800 onwards as "Excellency."

Schiller's letter of 16 October 1804 had to have brought Cotta to the
goal of his initial desires. The reason for jubilation was the news, so impatiently awaited, that Goethe was ready to let him publish a complete edition
of his works. Schiller told him:

Goethe is now thinking of the publication of his collected works in a pocket edition, without decoration or pomp. According to the information I have received from him his intention is to coordinate the work so that all the volumes will appear in the space of a year and a half, and in five years, calculated from the first consignment, the rights to a new edition will become his. The publisher would certainly have to get a move on to sell the work in this short space of time. I sounded him out and he seems to be asking not less that 4 Carolins a printed signature and he reckons the whole thing will be 380–400 signatures. A few unpublished things from his early youth are among them, and he is also thinking of including as much of *Faust* as he has completed, if he has not by then got to the point of completing it. Think about whether you want to accept his offer and, if you are interested, it would be a good idea to ask him, in general terms, for a work for publication, so that he will in this way be induced to offer you his complete works.

Was Schiller not entirely sure of himself when he recommended that Cotta not ask Goethe for his collected works but only "in general terms" for a "work to be published"? Schiller, the tactician, had to doubt whether Goethe was in a position to make good on what they had been discussing. Schiller met Goethe on 1 October, probably to discuss the production of *Homage to the Arts*. Schiller must have raised the idea of an edition of the collected works in their conversation, for Goethe sent Schiller the following day "an essay about the suggestion you made yesterday! Please be so kind as to think it through and give me the benefit of your good advice!" But under no circumstances did he want Cotta to be given the news at that time. It was for this reason that Schiller felt himself impelled to advise Cotta to be cautious.

The plan that Goethe wrote down at Schiller's suggestion is preserved. Goethe had dictated it to his secretary Geist, and Schiller had written a commentary.

Goethe's draft is very decided both as regards the layout of the edition and his royalties:

The undersigned intends to publish his writings: there should be no talk of a complete de luxe edition but rather of a neat and tasteful paperback edition, in German characters. The same would contain all my aesthetic works worthy of being preserved for a time, among which there will be some unpublished works.

The First Complete Edition

The following works are to be divided into sixteen, or if you prefer, twelve volumes:

The Mood of the Beloved
The Accomplices
Mahomet
Tancred

Berlichingen
Egmont
Stella
Clavigo

Iphigenia
Tasso
Eugenia

Claudine
Erwin and Elmira
Jery and Bädely
Lila
The Siblings

The Cophta
The Triumph of Sensibility
The Birds
What We Are Performing
The Bourgeois General

Faust

Werther
Wilhelm Meister

Hermann and Dorothea
Reynard the Fox

Shorter Poems

Shorter Prose Works

To the volume containing *The Cophta* Goethe added *Fun, Cunning and Revenge* and *Magic Flute*. To *Faust* Schiller added a marginal note: "Puppet Play." After *Reynard the Fox* Goethe placed *Achilles*. Then he added:

> It should be noted here:
> *The Mood of the Beloved,* comedy in one act and alexandrines, is the oldest one of my works that has survived.
> Faust will appear once more as a fragment, which it will more or less always remain.
> All the works will be gone through for the purpose of correction, this will not impair their characterisitics, though one cannot rely entirely on one's own judgment, but with the aid of intelligent friends no pains will be spared. The author's intention is: To assign the rights of the edition to the publisher for five years from the start of printing, in such a way that if a start is made this winter the contract will last until 1810; however after this the author or his family have the right to publish a new edition.
> This is a first draft and can serve as a basis for further discussion.
> W. 2 October 1804   Goethe

Schiller's commentary of the same date runs:

> In my opinion the whole body of Goethe's works would be divided into three batches and delivered at three consecutive fairs.
> Each third, whether it consists of 4 or 5 volumes, would cost the purchaser 9 Reichsthaler, and consequently 6 Reichsthaler net. The purchaser will receive for these 9 Reichsthaler either 4 volumes of 32–36 signatures or 5 volumes of 25–30 signatures, in this way the size of the volumes is immaterial both to the selling price and to the contract with the author.
> If the publisher pays the author 1,000 ducats for each third, then he will break even if he sells 1,300 copies (the selling price for each third is 6 Reichsthaler net).
> However, since sales can be more accurately gauged in the case of the second and third consignments, then it would perhaps be advisable for both contracting parties only to enter into a provisional contract for the first consignment and to be guided in the following consignments by the volume of sales.

If the whole thing—for the purchaser's convenience—is made in four consignments then the selling price for each consignment could be set at 6 Reichsthaler, 4 Reichsthaler net. In this case the publisher would pay 2,250 Reichsthaler for each consignment and the amount of royalty would remain exactly the same. The only thing would be that the purchaser would be somewhat favored at the publisher's expense; but the latter would have hopes of greater sales.

I recognize that the royalty I am suggesting is twice what Wieland received for his works.

These documents sent to him on 2 October formed the basis of Schiller's letter to Cotta of 16 October 1804. Schiller did not mention any details in it; he gave a résumé of Goethe's memorandum and was, as we have mentioned, careful enough to advise Cotta only to ask Goethe for a "work to be published." Schiller, however, was aware of the uncertain legal position and he knew that Johann Friedrich Unger was pressing Goethe to publish the eighth volume of his *New Writings*. "I can," Goethe wrote to Zelter on 29 August 1803, "agree or refuse. I cannot refuse because I would like to complete the number, I cannot agree because I have promised my next works to Cotta with whom I have reason to be very pleased." Unger quite understandably did not relax his pressure and tried through the efforts of mutual friends to make Goethe change his mind. On 30 April 1804, Unger learned that A. W. von Schlegel had "talked a great deal with Goethe and I have taken the opportunity of reminding him of your requests, without being able to get him to give a definite answer. He does not seem interested in a new edition of his complete works." But Schlegel was wrong; Goethe was ready, but he wanted to publish the edition with Cotta, not with Unger. In the meanwhile the knot untied itself—Unger died on 26 December 1804. Göschen was later to make his presence felt by taking legal action against Cotta to assert some older rights to Goethe's works.

This was the background against which Schiller advised Cotta to proceed cautiously, and Cotta followed the advice. In his reply to Schiller on 26 October he thanked his "most valued friend" "for your kindness in telling me of Goethe's plans." Since he knew how important an edition of this sort could be for him and his firm, he in no way wanted to importune Goethe only to receive a refusal. "I may not and certainly do not want to let this opportunity escape, and I ask you out of your friendship for me to represent me in this matter." He was "happy with everything that you have told me up till now," and yet he had seen a snag in Schiller's idea (that the publisher would have to "get a move on") and he wanted to eliminate this snag right at the outset: "All I want is for G. to reckon not from the start of publication but from its completion and put this at 7 or even 6 years, rather than 5. I would also hope that at the end of this time I would have right of first refusal." There was another reason for Cotta's not letting himself be rushed into making a hurried request of Goethe, but for the rest he would like Schiller himself to get involved: "You will in any case know how best to handle the whole matter." After 26 October, Cotta heard nothing further about this, for him so important, matter. In a postscript to his letter of 4 December he asked Schiller: "You wrote me nothing about Goethe. You did receive my last?" Schiller replied on 13 December: "For a long time I have heard nothing from Goethe about his intention to publish his complete works; at least for the moment he does not seem to be thinking about it." However, at the end of December Schiller did give Cotta a hint, and as a result Cotta thought he could put the crucial question to Goethe, which he did on 7 January 1805. He cleverly played down the matter that was so important to him but came to the main point which he formulated in three lines. "Councillor Schiller has written to me about a great undertaking for which I would thank your Grace, and for which I especially recommend myself." Goethe replied on 15 January, rather calmly, that "many inner and external hindrances" had kept him from "sending news of himself to distant friends." The external hindrance was Goethe's involvement in the wedding of Crown Prince Carl Friedrich and the staging of *Homage to the Arts;* the inner was his state of health, for at this time he was suffering from a rather serious renal colic. Goethe did not go into details in his reply to Cotta. Since he knew from Schiller that Cotta would be visiting him in May on his way to Leipzig, his reply to the question about "the great undertaking" that was so important to Cotta could afford to be sibylline: "We are looking forward to your coming with pleasure so that we can discuss a few rather important matters with you."

However, it is clear from Goethe's letter that he did not know that Schiller had given such detailed information to Cotta. This may tie in with the fact that relations between Schiller and Goethe in the first months of the year 1805 were very complicated. Goethe knew that Schiller was seriously ill. In February Goethe caught pneumonia, and both of them were now writing from their beds. Goethe, "So tell me how you are?" And Schiller, "I am glad to get a few lines from you again and it revives my belief that there can be a return of the old times, though I often despair of that. The two harsh blows to which I have had to submit in a space of seven months have shaken me to the roots, and I shall be hard put to it to recover." Both of them appeared to have regained their health by 1 March 1805, and Schiller visited "his dear Goethe."[1]

On 19 April, he and Schiller once more returned to the question of the legal situation. "Since on the occasion of Cotta's next probable visit here there could be talk of an edition of my works, I find it necessary to acquaint you with my former relationship with Göschen. Your friendship and insight into the business relieve me of the task of looking through these unpleasant papers at the moment. Besides, I notice that Göschen printed an edition in 4 volumes with the false dates 1787 and 1791, something that we had never discussed." Göschen had repeatedly brought out individual works of Goethe in new editions; he had printed two each of *Clavigo* and *Götz,* three of *Egmont* and *Werther,* five of *Tasso* and seven of *Iphigenia* which Goethe did not find out about and for which he received no royalties. Schiller seems to have busied himself with Goethe's publishing contracts with Göschen and not to have discovered any obstacles to an agreement with Cotta. In any case Goethe thanked Schiller a day later for "looking through the papers." He was happy "that we are of one mind about these obligations." The two authors might be of one mind, but the two publishers gave violent expression to their different views. On 7 October 1805 Cotta received a letter from Göschen, in which the latter, justifiably, mentions that he had entered into a contract with Goethe for the works he had published that covered the "first and subsequent edition." Göschen uses the singular form, "subsequent edition," not "editions"; he could have claimed—in a strict interpretation— only the rights to the first and the subsequent (second) edition. This was unacceptable to Cotta. It was important to him that another point of view prevail, and he presents it in sovereign fashion, in his letter to Göschen of 18 October 1805: "It seems to me that with your edition of Wieland's works, you have given the German book trade a completely different turn; up to that point, if I am not mistaken, the relationship of writers to publishers had never been the subject of legal discussion; it was more of a friendly relation-ship in which the publisher's interest generally gained more than the authors', especially those whose works sold really well. You, with your firm, were the first to draw the attention of writers to the great advantages that justifiably accrued to them for their intellectual work, and you have—in the eyes of every just man—performed a service. Now, it is a natural consequence that the relationships that are now based on a legal foundation will be disadvantageous to many publishers, in a way that was formerly not the case. The law now takes the place of *mere goodwill* and therefore it seems to me that any appeal you make to the public against Herr von Goethe can gain you nothing. If, namely, it is a question—as you assure me and as I do not doubt—of your having a contract for the first and subsequent edition of the *older works* that you have published, then it seems to me that this contract is binding only if Herr Privy Councillor von Goethe were to publish these older works in a special edition; but since he wants to publish all his works you have as little ground for legal complaint as I, since many of Goethe's works will be published by me." Cotta also indicated that Goethe could prevent Göschen from publishing older works. He finishes his letter to Göschen with the words, "If there were something on your side that could justify a complaint against the publication of an edition of the complete works, you should have specified it expressly in your contract—that the works you published might never be included in a complete edition of all Goethe's works. If this is not the case you have, in my opinion, no grounds for complaint and Herr Privy Councillor Goethe can, indeed, insist that you do not bring out a new edition of his older works, because he no longer wishes to publish one, in order not to harm the publication of his complete works. Incidentally I am sending you this only as my comment, for your consideration, for on my side I can await everything in peace."

Thus Cotta carried on the controversy on the basis of a matter of principle: Does the publisher have the sole right of publication for one and all subsequent editions, and with no time limit—as was then the case—or does the author have a right of property and use that permits him to present his works in the format, form, and within the space of time that he wishes? In his fight over the rights to Wieland's works Göschen had, at that time, fought on the basis of the author's rights. Of course he was concerned with rights in works already published, precisely the right to be allowed to anthologize already published works in a complete edition. But Cotta went further, he claimed the right of the author himself to determine the content of a complete edition and the form of possible textual revisions, and for individual works to be regarded as new material in a new complete edition, as a new part of a whole. Goethe appeared satisfied with Cotta's explanation; it was "very proper and to the point, we shall now wait and see what further steps he takes." But on Göschen's side there were no further steps. Goethe told Cotta on 14 February 1806, "Herr Göschen has said nothing to me, and this would have been his first move. If I am not mistaken he feels that I have a question to ask of him that he cannot answer."

Cotta could now publish Goethe's works, but the two publishers remained at loggerheads. When the German Book Trade Exchange, after its founding in 1825, erected a building in Leipzig, two busts were set up next to each other in one of the lobbies, one of Göschen and one of Cotta. Viscount Goschen remarks about his grandfather's portrait, "the one, that of a generous and helpful friend in need in the early days when Schiller was struggling with the disagreeable aspects of life, the other that of a wealthy provider on his way from triumph to triumph. Assiduous and envious competitors for the favor of the most famous German poets during their lives, now share in peace the respect of posterity as great and outstanding figures in the annals of a profession rich in honors."

In the days between 19 and 26/27 April, Goethe's and Schiller's letters followed hard on the heels of one another. Goethe had drafted some notes for his translation of Diderot's *Rameau's Nephew,* Schiller made some comments, Goethe studied the suggestions and adopted most of them in his manuscript. He then sent the manuscript back to Schiller for him to forward to Göschen in Leipzig. He had, as he mentioned in his notes on 25 April, "many reservations," but he consoled himself with words from Ovid's *Tristia,* "sine me ibis Liber [the book will make its way without me] for I do not want to be present everywhere it goes." And he continued, "In the meantime I have begun dictating the History of the Theory of Color." On 26/27 April in his last letter to Schiller he sent a short plan for him to look over, but Schiller could no longer react.

On the afternoon of 9 May 1805 Johann Heinrich Meyer was visiting Goethe; he was called to the door to receive the news that Schiller had died at 5:45 p.m. Meyer did not have the heart to pass the news on to Goethe and left the house without saying farewell. Christiane too had learned of Schiller's death but said nothing of it to Goethe that afternoon or evening. Goethe did not learn of it until the following morning. We know about this from the description that Voss the Younger gave of Christiane's report. "Vulpius told him in the morning but as considerately as possible without mentioning the word death. Then Goethe turned sideways and started to cry without uttering a syllable."

"I thought I had lost myself," he wrote to Zelter three weeks after Schiller's death, "and now I lose a friend and half of my life in him." His son August talked of a "wound in my father's life that neither time nor his fellow men were able to heal." Goethe visited Frau von Stein the following day. She states how "irreparable a loss" Schiller would always be for Goethe. "He talked today," she noted, "so beautifully and originally about the physical and spiritual man." According to Weimar custom the burial took place in a simple pine coffin during the night of 12 May between midnight and 1 a.m. in the so-called *Landschaftsgewölbe* in the old churchyard of St. James's church in Weimar. Instead of the usual guild craftsmen, friends carried the coffin. Goethe excused himself on grounds of ill health. In his *Epilogue to Schiller's The Bell* he was to write: "I hear a terrible midnight tolling / dully and heavily swelling the mourning tones, / Is it possible? Does it mean our friend?"

One of the first letters to reach Goethe about Schiller's death came from Cotta. Cotta expressed "his sadness about the loss of our immortal friend" and continued "Permit me then to tell you of a plan! The theater here wants to dedicate a memorial to him and this gave me the idea of asking the public, in a manner that would show delicacy to the widow, to do this for her and to allow her to have the benefit of it. The management here is ready to do this, Berlin and Hamburg would probably follow suit and the results should not be inconsiderable. I heard that you were going to write something suitable for the theater there—could not my giving notice of that be the most suitable way of inviting the various managements to participate? I hasten to tell you the idea before I arrive in Weimar on the Saturday or Sunday after Ascension." Goethe replied on 1 June 1805:

> In reply to your question, most valued Herr Cotta, as to whether some memorial to our Schiller should be presented by the German theater, I can only say that at present I am in many ways encouraged to do this. My conviction is that art, when it unites with pain, should only stimulate the latter in order to alleviate it and resolve it into higher consolatory feelings, and it is in this sense that I shall try to represent less what we have lost than what remains to us.
>
> My plan is ready and I hope to carry it out in the near future, but

I would not know what deadline to set. If I succeed in producing a work that is not entirely unworthy of the task then I am inclined to let other theaters have it and for this purpose would gladly let you have the manuscript and the score.

Goethe's plan was made. His first thought after Schiller's death had been the completion of *Demetrius*. But the plan failed; his relations with the dead Schiller were detrimental to Goethe's powers of imagination. When he replied to Cotta he already had something else in mind. He wanted to produce a dramatized version of *The Bell* in Lauchstädt in Schiller's honor, and on 4 August he asked Carl Friedrich Zelter to visit him in Lauchstädt and name a "suitable symphony" by "some master or other." On 10 August 1805, after a performance of acts 3–5 of *Mary Stuart*, Schiller's *The Bell* was presented in dramatic form and Goethe's epilogue was recited by the actress Amalie Wolff-Malcolmi. On 12 August before leaving Lauchstädt, he wrote to Cotta, "The dramatic performance of *The Bell* had a powerful effect and far exceeded the public's expectation." Goethe said nothing about his ten-strophe epilogue, a versified summa of Schiller's achievements in his life and his work: "For he was ours! May the proud word / drown out in its power the noise of pain!" The last two lines of the poem are: "He shines before us disappearing like a comet, / Joining eternal light with his own light."

A second commemoration was arranged in Weimar on 9 May 1810 with scenes from Schiller's plays and the recitation of Goethe's epilogue that was expanded for the occasion. For the celebration on 10 May 1815 that was dedicated to Schiller and Iffland, Goethe added two further stanzas to the epilogue.

Goethe's actual poetic testament to Schiller was only written much later. The burial place was closed in 1826. On 24 September of that year, Goethe had Schiller's skull brought to his house—an unusual proceeding for Goethe if we think of his fear of the "catafalque," of dying, death, burial and decay. But Goethe had been interested in osteology for forty-five years; the human skull had interested him from the time of Lavater's physiognomical researches, and he had later been introduced by the anatomist and phrenologist Franz Joseph Gall into his theory of the skull. And so on 25/26 September 1826 he wrote the poem "It was in the stern charnel house," which was published for the first time in 1829 at the end of the second version of the *Journeyman Years,* after the prose sayings, "From Makarien's Archive." It was reprinted in volume 7 of the "Posthumous Works" in 1833, this time with the title *On Looking at Schiller's Skull.* In a letter to Zelter on 14 October 1827 Goethe calls the poem "Relics of Schiller," an unambiguous indication, important because Schiller's name does not appear in the poem. In the poem Goethe draws up the balance sheet of his eleven-year contact with Schiller. It refutes the opinion that the relationship was based fundamentally on antipathy. Goethe never offered to address Schiller in the familiar "Du" form, and he concealed works from him, for example, *The Natural Daughter.* Schiller often complained to friends of Goethe's lack of willpower, and his dilatoriness and his "domestic misery" would have always been unacceptable to Schiller. And yet on Goethe's account Schiller had turned down a brilliant opportunity to move to Berlin from Weimar, and in spite of all the insinuations, for example from the brothers Schlegel, Goethe had maintained his friendship with Schiller and used him time and again as an intermediary in dealings with Göschen and Cotta. Thus the relationship between the two rested on mutual freedom, on an equal intellectual partnership, and also, by and large, on a lightness and brightness in their contacts. Of course, Goethe had recognized that Schiller's inclination to philosophy, to Kant's theories, would have been detrimental to his—Goethe's—productivity, but as early as 1801 he expressed himself on the subject of Schiller's greatness. "Schiller," Goethe observed, "appears here, as always, in complete possession of his noble nature; he is as great at the tea-table as he would have been in parliament. Nothing bothers him, nothing confines him, nothing lowers the flight of his thoughts; he expresses freely, without consideration or reflection, whatever great views dwell within him. That was a real human being, and that's how one should be! We others on the other hand always feel limited. Persons, objects that surround us have their influence on us; the teaspoon embarrasses us if it is made of gold, because it should be made of silver, and paralyzed in this way by thousands of considerations we never get round to expressing freely what is great within our natures. We are the slaves of objects and appear petty or significant according to whether these cramp us or give us room to expand freely." When Eckermann compared Schiller with the new tragedians, Goethe had the answer pat: "Schiller was able to take up whatever position he liked, he was unable to do anything that did not turn out far greater than the best that these new people can produce: when Schiller cut his nails he was greater than these gentlemen." The poem about the relics—about Schiller's almost holy remains resting in precious memory—

expresses such respect, such greatness. In the midst of such a "rigid multitude" the poem preserves "an image inestimably beautiful" and it was "as if a spring of life flowed from death."

The poem moves to a climax in the last four lines, God—Nature—can reveal itself to mankind: the idea of the whole is present in spirit, a "divinely conceived path" expresses the spirit and the whole. Goethe also gives expression to the special position of the last four lines by expanding the last tercet of the poem into four lines.

Schiller had been "as dear a mediator as he was successful" in Goethe's "concerns" with Cotta, but of course Goethe esteemed his poetic and intellectual achievements more highly.

Dorothea Kuhn assumes that the meeting between Goethe and Cotta that had been announced took place on 3 or 4 May 1805, and there would certainly have been a discussion of Goethe's memorandum about the complete works. Goethe's "Memorandum" is dated 1 May. Cotta announced his arrival for 26 May in a letter from Leipzig that we have already mentioned. Schiller had died on 9 May, and Cotta had expressed the wish to be "active on behalf of his survivors," saying he considered this "the legacy left him by the unforgettable one." But however great the loss caused by the death of one of the firm's authors—and of a friend—might be, Cotta knew what an essential role Schiller had played in Goethe's relationship with him, the role of the scout, the mediator, the stimulator, the admonisher, and the reconciler. It was for this reason that—in his letter—he made his most important request, "I can deal with my sorrow over the loss of our immortal friend myself, I am therefore suppressing everything else and asking only that I now find in you the sympathetic representative of yourself." The visit that had been announced for 26 May did not take place. True, Cotta was in Weimar that evening, but he did not meet with Goethe, who was ill. On the other hand, we can also assume that he did not want to, was not able to, talk to Cotta about Schiller's death. On 14 June he sent his memorandum about the complete edition off to Tübingen, the "Promemoria that Herr Cotta already knows," together with an addition containing a "hearty greeting and hopes for a safe return home in every sense." The new memorandum differs in a few points—having to do with the division into volumes—from the draft that Goethe had sent Schiller on 2 October 1804, as his "essay."

The differences between this and the first plan are that Goethe changed both his plan for the volumes and their order. The essential changes concern the poems he preferred to have in the first volume and in the *Journeyman Years,* intended for volumes 2 and 3. He dictated his new conception to Riemer, and the plan is preserved in Riemer's handwriting with Goethe's own signature; what is new, or unpublished, is underlined in red (italic here).

I. Miscellaneous Poems; *Some new.*
II. Wilhelm Meister. First and Second Volume.
III. Wilhelm Meister Third and Fourth Volume.
IV. *The Mood of the Beloved.* The Accomplices. The Siblings. Mahomet. Tancred. *Elpenor. Fragment.*
V. Götz von Berlichingen. Egmont. Stella. Clavigo.
VI. Iphigenia. Tasso. Eugenie.
VII. Claudine. Erwin and Elmire. Jery and Bäthly. Lila.
VIII. Cophta. Triumph of Sensibility. Birds. Bourgeois General. What we bring.
IX. Reynard the Fox. Herrmann and Dorothea (*revised according to new prosodic conviction*). Achilles, *First Canto.*
X. Faust. Fragment *enlarged by a half.* Puppet play. *Enlarged.* Other analogous poems, old and *new.*
XI. Werther. Shorter prose works.
XII. Similar.

This was the position on 1 May 1805. On 14 June, Goethe added:

I have only to add to the existing memorandum, that Herr Cotta is already familiar with, the following:
The rights to this edition will extend over five to six years.
I would like to have for this
 Ten thousand thalers
Made up as follows: 1,000 on receipt of the first manuscript, the rest at three successive Easter fairs, 1806, 1807, 1808, 3,000 Saxon Reichstalers on each occasion.

Cotta accepted Goethe's proposals on 5 July but included five suggestions for alterations and closed the letter with these words: "I flatter myself that on my return towards the end of the month I shall receive confirmation of the above from your grace, since I believe that everything is based on fairness and, as I flatter myself, my ideas are known to your Excellency as not being disadvantageous." Goethe sent his confirmation on 12 August from Bad

Lauchstädt, where he had been responsible, on behalf of the court of Weimar, for the above-mentioned productions in Schiller's honor at the theater in Lauchstädt. Goethe's "Declaration" gives a precise statement of his view of Cotta's five suggested alterations; this makes clear how important the contractual side of the complete edition was.

COTTA: (1). "I will assume the publication of your works, so graciously offered, for 10,000 Saxon thalers, at the times agreed, but as the whole thing involves significant capital, I stipulate (1) that the rights for this edition be reckoned as lasting for 6 years from the publication of the last installment; that is e.g. if the final installment appears at Easter 1808, then I have rights to the edition until Easter 1814."

GOETHE ad (1). "Since in the case of an agreement it is important for both sides to be sure what is involved, I would like the duration of the rights to be measured from the first installment. However, I am happy that this extend over eight years, thus, e.g., from Easter 1806 to Easter 1814."

A significant change. Cotta wanted to have six years from the appearance of the *last* installment. Goethe, having learned by experience, could imagine that, for one reason or another, whether it were delays caused by publishers, printers, or the circumstances of the day, or ones that were the fault of the author, this final installment could be held up for a long time, perhaps for years, and he would then have to grant rights for a further six years. So he stuck to his original suggestion: the duration of the contract begins with the first installment and ends—and here he made a new suggestion—not six, but eight years later. He acted cleverly in the process and arrived at the same date as Cotta.

COTTA: (2). "I am not bound exclusively to the fixed, neat, and tasteful edition with gothic script, but may be allowed to choose other formats if, e.g. I find it advisable to come out with a pocket edition.

GOETHE ad (2). "I am satisfied."

In my opinion Goethe did not see through Cotta's thinking. The expression, "other formats" is unclear. Is it a question here of the pocket edition or of an edition with a typeface other than Fraktur? Perhaps the cause of later irritation lies in this lack of clarity.

COTTA: (3). "After the passage of six years I should have preference over
every other publisher if my terms are the same."

GOETHE ad (3). "I am also in agreement (should read eight years not six)."

COTTA: (4). "You will represent me vis-à-vis your former publishers,
Göschen, Unger—"

GOETHE ad (4). "When Schiller asked me about the publication of my works,
I informed him about all my former arrangements; he then said that there
was no basis for an objection, and I have a note from him to this effect.
If meanwhile anything of the sort should happen, please permit me to
inform you and take your advice."

This point was disagreeable to Goethe. He had asked Schiller on 19
April 1805 to take a look at his "unpleasant papers" in connection with
Göschen. The point about representation, that is, the release of rights that
Göschen, or possibly Unger, could have made legally tenable, remained un-
clear.

COTTA: (5). "No new edition will be printed until the first has been sold out,
in case this should take even longer than six years."

GOETHE ad (5). "This condition is, as the writing indicates, added later
and in your haste to add it you probably did not realize that this point
negates the first. In order that the author not have to worry about the size
of the edition or the way in which the publisher offers the works to the
public, a time was determined that will eliminate all misunderstandings.
But the deadline would be lifted by number (5), by means of which a
great many complications could arise."

Here Goethe had very clearly foreseen a possible conflict. First of all
Cotta has confused the agreed eight years with six, and second he had to
distinguish clearly between a printing and an edition. Apparently what Cotta
wanted was the following: If the sale of the edition were to take longer than
six, or eight, years from the beginning of the first installment, then no other
publisher, whom Goethe could nominate in accordance with paragraph 1,
could come out with an edition. Goethe rightly sees a contradiction to the
agreement in paragraph 1 that could lead to misunderstandings. The author,
justifiably, does not want to be burdened with problems of the size of the
printing and of sales. Cotta on the other hand has to regard the restricted
term of the contract—in view of the royalties that have to be paid—as

essential, and he fears, in addition, that Göschen and Unger "will do their utmost to sell quickly the stock of old and new writings in the cheap edition, costing 9 Reichstalers, at reduced prices, thus taking part of my public away from me for the immediate future." Dorothea Kuhn comments on this contractual process: "It is important in this connection that Goethe emphasizes that the size of the edition is the publisher's concern and that he thus has the rights to duplicate printings; but not to a new edition after the end of the contract's duration." But there is no talk at all of a new "edition"; during the life of the contract Cotta can only come out with as many printings as he will. But there is in no case an agreement on Goethe's part for "duplicate printings," whether these are altered or not. After Goethe's objection, Cotta took back point 5, but it is wrong for Dorothea Kuhn to conclude that Goethe for his part had "finally communicated a confirmation" in his letter of 18 September.

Laconic, imperative, succinct—Goethe remained true to himself, but when the fundamental principles had been clarified in the negotiations and he had reached agreement, then trust and goodwill had to enter in. As we have mentioned, he had required in the *Elective Affinities*—that was written only shortly afterwards—that business and life be separated; the former called for seriousness and rigor, the latter arbitrariness. "Business needs pure consequentiality, whereas life often needs inconsequentiality, indeed such inconsequentiality is pleasant and cheering." And: "Business is like dancing: persons who keep in step are bound to become indispensable to one another; a mutual goodwill must spring from this."

The extent to which Goethe felt this goodwill is shown in his letter of 30 September to "The most esteemed Herr Cotta," which seems to me characteristic of Goethe the author, characteristic for the relationship he wished to have with his publisher, and I should like to quote it verbatim:

Wilhelm Meister was sent off by today's post. As we have already combined two of the previous volumes into one, this will now constitute the second and third volume of the edition. Most esteemed Herr Cotta, you can now think about the printing and the whole layout, perhaps you will send me a sample of the type and the paper. I hope that the whole will have a pleasant appearance.

But I am not so concerned about that as about typographical accuracy, and for this I plead most urgently. You can see that the copy has been gone through and corrected with the greatest care, and I should be in despair if it were once again to appear in garbled form. Please be good enough to entrust the proofreading to an exceptionally careful man, furthermore I expressly wish that the copy I have sent be printed exactly as it is, that nothing be changed in spelling, punctuation or otherwise; even if there were still to be a mistake, it would be better to print that. Enough, I wish for and ask nothing more than that the original I have now sent be copied exactly as it is.

The shorter poems which are to constitute the first volume have all been rewritten in manuscript and should appear first in order. I think that, in spite of the war, these things can be entrusted to the post.

I have still not made up my mind as to what I shall put in the fourth volume. If it is at all possible I shall come out straightaway with Faust. He and the other woodcut-like jokes make a good whole and would arouse lively interest in the very first installment. Tell me the very latest date by which you have to have the manuscript for the fourth volume, so that I can make a more or less rough calculation.

Let me have a word or two about the look and state of affairs in your area and let me know at once when the Wilhelm Meister install-ment arrives.

To which I bid a hearty farewell!

The Origin of the   In March 1807 three different editions of the first four
"Works" and Cotta's   volumes of the *Works* are ready, with 1806 as the date
"Let's hope for the   of publication, but the edition bound in vellum is
best and be ready for   delayed because of carelessness on the part of the
the worst!"   printer, for the printer had, mistakenly, used two sorts
                               of paper for this edition. Cotta therefore had to repeat

the printing process, so that the vellum edition could not be ready till May. The promised copies reach Goethe on the afternoon of 16 March. Two days later he writes to Cotta that the different editions "look really good." But he must express his regret about the delay in the vellum copies: "I regret the mistake about the vellum copies because this will lessen the number of those bibliophiles who would have been inclined to spend something." The "lessen" is not quite understandable, for we know from bibliophile amateurs that they often have to wait for books because of special sorts of binding. On the whole, though, a moderate reaction! "The applause," Cotta writes on 5 April, "for the copies that I sent was pleasing to my ears." This is the only remark he makes about the edition, otherwise his letter deals with other matters. He speaks of his "humble visit" on the third Sunday after Easter. "I can confess at this point that the enjoyment of this pleasure is really one of the main reasons for making the journey; for what book business am I going to do in Leipzig?" Pure exaggeration! In spite of terrible burdens imposed by the war, Cotta is offering at the Easter Fair no fewer than five continuing journals and ten new, in part multivolume, works. It is this Easter production that causes a man like Carl August Böttiger to write to Cotta, "Incidentally when I look at the list of new works, I once again admire your stupendous energy. Truly what Napoleon is among the crowned heads and the anointed of the Lord, you are among booksellers." The comparison with Napoleon was made repeatedly by his contemporaries, sometimes admiringly but also polemically and maliciously. The label still persists.

But why so little fuss on Goethe's and Cotta's part when the desired fruits of the relationship were at last available? Certainly this has a lot to do with the times. It was also in large part connected with Goethe's changing state of health, as well as with the fact that he could not proceed as quickly as he had thought with revising the texts that he intended to include in the works. It was also connected with the extremely laborious process of writing the *Theory of Color,* but it was affected most of all by Goethe's evaluation of the conditions of the time and his attitude towards Napoleon. Contemporaries did not know whether to see in Napoleon a genius or a demon, whether he was an oppressor or a liberator. Cotta's view vacillated as well. He wrote to Goethe on 12 November 1805: "Napoleon will—look at him as you will—stand as something extraordinary. . . . The spirit continually conquers what is otherwise merely dead power. Let us hope for the best and be ready for the worst! In fact at the moment this is not just an election slogan of mine, but a norm for my business." Napoleon had been invading the German lands with his army from 1805 onwards. At first, only Austria and Russia were the enemy; Prussia, and with it the other German princes, hesitated a long time before declaring war. The French had now once more encircled an army in Ulm and this army was forced to surrender on 24 October. Goethe refers to this in a letter to Cotta on 25 November 1805: "While the strangest things are happening on the Danube, our Thuringia is filling up with soldiers. The incalculability of the circumstances leaves fear and hope in suspense and everyone is simply seeking to survive for the moment." The "fatherland's misfortune" was the battle of Austerlitz, on 2 December 1805, in which Napoleon disastrously defeated Emperor Alexander of Russia and Franz I of Austria.

"We are alive"—this is the emphatic way in which Goethe's letter to Cotta of 20 October 1806 begins. It was written after the battle of Jena and the pillaging and burning of Weimar. "Our house was saved from looting and fire as if by a miracle. . . . The Emperor arrived on 15 October 1806." Cotta, for his part, had written to Goethe on 7 February 1806 and given him a "sign of life": "I am not in the kingdom of the dead, but also not in the kingdom of the cheerful: for now I am oppressed by my fatherland's misfortune."

Actually it was a miracle that, given the circumstances of the time, the edition of the works should have been produced at all. Goethe was working with Riemer on the printer's copies and the proofs that, because of the postal situation, could understandably only be sent back and forth between Weimar and Tübingen with substantial delays. He kept demanding sample extracts both of the typography and of the way the printing was being controlled. "Of course it will be a long time before the south German printing presses equal, in a certain gallant manner, the north German ones." This must not have pleased Cotta, for in the circumstances of the war there could be no question of producing the work in north Germany, and the south German printers were working under the greatest difficulties.

Goethe did not get on as fast as he would have wished with the versions that he wanted to make for the edition of the works; for almost a year he had worked on *Faust* with Riemer, in the hope that it could still be published in the fourth volume of the "dramas," but the hope fell through; it was to appear, as originally intended, in the tenth volume. Cotta did not want to wait too long to continue work on what was for him so important an edition and suggested publishing a separate edition. Goethe agreed: "the more widely it is scattered, the better it is." But he did not agree with Cotta's idea of including pictures in the edition. "I thought we should publish *Faust* without woodcuts and pictures," he writes on 25 November 1805, "it is so difficult to produce anything that is suited to the sense and tone of a poem like this. Etchings and poetry are mutual parodies of one another. I think that the sorcerer must look after himself." And in truth the sorcerer did just that.

The work on the still fragmentary *Elpenor* also dragged on. After his stay in Carlsbad, Goethe was working in August on a new version but gave it up, finally commissioning Riemer to do the iambic version and reserving the "final redaction" for himself. On 27 October 1806 the manuscript was sent off to Tübingen.

At this time Goethe was continuing, with the greatest difficulty, to investigate the "theory of color." Goethe was an author who had constantly to put pressure on himself when he was writing; it often happened that a part of a work that he had just written was being set, even being printed, in the hope that this would inspire him to complete the rest quickly, as we saw in the case of *Wilhelm Meister.* "Six signatures of the 'Theory of Color' have been printed, three of the first and three of the second part. I now see that I cannot complete the whole work in less than a year. I am saying this in advance so that you will not announce it for Easter." The two volumes of the *Theory of Color* appeared in 1808 and 1810 in two volumes of text and a volume of tables.

Goethe constantly urged Cotta to be "accurate in printing" and asked him once more, "insistently," to keep an eye on this. In this connection the admonition was necessary. "Furthermore please print my name as Goethe and not Göthe." Strange that this was still necessary in 1806. But Goethe was also himself at fault for this: Göschen and Unger and the pirates, too, had reproduced Goethe's name in different ways; as Goethe often took the models for his copy from old printings or even from pirated editions, different spellings of his name were constantly occurring.

Authors in general have an ambivalent relationship to the products of a publishing house with which they publish. On the one hand they appreciate being published by a firm that produces good, progressive, forward-looking books; on the other, every book besides their own that the publisher publishes is one too many. They watch with special jealousy what seems to be of particular importance to the publisher. It is astonishing how often and how urgently Cotta told Goethe of his "concern" (for contributions to the *Ladies Calendar*). And he persistently asked, even in those hard times, for texts that Goethe did not want to give up so easily, poems and "suitable things" from *Faust.* We can understand Cotta; the *Ladies Calendar* sold well, and the calendar business was absolutely necessary, for there were many books that he published on which he could scarcely make any profit. Every year he published four calendars, the *Card Almanac,* the *Almanac des Dames,* a *State History of Europe* edited in the form of a calendar, and *The Pocket*

Book for Ladies. When Cotta turned to Goethe on 6 February 1806 saying that he was "once again living in the period when calendars were being prepared and was therefore taking the liberty of daring to ask you to do me the pleasure of giving me a contribution for my *Ladies Calendar,*" Goethe thought he could not but fulfil the request. But once again he reacted in his own way. He did not send a poem or a piece from one of the works that was important to him, but something from less important works that he nevertheless set store by. One gains the impression that he did not want to appear in the *Ladies Calendar.* But with Cotta constantly calling his "kind attention" to the *Ladies Calendar,* Goethe replied firmly on 24 January 1808 and confessed his "apprehensions." "Permit me to express an apprehension that I harbor towards this little book. It is the arrangement by which etchings that do not belong to the text are introduced into it. It may be that others are not so sensitive, but I do not deny that I find it painful even in other people's work that, when I am reading, with a ready interest, a nice little novel, a picture of the Virgin or a scene from Wallenstein's Camp intervenes. Please excuse this remark. But I would rather confess my idiosyncrasy than fear that you suspect me of not fulfilling your wishes either out of neglect or unfriendliness." Cotta should have known Goethe's attitude, for the latter had actually told him of it a little while before when the addition of pictures to *Faust* had been discussed.

The political motivations and points of view that the publisher states or that the works of his authors express can also make the relationship of author to publisher difficult. Certainly, Cotta's second most important activity was a political one. He was a member of the Würtemberg state parliament and distinguished himself especially in his country's customs negotiations and, as we shall see, in questions of copyright and publishing rights. Every publisher is also tempted to express directly, in a programmatic periodical, the message that is indirectly contained in the sum total of his books, but even when there is a certain political consensus among authors of a given publisher, there is simply never unity on all contemporary questions—in attitudes to politics, history, ethics, religion, and certainly not in questions of literary judgment. While the publisher must be open and liberal in support of the freedom of others, ready to support the opinions of the other person even if he does not share them, the author for his part can and must go his own way, and do so even if it is unrecognizable or tortuous, a false trail or the wrong track; even if he makes many changes of direction, he cannot do otherwise, he has to follow his star.

Cotta had founded his *Allgemeine Zeitung* in Tübingen in 1798 and then transferred it to Stuttgart as the daily *Allgemeine Zeitung,* but as the contributions were always causing offense to the political censor, the place of publication and the editorship had to be moved to Ulm and Augsburg. In spite of all difficulties, Cotta held on to the newspaper. His basic idea was a nonparty, European newspaper appearing daily and he wanted no one but Schiller as the editor; but the plan had failed, the literary monthly *Die Horen* that was very close to Schiller's heart also had to be given up. In spite of this Cotta kept on hoping to add to the *Allgemeine Zeitung,* the political daily—his "institution," his "sheet"—a further "institution" that was to be exclusively an organ for literary publications. This organ was from the beginning to be totally nonpolitical—a contradiction in itself, since every good piece of literature is new and therefore strange, is critical and, as a result, political. Finally the idea gave rise to the *Morgenblatt für gebildete Stände,* and it appeared daily from 1 January 1807. Cotta had told Goethe on 15 August 1806, "Come the New Year I am thinking of founding a similar institution to *Der Freimüthige* [The Candid One] for Southern Germany; might I not flatter myself that you would be an active participant in it?" There was no answer from Goethe. This letter was—as we have mentioned—written at the time when the war situation in Weimar was at its most difficult and Cotta should have known that a mention of *Der Freimüthige* would frighten Goethe off rather than attract him. *Der Freimüthige* was a "Berlin newspaper for educated, impartial readers" that had been appearing since 1803 under Kotzebue's editorship. It was a scandal sheet, devoted first and foremost to anything topical. Goethe's friend, and later antagonist, Carl August Böttiger was a collaborator on the paper; that alone should have made Cotta suspicious, but the fact that the paper had on several occasions made critical and malicious comments about Goethe should have been absolutely enough to keep him from the project. However, Cotta repeated his request in October 1806: "With the coming of peace I am thinking of bringing out a nonpolitical paper. . . . Might I hope that you would graciously join it and could you please me by sending some contributions which I would all too gladly start off with?" No answer from Goethe. However in an advertisement in the *Allgemeine Zeitung* Cotta distinguished his interests from *Der Freimüthige.* The purpose of the *Morgenblatt für gebildete Stände* was "to found an institution that will embrace everything—with the exception of political subjects—that can be of interest to educated people, and it shall have no other inclination but to disseminate such knowledge as is necessary for spiritual and moral culture and, by means of entertainment, provide the most pleasant of educations."

Cotta now wanted expressly to distinguish himself from other organs, particularly *Der Freimüthige,* and announced his intention "to make truth, circumspection, and humanity the principles of all his judgments." But Goethe, who had been regularly receiving free copies from Cotta since the paper first appeared, still refused to react. When Cotta "flattered" him once again on 2 February 1807 by asking Goethe "to participate in this institution," Goethe did put a few contributions at his disposal for the year 1807, admittedly once again ephemeral works rather than central ones.

A painful—and continuing—source of friction for Goethe was Cotta's *Allgemeine Zeitung* with its reportage from Weimar. It was a report of this sort that led to the first serious quarrel between Goethe and Cotta; but because both sides expressed themselves openly and clearly, work on the edition was able to continue.

The first four volumes of the edition of the works appeared in March 1807 with the date 1806 (volumes 5–7, 1807; volumes 8–12, 1808). Even while the last volumes were still being set Goethe expressed his satisfaction with the fact "that in the business we have in common, I am able to place my own and my family's interests entirely in your hands." He informed Cotta that he was able "to complete a novel . . . that will probably fill a couple of pleasant volumes. While reading it aloud I was able to cherish the hope that it would be well received in the future. The novel is a very pleasing, comprehensible genre that is also entertaining to the author. I really fancy presenting more of what I have to say in this form than I have done in the past." This was the way in which Goethe gave notice of his *Elective Affinities.* It is a good idea for an author to encourage his publisher and not to expect agreement, animation, and encouragement to come from his side alone.

The Elective Affinities was originally intended as a narrative insert into *The Journeyman Years.* Goethe started dictating it while taking the cure at Carlsbad in June 1808; he dictated the whole of the first part and the end of the second part in July. It was at this time that he made his announcement about the novel to Cotta. He took up the manuscript again in Jena in April 1809 and worked at corrections, expansions, and reformulations. Again he put pressure on himself to hurry by having the first parts printed from the end of July 1809 onwards. The first two volumes appeared at the autumn fair in 1809. They were then included in the collected works as volume 13 and this concluded the edition as Goethe and Cotta reached quick agreement on royalties.

What was it, then, that motivated Goethe to make the novel *The Elective Affinities* out of the story "The Elective Affinities"? "Leisure" and "humor" were what he felt as he dictated the novel to Riemer. I am sure, however, that the shock of contemporary events in 1806 that brought about his decision to marry and the shock of the reaction to the marriage motivated him. "In the uncertain moments of the war" was the way Goethe had rationalized his marriage, "when all other bonds are dissolved, you are thrust back onto domestic ones." The exact opposite is the case in *The Elective Affinities;* there the "traces of gloomy passionate necessity" lead to a tragic ending. Goethe himself announced the novel in the *Morgenblatt,* 4 September 1809: "[The author] has been able to observe that science often uses ethical similes to bring closer something that is far removed from the circle of human knowledge; and so he has, in a moral situation, been able to retrace a chemical simile back to its intellectual origin, the more so as there is only *one* Nature and the traces of gloomily passionate necessity inexorably traverse the kingdom of Reason and Freedom and can be eliminated only by a higher hand, and probably not in this life." There is an indication of a tragic ending here but the story is not as simple as that nor as easily understood. Not all interpreters are agreed that this novel, whose protagonists have entered into, or wish to enter into, marriages is a novel about marriage. "The subject of *The Elective Affinities* is not marriage," nor is it "true love."[2] Marriage or not marriage, marriage for a limited time, or marriage without a license, these are the topics addressed in the novel. Reading the novel today we are fascinated by its artistic sense, its masterly epic structure, the unity of place, the total consistency of its unusual plot, its figures that point far beyond it. But above all else the novel speaks to us today by the force of its ironic brokenness. Thus it is the character Mittler ("mediator"), that "strange," "peculiar," "irksome" man, who, as a mediator, collapses in the end because he is unable to "mediate." "Marriage is the beginning and the peak of all culture." A saying that universally and up to today reflects the power of an institution that sets its stamp upon a culture. But there is an immediate caveat in Mittler's next sentence: "It [marriage] makes the coarse man mild, and the most educated man has no better opportunity of demonstrating his mildness." In the course of discussions between the characters in the novel, one character makes an unusual suggestion, that marriages should be contracted for only five years; we would have to think that this possibility would be discussed seriously but it is immediately sacrificed to conversation—the narrator's irony. In Carlsbad, and in other places, Goethe saw, what were for his time, completely "free morals," and in the summer of 1807 he astonished Reinhard, the senior chaplain at the Saxon court, by his strict principles "in regard to marriage." In his "poetic self-confession" Goethe wrote: "No one fails to recognize in this novel a deep passionate wound that refuses to close itself by healing, a heart that fears to enjoy." However we may not regard the novel as exclusively autobiographical. But it is true that in *The Elective Affinities* (in which there is far less "choice" than compulsion) "there is not a stroke that has not *been* experienced but none *as* it has been experienced."

And so volume 13 of the works appeared in 1813. As we have mentioned, the edition was presented in installments: 1–4, 5–7, 8–12 and finally volume 13. In the process a problem arose for the publisher (and the author): the demand was greater than Cotta had expected and so for the second installment (vols. 5–7), he had to have a larger print run than for the first, and then an even bigger one for the third installment (vols. 8–12) than for the first two. In order to keep the edition complete, it was therefore necessary to reprint the first installment (vols. 1–4) at the same time as the second, and again reprint installments 1 and 2 when the third was printed. Since, as we have mentioned, the printers could not keep the forms, the whole thing had to be reset and in this way typographical errors occurred. As far as I am concerned, there is no question as to the legality of Cotta's producing these reprints. But in the firm's advertisement in 1808 there was a mistake:

> Goethe (von) complete works, 12 volumes, octavo, 2nd edition, white
> paper, subscription price 2 Carolines, ordinary paper 1 1/2 Carolines.

The advertisement announces a *second* edition of the *octavo edition* to which Cotta did not have the rights. It was presumably not a question of a completely new edition, but of mixed copies with reprints of individual signatures that were necessary for the complete edition. Nevertheless as far as the contractual agreements were concerned this made Goethe feel uneasy. Perhaps Cotta was also not entirely sure of himself; in any case he made a voluntary royalty payment in August 1808. The genesis of Edition A has a complicated history. The edition of the *Works* had a mixed reception. The review in the *Allgemeine Literatur Zeitung* had said of the first installment, "of the three editions advertised in an announcement, something went wrong with the one on vellum and so it did not appear at all; the one on so-called ordinary paper however deserves not to be called an edition on vellum but on *papier vilain,*[3] and we do not think the one on white paper much better. Bad as the gray, thin, spotted paper is, the printing is as bad." Goethe had at first agreed to the quality of the printing of the advance sheets, but in the course of time what came out in the printing was also not to his liking.

Goethe complained to Cotta on 22 August 1811 about a pirated version in Vienna. Seventeen volumes of Goethe's *Complete Works* had been published on commission by the Viennese publisher Geistinger (the nine further volumes appeared over the years until 1817). Goethe was annoyed at the incorrectness of the text and the way it was arranged, which was different from Cotta's edition of the *Works.* Cotta reacted with the consideration to which his contract with Goethe entitled him. "Incidentally, in order to give the pirates something to do as well," he wrote to Goethe on 17 September 1811, "I intend publishing a pocket edition of your works in 8 point type and advertising it for 3 Laubtaler." The answer to this was so important to Goethe that he wrote back immediately and sent it by express mounted courier and asked Cotta also to reply by courier. Goethe's letter of 28 September 1811 is a masterpiece of an author's diplomatic art. Goethe did not, in fact, agree with this "copy" of "my works in a smaller format"; that it should appear so long after the octavo edition seemed to him "in many ways questionable." Because of his work on his autobiography, he had apparently come upon new materials that he wanted to see included in the complete edition of his works. "Would it not be better, more effective and more advantageous," he wrote in his letter, "to move in the direction of a complete and accurate edition, that could be all the more complete in that my confessions pave the way to putting together a lot that would not stand on its own as a part of the whole?" Cotta answered, three days later, on 1 October. He did not think that a new complete edition was "advisable," and he gave good reasons for this. The owners of the first edition would scarcely buy a second one in so short a space of time. Goethe's new works, *Literature and Truth* and *The Journeyman Years,* would have to be included in the new edition and could not be published previously as individual editions; further, he must point out "that times in the book trade were not so good as not to make it advisable to wait a few years, until things got better and I am more secure, or completely secure, in France and Austria, against pirated versions." This was the only way Cotta could react. His contract secured him the rights to sell the first edition until 1815. If there were to be a new edition, a new contract would have to be negotiated, and for the firm this would mean, first of all, the uncertainty of obtaining an agreement for the new edition at all and, secondly, a new royalties clause. Cotta had the danger of competition in mind when he wrote that he very much wished that Goethe would have "the grace to settle the future relationship vis-à-vis a new edition, at least as far as we are concerned."

But Goethe held fast to his position. He wrote to Cotta on 14 October 1811 that he would prefer to discuss the whole question in person. And then he returned once more to the announcement of the 1808 edition, saying that he had at the time not reacted because according to the contract Cotta still had six years in which to sell the edition and because he "owed Cotta so much that called up in him a lively gratitude." "But if now, shortly before the contract runs out"—and this clearly proclaimed the end of his gratitude—"a new edition were to appear, almost identical with the original and offered cheaply to the public, then I can see that a carefully prepared, accurate and complete edition of my works—something I should still like to live to see—would be postponed indefinitely, especially when I think of the pirated version that already exists and the rigors of the times." And for the first time, understandably enough when such fundamental issues are at stake, the question of the security of his own existence is raised:

> My embarrassment is increased by the fact that my family to whom—in view of the mortality of a human being—I am accustomed to give notice of my economic conditions, regard this event with especial suspicion and I do not see myself as being in a position to mitigate it. Perhaps these worries arise out of an ignorance of business procedures and would be removed in a verbal exchange.
>
> I believe, in view of our excellent and intimate relationship, that it is my duty to reveal this objection to your honor and I will not deny that I looked on my proposal to advance the new edition as a means of balancing things out, whereby the two years you have left would have to be taken into consideration equitably in some way or another.

Again, imperative, laconic, succinct. Cotta is impressed and for the time being gives up the idea of a pocket edition. Of course it nags at him, one can sense it in the letters, and on 2 November 1811 he conjures up the old relationship and adds a threat: "I admit to you on this occasion that it is only the excellent, and to me so flattering, relationship with you and with

Schiller that keeps me in the book trade, otherwise I would retire from a turmoil that has been a school of so many bitter experiences for me and which can only be cherished by and of value to me in the relationship that I have mentioned."

On 7 March 1812 Cotta reverts to the pocket edition, this time from Stuttgart, where the firm had in the meantime moved. Cotta mentions that the pirated edition in Vienna is now "worming its way" into Berlin and that the best defense against it would be a pocket edition. Goethe clings to the negative attitude expressed in his letter of 17 March, the pocket edition would not be profitable for him and he could not see how the harm that threatened him could be averted. "How can my profit be linked to your own? I amaze myself when I use the word 'profit'; I paid no attention to it in my youth, little in my middle years and still do not know how to take hold of it. And yet I am forced to think of it if, after a trying and modest life, I am not to leave the stage burdened with debts. . . . I allowed myself to use it this time in order to convince you that my hesitation arises not because my views have changed but because my circumstances have."

A delicate situation. His contract with Goethe did give Cotta the right to issue a pocket edition, but he refrained from doing so, probably having in mind his experience that a publisher, even when he has good reasons, may not act contrary to the wishes of his author in matters of great importance. This was the end of the undertaking that saw Cotta's publication of the first complete edition of the works. On 12 November 1812 Goethe sent him a plan for a new edition that was to contain 21 volumes, but Cotta did not respond to the suggestion. He writes to Goethe on 6 December 1812, "Meanwhile before we attempt to publish this we shall have to await the end of the present conflict that is having a much too disadvantageous effect especially on this branch of business." Napoleon had penetrated deep into Russia. We know Goethe's response (14 November 1812 to Reinhard), "It means nothing to me that Moscow has been burned to the ground." But this was the beginning of the fall of Napoleon and his German auxiliary troops in Russia. Cotta was well advised to await developments.

Cotta and Goethe's   Two years earlier Goethe had acquainted Cotta with
"Subsidiary Works"   two undertakings that were of importance to him. He
   had invited Cotta to Jena, and the visit took place in
Knebel's house. Goethe first informed Cotta that he had, in accordance with

their agreement, sent the completed manuscript of the *Theory of Color* to the Karl Friedrich Ernst Frommann printing works in Jena, where it was printed and bound; the two volumes then appeared at the Easter Fair in 1810. Cotta had to "recognize with great gratitude that I am also the publisher of this work, unique of its kind," and he offered Goethe 1,200 thalers as a royalty. At the time Cotta could not know how right he was to be the publisher of "this work unique of its kind." Goethe regarded his treatise on light and color as an important part of his life's work, and yet he had to experience the fact that it was this above all that was to become his greatest disappointment, a disappointment he had to confront until his dying day. "I am not in the least conceited about anything I have achieved as a poet," but he had "put half a lifetime's effort into his *Theory of Color.*" But when Eckermann provoked him, in 1823, by remarking that Goethe alone stood by his theory, his rejoinder was "for the past twenty years the great Newton and all the mathematicians and exalted calculators with him were definitely in error as far as the theory of color goes and I alone, among millions, was the only one to know the rights of this great natural object? It is well known," he goes on, "that in order to be an epoch-maker in the world you need to know two things, first that you have a good head and secondly that you are creating a great heritage." His heritage, he opined, was Newton's error. Questions of science are always questions of human existence and its development; when Eckermann asked him in 1828 how, and for how long, this development was to extend, Goethe made his apocalyptic prognosis: "I see the time coming when God will no longer be pleased with it [humanity] and he will once again have to destroy everything for a rejuvenated creation. I am certain that everything is set up to that end and the time and the hour of this epoch of rejuvenation have been set down in the distant future." But, Goethe continued, in an especially good and exalted mood, "We could go on living on this dear old patch for thousand of years, just as it is, and have all sorts of fun." The documents on the effect of the *Theory of Color* are absolutely legion. The last significant work—that probably closes the discussion—is Albrecht Schöne's book of 1987 that interprets the "theory of color" as the "theology of color." Schöne takes the view that Goethe had written sentences of disturbing actuality. We "who were born later and who have become capable of destroying both nature and ourselves, will have to read this strange and objectionable work with new eyes—as though it were written for them and contained in its error an unhoped for truth."[4]

Although the problematic of the *Theory of Color* was unknown to Cotta, he spoke effusively of his visit on May 11 1810. He noted his "inmost thanks" for "the great pleasure" of "the pleasant evening in Jena" and the happiness of the "unforgettable hours spent with your Excellency in Jena."

The second project that Goethe presented to Cotta during his visit was "the important undertaking of an autobiography" that he intended to publish in two parts. Goethe had first mentioned his plan to write an autobiography to Schiller on 19 January 1802: "In the course of some reflections . . . it occurred to me what an interesting work you could write, if you were good-humoredly to record your experiences making use of the insights that the years afford you." On 26 February 1806 in the *Jena Allgemeine Literaturzeitung* he reviewed an anthology edited by S. M. Lowe, *Portraits of Berlin Scholars Alive at This Moment:* "The demands made of living scholars to write short autobiographies with a view to making a gift to the public is a very happy thought. . . . there are two ways of writing history, one for those who know and one for those who don't. . . . The second way is the one where we—even though we intend to present a great unity—are in duty bound to hand down individual events without ceasing." This seems to have been the program for *Literature and Truth.* As early as the time when he was preparing the first edition of his collected works for Cotta, Goethe had the impression that his productions were incomplete, provisional, even fragmentary and was for a long time reluctant to release the works to the printer. The destruction in Weimar in October 1806 after the battle of Jena was however the spur to overcoming his delays. He wrote to Cotta on 24 October 1806, "In that unhappy night, my papers were my greatest concern, and rightly so, for in other houses the plunderers handled them very badly and if they did not actually tear everything up they strewed them all over the place. After I have survived this epoch I shall be in all the greater hurry to get my manuscripts printed. I shall no longer delay; the easy-going hours in which we flattered ourselves with hopes of completing what we were attempting and of bringing to fruition what had only been planned are gone."

There is one more important statement from the year 1806. Earlier in the year he wrote, "after the great gap that Schiller's death made in my life, my attention has been drawn in a more lively fashion to the memory of the past, and I feel, in a way passionately, what a duty I have to preserve the memory of what seems to have been lost for ever."

So Goethe had the "greatest concern" for his work and for his state of health, and he regarded the end of the Holy Roman Empire of the German nation and the Napoleonic Wars as a historical turning point. He thought he recognized a change in public taste as it turned more and more to the Romantics, whose statements were alien to him. All this put increasing pressure on him to represent and historicize himself. In the fictional letter in the foreword to *Literature and Truth* Goethe also speaks of his new attitude towards the public: "For though, at an earlier age, we pursue our own course with passion, impatiently rejecting other people's claims to our attention for fear of being distracted, these claims prove to be most beneficial for us in our later years when a generous expression of interest may quicken us and stir us to new activity."

In the year 1807 Goethe was constantly regaling Riemer with accounts of experiences that he had had in his childhood and youth. He told stories of student pranks in Leipzig, he told others about "the golden age in Weimar," and on his return to Weimar from Jena in December he told Riemer, his traveling companion, "the story of his love for Lili Schönemann." But still Goethe did not get down to writing his autobiography. It is true that the first edition of his collected works was complete in 1808 and he began "to be historical to himself." *The Elective Affinities* was still not ready and he still had to work on his "main task," *The Theory of Color.* But as early as 11 October 1809 Goethe wrote, or rather dictated, a fragmentary scheme for his autobiography; he continued working on this until December 1809; it embraced the years 1742–1809; the first historical dates in it were for the coronation of Charles VII, in 1742; the final works mentioned in the scheme were "Pandora's Return"—Goethe's first festival play, *Pandora,* that appeared originally in the first two numbers of the journal *Prometheus* with the title of *Pandora's Return—The Elective Affinities* and the *History of the Theory of Color.*

That was the situation during Cotta's visit when Goethe told him about the projected autobiography. Cotta spontaneously declared himself ready to publish it. A year later they agreed upon the royalties, Goethe was to receive 1,500 Imperial thalers for every volume. Goethe had reacted particularly well to Cotta's visit and it proved an inspiration for the autobiography, for he wrote to him in May 1811: "My pleasure in continuing my biographical writings has increased since your visit. I hope, by means of these innocent confessions, to enter into new and lively contact with all those who wish me well and to revive and make interesting again—especially for my friends—

what up to now I have best been able to do and achieve." Immediately after Cotta's visit Goethe had, in fact, energetically taken up the idea of writing down his autobioigraphy. He made numerous notes about it in his diary. On 25 October 1810 he wrote to Bettine Brentano, "I want to confess to you that I am in the process of writing my confessions; it may be that a novel or a story will come out of this, we cannot foresee; but in any case I need your help. My dear mother and many others are dead who might have been able to recall for me the past that I have mostly forgotten. Now, you lived quite a time with my dear mother, you heard her stories and anecdotes over and over again and you carry and nurture everything fresh in your memory. So sit down at once and write down anything relating to me and my family and in doing so you will give me great pleasure and put me under an obligation to you." Thus Bettine was also a part of that "magic apparatus" of which Goethe had spoken in the annals of the year 1811— historical sources, reports, letters, diaries, and information from friends.

The collection of materials was completed in January 1811. But he was still working on the biography of Philipp Hackert; on Monday, 28 January, he arranged "the last third of Hackert's biography" (it appeared in 1811; "*Philipp Hackert.* Biographical sketch mostly on the basis of his own sketches, written by Goethe"). On Tuesday 29 January, there is an entry in his diary, "My own biography." On 2 April 1811 the autobiographical work was "read aloud to the ladies." In May 1811 the first part was completed and divided into books. The first book went to Frommann to be printed on 17 July; the remaining four books followed at short intervals until 7 September. As titles Riemer had suggested to Goethe, "From my Life" and "Truth and Literature." Goethe accepted them eagerly and called it "Literature and Truth," for "the sake of euphony, because in that combination two similar letters oppose each other and cohere." On 26 October the work appeared in Cotta's bookshop in Stuttgart in good time for the autumn fair; it was entitled "*From My Life. Literature and Truth. By Goethe, Part I.*" Cotta sent the 1,500 Reichsthalers royalty to Weimar in October.

A year later, a letter from Goethe arrived for Cotta. How he (Goethe) "wished the noble Schiller were still alive, he was a mediator in our affairs as dear as he was fortunate." "For my part I feel pain at having to discuss business matters with persons with whom you only wish to maintain an unsullied relationship. That was probably the reason why our last meeting left us both feeling dissatisfied and now I feel the need to make up for what

I did not reveal at that time." After this introduction, Goethe went on to say that it would only be possible for him to continue work on, and publish the second volume of, his autobiography if Cotta were to give him a royalty of 2,000 thalers for this volume and also pay him a further 500 for the first volume. "I am referring to everything I previously said about my position and I will only add that once again pressing circumstances cause me to hasten to make a declaration which I do with reluctance." Cotta fulfilled Goethe's wish. The latter sent his manuscript to Stuttgart at the end of 1812 and in this way the second volume could appear in time for the Easter Fair in 1813.

There is no record of whether Cotta read Goethe's statements about writing that come at the end of Part 2: "Writing is a misuse of language, reading silently to oneself a sad surrogate for speech. People exert all the effect they can on others by virtue of their personalities." True, Goethe immediately relativizes this harsh verdict,[5] but he came back to the thought in his preparations for the *West-East Divan,* where he writes his appreciation of ancient Persian poetry: "What importance the word had then, because it was the spoken word." Talking, speaking, telling, singing, and listening were always essential to the young Goethe as well as to the Goethe looking back at his youth.

Part 3 of *Literature and Truth* appeared in May 1814. And this part marked, for the time being, the completion of the autobiography, for Goethe now interrupted his self-historicizing for five years. Again a new work came to the forefront, *The West-East Divan,* and with it new personal experiences. But because, when depicting the Lili experience, he was reluctant to write highly personal details about Lili von Türkheim, who was still alive at the time (she died in May 1817), the continuation of the work was delayed. Instead he preferred working on the *Italian Journey,* which appeared in 1816/1817 in two volumes entitled "From My Life. Literature and Truth. By Goethe. Section 2, Parts 1 and 2. I too in Arcadia." It was not until the appearance of the second part, "The Second Roman Sojourn," in the final authorized edition of his works (1829) that the whole was entitled *Italian Journey.* Goethe now undertook the description of his later years in Weimar, but for this he chose the chronicle-like form of "annals." According to an advertisement for the final authorized edition, an autobiography was to be included that would assemble all the previous autobiographical works. But that did not happen. It was not until 1821, when the *Journeyman Years* had, at least for the time being, been completed that Goethe resumed work on

Literature and Truth. In February 1825 he resumed work on *Faust* and, until
the summer of 1831, this was the work that now became his chief concern.
He records in his diary in November 1830: "I was reading the third volume
of my life and undertook preliminary work on the fourth volume. I was in
the process of recalling conditions at that time and arranged the manuscript
in a new portfolio, so as to be able to see it better." On 3 March he again
began a "serious attack" on this work. He succeeded in doing this until 12
October 1831, and shortly before his death Goethe was able to complete, as
his last work, the story of his youth. The fourth part first appeared in 1833
in the eighth volume of the posthumous section of the final edition.

Excursus: Reflected in   If we survey the first ten years of the author-publisher
the Correspondence   relationship between Goethe and Cotta, we come
away with the impression of an extraordinarily fruitful
and solid association. Cotta had been a very close friend of Schiller, but with
Goethe the footing was more that of a partner. There was, it is true, a certain
distance resulting both from the admiration that Cotta felt for Goethe as an
author and from Goethe's social position. Both of them played a game, each
had his role—one the author, the other the publisher—and each respected
the other. Goethe demanded a lot, but never the impossible. Cotta was able
to fulfil his demands—in spite of the problems that faced book production
and the book trade at the time—more easily than he sometimes asserted.
Thanks to Goethe and Schiller he was able to create a magnificent publishing
program. The most important authors of the time were published by his
firm: Herder, Hölderlin, Wieland, Jean Paul, Schelling, Fichte, and others.
Cotta was *the* publisher of "Modern Classics" in those years. Goethe was
sure of his position and of himself. Cotta's suggestion that he might leave
publishing if he could no longer take care of Goethe's works would certainly
have been unpleasant for Goethe, but not a threat to his existence. All of
this lent sovereignty and calm to their communications. It is not as though
the correspondence between the two was simply a collection of business
letters. One critic's judgment was that the letters are not entertaining; only
in exceptional cases was there a literary brilliance about them. They signified
the end of a "lovingly nurtured legend" of the German book trade, the
legend that "two princes of their respective disciplines faced each other as
equal partners." Cotta, according to this critic,[6] was always for Goethe "just

a business partner and never an interlocutor, and what the German book trade celebrated as their much vaunted cooperation was only possible because the publisher did everything the author asked." If this was the case it was not such a bad position for a publisher to be in! But even the most experienced publisher can only fulfill an author's wishes to their mutual advantage if he is in agreement with him, his work and its challenges; even if he does not exactly approve of the works' perhaps offensive innovations, idiosyncrasies, sensitivities, judgments, and prejudices, he at least understands them and can take responsibility for them. And the author too must have understanding—even if he does not agree with it—for what the publisher stands for as far as the group of authors created by the publisher is concerned. For me the letters have the sheen of immediacy, the concrete, the authentic; given the unique phenomenon of Goethe, who was conscious of his uniqueness and made use of it, there is simply no question of intellectual equality.

In any case Cotta was an important correspondent for Goethe to have. The correspondence bears witness to this in that, time and again, it goes beyond mere matters of publishing to treat topical themes and problems and also contains reports of important happenings. I would like to emphasize three such events.

Napoleon: "The   Goethe did not talk about Napoleon very often, not
greatest phenomenon even about his personal meeting with him; his reports
that was possible   always contain elements of the mysterious. But there
in history"   is no portrayal as clear as the one he gave Cotta.

Goethe met Napoleon in Erfurt in 1808. It was there, from 27 September to 14 October, that Napoleon had gathered around him Czar Alexander I and the kings—appointed by his favor—of Saxony, Bavaria, Würtemberg, and Westphalia, the princes of the Rhenish Alliance and the brother of the King of Prussia. Napoleon held court in the truest sense of the word and was carrying on realpolitik at the same time. German intellectuals hailed him; Kassel was to become a new German capital. Johannes von Müller welcomed the plan, he himself was to write the standard work on Napoleon; Jakob Grimm was designated librarian in Kassel and Beethoven the musical director, but the Viennese prevented this (they were willing to give Beethoven a pension for life if he remained in Vienna).

Carl August, who knew at the time that the independence of his duchy was hanging on a silken thread, wanted as impressive a representation of his territory as possible in Erfurt and so he asked Goethe to be present. Napoleon gave Goethe an audience on 2 October in his headquarters. According to Goethe's entries in his diary he scarcely seemed interested in meeting Napoleon at the time. His chief wish was to stay with "Serenissimo," the crown prince, the hereditary duke who after the fall of Napoleon became the archduke, and with whom Goethe had been close friends since his youth. Goethe notes: "2 [October. Erfurt] To the levée. Afterwards with the Emperor."—and that is the end of the entry. The conversation—carried on in French—lasted scarcely an hour; biographers and scholars have collected what little authentic material there is. What we know for certain is that Napoleon greeted him with the words "Voilà un homme"—these were "the emperor's wonderful words with which he received me" as Goethe told Reinhard on 14 November 1808. Napoleon invited him to Paris, and the thought of a journey to Paris occupied Goethe for a long time. Otherwise he said nothing at that time about the meeting. Chancellor von Müller reported this in his memoirs: "For a long time, *Goethe* observed a deep silence about what happened in the audience, whether because it was completely characteristic of him not to speak lightly of happenings that were important and personal to him or whether from modesty and delicacy. But you could soon tell that *Napoleon's* statement had made a great impression on him, although he knew how to avoid, in very clever fashion, the Duke's [Carl August] questions as to the content of the conversation." There can be no question of Goethe's being deeply impressed. The admiration that he already felt was given a new basis, and his assessment of Napoleon, in a letter, as the "greatest phenomenon that was possible in history" was confirmed. As far as he was concerned, Napoleon was simply an incorporation of the dæmonic, which was, in Goethe's view, a combination of genius and productivity.

To translate the word "genius" as "dæmon" when referring to Napoleon is a bold stroke, but perhaps every genius who acts politically and leaves his trace and impact upon the centuries is a dæmon. What Goethe stated in retrospect in 1829 is precisely what he would have felt in 1808: "Thus I cannot resist the thought that in order to tease humanity and to fool it dæmons also come up with individual figures who are so attractive that everyone strives to emulate them, and so great that they are inaccessible." In this connection Goethe adduced Raphael, Mozart, and Shakespeare and mentioned their "great innate quality": "And so Napoleon stands there inaccessible."

On 14 October Goethe received the Croix de la légion d'honneur. He always wore the order on official occasions and did not discard it even after Napoleon had been defeated and exiled; when friends drew his attention to this, Goethe cried spontaneously, "What would you have? I didn't write my love songs and my *Werther* a second time either." Napoleon was for Goethe *the* challenge. Napoleon was "inaccessible," "incomparable," and Goethe saw it as his task to stand by him. It was to Cotta of all people that he confided the details of this, for him, so important experience. It was important for Cotta to know how much Napoleon valued Goethe, and this was the way in which Napoleon's verdict was to be made public, since Goethe spoke of "many friends" who were sympathetic. "I was convinced that so many of my friends, and especially you, would take a lively interest in all the good things that happen to me: and I will gladly acknowledge that, in my whole life, nothing loftier or more pleasing could have happened to me than to stand before the French emperor and in such a way. Without going into details of the conversation, I can say that a person of rank has never received me in such a manner, in that he, if I may use the expression, treated me as an equal and clearly expressed the view that I was an appropriate interlocutor."

Nowhere else, and never again, did Goethe ever express himself so emphatically about Napoleon and about Napoleon's attitude towards him and never again did he compare his work and himself with that incomparable person. Goethe had to suffer criticism from those who saw in Napoleon only the conqueror and the tyrant from whom it was their duty to free themselves. He defended himself against those who lamented, who complained about something "that no one in Germany had seen in his whole life, much less concerned himself with." The jingoistic emphasis upon things German that developed during the so-called wars for freedom was repellent to him; to him this was all provincialism. Later, it is true, he expressed himself more positively about "his Germans'" will to self-assertion and in his notes to *The Awakening of Epimedes* practiced a sort of self-criticism of his previous admiration for Napoleon.

Christiane, "my dear little friend" It is understandable that Goethe's relationship to Christiane Vulpius, who was later to become his wife, was too spectacular to be kept from the public as a purely private matter. Even today his biographers mention 12 July 1788 as the date of Goethe's first meeting with the twenty-three-year old and simultaneously as the date of their first physical union.[7] But otherwise this relationship is still a touchy business for biographers. In patronizing fashion they allow the Olympian a fling—the price of genius must be paid. In my opinion it is Goethe himself who is in large measure responsible for this misjudgment. He had the right to conceal his "domestic sweetheart," to keep her for himself and remove her from the public gaze, but then he himself made some very strange remarks about the relationship. First of all he concealed it from Frau von Stein for more than a year. When she did find out about it on 8 June 1789 through her son Fritz, Goethe's pupil, she broke off all relations with him. Charlotte von Stein was deeply angered and doubly enraged at Goethe's reaction to her: "And what sort of a relationship is it? Who is diminished by it? Who lays claim to the feelings that I grant the poor creature?" "The poor creature," "the dear little one," "my little friend," "the little child of Nature," these are the words Goethe used to his contemporaries and to posterity about the disrespectful way in which people sized up Christiane, and they are words susceptible of misunderstanding.

Weimar society really felt that the "housekeeper" was a nonperson. Goethe's friends shared his silence and even Schiller simply did not acknowledge Christiane. There is no doubt that this "poor creature" loved Goethe, that he was everything to her. They lived together for twenty-eight years, she bore him five children, and for her whole life she was—as she characterized herself—a true domestic treasure for her "dear Privy Councillor." Goethe, too, was very satisfied with the measure of her domesticity, the way she preserved his privacy, the way she cared for him and served him, but also with her tenderness and sensuality. Did he show her adequately how satisfied he was? Whatever the truth, Christiane suffered because she knew what society said about her, that she was unworthy, stupid, loud-mouthed—a drinker—to whom Goethe had attached himself. She also suffered under Goethe's relationships with other women, under the news that spilled over from Carlsbad and Jena to Weimar, and she was in no position to know that most of these affairs were platonic. "What do you want with all the things you look at. It's too much. But do not forget me your oldest love, and I beg you, think of yourself sometimes, meanwhile I shall trust you completely, let people say what they will. For you alone are the one who thinks of me"—this is what Christiane wrote in one of her letters.

The relationship became a scandal (at least temporarily), when Goethe surprised everyone by marrying Christiane. But let us recall Goethe's situation. There was a war on, and as a Prussian general Carl August had to mobilize his forces. However, on 14 October, Napoleon totally defeated the Prussian armies on Weimar territory at the battles of Jena and Auerstädt. Goethe's view of the day is recorded in his diary: "Early cannonade at Jena, after that a battle at Kötschau. Rout of the Prussians. At 5 o'clock in the evening cannon balls were flying through the roofs. At 5:30 entry of the chasseurs. 7 fire, looting, terrible night. Preservation of our house by fortitude and good fortune." He reported the happenings to Cotta over and over again. Anyone who opposed the looters was severely punished. Charlotte von Stein hid the severely wounded General von Schmettau, and her house was completely devastated. The house of Goethe's future brother-in-law, Vulpius, was looted. Rampaging hussars forced their way into Goethe's house during the night and threatened to knock him down. Riemer reports that Christiane faced up to the marauders resolutely, forced them out, and barred the door.

Something else happened on that 16 October. The privy council of Weimar, to which Goethe belonged, asked for an audience with Napoleon in the castle, to petition him to stop the looting and preserve the state of Saxon-Weimar. At the last minute Goethe begged to be excused—an astonishing move in a matter that was so important to the existence of his country—on the grounds of ill health. However, Goethe may not have had a good conscience at not being available in a matter of this sort. Later on he reacted in his own way when he met the inspector-general of French museums who had been appointed by Napoleon to requisition art treasures from the conquered lands for Paris. Goethe succeeded in protecting Weimar and Jena from what was probably the greatest art robbery of the time.

Fear for his life, "the greatest concern," "sympathy for friends' catastrophes," "times of testing," feelings of failure as a statesman, complete disorientation, uncertainty about the future of the structure of the Weimar state, uncertainty about the future as a whole, fear that his writing and his influence could now be at an end—those were the existential despairs that Goethe felt at this time. He had only one prop, his life's companion, Christiane; she was his "savior," she was active, cared for him, and also helped his friends who had been victims of the looters. For Goethe, who felt these days to be fatal, she was a picture of the vitally active. On Friday 17 October he wrote to the head of the consistory:

An old intention of mine has matured in these days and nights, I wish to recognize as my own, totally and officially, my little friend who has done so much for me and who has shared these hours of testing with me.

Tell me, esteemed sir and father how to go about our being married on Sunday or before. . . . Could you not perform the act yourself, I would like it to take place in the sacristy of the state church.

Goethe and Christiane were married there on Sunday, 19 October 1806. At first the news attracted attention only in Weimar. Charlotte von Stein, who had been hard hit by the looters, immediately voiced her mortification. "Schillers have lost but a little, Goethe nothing at all . . . and while the looting was taking place he was married publicly to his mistress in the church, and this was its last ecclesiastical act as all our churches are now field hospitals and ammunition dumps." The women of Weimar were beside themselves at Goethe's marriage to this unworthy person, and the malicious gossip about the allegedly stupid and alcoholic, common and loud-mouthed Christiane became outspoken. Charlotte von Schiller said derisively that Goethe had now got his "bigger half"; another woman observed in a letter, "Goethe said [with reference to the marriage] that in times of peace you may be able to ignore the law, but in times like the present it must be honored." Was he really concerned about honoring the law at this time? It is certainly characteristic of him that at the moment when all the conventions were falling apart, he would set an example of the conventional. Perhaps he also thought that this unusual marriage would be less noticeable and less falsely judged in times like those. But his main motive was certainly his thankfulness to Christiane; she had served him for twenty-eight years and had risked her life for him. He must have been concerned at that moment in making Christiane's and his son's existence secure by legalizing their relationship. Yet he must, in spite of everything, have been afraid. But why did Goethe have the date 14 October engraved on the wedding rings? It was Shakespeare's birthday and the date of the battle of Jena. Jena was not just a battle. Goethe foresaw the consequences: the possible dissolution of the Electorate of Saxony, the end of fortifications, desertion to the enemy, the sacrifice of political and moral positions. Napoleon "the dæmon" was ruling. As far as he was concerned a new epoch in his life began on the day he was married, and he described the time before this as his "antediluvian age."

We can understand Goethe's anger when he read the following announcement in Cotta's *Allegmeine Zeitung* a few weeks after his wedding, on 24 November 1806: "Weimar, 6 November. To the thunder of cannons, Goethe married his long-time housekeeper, Mlle Vulpius, and so she alone made a direct hit while thousands of other shots were misses. Only the uninformed can smile at this. It was very good of Goethe who does nothing in the usual way." There was another load of gossip purveyed in the *Allgemeine Zeitung* of 18 December. This time the target was Goethe's brother-in-law, Vulpius, and Johannes Daniel Falk, a writer, who had been living in Weimar since 1797, had had some slight contact with Goethe, and who left behind a work entitled "Goethe: A View from Closer Personal Contact."

Goethe was outraged. He dictated a letter on Christmas Day. He wrote about "the malicious way in which Vulpius and Christian Gottlob Voigt had been treated in the article"; it was "disgusting" if the "most vulgar gossip . . . is thrown back at us from the burning glass of a newspaper in Ulm." He asked Cotta to stop sending him the newspaper in the following year. In a masterly few sentences, Goethe summed up this letter that was never mailed, in a further letter to Cotta on the following day, "Yesterday, I dictated," Goethe wrote, "a long letter to you, most esteemed Herr Cotta, which I am however keeping, because it is not good to expatiate on unpleasant things. I just want to draw your attention to a few things, the way in which for some time *Weimar,* its conditions, its nobility, its private inhabitants have been improperly and indecently treated; 352 of them can bear witness to this. If you consider the good things that we have planned to be important, if you sense the beauty of our relationship in its totality, then you will put a stop to this gossip, which could very soon terminate a mutual trust. No more! G."

Cotta had also been surprised by the announcement in his newspaper, and he had almost had a "stroke" when he read the "infamous notice" in the *Allgemeine Zeitung* that had been accepted by the editor through some "incomprehensible blunder." True, Goethe's letter had been a personal insult. Cotta wrote a lengthy letter to him on 9 January 1807 in which he says, among other things,

> But nothing, nothing caused me such pain and disturbed me so much as that crazily misinformed piece of news about Weimar—and now there is added to this pain and disturbance an inner sorrow caused by

your letter. I am speaking now as one person to another, as one man to another—you did not spare me in the writing of it; for I am innocent and in the long years that I have had the fortune to be known to you, nothing can have taken place in which you could not recognize in me a deep admirer, a man of deep sensibility and one who was inmostly devoted to you. If instead of writing, "If you sense the beauty of our relationship," you had said, "since you . . . feel . . . ," then the terribly unpleasant nature of this business would have been nicely mitigated for me by your true estimate of me; now I am not only angry but sad as well.

Cotta's behavior in all this was inept. A publisher is simply never "innocent"; he must take responsibility for whatever appears under his imprint. Goethe, who in spite of everything did not want to interfere with the processes involved in the production of his works, made a concession in his letter of 23 January, "If there was, for you too, something unpleasant in my letter, ascribe it to our position not to my attitudes. To be downtrodden by Prussians, plundered by the French, and despised by South Germans and all that in the space of about fourteen days was a pretty tough test. Let us hope that when we meet again in happier circumstances we can talk about all this evil as though it were in the past." But he could not stop airing his complaint. He wrote to Cotta on 24 January, "it is really sad that in times of such great suffering evil is increased by those who simply relate it, but who should not mention it. But the nature of the daily newspaper is such that nothing good can be expected from it any longer. Forgive me for complaining again; but I could not avoid this obligation and please remain assured of my old unchangeable point of view." As we mentioned, work on the edition continued in spite of this serious difference, even if Goethe did remain prickly on the subject.

One thing is certain: Goethe did not protect Christiane enough throughout the whole business. When her brother told her of the latest piece of malice she turned to Goethe in Jena and he calmed her down, writing on 2 July 1808, "The fact that they have said bad things about you in Weimar is something that you must not fight. This is simply the way things are in the world, no one likes to cede advantages to the other person, whatever form they may take, and since they cannot be taken away they are minimized or denied, or simply contradicted. Therefore, enjoy what good fortune has given you and what you have acquired and try to hold on to it. We shall persist in our love and arrange things ever more simply and better, so that we can live according to our own lights and without bothering about other people."

Goethe again reacted completely in his own fashion. He accepted the advantages that Christiane offered him, he needed them for the type of life he led. He swept aside the rumors, the mutterings of society, and clung to the relationship without any doubts at all—this was his contribution. And Christiane now entered his poetic household. He had remembered her early on in the *Roman Elegies*. In 1798 he honored her with the poem "The Metamorphosis of Plants." Many of the Christiane-poems, "The Visit," "Morning Plaints," "The Happy Spouses," embed his attraction to her in this "higher world." On the twenty-fifth anniversary of their meeting—on their informal silver wedding day, that is—Goethe, who was away on a journey at the time, sent her the poem "Found": "I saw in the shadow / a little flower / sparkling like stars / beautiful as little eyes." The letter was addressed to Frau von Goethe and dated 26 August 1813. The "I" transplants this little flower into the garden of the beautiful house, "now it is always sending out shoots / and thus it goes on blooming." And shortly before this he had written the poem "Birds of Feather": The flower was "blooming in charming fashion / a bee came to it and nibbled gently; / they must both exist / for one another." Goethe not only preserved Christiane in his poetry, there are also several drawings of her—mainly in the first two decades of their relationship—that Goethe did not complete. Most of them are stylized in an old-fashioned manner, the artist trying to create an ideal that goes beyond the likeness.

Much in Goethe's relationship to Christiane remains a typically Goethean secret. It was not to be "found out." But greater justice was to be paid to the relationship. There is no doubt that the years during which the relationship lasted meant more to Goethe than is apparent from immediate sources. For me one example of this is Goethe's poem "Diary" from the year 1810, in which the "mistress" is sovereign over his sensual life.

Yet, again and again, we marvel at how little Goethe protected Christiane. On 13 September 1811 Christiane von Goethe and Bettine von Arnim went to an art exhibition together; the exhibition had been arranged by Goethe's adviser in artistic matters, Johann Heinrich Meyer, and Bettine spoke slightingly of him. Christiane thought that her former housemate had been insulted and responded in a loud voice. There is no record of how far the argument went or whether they actually came to blows. In any case Bettine's glasses were broken. The women of Weimar enjoyed a scandal about Goethe's "bigger half" and it was reported that Bettine "told the whole of Weimar that a blood suasage had gone mad and had bitten her . . . and really the Goethe woman looked like nothing so much as a blood sausage." Goethe finally reacted to this and forbade the Arnims his house.

Perhaps he should have acted more decisively earlier. He cried "No further!" to Cotta; in the letter that he did not send to him, Goethe "reproaches himself for having passed over some unpleasantness on an earlier occasion: I am annoyed with myself, not for saying it now, but for not having drawn your attention to it earlier."

When Goethe made Christiane the wife of a privy councillor, she was already in her forties. Goethe felt forced to do what he had up till then avoided, which was to criticize Christiane's peculiarities, but on the other hand he helped her by appointing Caroline Ulrich as her companion and chaperon. "Uli" was experienced in the ways of society and was in a position to shelter Christiane from at least the harshest reproaches. True, the marriage became increasingly the product of Goethe's art of living. He left Weimar more and more frequently to go to Jena, to take the waters, to travel. Whenever they met in the final years of their life together it seemed as though a deeper relationship was at an end. While Goethe was staying in Frankfurt that summer he wrote Christiane reports of his meeting with Marianne Willemer, daughter of the family in whose house he was a guest. They are letters that were kept strictly personal. But did Goethe really miss Christiane? And what must his servant Carl Stadelmann have thought when Goethe dictated such letters to him? Christiane, too, no longer answered in her own hand but left it to her companion, Uli. Goethe remained for Christiane the "dear Privy Councillor," and the two of them together played the "parts" of privy councillor and privy councillor's wife.

On 22 May 1816, two weeks before her death, Christiane wrote Goethe a letter that ends with the words, "Farewell, remember me." The postscript that she added reveals her concern for her "dear Privy Councillor." "At this time there is no *champagne* to be found in our cellar, Ramman did not send me any. I am sending 2 bottles of *Wertheimer* along with this."

After a long illness and terrible death throes, Christiane died on 6 June 1816 about midday. Goethe's diary for the day reads: "Slept well. . . . Approaching death of my wife. . . . The last terrible struggle in her nature. She died towards midday. Emptiness and the silence of death inside and outside me. Arrival of the festive procession of Princess Ida and Bernhard . . . evening brilliant illumination of the town. My wife taken to the mortuary around midnight. I spent the whole day in bed." On 8 June he records, "My wife buried at 4 in the morning." Both of these entries appear to be strange enough; on the one hand, "emptiness and the silence of death"; this was the day he wrote the quatrain "O, sun you try in vain / to shine through the gloomy clouds / The whole harvest of my life / is to weep for her loss" and, to Sulpice Boisserée (24 June 1816), "my condition borders on . . . despair"; on the other hand, on the same day he mentions the festive entry of Princess Ida of Saxe-Meiningen and her husband, and in addition he was impressed by the "brilliant illumination of the town." At this time Goethe was working on the *West–East Divan* and his thoughts may have been with Marianne Willemer and that very strange relationship. He had always felt at home with Christiane's naturalness. Even if there were internal and external distances in their marriage, it did last for twenty-eight years. We are generally only aware of the facade of a marriage, but their correspondence does set a tone of married closeness.

Few people were concerned about Christiane's death. But an exchange of correspondence between two ladies acquainted with her is significant. "It offends me," said one writer "that no one thinks of her death with sympathy, that everything—the many good things that formed part of her—is forgotten and people only mention her faults, even those people to whom she was good and who heaped flattery on her while she was alive." Her friend replied, "What I found pleasant about the dead woman is that she would never listen when people said nasty things about others; and her conversation, to the extent that I knew her, was always such that I found it easy to explain why her unpretentious, happy, utterly natural mind could interest our Goethe, who presented his wife to me with the words: 'the woman who comes with the recommendation that since she first set foot in my house, I have nothing but joy to thank her for.' "

For twenty-eight years he had her to thank for pleasures and joy—certainly a long time in the life of a person. For twenty-eight years she made it possible for him to lead his life the way he wanted. The house on the Frauenplan had been Goethe's productive and comfortable dwelling and workplace.

Goethe as   Cotta, too, just as publishers do today, tried to dis-
Publisher's Reader cover authors by means of competitions. On 2 January
            1807, competitions sponsored by the firm of Cotta
were announced in the *Morgenblatt.* A prize of 50 ducats was offered for
"The best satire in rhymed verses on Egoism"; for "the best tragedy," 200
ducats as a first prize and 50 as a second; for the "best comedy," as much
as 300 ducats for the first prize and 75 for the second. The different commercial value of the different genres is interesting: for a satire with a prescribed
subject, the lowest prize; a comedy with its value as entertainment gets a
higher prize than a tragedy. Cotta was very concerned that there should be
a lot of publicity, and as a result the judges were to enjoy the highest possible
public authority and were to be named when the prizes were awarded. On
20 August 1808 he set his sights on the highest of all and asked Goethe:
"Several tragedies have been submitted to the editor of the *Morgenblatt* in
the prize competition, among which there are two or three of outstanding
merit; might I have the audacity to send them to your honor for a decision?"
Astonishingly, Goethe agreed. "If you like to send me the tragedies, I will
give you my honest opinion about them."

Several satires were entered in the competition, but Georg Reinbeck, the
editor of the *Morgenblatt,* did not think they merited a prize. In the case of
the tragedies the harvest was also rather poor; however, a second prize was
awarded. Reinbeck had selected four tragedies that were now to be sent to
the "competent judge" Goethe. The editor recommended that Cotta publish
these works; they were, he said, "a pleasing phenomenon in our literature."

Goethe's judgment, given on 14 November 1808, is once again "laconic,
precise, succinct": "I immediately read through the four tragedies that you
sent me and I can, as you can probably imagine [a wonderful *captatio benevo-
lentiae,* since Cotta had after all written of the 'outstanding value' of the
plays] say little that is cheering: I well understand that there is a form of
mild criticism that may apply to things of this sort and evaluate them courte-
ously, but for me they do not exist and had such manuscripts come into my
hands by chance I would have set them aside after reading the first few
pages." And he continues, "In all of the four plays that are presently under
discussion, there is the least possible trace of vigorous sensuality, flourishing
imagination, uplift of heart and soul and of much else that belongs to literature." He hopes that his remarks will not be used publicly—"Why should
we be cruel to the mediocre?"—and thus he refuses to have his opinions

published, as the *Morgenblatt* had promised. Reinbeck, the editor, did not agree with Goethe's verdict: "it was obviously one-sided," he is not "able to trust Goethe's verdict completely," "there is an injustice at work here," and finally "The results will show that these four plays will not go unheeded in our literature." Well, they did remain unheeded; the editor was wrong, Goethe was right. The *Morgenblatt* announced the results as follows: "In spite of the unmistakable and praiseworthy efforts of the authors and despite many beautiful details none of these four tragedies has the right to lay claim to an important place in our dramatic literature. Most of them lack—even though there is a praiseworthy regularity and simplicity—that Promethean spark, that depth of feeling with which alone a work of art breathes life."

It was the only time that Cotta tried to use Goethe more or less as a reader. Goethe then goes on to say something in his letter to Cotta that, for me at least, is important, essential: "For while true works of art bring their own theory along with them and provide us with the measure by which they should be judged, in the case of such stumbling attempts of half-trained dilettantes it would be necessary to set up a theoretical model, against which their inadmissibility would soon be revealed." Once more he stated his "conviction," "that not one of these entries was worthy of any sort of prize, for if we want to we can label them all absurd from the dramatic, theatrical, and tragic point of view."

The standard for judging a manuscript lay, then, in itself, because every literary work contains its own theory. An astonishing verdict from the point of view of the theory of art![8] Goethe's statements to Cotta in his function as reader, critic, or judge refer implicitly to his own theory of art. Goethe never developed an aesthetic theory of this sort or even a "theoretical model" discursively and abstractly. "What the poetic spirit creates," Goethe said, "must be received by a poetic nature. A cold analytical approach destroys literature and does not create reality. Only shards remain that serve no purpose and are only inconveniences." Kant's *Critique of Judgment* appeared in 1790. Its inexorability stimulated people's feelings, Schiller praised it, Herder and Wieland rejected it, Goethe refused to accept it. In art people must *feel,* they may not be limited by reason and learning. Goethe speaks of the prince in *Werther:* "He also values my (Werther's) mind, my talents more than this heart, but that is my only pride, that alone is the source of everything, all power, all happiness and all misery. Oh, what I know, everyone can know—I alone have my heart." And yet, Goethe's statements about art, literature, and aesthetics run through his most diverse writings in the wide variety of his areas of work, from the theory of color through the fine arts and his belletristic prose to, of course, his explicitly critical works. His literary prose in particular reveals a multitude of aesthetic statements that also lay the foundations of literature. Goethe's reflections on art have an enormous effect in spite of—or perhaps because of—their only being able to be arrived at inductively; we recall the repeated efforts of literary historians to discover a theory of literary genres. In view of the cosmos that Goethe's reflections on art open up to us, some limitation is in order. This is the place to cast an eye on those elements of his thoughts on the theory of art that are illuminated by his "reader's recommendation" for Cotta.

Goethe's hostile stance towards the purely rational Enlightenment and towards every form of regular poetics—characteristic of all his work—leads to a wide-ranging determination of the basic function of all art. In the epistolary narrative—all too frequently and unjustly overlooked—entitled *The Collector and His Family* (1788/1789) we read (in the eighth letter), "True art can only derive from an inner link between playfulness and seriousness." In the sixth letter the truth of art is also mentioned: "and yet there is a common point in which the effect of all arts, literary or fine arts, meet, from which all their laws emanate—and this is?—human feelings." And to forestall any attempt to reduce man to mere rational activity, Goethe adds: "But the human being is not just a thinking being, he is at the same time a feeling one. He is a whole, a unit of diverse forces that are inwardly connected, and the work of art must speak to this rich unity, correspond to this diversity within him." In order to explain this aspect of the effect of the work of art he appends to the passage that we have cited a sketch of an ideally typical way in which every successful work of art comes about: art starts out with an artist's particular, unique experience. If the artist were to confine himself to the reproduction of these externals, his work would be mere repetition. If the artist abstracted from the individual and aimed at the representation of the generic concept, then all he would produce would be a scholarly essay. If he strove, by going beyond this, for the ideal of all genres, for the absolute that manifests itself in that ideal, then he is and remains a philosopher. A successful work of art can be produced only when the artist, having passed through all these stages, represents all the foregoing aspects on the basis of a unique experience and refers them all back to it. For this cycle to be made apparent through the individual work, it has need of the beautiful. "The human spirit finds itself in a magnificent position when it reveres, when it worships, when it elevates a subject and is elevated by it. But it must not remain in this situation for long; the concept of genre leaves it cold, the ideal elevates it above itself, but now it wishes to go back into itself once more, it would like to enjoy the earlier attraction that it had felt towards the individual, without returning to the individual's narrowness; at the same time, it does not wish to relinquish the significant, that which lifts up the spirit. What would become of it in this state, if beauty were not to enter into it and solve the riddle favorably! A beautiful work of art has gone through the whole cycle, it is now once more a sort of individual that we embrace with a taste for it, that we can make into our own."

Against the background of this understanding of the origin and effect of art, Goethe is able to typify different modes of failing to achieve the ideal—and possibly the authors of the manuscripts that were criticized negatively by him can be put into one of these categories; imitators miss the truth that is inherent in art, since they confine themselves to the reproduction of reality, while others divorce themselves entirely from experience and rely entirely on their imagination. Some writers take no account of the individual but aim solely for the general, whereas others consider that the general can be represented in any form whatever. Minor artists are unable to create a whole because they are too steeped in detail, while those who write sketches do, it is true, unfold the context in fits and starts, but can never carry it out to the end in concrete form.

This normative model seems at first sight to contradict Goethe's statement that "genuine works of art contain their own theory." But this apparent contradiction can be resolved if the forces involved in the creation and the effect of the work of art that have just been elaborated are seen in relation to one another. The work of art must affect the individual as unity in diversity; the artist starts off on the basis of his experience and this leads cyclically through the general back to the particular. This is made possible only by means of the creation of artistic beauty. Thus, for Goethe, experience is the origin of every work of art, but he does not understand experience as something that takes place passively; it is something active. Experience is produced by the artist, brought forth, created. The origin of art determines its relationship to external nature, to its object. The experience produced by the artist has the effect "of enabling him to penetrate not only into the depths of objects but also into the depths of his own spirit, so that he produces in his works something that is not just simple and superficial but is also, in competition with Nature, something that is spiritual and organic and enables him to furnish his work with a content and a form whereby it can appear at one and the same time as something natural and supernatural." Art is thus determined by its intellectual-organic character and the indissoluble and mutual penetration of form and content. For Goethe form and content are not polar opposites; they are different aspects of a single "artistic truth." Nothing that is experienced, no material, is without form, just as every material has a form within itself. While the artist in his work of art works out the inner form of the experience created by him and, in so doing, gives the inner form of his experience a general form, he creates the content of the work which, because it rests upon a particular experience, is individual, but is nevertheless general because of its inner form. Thus, art must proceed from the experience of nature, but must mediate this experience through the work of art. Consequently, Goethe can say, "Poetry points to the secrets of Nature and tries to solve them by images." Three aspects of the metamorphosis that is brought about by the work of art can be distinguished: truth, beauty, and perfection. Truth denotes the force of the transformation that makes clear the necessary relationship of the individual to the general. Beauty denotes the sensually perceptible quality of the work of art, the creation of the picture. Perfection denotes the correspondence of inner and outer form.

The organic coherence of the work of art is determined in these aspects by the power of the "artistically true" in the Goethean sense; the individual thing (the experience produced by the artist) simultaneously contains the whole because of its inner form. And the whole is only recognizable as the whole because it rests upon the conception of the individual thing with respect to coherence. Consequently, every work of art—assuming that we are dealing with a true work of art—is the unity of the general and the particular in an individual unity. Seen as a whole every individual work of art is thus a symbol, of whose power Goethe says: "Symbolism changes the phenomenon into an idea, the idea into an image, and in such a way that the idea in the image remains infinitely effective and unattainable and, even if expressed in all languages, would remain inexpressible."

In order for a work of art to become a symbol, we demand that the artist create his own style. Style is for Goethe the highest mark of art. "The result of a genuine method is called style, in contrast to manner. Style raises the individual to the highest point that the genre is capable of attaining; for this reason all great [(!] artists draw near to one another in their best works." And, "It is simply important for us to hold the word style in the highest honor, so that we are left with an expression with which to designate the highest level that art has ever reached and ever can reach." In *Truth and Method* Hans-Georg Gadamer has given an impressive description of the significance of the concept of style for Goethe's view of art: "An artist creates a style for himself to the extent that he is no longer lovingly imitating, but is creating a language for himself at the same time. Although he binds himself to the given phenomenon, this does not fetter him, it is a way in which he can express himself. As infrequent as the agreement between 'true imitation' and individual manner (the way he conceives things) may be it is precisely this that constitutes style."

This short illumination of Goethe's theory of art makes clear that there is a strict difference between it and any sort of regulated poetics and aesthetics. An individual work of art cannot be understood in relation to the circumstances of its creation, nor in its relation to a literary tradition, nor in relation to other works of the same artist, and in no circumstances by rules or, to use Goethe's word, "laws," that exist outside itself. Rather the artist endows his work—when he creates a symbol out of it by means of his style—with his own principles that are valid for this one work, laws that are valid only in this one case. It becomes understandable and susceptible of criticism only when the reader has grasped the inner form of the symbol and can relate the particular and the general, the idea and the concept, to one another.

As a result, Goethe's comment to Cotta—put most succinctly—contains the fundamental principles of his aesthetics. It is only the immersion in the individual work of art and the acceptance of its structure, without any prejudice, that is the measure of this criticism.

For me, a yardstick of this sort that holds that the individual work of art must be judged from within itself, is of great importance. How could and how can a publisher, like a publisher's reader, evaluate the manuscripts that he receives every day? What standards are to be applied? The question most frequently asked of me by the public runs: "What criteria do you employ to evaluate the manuscripts that are offered to you; is there an objective standard by which the works of all writers, young and unknown and older and prominent, can be measured?" I often have to disappoint the questioners with the answer that there is no standard that can be imposed from outside, there cannot be. The decisive criteria, as I have said on innumerable occasions, are the ones inherent in the manuscript itself (or ones that are not inherent in it), substance and quality, the substance of the experiences, personal observations, and feelings that the author communicates to his reader and makes his own through the quality of his language and form.

I am now able to substantiate my own personal attitude by quoting Goethe's view, according to which the essentials are "vigorous sensuality, flourishing imagination, the uplifting of heart and spirit" and also at the same time the formal ability to turn these into literary forms.

The Second Complete Edition

"The Fate of   GOETHE HAD WRITTEN to Cotta on 12 November 1812
the Germans"—   suggesting a new edition of his works. Cotta had put
November 1812 to   off making a decision about this until the end of hos-
December 1814   tilities which, as he said, "were having a most disadvantageous effect on this branch of commerce." In
the meantime, in another letter to Cotta dated 7 February 1814, Goethe had
said that "he had undertaken the editing and revision of his works" as his
winter's work; "a complete sample should be ready when more favorable
circumstances call for and permit publication." This was to be the case on
21 December 1814.

The period from November 1812 to December 1814 was a very eventful
one not only for Goethe but for the whole world. It was the period of the
wars of liberation in which the German lands, Italy, and Spain freed themselves from French rule and prepared an end to the Napoleonic Empire.
Napoleon passed through Weimar, incognito, on 15 December 1812 on his
flight from Russia. He sent greetings to Goethe through his ambassador.
Goethe was not ready to join in the general anti-Napoleonic mood; he still
saw him as a dominating historical force. He was unable to discern any new
system that could replace the old one, no order that could follow on disorder,
and he did not trust the patriotic feelings that were being more and more
stridently expressed.

These were turbulent times for Goethe and for Weimar. Goethe had left
Weimar, on the advice of his friends, on Easter Saturday 17 April. He left
early, at six o'clock, in a coach with his secretary John, and they drove in
the direction of Bohemia; he was disguised and carried a Prussian passport.

He was recognized by a "section of the Prussian corps of irregulars, the Black Rangers" who asked him to bless their weapons. "Go with God, and the very best to your lively German courage," said Goethe. On the following day he arrived in Dresden at the house of Christian Körner where he met Ernst Moritz Arndt. The latter gave full rein to his hatred of the French, and Goethe shouted at him in anger: "Just shake your chains, the man [Napoleon] is too great for you, you will never break them."

Goethe was back in Weimar in August 1813, and in October soldiers of different armies began to be billeted there. On 23 October the Austrian general of artillery, Colloredo, was billeted on him and was very annoyed that Goethe received him wearing the French order of the Légion d'honneur! Colloredo got his revenge by inviting twenty-four people to dinner every day at Goethe's expense. On 29 October Goethe writes to Cotta: "the fact is that the horror passed me and my family by and we have nothing to complain about." Cotta expresses his happiness about the fortunate outcome of "those fateful days." He adds the hope that "these days will be harbingers of a more pleasant time that it would have been entirely within Napoleon's power to achieve without the need for so much bloodshed and distress! This seems to me the greatest cause for blame, for it all depended on him, he could have become the savior of the world." What Cotta probably had in mind as he recalled this was that he had always believed that Napoleon had "higher aims" in mind than merely conquering countries.

But the letter of 29 October held a surprise for Cotta. "I want you to consider publishing a pocket edition of *Hermann and Dorothea* and distributing it at low cost." Goethe saw, justifiably, that this was a favorable juncture for the epic to exert a new influence as a counterpoint to the disturbances of war and to remind people of the older virtues of order and the status quo. Cotta was happy with Goethe's suggestion. He had long awaited such a permission, for the house of Vieweg had reprinted *Hermann and Dorothea* continuously since its appearance in 1798, interpreting their agreement with Goethe very arbitrarily and constantly demanding their rights. Cotta fulfilled Goethe's wish immediately and printed the book in his own printing works in Stuttgart and delivered it in February 1814. Cotta chose a larger format than Vieweg's for his edition, so that the work should have a more beautiful appearance and particularly to avoid breaking up the hexameters.

Even if Goethe did think on 29 October 1813 that the horror had passed him and his family by, his troubles were not at an end. There were still remnants of French troops in Leipzig, most of them chased south by Russian troops. On 6 November Goethe was once again in trouble, "twelve men—Don Cossacks" forced their way into his house. But he was able to free himself from them. Meanwhile it had become clear that Napoleon had definitely been defeated.

The Napoleonic order in Germany collapsed, and Napoleon abdicated in Fontainebleau on 6 April 1814. During the night of 11 April he tried unsuccessfully to commit suicide by taking poison. On 20 April he went into exile on Elba. In Europe people were of the impression that they had now reached a state of peace that would represent some sort of balance in Europe after the bankruptcy of Napoleon's Europe policy.

It was this sort of peace euphoria that caused the director of the Royal theater in Berlin, August Wilhelm Iffland, to approach the Weimar court chancellor and ask him to find out whether Goethe would be willing to write a festival play to celebrate the return of those who had defeated Napoleon. Goethe thought the proposal over "for twenty-four hours from every possible angle," rejected it, and then quickly changed his mind. Iffland responded enthusiastically to Goethe's readiness. "It seems to me that no work of such magnitude as the present liberation of Germany has been undertaken since Luther's Reformation . . . , there could be no loftier celebration than to have the first man of the nation write about the event." In a space of eight days while in Berka, Goethe drafted "The Awakening of Epimenides," sent it to Iffland for his comments and worked, in his words, day and night to complete it, so that as early as 15 June the first parts, among them the lyrical ones that were intended to be set to music, were ready to be sent to Berlin by express messenger. Iffland's idea was to print the work in Berlin at Duncker und Humblot's. Goethe agreed and also said that he would not reprint the work himself before the Easter Fair of the following year. His suggestion was to make a pleasing quarto edition, and in addition he advised the publication of a pocket edition. The composer Bernhard Anselm Weber and the publisher Carl Friedrich Duncker went to Bad Berka where Goethe was continuing to work jointly with Riemer, even though the latter was technically no longer in Goethe's employ. The manuscript was sent to Berlin on 12 July. "At the end it caused me the greatest pain," Goethe wrote to Knebel on 9 July 1814, "for until a child which has been born in this way is baptized there is no end to the difficulties." However, he hoped that he had undertaken this work not merely for Berlin but for the future.

It is easy to understand why Goethe should have first rejected the idea of writing, in the space of four weeks, a piece that—in view of the circumstances—would be so exposed. Feeling and instinct warned him against it; on the other hand, he was now under pressure to state his convictions about the freedom movements and the wars of 1813 and 1814. From the beginning he had in mind a large-scale opera-like piece in which music was to play the main part, but he also wanted to call attention to the other theatrical arts—decor, choreography, and costumes. *"The Awakening of Epimenides* can justifiably be called a *festival production,"* he wrote to the composer Weber on 21 December 1814, "in that it will first be produced for an important festival and if it is favorably received can only be repeated on festive occasions." The "axis around which my piece revolves" (to Zelter on 15 April 1815) is formed by the figure of the Greek Epimenides who, according to the legend, was grazing his father's herds when he fell into a fifty-six-year-long sleep and afterwards became the prophet of his people. Does Epimenides excuse his absence from active participation by a mythical sleep? At the opening of the play we read, "the poet is trying to act as midwife at the birth of fate." Goethe also tries this later in the *West-East Divan.* Goethe had already written a festival play, *Pandora,* in celebration of the Peace of Tilsit. It was published in 1808 in the periodical *Prometheus,* whose great aim was to reinvigorate German intellectual life after the year 1806. Lines 1 to 400 appeared in the first number, but a section in the middle of the poem, lines 277–91, is missing. Meanwhile the editors had quarreled with the publisher, Joseph Geistinger. It is not clear how Geistinger managed to obtain some sort of permission from Goethe to print the entire play but it appeared in 1810 under the title *"Pandora* by Goethe, A pocket book for the year 1810." Geistinger maintained that he paid Goethe an honorarium. Thus, the greatest of all Viennese pirates published at least one of Goethe's works "legally."

Pandora addresses both the endangerment and the hopes of mankind. Goethe had worked on the play from October 1807 to June 1808. Wilhelm von Humboldt, who received it from Goethe, spoke of it as one of the "most marvelous of Goethe's works." The play contrasts two unequal brothers, the cold, restless, enterprising Prometheus and the sensitive, unhappy, idle Epimetheus. According to the myth, Pandora comes down to earth with a vessel which contains all mankind's evils and diseases, in order to punish mankind for Prometheus's crime of stealing fire. Prometheus warns his brother but Epimetheus marries Pandora.

The play was originally to be called "Pandora's Return," but Goethe was unable to complete it in that form. All that remains is a short sketch, written on 18 May 1808. Goethe did not take the work up again, as work on *The Elective Affinities* forced the festival play into the background, and after *Epimenides,* in which the vision of a new and ideal cultural epoch for mankind is conjured up, he was again unable to resume work on "Pandora's Return."

It is however evident that *Epimenides* was the work Goethe had in mind when he decided after all to go along with Iffland's request. He took advantage of the opportunity, he wrote to Iffland in June 1814, "to express to the nation, the way in which I have felt and still feel pain and pleasure with them."

In the play *Epimenides* the demon of repression first gains a victory, supported by reaction—the demon of cunning—and enchains love and belief. But then a massive movement rises up from below, the choir of hope and unity lends its assistance, a youthful prince overthrows the tyrant and points the way to freedom and unity. Epimenides realizes that "it is beautiful to entrust oneself to the supreme being. . . . He taught me to know what is taking place at present." The allusion to the present is the meaning of the play. And the choir knows it too: "Now we are Germans again / Now we are great again."

Goethe had hurried to complete the text in July 1814, but work on the book was delayed and there was no deadline in sight for the production. The reasons for this remain unknown. Goethe, however, was very annoyed at the delay and believed that the meaning of the play had been superseded by the events of 1814/1815. The Congress of Vienna met in October 1814 and terminated with the signing of the acts of the congress on 9 June 1815— before the final and definitive victory of Waterloo. The diplomats pushed to one side what the freedom movement had longed for, the freedom and unity of the German nation.

The results of the Congress of Vienna must also have confirmed Goethe's political attitude in all these years. Freedom and equality, he had written at the beginning of 1789, are now possible in the dizziness of madness; a quarter of a century later freedom and equality had still not been achieved. Revolution and restoration seem to belong together; their dialectic seems to determine the history of the modern world.

The production of *Epimenides* was repeatedly postponed. Iffland died on 22 September 1814. The new director, Count Carl Friedrich Moritz Paul von Brühl, was closely connected with Weimar and was in favor of the production. It was now supposed to take place on 30 March 1815, on the anniversary of the storming of Paris. But what a date that was! Napoleon was en route from Elba to Paris; the Congress of Vienna, at which national horse-trading was increasingly gaining the upper hand, gave the victorious countries no rights whatsoever—this was all in contrast to Epimenides' hope. Goethe expressed the fear that he had expressed epigrammatically to the directors of the Berlin theater while it was waiting for the production of the play: "Epimenides will, I think, awake in Berlin too early and too late." Duncker, having received the final proofs on 8 March, wrote to Goethe on the twenty-fifth, "The time for the production of your Epimenides is now so imminent that I have had to put the presses, and myself, to work hard so that I can complete it for the first performance by next Thursday, 30 March." However, Goethe learned that, at the wish of the theater director, a professor had been asked to write a "foreword to the audience," "in order to put the public in a position in which it can view this great dramatic poem properly and enjoy it more deeply." When the book appeared on 30 March, *The Awakening of Epimenides. A festival play by Goethe,* it was indeed preceded by an eight-page foreword, signed "K.L." As far as I know this is the first time that a first edition of a work by Goethe appeared with a foreword by a third party and without Goethe's even having seen the text of it! The publisher and the writer of the foreword were lucky. On 13 April, Goethe wrote to the latter, "the intention of the very successful foreword, in its three parts, is commensurate with my final intention and could not fail to bring about a more rapid and more favorable reception."

The performance did finally take place on 30 March. Goethe informed his friend Knebel on 5 April, "Epimenides finally awoke in Berlin on 30 March, just at the right moment to repeat symbolically what the Germans have so often heard in dry prose, that they have suffered the unbearable for many years, but that they then liberated themselves from this suffering in magnificent fashion. Everyone will add that new energy is needed to protect what has been achieved and to maintain it."

The play was not given many performances in Berlin. There were three in Weimar, and the text was published by Duncker and Humblot under the title "*The Awakening of Epimenides. A festival play by Goethe.*" There was also a libretto of the first edition that was sold at the box office at the first performances in Berlin and Weimar, after which this version of the *Epimen-ides* was not printed again during Goethe's lifetime. The choral song from this first version, "Arise brothers! to free the world," was published separately under the title *Forwards Choir* in the collection *Awakened Europe,* in Berlin in 1814 and in Cotta's *Morgenblatt* on 17 November 1814.[1]

Goethe was disappointed at the cool reception; the allegorical introduction had made things more difficult for the public, even Knebel was of the opinion that "much in the allegory was too fine and therefore too indefinite for the viewer."

Later, after Goethe's death, an additional strophe was added to the play. It is among the *Tame Xenien* that Goethe had retained and that were only published posthumously, and was presumably written after the conclusion of the Congress of Vienna. These lines express Goethe's disappointment at the fact that the great expectations of the *Epimenides* were not fulfilled and that basically the Congress of Vienna merely confirmed existing conditions. Goethe did not want be counted as a "friend of the status quo," but this is the accusation he had to counter over and over again. He was later called "a prince's slave," "despot's servant," and an "obstructive force."

Goethe's awakening is different from that of Epimenides in his cave. Did he know the Chinese saying: "Before the extreme is reached, nothing will turn into its opposite"? Goethe set his own individual world against the universe, set play against seriousness. In the midst of his work on *Epimenides,* he suddenly notes in his diary on 7 June 1814: "Hafi's Divan."

The *"Divan"* (1814–1819)   Goethe cloaks his Divan-game, both its historical background and its autobiographical character, in secrecy. It is therefore of special significance, that he should be anxious to tell his publisher about the most important piece of evidence for the genesis of the work that was now interfering with the new edition of his *Works.* In a letter to Cotta that he never sent off he writes, "I have written a lot in the sense and manner of the Orient. In doing this my intention is to link, in a playful manner, the West and the East, past and present, Persian and German, and to let the customs and modes of thought of both sides interact." Goethe mentions with thanks Cotta's gift of the previous year. In 1814 Cotta had had the "grace" to send Goethe "a few novelties from his publishing house." Among these novelties was a book,

The Divan of Mohammed Shemedseddin-Hafis. In 1815 Goethe makes a note of the impression the work made on him when he read it: "As early as last year I received all *Hafiz*'s poems in *Hammer*'s translation and though I had previously not been able to get anything out of individual translations of this magnificent poet's poems . . . they now produced an all the more lively effect upon me. Whatever similar themes or meanings had been nourished and preserved in my own work made their mark on me and all the more forcefully because I felt the utmost necessity to flee from the real world that was a menace to itself both overtly and in secret into an ideal one in which I could participate as I pleased, as I was able, and as I wished to." A revealing remark about the triggering of Goethe's creative process.

What was it about Hafiz that Goethe found so fascinating? Hafiz ("who knows the Koran by heart") was born in Shiraz in 1326 and died there in 1390. Like Goethe he was in the service of princes. He praised the princes but also criticized them, and he was influential in lifting, temporarily, the ban on the drinking of wine. "Shah Sedshan" in the "Book of Observations" is Carl August in Weimar; the wish is that his empire shall flourish, and the onlooker feels it to be his "greatest good" "to have found a lord." Just as Goethe met Napoleon, so Hafiz met the leader of the second Mongol invasion, Timur Lenk. The figure of Timur in the "Book of Timur" alludes without question to Napoleon. In his conversation Goethe commented: "Acquisition of orientalism—Napoleon, our age offers rich material for this. Timur. Genghis Khan, natural forces appearing in similar form in a human being."[2] Thus in the poem *The Winter and Timur* it is not human beings who destroy the dictator, but the forces of nature. In *Poetry and Truth* the demonic is a "force that thwarts the moral order of the world" and it cannot be subdued by human beings but only by the "universe itself." According to legend, Timur reproached Hafiz for blasphemy, because he had written that angels in a tavern had drenched with wine the lump of clay that was Adam, thus determining that human beings would be constantly drunk. It is alleged that Hafiz replied to Timur that he intended the drinking of wine to represent perception and the inn to represent the place of perception. Wine, he says, points to the celestial origin of mankind; the game of love on earth is only a prelude to the heavenly one, and human longing is also a longing for the celestial origin of mankind. In "An Hafiz," one of the last poems to be written for the *Divan,* in Carlsbad on 11 September 1818 (Goethe had just learned from Willemer that the latter's wife, Marianne, was in despair, sick and melancholic, and that he had received a letter from her expressing her deep suffering), we read:

> What all wish for you know already
> And have understood it:
> For longing holds us all, from dust to throne,
> In strait bonds.

Goethe admired Hafiz's piety. Death for Hafiz is only the gate to union with God. His lines, "No matter how many lovers his boundless beauty kills, new throngs of lovers arise for him at once from the other world," are famous. Goethe admired piety and sensuality in Hafiz, his "twin brother." Above all he admired his unmatched mastery of the ghazal, a poem operating simultaneously on two levels, the secular and the mystical. The individual couplets, complete in themselves, and linked contrapuntally, contain a rich variety of themes while at the same time achieving great poetic unity. What the Bible was for Goethe, the Koran was for Hafiz, and it is not by chance that in *Notes and Essays* we read under the title *From the Old Testament:* "Since all our wanderings in the Orient were occasioned by Holy Writ, we always come back to them as to the most refreshing of spring waters, although they are somewhat clouded in places, hidden in the earth, but then springing up again pure and fresh." Goethe repeatedly comes back to the Bible, even to episodes in Christ's passion. We know from *Poetry and Truth,* which was written at about the same time, how much Goethe was affected by the impression of Jesus' countenance on Veronica's veil, a countenance that was "by no means that of someone suffering in the present but of a gloriously transfigured being radiating heavenly life." The poem *Epithet* from the Book of Hafiz, a dialogue between the poet and Hafiz, refers to this. Hafiz, like Goethe, had to protect his religiousness against the self-righteous and orthodox, against "negation, hindrance and plunder." Sulpice Boisserée once confided in Goethe that Hafiz was for him "another Voltaire," "an arch-enlightener," greatly impudent—"I am not going to enter your heaven unless I can install a couple of houris there." In the poem that was originally called "Revocation" and later published under the very significant title "Hint," we read: "The word spreads out like a fan!" and in this way Goethe, too, opposed "negation and hindrance" and emphasized repeatedly that religiousness did not necessarily entail a darkening of life. Hafiz and Goethe both affirm life; their profundity is compatible with gaiety, indeed sometimes with frivolity. The element of cheerfulness is characteristic of both of them, they want to bear a cheerful image of faith.[3]

Goethe found Hafiz lively. He took what was important to him from his poetry, or its Persian models, and changed it into his great song of "Perish and Be!" He takes the image of the candle that becomes a flame, and the simile of the butterfly that burns itself to death as it is purified, from the Persian models for Hafiz' *Divan.* These images and similes become symbols of change and also of purification, images of his own existence. The earth is not a dark place for him, he is not a melancholy guest. When Suleika says: "Let the highest happiness of the children of earth / be the personality alone," Hatem answers, "Maybe! that's what's intended / But I am on another track: / It is only in Suleika / That I find all earthly happiness united."[4]

On 21 June 1814, two weeks after he had mentioned the *Divan* in his diary, he wrote *Create and Animate,* the first poem in the context of the *Divan*-cycle. At first the rough verses are far from pleasing, then we see that Goethe had taken the idea for the poem from a Persian model. Here the newborn child is half a "clod" until Noah finds the truth—wine—in the tankard, and the "clod" is animated the moment it "moistens" itself with wine.[5] The topoi of singing and drinking, of the lover and longing for the divine, were important for both Hafiz and for Goethe.

On 25 July, Goethe started his journey, a flight backwards and forwards, back to his old home, past the places of all his loves, forward with the secure "phenomenon": "but you will love." The introductory poem to the *Divan,* written in Weimar on Christmas Eve 1814, bears the title *Hegire,* the French form of the Arabic *Hijrah,* flight, a reference to Muhammad's *Hijrah.* Goethe followed the prophet's example; Muhammad's departure from Mecca and his emigration to Medina in 622 marks the beginning of the Moslem reckoning of time. In Goethe's vision the one who is writing the *Divan* poems commences an emigration, an epoch in his life's work.

> There in purity and justice
> I will penetrate to the origin
> Of mankind,
> When it first received from God
> The heavenly doctrine in earthly tongues,
> And did not rack its brains over it.

This refers unambiguously to the Koran as well as to the Bible. Muhammad was for Goethe a prophet, in immediate contact with God, and so he had no need to read or write. This was absolutely unessential for Goethe; in his various extracts from the Koran he noted "Mahomet was nothing but an ambassador," he was only "a preacher," and he goes to say that faith is broad, it is thought alone that is narrow. Goethe puts this in a totally Islamic fashion:

> Just as the word was so important there,
> Because it was a spoken word.[6]

As we know, Muhammad, like Jesus, left nothing written in his own hand. Thus his words, like those of Christ, are poetic words in the original sense: "Hovering round the gates of Paradise / always knocking softly, / Asking eternal life for themselves."

Goethe's journey is productive; on the first day he writes two poems and on the second nine. He is in Frankfurt on 28 July, where, passing his family house, he hears the old grandfather clock chime. The poem in the manuscript that is entitled "The Book of Sadf Ghasele I"—later to be called "Self-Sacrifice" and then in the *Pocket Book for Ladies for the year 1817,* "Completion," and in the published version of the *Divan,* "Longing"—appears days later with the caption "W[ies] B[aden] 31 Jul[y] 1814":

> Tell it to no one only the sages,
> For the crowd too lightly mocks.
> I will praise what lives,
> And longs for death in flames.
>
> In the freshness of nights of love,
> That bred you, and where you bred,
> An alien feeling attacks you
> When the silent candle gleams.
>
> No longer do you stay embraced
> In the shadow of the dark,
> And new longing pulls you up
> To a higher union.
>
> No distance makes you difficult
> You come flying and enchanted,

And at last desiring light,
You the butterfly are burned.

And as long as you do not have that,
This: "Perish and Be!"
You are only a melancholy guest
On this dark earth.

Life is praised in a quiet, relaxed manner in the four-line strophes with trochaic meter and alternating rhymes, the strophic form most frequently used in the *Divan* (and incidentally the strophic form most commonly employed for narrative romance cycles in German literature). Goethe borrowed motifs from Hafiz's Persian models, images and similes of purification and change. "What, if not change, is your pressing task?" Rilke was to ask on one occasion, and Goethe proclaims this in the final strophe, where the trochees are shortened. The person writing this in Wiesbaden on 31 July 1814 is certainly no melancholy guest and does not experience the earth as dark; he is on "another track." "Only in Suleika, do I find all earthly joy united." A few days later in Wiesbaden, Goethe met with Johann Jakob von Willemer who introduced him fleetingly to "Demoiselle Jung"—Marianne, who was to be his spiritual partner, his "dear little one," in the *Divan*. They met again in September at Willemer's country house near Frankfurt. The day is "most beautiful . . . Marianne well," Goethe writes to Weimar. Willemer also visited Goethe in Heidelberg that same month, the "women" come later; Willemer must have used the occasion for a tête-à-tête with Goethe about Willemer's intention to marry Marianne. Goethe, remembering the situation of his earlier love poems, strengthened him in his resolve. Willemer and Marianne married on 27 September 1814, hastily, precipitately, without delay and without banns; because Marianne cannot produce her birth certificate she will not be granted Frankfurt citizenship. Goethe is in no hurry to tell Christiane about the marriage, it is not until October that he dictates a letter for Christiane: "Went to Frau Geheimrätin Willemer for the evening: for our worthy friend is now married *in forma*. She is as kind and good as before. He was not at home." Goethe is in Frankfurt where he remains until 20 October; he also visits Marianne on that day.

In the summer months of 1814 Goethe wrote a number of poems; they constitute "a small whole that can be expanded when my mood is lively once again," he wrote on 29 August. First called "The poems to Hafiz," the collection was renamed "German Divan." On Christmas Eve he wrote the poem "Hegire," planned retroactively as introduction and prologue, and at the same time the poem "Good Night!," that forms a sort of epilogue. Goethe presents us in "Hegire" with a sort of poetic self-characterization, while at the same he wishes to conjure up a past in which "thrones burst and empires tremble." He wants to try once again "in this period to measure our petty private circumstances by the enormous yardstick of world history." He wants to link his personal experience to the political events of this period in which one epoch came to an end and a new one began, in which Napoleon rose and fell, in which the Holy Roman Empire perished and an attempt was made to create a new order of peace. Thus almost unawares the poems of the *Divan* became for him "the vehicle of his political creeds." But now he wanted—as he says in "Good Night!"—to lay his poems "upon the bosom of his people," so that "what was new" "should continue to grow on every side." This seemed to constitute the end of the *German Divan* complex. On 30 May 1815, in the so-called Wiesbaden index, Goethe added 47 more poems (among them ones still to be written) to the 53 poems that had been written up to the end of 1814. What Goethe did not suspect was that the work was just beginning.

In the following months Goethe carried on a systematic study of all the works about the Orient that he could lay his hands on, first *Treasures of the Orient* and *History of Persian Rhetorics,* both by the translator of the Persian *Divan.* He read reports of journeys, had conversations with orientalists and bought oriental manuscripts for the ducal library. As he could not read Hafiz in the original, he devoted himself "energetically" to "calligraphy."[7] He studied sources, like the famous seven Arabic poems *The Moallakat* (that hang in the mosque in Mecca and appeared in German in 1802, "The brightly shining pleiades in the poetic sky of Arabia"); he read Marco Polo's account of his travels and read and reread Hafiz's *Divan* and the Koran. Goethe listed his most important sources in an unusual dedicatory page.

His "Notes and Essays" resulted from these studies. In the first edition they were entitled "For a Better Understanding" and included the lines: "Anyone who wishes to understand poetry, / Must go to the land of poetry / Anyone who wishes to understand the poet / must go to the poet's country."

The introduction contains the statement "Everything in its time." The "Notes and Essays" are more than a guide to better understanding, however.

They are called, with absolute justification, the independent second part of the *Divan*. Today we have complete information about Goethe's oriental studies in the book by Katharina Mommsen, *Goethe und die arabische Welt*.[8] According to Mommsen, Goethe picked up the male as well as the female side of the Arabian spirit. Scheherazade stands as a muse at Goethe's side, Muhammad and the Koran inspire him; he is equally fascinated by the nomadic lifestyle of the bedouins, their closeness to nature, their rich imagination, their courage, their hospitality, their vital force. It is extremely revealing that proverbial Arabic sayings were Goethe's companions to the end of his life. The motto of the "Book of the Singer" that is placed at the very beginning of the *Divan* is based on the proverbial Arabic saying "As beautiful as the age of the Barmecides," which Goethe had found in a book about the prophet Muhammad. He took it and made use of it for a very cryptic personal statement: "For twenty years, I took things as they came, / and enjoyed what was given me; / A series of things totally beautiful, / like the age of the Barmecides" (an important epoch of the eighth century both in politics and literature when this important family was exerting its influence in Baghdad and upon the caliphs). In the chapter "Older Persians" in "Notes and Essays," Goethe tells us that the Barmecides came from the fire-worshippers in Balch. The family shone for a very long time as influential servants of the state, until finally they were extirpated and driven out. "For this reason the period when the Barmecides wielded influence in Baghdad remains its most brilliant . . . of which men can only hope . . . that after a short time it will perhaps arise again on foreign shores and in similar circumstances." Goethe was impressed by the fact that a proverb could express such high praise for a family that was of a different creed, but he must chiefly have been struck by the fact that, in the case of the Barmecides, we are dealing with "influential servants of the state." Here, *nolens volens,* Goethe must have thought of a comparison between Baghdad and Weimar and seen in himself a servant of the state of this sort. Thus, as in the case of the old Persians and Hafiz, Goethe wants to lay his poetry on the bosom of his people, and he also wants to achieve great things with his poetry. Writing poetry is, it is true, a "presumption," but "If the poet's pure hand goes to the well / water will form into a ball."

Though Goethe went via Frankfurt to Wiesbaden in May 1815 he did not see the Willemers and was obviously in no hurry to see them again. He continues to work on the *Divan;* it is here that he writes the first Suleika poems. It is a time of political and military unrest. He does not meet the

Willemers again until 12 August in Frankfurt. Goethe has Hafiz's *Divan* in his luggage as a gift for Marianne—it is to be a momentous gift. His birthday was celebrated at the Willemer home on 28 August, a difficult undertaking as he did not like this sort of celebration. It was the first birthday for years that he had celebrated in Frankfurt and it was the last. In his diary for the day he writes mysteriously and evocatively: "Divan. Beginning—end." He starts writing the book "Suleika" and with it the names of the protagonists: "Since you are now called Suleika / I should also have a name. / If you praise your beloved, / Hatem! that shall be the name." Goethe took the name Hatem from Saudi's poems: Hatem from the house of Thai was "the most generous of all Arabs." Goethe also took the introductory words from an Osman poet, who mentions that he dreamed of the moon in the night but that unexpectedly "the sun" rose. The sun. The other track. On 12 September Marianne received from Goethe the first poem directly addressed to her: "Hatem": "Opportunity does not create thieves, / it is itself the greatest thief, / for it stole the remains of the love / that was still in my heart." "His life," he says, now "expected" something of her and he enjoyed "a renewed skill" in her arms. This was an unambiguous declaration, the poetic form was nothing but a final effort to achieve distance. Goethe, the experienced man, spoke freely, explained himself, could imagine what was going on in Marianne's mind; she whose feelings had been unfulfilled throughout her life now found fulfillment in the man whom she revered so highly. Today we have to recognize that Goethe, the wonderful director of his own life's work of art, was assisting in staging the collapse of a relationship between two people linked in another way.

Marianne, and this is what is miraculous about this book, replied four days later with a poem that responds just as clearly to the love that is offered her, a poem that demonstrates poetic force and does honor to its recipient. It is also one that gives a new word to the German language—*hochbeglückt* ("blissfully happy"). It marks the beginning of a poetic antiphony: "*Suleika.* Blissfully happy in your love / I do not scold opportunity; / If it once played the thief to me / how such a theft rejoices me!/. . . Do not jest! Not a word about growing poorer! / Does not love enrich us?/ If I hold you in my arms / my joy is the equal of all."

The master accepted this token of homage, he made a few corrections, copied it, and added it to the other manuscripts. Later scholars held that Marianne had rewritten an earlier version by Goethe, but this can no longer be verified. The original is lost and, as evidence of authorship, we have Marianne's letter to Herman Grimm in 1856. But now Goethe also knew what he had begun. It was his "Duodrama." And he reacted as he had always reacted, by taking flight. But Hafiz's *Divan* had started a creative process in Marianne. It is astonishing how rapidly and intensely she empathized with Hafiz's work and how she learned the art that Goethe, in "Notes and Essays," described under the rubric "cipher":[9] "Two people agree upon a book, combine page numbers and lines into a letter, and are certain that the recipient will work out the meaning with little trouble."

In Goethe's and Marianne's "cipher" letters the individual strophes and lines from Hafiz's poems are so artfully composed, that beyond the protestations of love, beyond an intellectual game, "Songs of the most sublime expression" were written. Goethe pasted three of the four "cipher" letters that have been preserved into his copy of the *Divan*.

Goethe left for Heidelberg on 18 September 1815; he did not tell his friend that his return journey to Weimar would not be by way of Frankfurt. The Willemers visited him in Heidelberg on 23 September, Marianne giving him the poem "If the East wind brings happy tidings." Once more they experience "joyous feelings," happy days.

He takes Marianne into the castle garden, draws her attention to the ginkgo tree (he had already sent Marianne a leaf from the tree while she was in Frankfurt). The ginko is a coniferous tree; originally indigenous to China and Japan and revered there in the gardens of temples and monasteries as a holy tree, it was brought to Europe in the eighteenth century and in about 1780 to Heidelberg. Its leaves are divided in the middle, so that it might appear that they were two leaves that had grown together. Goethe sees in this that secret meaning of which he writes in the first strophe of his poem "Ginkgo biloba."[10] According to Boisserée, Goethe sent the leaf to Marianne from Frankfurt "as a symbol of friendship . . . we do not know whether it is one divided into two, or two that are joined into one."

On the last day in Heidelberg, the Willemers and Goethe are walking through the park. He takes Marianne aside and leads her to the well, where, in the sand, he writes in Arabic script that he had learned the day before, the name "Suleika": "Inscribed in the moving dust / the wind blows above it; but its power / stretches to the middle of the earth / fettered to the ground." The day after, on 26 September, the Willemers leave Heidelberg, always conscious of the fact that though they will not see Goethe on his homeward journey they will on other occasions. But he knows differently. Goethe plunges into his Persian studies. On the day after the Willemers' departure he visits the antiquary Georg Friedrich Creuzer, to whom he talks about the symbolic content of Greek and Asian myths and compared the double meaning of the myths with the "single and double" of the ginkgo tree. The second and third strophes of the poem talk about this; the questions asked in the poem are rhetorical. "Is it two that chose each other, to be recognized as one?" and "do you not feel in my songs / that I am one and twofold?" Was Marianne to learn his real being from his poems and not from his personal actions? A few days later, still in Heidelberg, he writes Hatem's poem, "Curls, hold me prisoner!" (Whose curls are they, Marianne's or Christiane's?) Goethe is playing his poetic game here, he rhymes in such a way that at the place where the name Goethe should crop up, the name Hatem appears; "You shame, like the dawn, / the grave wall of those mountain tops / and once more Hatem feels / the breath of Spring and summer's heat."[11] The poem of Suleika's that follows, "I will never lose you!" that ends with the famous lines, "For life is love, and the life of life is spirit," were long ascribed to Marianne. But this is not a woman's sentiment, and an early draft by Goethe for this poem was found among Boisserée's papers. It is possible that it was inspired by Marianne, for in her letter to Hermann Grimm she wrote, "I inspired, occasioned and experienced a great deal."[12] The other poem, "West wind how I envy your dampened wings, / for you could bring him news / of what I suffer in our separation," was written by Marianne as a counterpoint to the Heidelberg "Song of the East Wind." Eckermann, who did not know who wrote it, praised it in his book *Essays on Poetry with Special Reference to Goethe* as something typical of the master and rightly praised the closing lines, "Tell him, but tell him humbly / that his love is my life / a joyous feeling of both / will bring me close to him."

A poetic exchange of this sort is unique in the history of literature. Of course there are the great (literary) lovers and loved ones, Beatrice, Laura, Diotima; there are poetic exchanges between teachers and pupils, but hardly any examples of such *mutual productivity* on such a high poetic level. I remember, after the appearance of Bertolt Brecht's *Collected Poems,* an actress wanted to sue the publisher Suhrkamp because a poem had been included that was not by Brecht but by her; that was true enough but by making a few corrections Brecht had made the poem into his own; nevertheless we did not include the poem in the second edition.

Goethe and Marianne von Willemer did not see each other again. On 20 July 1816, a few weeks after Christiane's death, Goethe accepted Cotta's invitation to make a trip to Baden-Baden via Frankfurt, but shortly after leaving Weimar the coach overturned. Goethe, though not injured, returned to Weimar.

On 6 October 1815 Goethe rearranged the collection of poems, particularly the Suleika poems that now appeared as a complete group. Goethe's manuscripts were copied and made ready for the press. On 14 February 1816 Goethe's "self advertisement" appeared in the *Morgenblatt No. 48*: "The poet sees himself as a traveller. He has already arrived in the Orient. He delights in the mores, the customs, objects, religious views and opinions, he does not even reject the suspicion that he is himself a Moslem."

But although production had begun, the poetic plan of the *Divan* was still not complete. Goethe took up his scholarly pursuits once more; in the course of these he wrote significant reflections on art and life, history and society, and developed new ideas on the position of rhetoric. Goethe's statements about the technique of translation are outstanding and still valid to this day. His demands should be seen as a challenge by every translator: "The translation, should be made identical with the original . . . , so that the one should not take the place of the other, but should prevail in place of the other." [13]

Religion and piety again became one of Goethe's great themes. He states that the "Old Parsees'" worship of God was based entirely on the contemplation of Nature. Their "so delicate religion" is oriented towards the "omnipresence of God in the works of the sensual world." In this Goethe could find total agreement with his own religious ideas: God is present in all the creations of the world, religion as *re-ligio* to Nature, as an openness that cannot be limited by any confessional barriers. He himself had never "found a religious belief to which he could totally subscribe." But now he discovered that he had "always wanted to qualify as a Hypsistarian." "Now in my old age I learn about a sect called Hypsistarians who, sandwiched between pagans, Jews and Christians declared that they valued, admired, respected the best, the most perfect, that they learned about and, insofar as it was closely linked to the divinity, to worship it. Then a cheerful light suddenly dawned on me from a dark age, for I felt that all my life I had been aiming to qualify as a Hypsistarian; but no small effort is involved; for how does one become aware, within the limits of one's own individuality, of the most excellent?" [14]

As a result of this work "Notes and Essays" expanded into a more and more significant and independent part of the *Divan*. Goethe now divided the book into two halves. On 23 September he wrote the final poem: "The Higher and the Highest."

Then Frommann in Jena began the process of production—a highly complicated one. Goethe himself made fair copies of the completed poems in black ink in Roman script; 184 pages have been preserved. In all, 300 texts for the *Divan* have been preserved in Goethe's own hand. He kept for himself the texts that he wrote down in his own hand and always regarded them as a "personal copy," not as a "printer's manuscript," and he read to his friends from it. Goethe took a lot of trouble with the preparation of the manuscript, and from the beginning of 1818 he was mainly in Jena, where the work was being printed. While the work was in the press he rearranged the books of poems and reduced them to twelve and he was constantly inserting new manuscripts into the already paginated printed manuscript. He also kept revising the poems while they were being printed and sent the proofs on to the orientalist J. G. L. Kosegarten, who made the Arabic title page for the first edition, to check the oriental names. Goethe carried on the correspondence with Frommann personally. Though Goethe and Cotta only exchanged a few letters during these weeks and months, on 11 August 1819 Goethe was able to report, "The *Divan* is now finally assembled and I am very pleased to be finished with it as the work became more and more difficult as things progressed."

The first edition appeared in the summer of 1819 in a run of 2,000 copies (30 copies were printed on vellum). Goethe received royalties of 2,000 thalers. The octavo copies contained 556 pages. After the index, on pages 555 and 556, there were two further poems in an Arabic translation by Kosegarten printed alternately in Arabic and German. The first is entitled "Silvestre de Sacy" and was conceived as a tribute to the most famous French orientalist, Baron Antoine Isaac Silvestre de Sacy, the founder of Arabic studies and research on Islam in Europe at the beginning of the nineteenth century.

Each poem starts on a new page; only the short aphorisms are grouped together as in Goethe's manuscript and longer poems are divided equally over a number of pages. Each book begins on a right-hand page and ends on a left-hand one. Unfortunately there were numerous typographical errors in the first edition, errors that were overlooked by Goethe and his associates as well as errors that have to be ascribed to the proofreader at Frommann's printing house where Goethe's punctuation and spelling had been corrected with "discretion." Goethe sent a corrected version to Frommann on 21 January to be forwarded to Vienna, so that they could produce a "completely clean edition" (this Viennese edition corrected a few errors). The *Divan* originally appeared in volume 21 of the "Original Edition." The individual edition dated 1819 is a separate edition which was taken from volume 21 of that "Original Edition." Later, a scholar who was one of Goethe's advisers, Karl Wilhelm Göttling, was commissioned to undertake a revision of the texts for the final edition, but even here the text is not completely accurate. *Divan* poems from Goethe's unpublished works first appeared in *Goethe's Poetic and Prose Works in Two Volumes,* Stuttgart and Tübingen 1836, and in 1842 further poems appeared in volume 16 of the *Posthumous Works* and were added to the final authorized edition. The whole textual history is complicated, since some of the manuscripts that were at Eckermann and Riemer's disposal have disappeared. Thus, till the present day we cannot be certain whether Goethe's "completely clean edition" exists; perhaps we do not have a completely authentic text, perhaps not even the best, but we do have a text that accounts for the effect of the book.

When the book appeared in 1819 it had little effect on the public. Times had changed, "Young Germany,"[15] the Carlsbad Decrees, stricter censorship regulations had politicized the literature of the time. Goethe, the author, had more enemies than friends. In the "Literary Supplement for the Year 1820" of the Cotta *Morgenblatt,* a reviewer wrote, "In short the scholarly periodicals may preach what they like about mediation between occidental and oriental literature; this book is one of the strangest that Goethe has written; it is, so to speak, a riddle without a solution." Another writer classed the *Divan* among the "rotten herrings." A united front of opponents was formed; pamphleteers polemicized and wrote scornful satires. A letter by Ludwig Börne stated, "Have finished Goethe's *West-östlicher Divan.* I had to read it with my mind; I tried earlier to read it with my heart but I did not succeed. . . . Among all the delicacies of the oriental bazaar it is the tame service of obstinate rulers that Goethe has taken possession of most greedily. He found everything else but this was what he was looking for. Goethe is the rhymed servant just as Hegel is the unrhymed."[16] Heine defended Goethe against this charge; writing after his death, in 1835, he says: "Goethe has here put into verse the most intoxicating delight in life and his verses are so light, so happy, so airy, so ethereal that one is amazed that such a thing was possible in the German language." And talking of the prose of *Notes and Essays* he continued, "But the prose too is often as magical, as full of presentiment as the sky when twilight has lifted, and Goethe's great thoughts appear, pure and golden, like the stars. The magic of this book is indescribable."[17]

The *West-östliche Divan,* however, did not receive its due attention nor was it properly understood either when it appeared or a hundred years later. It has been pointed out over and over again that, up to the beginning of World War I, copies of the first edition could be found in bookstores or obtained from Cotta. It was a long time before it was discovered that Goethe had created something for which a few years later he used the expression, taken from Wieland: "world literature." "National literature does not mean very much now," he said to Eckermann on 31 January 1827, "The epoch of world literature is at hand and everyone must do his part to hasten this epoch." He did, but it is true that his contemporaries did not recognize the fact. "Pro captu lectoris habent libelli sua fata"; this famous quotation was translated by Goethe as "Books too have their *experience.*"[18]

Goethe on   On 24 December 1814, Goethe wrote the poem:
21 December 1814   "While loving, drinking, singing / Chiser's spring will rejuvenate you." It was in such high spirits, conjuring up Chiser, the guardian of the spring of life, who promised Hafiz immortal fame, that Goethe wrote Cotta the letter we have already mentioned. But the progress of the Congress of Vienna was not such as to allow him to make a decision to embark upon larger undertakings. "Since in the meantime, honored Sir, the fact that you raise my greatest hopes and express the wish that you will shortly witness the re-appearance of my works points to a peaceful issue, please allow me to express myself at length about so important a matter." And he did express himself at length but as always imperatively. The new edition, he says, was to bring him higher royalties than the first one because "this time he would agree to twenty volumes," and "it might possibly be the last time that the pleasure deriving from my whole life's work will fall to my share personally, a pleasure that I look forward to all the more eagerly as, on all my journeys this year, I have clearly heard the public express the desire to be able finally to buy my works as a complete set." That is one thing. The other: he regards himself, justifiably, as part of history, just as life

and work form a whole. "My biographical publications have had the effect that I hoped for, inasmuch as, in addition to the interest that is shown in my works in the ethical and aesthetic sense, people, in their efforts to use them to their own greater advantage, now look in them for the stages of my growth, as so many younger people admit openly and with pleasure that they have modeled themselves on me. For this reason therefore I have received so many and varied requests in the past year—since the publication of the third volume—that I shall be able to fulfill them at least in part with the present edition." These, then, were the points of view that led him to demand higher royalties, 20 volumes, and the assumption that this was the last time that he would be in a position to undertake such an edition that should contain, as new texts, his "biographical publications." "In making these observations, I will freely admit that I think that the sum of sixteen thousand Saxon thalers is reasonable for what I intend to deliver and produce, in view of which I gladly accept the deadline of Easter 1823, just as I accept the fact that when this agreement expires you will have the prior right of first refusal over other publishers offering the same conditions."

He had prepared the works, he said, and a few manuscripts could be sent off immediately, if these conditions were agreeable. "In the contemplation of further kind memories, yours sincerely, Goethe." Cotta, who was attending the Congress in Vienna, answers on 11 January 1815. He does not wish to miss a single day's post in replying to Goethe that "It will always be a pleasure for me to fulfill your wishes and the sum of 16,000 thalers shall be the basis of the contract between us that I am asking to have drawn up and sent to me." Otherwise his letter is concerned with other things. Cotta believes that as far as "our most dangerous enemy, piracy," is concerned, there is hope in Germany at least, but not in Austria, where there is no one who "understands the terrible nature of this piratical work."

On 20 February 1815, Goethe sends "The Draft of a Contract for your kind examination"; the "Draft of an Announcement"; a "Table of Contents of the twenty volumes"; printing directions for the first two volumes; and a "note" of his "readiness to cooperate with the *Damen Calendar* and the *Morgenblatt.*"

The draft of the contract is essentially what had been set out in the letter of 21 December 1814. What is new is an offer: "I am not averse to leaving part of the sum in your hands, at an interest of 5%—either party having the right to cancel the arrangement at their will—if this would be a convenience to the publisher." An interesting suggestion—the author is using his publisher as a bank, the publisher can use the money, but he has to pay 5% interest. As far as I know, Goethe is introducing here an arrangement that was seldom used at the time, but which would be used more and more frequently as time went on. Today this does work in some cases as a financial relief for an author, but it can result in tax problems.

In Goethe's "Draft of an Announcement" he mentions "that it will also communicate much that can be introduced, and made both intelligible and enjoyable, by an author's confessions about his life, which can in the future achieve a greater harmony." Cotta was naturally aware that he was asking something of the people who had bought the first edition, for the new edition really offered little that was new. And so Cotta inserted the following announcement in the *Intelligenzblatt,* No. 1 (1816):

> The owners of the first edition will be taken care of in the following manner; they should set their first volume aside and take in its place the first two new volumes, labeled Volume I, Part i, and Volume I, part ii. The volume numbers then run to volume 13 that contains the *Elective Affinities.*
>
> An individual volume 14 will then be printed for them, and this will contain new material already inserted into the earlier volumes. From volume 15 onwards the final six volumes of the *new edition* follow without interruption, so that in this way the owners of the *first edition* will receive nine volumes.

Together with his draft of the announcement Goethe sent notes to the first two volumes to the foreman-compositor, the typesetter, and the make-up man. Research shows that 16 to 18 people under the direction of Wilhelm Reichel were employed in Cotta's Stuttgart printing house. As soon as the manuscript had been approved by the censor, a typesetter and printer went to work on the edition and Reichel himself was responsible for the proofs, sent the galleys to the publisher for inspection and the imprimatur. At first Cotta, and then a colleague, undertook the proofreading and gave permission to print.

Goethe's readiness to collaborate on the *Damen Calendar* and the *Morgenblatt* must have pleased Cotta very much. Goethe explained that it was not "stubbornness" that had prevented his participating more frequently. "It is not easy to be influential in German literature if you do not concentrate your powers together, indeed we can see in the many daily and weekly papers that much that is good is swallowed up and reduced to the level of lesser work and this is in the nature of things and simply cannot be changed." However, Goethe wrote more articles than ever before for Cotta's periodicals: true, he often used them to announce his own works: on behalf of the new edition in the *Morgenblatt,* for the announcement of the *West-östlicher Divan,* and for the "Epilogue to Schiller's 'Bell.'"

On 18 March 1815, Cotta told Goethe that he was summoned to the first meeting of the diet on 15 March 1815 and was appointed its spokesman. Goethe wrote to him on 27 March that he was delighted at "Cotta's continued activity and for the whole: there is certainly at the moment nothing more meritorious than to work for the welfare of individual states, because everything important that is achieved benefits everyone both as an example and an inspiration." Later on he was to change his opinion, but on the 27 March he sent "with today's post a packet wrapped in a waxed cloth" and this contained the first four volumes of his works, two volumes of poems and two volumes of *Wilhelm Meister.* On 2 June Cotta sent the publisher's contract to Goethe confirming the publisher's agreement to all the demands in Goethe's draft. The document was signed on 15 June. Cotta had not managed to get the rights to produce a pocket edition from Goethe. Goethe had had his experiences with the first edition and persisted in refusing the rights.

Communications between the two were limited in 1815 because of Cotta's political activities; letters became shorter and two visits that had been planned did not take place. The first two volumes of the new edition appeared for the autumn fair, and a year later the second batch with volumes 3–8 came out. Goethe was satisfied with the typographical quality: "Dear Sir, I am grateful that the copies of the second batch arrived safely. The printing and the paper are good, we should also give high praise to the designer for dividing up the poems, especially *Epeminedes,* without using up too much space" (to Cotta 22 October 1822). Volumes 9–14 appeared in 1817, volumes 12–18 in 1818, and the edition was completed with volumes 19 and 20 in 1819.

The demand for the edition was even greater than Cotta had expected; in 1817 when volumes 1–8 had already been printed and volumes 9 and 10 were at the printer's the run was increased—the first eight volumes and signatures 1–17 of volume 9 and signatures 1–5 of volume 10 had to be reset.

Volume 20 included an unforeseen supplement. In his letter to Cotta of

26 February 1816 Goethe had written about "uncalled for advisers" who, though it is true they were not named, had "made the absurd demand that the new edition be arranged chronologically." He asked Cotta not to take this matter up in his papers as he was himself thinking of writing a short essay. It appeared in the *Morgenblatt* on 26 April 1816 under the title *On the New Edition of Goethe's Works*.

Goethe's reflections are important, they treat a question that still bothers his editors today. How was Goethe to arrange his works, how should they be handed down? How does today's reader want to read Goethe's works? In the chronological order of their writing, according to their thematic context, or according to literary genre? In the case of Goethe, and essentially only in his case (Lessing is perhaps an exception), there is a further element, the constant link with biographical events. Goethe expresses himself emphatically, stating that it is true that in the edition of Schiller's works there is an example of chronological arrangement but on a different basis, since in Schiller's case the periods of his development are clear-cut; he wrote his works in a relatively short space of time. "Goethe's works on the other hand" are

> the product of a talent that does not develop by stages and also does not gad about but seeks to reach all sides simultaneously, from a central point, and endeavors to have an effect both close at hand and at a distance, will leave many a well-trodden path for ever and will stay on others for a long time. Anyone can see that in such a process the most peculiar mixture would have to emerge if you were to assemble in one volume what was occupying the author at any given moment, even if it were possible to separate the most diverse productions in such a manner that they could be juxtaposed again afterwards according to the time of their origin.

> But this is not feasible, because a considerable time frequently elapsed between the planning, the beginning, and the completion of larger scale and even of small scale works and even as the works were being published partial changes were being made. Gaps in them were filled and a final form was decided upon only as they were being revised and edited, and as the instant at which they started off on their way to publication suggested.

These then were the reasons for a genre-oriented edition in March 1816.

As early as May 1818 Goethe had told Cotta that he intended to add a short chronological survey of his works, for the interested reader, in the final volume of the edition. Volume 20 was already at the printers when, on 23 January 1819, Cotta reminded Goethe of this "chronological survey" as well as of an "index." On the strength of this "encouraging letter" Goethe replied, on 20 February 1819, that he "had once more attacked the highly precarious and difficult task—often undertaken—of rendering a chronological account of my works, and I hope to send you, within fourteen days, if not the whole thing at least a part of it. As has already been said in the *Morgenblatt,* my works cannot be separated from my life and for this reason I have already written five biographical volumes." And on 3 March 1819, "After working uninterruptedly for eight weeks without getting beyond the end of the last century I have resolved to send you . . . *The Summary Chronology of Goethe's Works.* The essay will explain more about this; may time, desire, and strength promote the rest." In the supplement of March 1819, Goethe explains, once more excusing himself, why a presentation of the chronological order of his works is so difficult. What has been published of his efforts are only "details that are rooted in the soil of a life and grew there, where action and learning, talking and writing formed, by their constant activity, a skein that is hard to unravel." And he goes on: "I therefore encountered many difficulties when I wanted, at least partially, to live up to my agreement. I tried to designate the occasions, the stimuli, I tried to link the public with the private, what was communicated with what was omitted, by means of aesthetic and moral confessions; I tried to fill in gaps, to disclose what had succeeded and what had failed together with several preparatory works and to point out, in the process, the way in which a great deal that had been collected for one purpose was used for another, indeed was even wasted. But hardly had I progressed a few lustra in my efforts to present the progress of my life in a logical sequence than it became all too clear that so cursory a treatment would be out of place here, instead it had to be like what had been presented in the five biographical volumes." There follows a short chronology of his works beginning in 1769 with the *Mood of the Beloved* and ending in 1818 with the third volume of *On Art and Antiquity,* the fourth volume of which is "delayed" until 1819. The question of the chronological arrangement of Goethe's works is still alive today.

"Where the law is The relationship between Goethe and Cotta in the
of no help, we must decade in which the second complete edition was
listen to cunning. But published was virtually without friction. Both made
too much cunning the effort to realize what they both wanted and what
often leads to had been mutually agreed upon. But these years were
stumbling." marked by the great political and military upheavals
(1815–1819) of the time and were also determined by far-reaching
events in Goethe's life and environment. Goethe be-
came a minister of state on 12 December 1815. He was given his own depart-
ment, organized in accordance with his own wishes, which by the end of
1817 was responsible for eleven institutes; this arrangement also made it
possible for him—according to a very remarkable memorandum dated 19
December 1815[19]—to make permanent appointments, of his son August as
an assistant, of Kräuter as his secretary, and of John as a clerk. Christiane
died on 6 June 1816 "towards midday." Caroline Ulrich, the trusted friend
of the family, had left there in 1814 when she married Riemer; Goethe's son
August was married to Ottilie von Pogwisch on 17 June 1817. But the quiet
family life that Goethe had sought for his old age did not materialize.

Goethe's life, then, was unsettled at this time. Cotta's life too was unsettled; more of his time was taken up with politics than he wished. "If I could
only see an end to my thorny political career," he complained to Goethe on
26 September 1816. Goethe sent him his "sincerest sympathy . . . that I feel
when I learn what you have to put up with because of your truly patriotic
and moderate opinions. Recent events as reported in the *Allgemeine Zeitung*
have pained me deeply. True it must be said that one has oneself experienced
similar scenes in similar circumstances, but should one then abandon all hope
of the world's ever adopting a more reasonable attitude and of the conflict
between power and force ever being set aside?" On 2 September 1817 Cotta
was able to tell Goethe that "after a long absence from home" he can "actually return to his business and his scholarship, while political life, thank
Heavens! is now a closed book for me." Also he luckily escaped injury, "as
a horse turned head over heels with me on it . . . one of the most miraculous
of rescues." He has therefore been granted a sort of "double resurrection,"
political and physical, and he can now, as his first task, devote himself to
Goethe's work. Goethe reacts quite typically; he will not "deny that your
politically unsettled career depresses me not merely on your account but has
pained me on my own account as well." And he hopes that "after such a

successful outcome to all your efforts you will be able to pay some attention to national literature and will be able to accompany me sympathetically on my paths no matter how far they may lead." Cotta planned to publish a *Musenalmanach*[20] and both the editor and Cotta wanted a contribution from Goethe. Goethe declined, because he did not want to split up the things he was working on. But he also told Cotta that he had rejected "innumerable unreasonable demands of this sort even under the most favorable terms," that is, he had rejected offers worth a considerable amount in royalties from other publishers. And it must have pleased Cotta to read that the rejection was made simply "because . . . I do not wish to damage our relationship." This, the mutual effort to stay in a pleasant relationship with one another and not to undertake anything that could have a negative influence on it, was the basis of the relationship.

At length however a discordant note is sounded. An unfortunate and unavoidable event occurs that could easily have proved fatal. The cause was what Cotta had always called "our most dangerous enemy"—piracy. As early as January 1810 there was a rumor circulating that the Viennese printer Geistinger was to reprint Goethe's *Complete Works.* Cotta had repeatedly tried, but in vain, to prevent this reprint. On 10 January 1810 it had been reported to him that the volumes Geistinger—"that thieving pirate"—was producing "were edited in the most shameful manner, without sense or order." In fact Goethe's *Complete Works* in 26 volumes appeared in Vienna between 1810 and 1817 bearing the imprint "Printed by Anton Strauss. Commissioned by Geistinger." On 19 March 1816, Cotta decided to take countermeasures and told Goethe in a note: "In order to control piracy I shall have to publish an edition in Vienna." However he immediately watered down this important piece of information: "at the moment they simply want to insert a copperplate engraved frontispiece . . . and a . . . portrait of your Excellency." In his reply, dated 25 March 1816, Goethe responded to this piece of news in the following words: "I can only approve the Viennese edition, where the law is of no help we must listen to cunning." He sent Cotta the portrait painted the year before that was now to be used as a title vignette in the new edition; in a postscript to his letter to Cotta on 22 October 1816 he asked that the original be changed very slightly as his "left eye is a little larger than the right."

It was a completely sensible act of Cotta's to arrange with the Austrian publisher Carl Armbruster and his associate Kaulfuss to publish an edition in Vienna. Armbruster had applied to the Imperial censorship office on 28 November 1819 for permission to include the *West-östliche Divan* in "the original edition of Goethe's works that is being published here." This was the way to stop a pirated version in Austria, for the head of the office told Armbruster on 1 December 1819, "According to the censorship regulation of 12 October 1810, no work may be reprinted the manuscript of which has been censored here and which can be shown to have been published in the Austrian monarchy."

So Cotta had a few of the volumes that had appeared in Stuttgart printed in Vienna and organized a separate edition to be published there; this protected him against unlawful reprints. The Viennese edition—2,500 copies were printed—is instructive for the printing and textual history of Goethe's works: "*Goethe's Works.* Volumes 1–26. Original Edition. Vienna 1816–1822. Published by Chr. Kaulfuss and C. Armbruster. Stuttgart. J.C.Cotta's Bookshop. Printed by Anton Strauss." Several texts that had been printed in Stuttgart and contained errors could be cleaned up in the Viennese edition, as we have pointed out above. On the other hand, completely new problems now arose. Because the Viennese proofreaders undertook changes on their own account, the Viennese edition makes use of a very individual orthography and punctuation that are closely linked to the locality and the publishing house. The advance sheets for the printing of the *Italian Journey,* in volumes 23 and 24 of the Viennese edition, went from the Frommann printing press in Jena to Vienna because Goethe's printed manuscript was no longer there. Goethe's corrected proofs, of which Frommann speaks in his letters to Cotta, were the proof sheets of the first printing of the work that was brought out by Cotta, but like several of Goethe's individual works that Cotta published it was printed in Jena by Frommann. Goethe undertook a number of changes in these proof sheets, thus superseding the printed manuscript. The printing of the *Divan* in the Viennese edition occupies a special place, and it appeared there illegally—that is, not approved by Cotta—as volume 21. Goethe had preserved the manuscript, which was the basis of the first printing, and sent it to Vienna as a model for the typesetters. "Dear Sir, You are to receive herewith the manuscript of the Divan, together with a corrected printed copy; but it would be excellent to direct the attention of the Viennese printers and proofreaders to the latter because at the moment it is much more reliable than the manuscript." The

Viennese edition, then, relies on a better original than the original edition published by Cotta did and is, in a number of cases, more accurate and closer to the original than the Stuttgart edition.

Goethe understood the special situation with regard to piracy in Austria and therefore approved of Cotta's project. But Cotta had made a big mistake in not informing Goethe about the origin of this edition, although he must have known how much Goethe was interested in the details of the production of a book; he had also offered Goethe neither free copies nor royalties for this edition. And thus it was that Goethe had forgotten the agreements, the preparations, in fact the whole Viennese undertaking, and this was how the disaster in the Johanna Franieck bookstore in Carlsbad—whose head was very experienced in matters of the production of Goethe's published works— occurred. On 21 September Goethe writes to Cotta after a stay in Carlsbad that he had indeed found "more beneficence and recovery" in the "healing waters" than "he could have hoped for" but that nevertheless "irksome moments came as a surprise to him."

I found myself in the company of several friends and strangers in a bookstore, the Iron Cross, in Carlsbad; they had been offered the final volume of an edition of my works, published last year in Vienna and Stuttgart. They were ready to buy it and asked me what I thought of the reprint under consideration. I answered, perhaps too naively, that I knew nothing about it! And on closer examination it appeared some-what irksome to see before my own eyes an *Original Edition* of which the author has no knowledge and in which the publisher does not iden-tify himself. Afterwards a cursory glance through it was enough to con-vince me that the most blatant typographical errors from the first re-prints were multiplied here and at the same time perpetuated.

Those present asked me further: how was it that there were only twenty parts available of the real edition, whereas there were twenty-six parts of the reprint. Something that placed those who owned the earlier edition at a great disadvantage. A question which I was also not in a position to answer, which made me appear indifferent, careless and rash in a most personal matter.

Please be good enough to explain this to me and set my mind at rest, for I may assure you that this is the only unpleasant impression I have brought home from the whole of this year's summer vacation that was otherwise so pleasant. I shall refrain from everything else and hardly need to add the assurance, that for my own part as long as I remain on earth I would, for the sake of my family, like to maintain without blemish the relationship that exists between us and that is so valuable and reminiscent of Schiller's mediation.

Cotta answers on 18 October. He first makes reference to the healing waters, but then writes that he was "doubly" pained by the fact that the Viennese edition had caused Goethe "annoyance" and he adds (and this is an expression of his bad conscience): "This has been, for a year and a day, my most unpleasant daily torment." Why did he not admit this to Goethe earlier? Why was this not a topic of conversation on 15 May 1823 when Cotta visited Goethe on his way to the Leipzig fair? Now he had to explain what he had only hinted at, that in order to control piracy in Austria he had printed a cheap edition in association with Armbruster in Vienna, "and I thought I had written to Your Excellency about this." Cotta recalls his letter of 25 March 1816 exactly. He now had to confess to Goethe as well that he had quarreled with Armbruster about the treatment of the *Divan,* something that was to lead to a suit and an arbitrated judgment. After the appearance of the twentieth volume of Goethe's works, Cotta had informed Armbruster that this was the end of the edition, but Armbruster reminded him of the competition from Geistinger's pirated version and insisted that the edition be continued with the *West-östlicher Divan.* There is no definitive explanation of the incident and it also remains unclear who was in charge of the Viennese undertaking. Cotta, it is true, had helped to finance the edition, but there was too little clarity about the situation for him to have been able to close off the project so rapidly. He mentioned to Goethe that the loss of money "that is very significant" pained him less than "the annoying hours this whole business has caused you—we must console ourselves with the fact that it would be impossible for another Austrian reprint to be made." Cotta knew what was at stake, he knew that Goethe was preparing another edition and that he was free to choose his own publisher. This is probably the reason he expressed the hope that Goethe "[was] convinced by earlier events that I must, and do, set the greatest store by remaining in this relationship with you." Goethe reacted slowly on 14 January 1824; he had been sick for a long time with a "most severe catarrh." Cotta's explanations, Goethe wrote, "were bound to revive all the painful feelings of which a German author is, throughout his life, all too frequently reminded and which on this occasion threw as black a pall as possible over the melancholy spirit."

It is clear that these "painful feelings" could not disappear overnight. If an author's relationship to his publisher, which is in any case a burdensome one, is seriously disturbed at any point there is an aftereffect. Goethe recalled the whole thing again two years later when the question of who was to publish the "final edition" had to be decided. The art historian Johann Sulpiz Boisserée, who at this time was one of Goethe's closest friends, was negotiating with publishers on Goethe's behalf. "You can imagine," Goethe wrote to Boisserée, "how much it would pain me to have to give up a relationship that is so firmly established; but at my great and often threatened age I am forced to make a rapid decision." There is a draft of a letter to Boisserée written by Goethe's secretary John; the letter was not sent off. In it Goethe says, "I too have the highest hopes that my relationship with Herr Cotta can be restored to its previous vitality: after the miserable Viennese reprinting neither side has been able to reestablish a proper trust."

It is of course understandable that Goethe did not forget the matter. But in a relationship as difficult as that of an author with his publisher, and vice versa, disappointment, unpleasant events, unhappy developments, as long as they are not the expression of wilful intent, can be lived through and can be overcome. Every human relationship, and this is true of the author-publisher relationship as well, only really proves itself in times of stress.

SEVEN

The Final Authorized Edition:
"The Most Important Matter of My Life"

ᐰᑯᐰᑯ

From "passionate
empiricism into the
more pure circle of
historical light"

GOETHE'S REACTIONS TO topical happenings are characteristic of him. It was the time when Goethe was
once more involved with the complex matter of *The
Journeyman Years.* The first version of *Wilhelm Meister's Journeyman Years* had appeared at the Easter
Fair in 1821; the press immediately attacked the book and it was also criticized by its readers. People preferred reading the product with the same title
by Johann Friedrich Wilhelm Pustkuchen, the theologian and writer, who
made fun of the "freedoms" of *The Journeyman Years* and launched strong
attacks on Goethe in several passages of his book. Pustkuchen became a
public success. It was in vain that critics voiced their opposition to this
botched piece of work; they succeeded in achieving the opposite effect, for
the antipathy that was felt towards Goethe at this time was merely intensified
by critical support. Goethe behaved as many authors do: outwardly it did
not seem to bother him; actually he was annoyed. At first he was restrained,
but in March 1822 he published "Well-disposed Sympathy for the 'Journeyman Years'" in the *Morgenblatt.* But he had already decided to rework it, a
task that was to occupy him until 1829. All the figures in the book know
that the "Purpose and Aim" of their existence—"A secret hidden by the
highest hand"—are to find their way by "thought and action"; they are
useful figures, active beings. The book is permeated by topoi of work, by
statements such as "competitive activity"; "what matters is that a person does
something excellently." "Action without talk must now be our watchword."

Goethe wanted to do something new and also something important for
the public at large. He intended not only to reinterpret the author-publisher

relationship, but also to determine afresh the situation of the contemporary author, of the author who regards writing as his profession.

In order for work on *Wilhelm Meister,* and on a new definitive edition, to continue "uninterrupted," he informed Cotta on 14 January 1824 that he had recruited "energetic, well-disposed helpers." He again talks of the chronicle of his life that is now to be expanded. "In its present form it now serves as a norm, just as all my papers, especially my correspondence, do, and these could some day be used and interlaced into the web of the events of my life . . . while the one, like the other, emerges from a dust-cloud of a passionate empiricism into the more pure circle of historical light." Goethe sees work ahead of him, work determined not only by the extent of his whole oeuvre but also by the revision of old texts and by the attempt that he is now making to complete various larger works. "But how these efforts, and the not insignificant expense involved in maintaining and paying my assistants, would finally benefit the author and his family, no less than they would the publisher, and to what extent a complete edition could be most rapidly prepared, you alone, dear Sir, can determine and indicate more closely, for which I would ask that you give me your well-informed opinion." And he ends his letter to Cotta of 14 January, "I who with ever the same confidence and the conviction of a successful cooperation have the honor to sign myself."

In his reply of 15 February Cotta appeared "extraordinarily pleased," for, on the one hand, the Viennese affair which was basically questionable and had been a burden to him seemed to be having no immediate consequences—there is even the possibility that he will publish a complete new edition—but on the other hand this "demands the most serious attention," "so that all the conditions that need to be mentioned and need to be attended to are observed and thought through." Cotta knows the problem, knows that the complete edition that he had published before this one can still be bought in the bookstores and suspects that he will have to pay unusual royalties for the rights. However he then mentions his "alliance" with Elisabeth von Gemmingen-Guttenberg, whom he will take as his second wife. He commends her to Goethe's friendship, saying that only the "unusual qualities" of Frau Elisabeth could bring him to make this decision: "what I sought and what I needed—an intellectually stimulating friend to be at my side in the evening of my days [Cotta is just under sixty]—I have certainly found." In fact Cotta's co-workers and a few authors confirm that Elisabeth had a beautiful soul, but his children by his first wife blame the enthusiasm of Cotta's new wife for Cotta's many new and not very profitable undertakings. Goethe congratulates him—the news of a "new and happy outlook for your life" has given him great joy.

Later Goethe often turned to Frau Cotta personally because she was in charge of the *Pocket Book for Ladies.* "Because of our common interest" he wanted to report for duty to Cotta once more. He told Cotta, however, of an inquiry by the publisher of the Weygand bookstore, who intended to "give the world a new edition of *The Sorrows of Werther*" and who had asked him for a "few words as a new foreword." Cotta urgently advised Goethe not to accept; the publisher's idea, he said, was "very presumptuous," he had no legal grounds for suggesting it, and it would thus be "more advisable" to "include" a new text in the complete edition. But Goethe was of a different mind. It was to be a jubilee edition, for fifty years had passed since *Werther* first appeared (authors too, as well as publishers—who are often criticized for it—are number fetishists!). On 25 March 1824 Goethe finished the proposed "poetic introduction." "Once more you dare much lamented shade / to appear in daylight." Again he found an intermediary to negotiate with the firm of Weygand for the poem and to obtain a royalty of fifty ducats (150 thalers) for five strophes of different length, consisting of fifty lines altogether. These fifty lines were sent to Weygand, who could now legitimately announce his "New Edition" for the year 1824 (though the printed date is 1825) as "introduced by the author himself."

The poem ends with the famous lines that, slightly altered, come from *Tasso:* "Half guilty and involved in such torments / Give him a God to tell what he is suffering." Goethe only addressed the theme of *Werther* later, when he actually gave the title "To Werther" to the poem—this "product of a highly passionate state"—and included it in 1827 in a collection of three poems with the title *Trilogy of Passion.*[1] "Weygand wanted to produce a new edition of my Werther and asked me for a foreword which was for me a most welcome occasion to write my poem to Werther. But as I still had some remnants of that passion in my heart, the poem took shape as though by itself as an introduction to that elegy." Goethe arranged the poems in the trilogy in reverse chronological order. The first poem, "To Werther," was written last (25 March 1824), the last poem, "Reconciliation," first (18 August 1823). He started writing drafts of the second poem, "The Elegy," on 5 September 1823 and had a fair copy two weeks later.

The biographical background, the work situation, the experience of love and life that lead to the *Trilogy of Passion* are well known. Goethe was very ill in February and March 1823, probably from a heart attack, but the illness went as it had come. When he reached Marienbad in June he felt like a changed man, a rejuvenated one; after writing *The Journeyman Years* he had been engaged mainly in scientific work and his poetic spring seemed to have dried up. He ironized himself as a scholar who "only" does research, "collects details,"[2] and who was now in spite of everything writing poems.

Again, probably for the third time, he meets Ulrike von Levetzow in Marienbad, falls so deeply in love that he asks Carl August to ask the Levetzow family and Ulrike whether she, scarcely twenty years old, would marry the seventy-four-year-old. The offer included a substantial financial settlement and the offer of a pension. Goethe receives a hesitating and vague refusal, and the Levetzow family leaves on 17 August 1823 for Carlsbad. A few days later Goethe turns up in Carlsbad, but on 5 September he records in his diary the final "tumultuous farewell." From Carlsbad he travels to Weimar; en route in the coach, he works on his "Marienbad Elegy," to which he gives as a motto the lines from *Tasso:* "And if man stays mute in his torment / A divinity let me say what I suffer." The poem is certainly one of Goethe's greatest lyric creations. Whether the generic description "elegy" is the right one is still disputed even today.[3] But the twenty-three strophes are certainly written with great artistry in a strict six-line stanza form. The symbolism of the last rhyme is characteristic: "They [the Gods] forced me to the generous mouth [Munde] / they separate me and destroy me [Grunde]."

When towards the end of the year Goethe had a severe relapse and recurrence of his heart disease, his friend Carl Zelter, the composer, had to read him the "Elegy" over and over again. Zelter himself has stated what his survival therapy was: "mental anguish" should help. And it helped. And work on literature helped. "Reconciliation" became, as the final poem in the trilogy, a significant apotheosis of reconciliation: "Passion brings suffering!" But music with its "angels' wings" brings reconciliation.

Goethe had often visited Marie Szymanowska, a pianist from St. Petersburg, in Marienbad and had tried to use her and her piano playing to heal his "morbid irritability." In Weimar from 30 October to 5 November 1823 Frau Szymanowska was able to comfort him with her playing and reconcile him to his fate; this is the biographical background to his placing "Reconciliation," the first poem composed (that he had given to Szymanowska in a French version), at the end as a symbolic highpoint. Then—"Oh, might it last for ever!— / The double joy of notes and love was felt." This applies to Ulrike, who remained unmarried until 1899 and commented in her old age on her relationship to Goethe: "It was not a love affair."

During those days in Marienbad Goethe had experienced anew the simultaneity of demonic genius and art, of passion and poetry, of despair and music. His novel *The Elective Affinities,* in which truly demonic depths of passion are plumbed, had no conciliatory art, no music. Now he could expose himself to the "Divine value of notes as well as tears." "The Elegy" ends with an expression of passion: "Already it rages and tears at me within my breast, / Where life and death are locked in grim combat."

Seven months after Goethe had written "The Elegy," Weygand came to ask him to write a foreword to the jubilee edition of *Werther.* Goethe took up the text again: Had he felt, experienced, expressed things like this half a century ago? For Werther there had been no solution outside the revelation of love; Werther half a century later does not allow himself to be destroyed by passion. He was granted "reconciliation" by nature and by art. Since Goethe places the poem *To Werther* at the beginning of the trilogy and as it is so personal, "The Elegy" becomes a self-portrait of the aged Goethe who has, it is true, found himself torn to pieces on the very edge of existence but still reconciled in the double joy of "notes and love."

"Thinking and Doing" Meanwhile the Marienbad experience, for all its poetic dressing, could not remain without consequences for Goethe's self-esteem. True, for him it is still a matter of change, metamorphosis, and renewal; he was to remark to Chancellor von Müller, on 24 April 1830: "Well, have I reached the age of eighty only to go on thinking the same thing all the time? Everyday I try to think something different, something *new* so as not to become boring. We must constantly change, renew ourselves, rejuvenate ourselves so that we don't become stick-in-the-muds." And yet: the Marienbad experience had shown him that there were limits, limits to his hope of rejuvenation, limits to his ability to experience a new erotic relationship, limits to his nature, limits to his physical consciousness, limits that his increasing age set upon him. This painful experience, the realization that for all the support of his friends and of other people, he was left alone, solitary, did not make him despair; on the

contrary a strong feeling of gratitude for life led him to face himself and "the challenges of the day." In a letter to Boisserée, his thirty-five-year younger friend, I discern the credo of the last decade of his life:

> Forgive me, my friend if I appear to be exalted; but since God and Nature have left me to myself for so many years, I know of no way of expressing my grateful appreciation better than by youthful activity. I want to show myself worthy of the good fortune that has been granted me—as long as it continues—and I spend day and night thinking how this can be, and acting so that it is, possible.
>
> Day and night is not just a phrase, since I devote many a nocturnal hour which—such is the fate of my advanced years—I spend sleeplessly, not to vague and general thoughts, but to thinking about precisely what I am going to do the next day, and the next morning I start on it in all honesty and do it as far as possible. Thus, in the days allotted me, I perhaps do and complete, in a sensible fashion, more than what one neglects at a time when one justifiably believes or imagines there will be another day and that there will always be another day.

A revealing insight for Goethe: to do *what is useful,* since, in the order of things, what is useless perishes.

Goethe's last decade is determined by his concentration both on what is close at hand and at the same time on the expanse of huge and distant intellectual spaces. The external distance, journeys, for example, beyond the immediate neighborhood of Weimar and Jena no longer take place. Weimar is and remains his world, he builds his house on the Frauenplan into a cosmopolitan city. Testimonies to his life and work are displayed, collections and books, gifts and diplomas, portraits and busts that had been made of him. It would be almost obvious to call this a museum of himself, but Goethe, of late a solitary person, is probably only building himself here a prop to help fulfil the demands of the day. A host of visitors seek admission; anyone who can come up with an introduction is admitted. Many who are permitted to cross the threshold of the house in the Frauenplan certainly gain the impression that his excellency is stiff and cold; people often take it amiss that he loves his decorations, that he likes to wear them. For many Germans he is not German enough, for many Christians not pious enough. Friedrich Wilhelm Riemer, Goethe's most important collaborator on the final authorized edition, remarks about these visitors' reactions: "You had to bring something if you wanted to take something away." And, "A watchful look, unconcealed attention, muted or apodictic response were certainly unlikely to be met with great openness on his part." Eckermann notes one of Goethe's statements in March 1830: "Sometimes I have to be proud, sometimes egotistical, sometimes full of envy towards younger talents, sometimes plunged into the joys of the senses, sometimes without Christianity, and now finally even without love for my country and my dear Germans."

Visits of writers to Goethe are especially precarious, but this is not only true of him. From my own experience I know how complicated such meetings are. At the entrance to Hermann Hesse's garden there was a notice: "No visits please." At my request Samuel Beckett received, within a short space of time, Edward Bond and Peter Handke; both of these eloquent writers lapsed into silence out of respect for Beckett's poetic authority and under the influence of Beckett's appearance and so the conversations were very one-sided. After this Beckett did not want to see any more writers. It is all too understandable that Goethe avoided meetings with writers of his time. He would however have liked to meet Lord Byron, who had dedicated his *Sardanapalus* to him in 1823. Byron regarded himself as a "literary vassal who presents his homage to the first of all living writers as to his liege lord—to him who had created the literature of his own country and had illuminated the whole of Europe." Goethe received the page with Byron's autograph dedication but the publisher had forgotten to include it in the printed book! Eckermann always stressed the intensity of Goethe's relationship to contemporary French literature. From 1826 onwards, Goethe subscribed to the French periodical *Le Globe* and had busied himself with the young French writers represented in it. It is true he had his difficulties with German writers. Eckermann mentions this in a remarkable entry on 14 March 1830:

> No one else came out of it better, most of them indeed worse and in England and France it is just the same as here. What did Molière not suffer and Rousseau and Voltaire! Calumnious tongues drove Byron out of England and he would finally have fled to the ends of the world, if an early death had not taken him from the philistines and their hatred. And what if loftier men followed the bigoted masses. No, *one* gifted person and *one* talent persecute each other. Platen annoys Heine and Heine Platen, and everyone tries to make the others hated and bad,

even though the world is large enough for peaceful coexistence and peaceful cooperation and everyone has an enemy in his own talent that causes him enough trouble.

Of course there were visitors who were very welcome: Zelter with whom he discussed the theory of composition and the composition of his own works, the brothers Humboldt (Goethe's last letter, of 17 March 1832, is addressed to Wilhelm von Humboldt), the botanist Friedrich Sigmund Voigt and Carl Vogel, Goethe's personal doctor from 1826 onwards, to whom Goethe transferred the supervision of the institutes for art and science after the death of his son August. Vogel knew Goethe intimately and published the treatise *Goethe's Last Illness* in 1833. Johann Heinrich Meyer who, with Zelter and Knebel, was among Goethe's closest friends was always willing to come and chat. Chancellor (Friedrich Theodor Adam Heinrich) von Müller was a favorite and spirited discussion partner. His *Conversations with Goethe* appeared posthumously in 1870 and present quite a different picture of Goethe from Eckermann's; in them Goethe speaks directly and pointedly, "with epigrammatic sharpness and biting criticism," as Müller noted. Goethe could express himself more clearly to him, a social equal, than he could to his secretaries and clerks. His relationship to Karl Ludwig Knebel was quite different; he had arranged Goethe's first meeting with Duke (later Prince) Carl August; their association continued until old age although Goethe chided him for his bad-tempered and hypochondriacal character ("Knebel is good, but uncertain and too eager to be idle and daydreaming"); nevertheless Goethe carried Knebel's translation of Lucretius with him for years and he distinguished it with a review. But, seen as a whole, visitors were a burden, only lightened by occasional "significant conversations" with scholars and friends. Thus between 1823 and 1826 he concentrated on what he called his "main business,"[4] on the preparation of the final authorized edition and the completion of *Faust*.

How did Goethe prepare for this "main business"? He did it, as always, in the most precise manner. He created an environment in his house that made it possible for him to work efficiently. He established an archive, sought out competent associates, and undertook the attempt, one that was to mark an epoch in book-marketing, to protect the complete edition of his works—an act that was to crown his life's work—by the receipt of privileges which would prevent pirating of the edition not only in the individual lands of Germany but in Austria too. When he had achieved this, he let publishers court him—to the point where it became an auction—only in the end to decide in favor of Cotta. His procedure is without compare.

However difficult and complicated his own family was for Goethe, he arranged things in such a way that he could on the one hand pursue his work and duties and on the other have some social life. Cooks and a changing group of servants were active in the household and were supervised, perhaps not to the extent he could have wished, by his daughter-in-law Ottilie, but mainly by the servant Stadelmann. A coachman looked after the equipage that he had bought in 1799 and that is still to be seen in the Goethehaus, a stately vehicle that was used for journeys and visits but also on representative occasions.

Excursus: "Goethe's Philipp Friedrich Seidel (who had already been a ser-
Well-Disposed vant of his father's), Christoph Sutor, Johann George
Assistants" Paul Götze, and Johann Ludwig Geist were his ser-
vants until 1804.

In 1814 Johann Carl Wilhelm Stadelmann entered Goethe's service and remained there until he was dismissed in 1826. Stadelmann was a character; he often accompanied Goethe on trips from which he sent the servants and the clerks orders in letters in which he tried, in grotesque fashion, to copy Goethe's style. Under Goethe's guidance he worked at mineralogy and geology, but he also worked on setting up the archives. He would probably have remained a servant until Goethe's death if he had confined himself to the enjoyment of the chemical experiment with the wine glass to show that—in certain circumstances—it reflected the rainbow and not the wine itself. He had to be dismissed. He ends up in the poorhouse, but even here he still drinks whenever he can lay hands on a groschen. When Goethe's hometown of Frankfurt wanted to erect a memorial to Goethe in 1844 people remembered Stadelmann and invited him to Frankfurt. He came dressed in one of Goethe's coats, sat in the front row at the celebration, but on his return hanged himself in the attic of the poorhouse. But Goethe is not to be reproached on this account.

Stadelmann was followed on 1 December 1826 by Gottlieb Friedrich Krause who remained until Goethe's death; Goethe had a good relationship with him.

Goethe's staff of assistants for the work on the final authorized edition was divided up hierarchically almost like a pyramid. At the foot there are the clerks, occasionally supported by associates from Bertuch's Industrial Office; above them the advisers and experts, Riemer, Göttling, Meyer, and Soret whom Goethe called his "living lexicons," in which he liked "looking things up." And then in special and elevated positions, Eckermann and Chancellor von Müller.

Goethe worked at this time with three clerks, or secretaries, John, Kräuter, and Schuchardt.[5]

Johann August Friedrich John was employed by Goethe from 1814 and also worked as a copyist in the Grand Ducal library. He probably wrote most of the letters that Goethe dictated.

Friedrich Theodor David Kräuter was a clerk in the same library and afterwards became a librarian. As library councillor he later ran the library that had been laxly cared for by Goethe's brother-in-law Vulpius. He was in Goethe's service from 1818 as a clerk and private secretary. As Goethe tells us in his *Biographical Details,* Kräuter, "a fresh young man, experienced in the business of libraries and archives," put his archives in order and made an initial index. He was the motive power behind all the work on the archives and thus something of a coordinator of the editorial staff. According to Eckermann, Goethe was very satisfied with him. Certainly, Kräuter was the one who occasionally rebelled against the totally uncreative work. "It is sad when, to be around great men, you lose all your independence; you are no longer permitted to have a will of your own, enough that you are the ball they play catch with according to their own whims." But Kräuter stuck to his work and played an important part in the progress of the edition.

Johann Christian Schuchardt, the last of Goethe's secretaries, was a lawyer and registrar at the institutes for science and the arts that were under Goethe's jurisdiction; later, in 1863, he became head of the Free Drawing Institute in Weimar. He had made a suggestion to Goethe as to how the collections should be arranged, and Goethe thought his suggestion "successful." On 20 February 1825 he was appointed secretary. Under Goethe's supervision he compiled the first scholarly inventories of the collections and in 1848/49 published a three-volume catalog[6] that for the first time revealed all the wealth and diversity contained in them. Goethe valued him highly; he personally made arrangements for his housing and, something that never happened to any other collaborator, visited him there on 23 June 1831.

Schuchardt observed Goethe very closely—the way in which he clasped his hands behind his back when he was walking up and down in his simple office with its wooden shelves and boxes, an oval table, and hard chairs. He was always enthusiastic about the ease with which Goethe could dictate; it was as if he were reading in his head from an already prepared paper, and he noted the gestures that accompanied the dictation. "With hands outspread and his body leaning to one side or the other he brought the subject into balance and into its proper place." If he was successful, he usually cried out, "That's right. Quite right!"

In the diary entries for these years we come across his name on almost every page. Thus Schuchardt was certainly the most valued collaborator among all the secretaries.

There is a clear distinction between clerks and secretaries on the one hand and experts on the other. The clerks and secretaries work during working hours and are paid accordingly. The gentlemen who advised Goethe were entertained outside working hours, for lunch, tea, or in the evening. As early as 8 September 1822 Goethe is able to tell Cotta:

> On the other hand, I can count myself lucky that a group of friends are most lively supporters and help me preserve and use what a good intellect had, both in my earlier and later life, granted me. During my absence this summer a repository has been put together which contains all the writings, works, and drafts of mine that have ever been printed or that have remained unpublished; here all my diaries written both at home and abroad, every fragment and what is more, from a certain year onwards, every letter that I have received, and the most important ones that I have sent, are stored in cupboards.
>
> I was surprised on my return by this arrangement and by a complete index and I am now negotiating with my older and younger friends as to how it might be used and how, if I were to be called away, care could be taken that nothing goes astray. I am reserving the right to tell you more about all this soon.
>
> Part of the winter, at least, will be dedicated to this business which we intend bringing to a high degree of completion and security. Without mentioning names we can assume that Councillor Meyer and Professor Riemer, collaborators for many years, will always be at my side.

In another place Goethe talks of the "assistance of excellent men." In fact this group of advisers were diligent, well-disposed, competent, and effective.

Friedrich Wilhelm Riemer, literary scholar and writer, was most closely connected with Goethe. From 1801 to 1803 he was a tutor in Wilhelm von Humboldt's house, in 1802/03 his *Greek-German Pocket Dictionary* appeared. Goethe appointed the barely thirty-year-old as tutor to his son August. He lived in Goethe's house and became an ever more trusted adviser in literary and philological questions, responsible for all matters to do with antiquity and classical philology. Because of a dispute with August, he left Goethe's house and became a high-school professor in 1812, a librarian in 1814 in the grand-ducal library in Weimar where he became senior librarian in 1836. In 1819 he once again worked for Goethe. Goethe entrusted him and Eckermann with the publication of his posthumous works; he paid out 800 thalers for their efforts, probably without an inkling of how many years the two, especially Eckermann, would have to work on the twenty volumes of posthumous writings. Riemer was indispensable to Goethe in the two "main pieces of business," for the final authorized edition as well as for the further work on *Faust,* something to which the diaries bear ample witness. Riemer rearranged the poems, verified the titles, compared the subtitles and the intermediate titles of the collections. Time and again there is a note in the diaries, "Faust with Riemer." Goethe thought highly of Riemer, "I admired his prudence and his deep knowledge of language." He approved of his marriage to Caroline Wilhelmine Johanna Ulrich, Christiane's companion. Goethe liked to talk about the "two women."

Karl Wilhelm Göttling, son of an apothecary, literary scholar and archeologist, was the circle's chief authority on correct orthography. He was a high-school professor in Rudolstadt and Neuwied and, from 1828, professor of classics and librarian in Jena. Goethe had met him on one of his trips to Jena, apparently in 1822; in any case he asked him at that time for a translation of Euripides' *Phaeton.* Goethe counted Göttling—whom he addressed as a "littérateur"—among his friends until his death.

The same is true of Johann Heinrich Meyer, the Swiss painter and art historian. Goethe had brought him to the drawing school in Weimar as a teacher, and he became director in 1807. Meyer was Goethe's closest adviser on art; the two died in the same year. Meyer lived in Goethe's house for ten years, from 1792 to 1802, and the plan for the *Propyläen* originated in a conversation with him and Schiller. There are contributions in Goethe's periodicals signed WKF, the initials standing for "The Weimar Friends of Art" (*Weimarer Kunstfreunde*), Goethe, Schiller, and Meyer, who edited one another's contributions. Meyer was closely concerned with revising the text of the art historical writings for the final authorized edition.

Fréderic Jacques (also Jean, Jakob) Soret, scientist, theologian, and writer from Geneva, was called to Weimar to become tutor to the hereditary duke, Karl Alexander. Goethe mentions him for the first time in December 1822. He took particular interest in Goethe's scientific writings and thus became involved as an adviser in this area. Soret was always consulted by Goethe when it was a question of judging translations of works into French. According to Eckermann, Soret frequently ate at Goethe's house and he was a frequent and welcome guest at evening social events. Besides this, his scientific knowledge offered numerous points of contact for a lasting companionship. As a careful mineralogist he put Goethe's crystals in order, and his knowledge of botany enabled him to translate Goethe's *Metamorphosis of the Plant* into French, thus ensuring a wider dissemination of that important work. Soret returned to Geneva in 1836.

All in all it was an astonishing, academically trained, and outstanding team that Goethe assembled for the preliminary work on and later for the completion of the final authorized edition.

At the peak of the pyramid of collaborators, however, was Johann Peter Eckermann. Eckermann was the most remarkable, most peculiar, and most effective of the collaborators. He did not come, as all the rest did, from a "house," but from a "hut," as the "last born of a second marriage" of a truly underprivileged family whose "main source of income . . . was a cow"—this is what he himself says in the Introduction to his book of conversations in which the author tells us "about himself and his origins and the way his relationship to Goethe came about." I find the expression of their special relationship in the account of their very first meeting. Eckermann, who had walked from Göttingen to Weimar, a distance of some 100 miles, with the actual goal of then walking back through the Rhineland area, saw Goethe on 10 June 1823 for the first time and notes under that date: "A noble figure! . . . the sort that one imagines an aging monarch to be . . . . I felt indescribably good in his presence; I felt calmed just as someone might feel who after much effort and long-nurtured hope finally sees his dearest wishes fulfilled . . . . (He) said that he wished to see me again and that he would send for me at a suitable hour . . . we parted with affection." This first entry already speaks volumes in its description of the first meeting with the revered writer and was already an expression of Eckermann's affection. Goethe too was apparently taken with the thirty-year-old, and Eckermann "was highly delighted, for his every word expressed goodwill."

Given his "origins," Eckermann could not have expected such a reception. He was born in 1792. In order to escape from his extremely poverty-stricken conditions he volunteered as a Hanover rifleman, then became a clerk and later a registrar in the military administration in Hanover. Meanwhile he attended high school and in 1821 he left the service. But, as he drew his pay for a further two years, he was able to study in Göttingen. However, he soon broke off his studies; he did not wish to become a lawyer but wanted to be a writer. Under the spell of Schiller's, Klopstock's and above all Goethe's lyric poetry he wrote poems that he sent to Goethe; he later wrote a drama. After this, according to his self-stylization, he read *Wilhelm Meister, Faust,* and "thought of nothing but Goethe." He later read the most "excellent pieces" by Shakespeare, Sophocles, and Homer. The personal wish of the autodidact Eckermann was to achieve something "excellent," especially in the areas of the poetic. He became increasingly interested in aesthetics and poetic theory and he turned his hand to writing essays until, finally, in 1822, he completed a manuscript entitled "Articles on Poetry with Special Reference to Goethe. He sent this to Goethe, too, but received no answer. And then that first memorable visit took place on 10 June 1823. Goethe was on his best behavior during the visit and completely captivated the young man, who was confused, astonished, and intimidated. Goethe personally arranged his lodgings in Weimar, ordered Secretary Kräuter to "show him around," but above all he praised Eckermann's poems and spoke highly appreciative words about his work on aesthetics. He promised that he would write "this very day . . . by express mail" to Cotta with the urgent recommendation that the latter should publish it.

In fact Goethe wrote to Cotta a day later in connection with his efforts to find collaborators for the "final edition." "Now, I have for some time had an eye on a certain young Eckermann from Hanover. I am sending you by express mail a manuscript that he would like your firm to publish . . . . the clarity and freedom of the manuscript are already engaging and the content appeals to me because the young man, like Schubart and Zauper,[7] has modeled himself on me. He is here at the moment and I think I will use him for certain preparatory work." This too is astonishing—just one day after their meeting Goethe knew that he wanted him as an associate.

From Eckermann's point of view, events must, after this, have raced ahead: the master's goodwill, the invitation to stay in Weimar and to visit him again, the praise for the manuscript, and finally the recommendation to

Cotta that was more than a recommendation, and to which the latter quickly acquiesced (the book appeared in October of the same year).[8] But there was still more; when they talked on the following day Eckermann received, without asking, a commission "so that we can get to know one another better."

The first commission, then. Goethe gave Eckermann the two volumes of the *Frankfurter Gelehrten Anzeige* for the years 1772 and 1773 that contained a number of reviews by Goethe that were not signed by him; Eckermann was to find out which they were. He was, said Goethe, in a position to do this, "as you know my ways and the way I think." And then there was a further appeal: "I want to know whether you are worthy of working on a future edition of my works." What a commission at only the second meeting and what trust in the judgment of the young man! Eckermann was not afraid to accept the commission; he wanted to test himself in these subjects and wanted nothing more than to succeed in acting completely according to Goethe's way of thinking. Goethe urged Eckermann, in the same conversation, to stay in Weimar until "I return in the autumn from Marienbad. I wrote yesterday already (that is after the first meeting and without consulting Eckermann!) to inquire about lodgings and things of that sort so that everything will be pleasant and comfortable for you." Eckermann found "nothing to object to in such suggestions" and agreed to everything. They did not arrange about payment. Eckermann was, as Martin Walser so appositely puts it in his drama of independence, "in Goethe's hands."[9]

Eckermann, who dedicated all his vigor and capacity for work to his service to Goethe, and accepted domestic misery in exchange, was forced by financial considerations to give up the forty birds that he kept in his room—significantly, diurnal birds of prey, falcons and sparrow hawks. He married Johanna Bertram, his "Hannele," to whom he became engaged in 1819, only in 1831; Goethe no more than tolerated her. She died three years later in childbirth. Eckermann gave up his own career (could he have been successful free of Goethe?), and this man, ready to make sacrifices, devoted but happy in his service, became Goethe's most intense collaborator and interlocutor. Was he, in the final analysis, a victim of Goethe's egoism, of Goethe's obsession with work, of Goethe's pressure, even of his addiction to the realization of his "main business," the final authorized edition and *Faust?* One thing is certain: Goethe paid him too little for the number of things he did, both for his work in the nine years up to Goethe's death as well as for the labor involved in preparing for the publication of the posthumous works. Eckermann was always forced to give private lessons, but he probably found fulfillment in his work for Goethe and he wished for nothing else than to act in accordance with Goethe's way of thinking. So he plunged into the work.

Goethe advised him about externals, changed the way he wore his hair, ordered clothes for him, instructed him in court manners, and above all always introduced him as "Doctor Eckermann" and addressed him as "Doctor" although the doctorate was a complete fiction. True, Goethe did make the fiction into a reality. When the University of Jena celebrated Goethe's fiftieth anniversary in office, in November 1825, they allowed him to propose two honorary doctors, one of whom was Eckermann. As far as Eckermann was concerned these were externals, he was only concerned with his work. "He's collecting my poems together like an ant," Goethe wrote, "Without him I would never have got to it, but it will be very nice . . . . he is collecting, sorting, arranging and he knows how to get something out of things with a great deal of affection . . . he is interested in things that are no longer of interest to me." Is there higher praise, is there greater satisfaction? Goethe discussed suggestions for editing his *Journey to Switzerland, 1797* with Eckermann, who made notes of what Goethe said in their conversations about it and then presented him with them. "You are on the right path," said Goethe, talking down to him. "You are unable to do anything off the cuff and superficially but have to be able to get to the root of your subject in peace, but this is the way the greatest things are achieved." These are the heights towards which Eckermann strived.

He lived for nine years for Goethe and the latter knew what he had in Eckermann, even if he only expressed this knowledge in his concern for him and not in generous payment. He confided his posthumous works to him and Riemer, he gave him the papers that he wanted to be kept confidential, he asked him whether it was a good idea to publish certain juvenilia, he left the editing of certain older writings to him, he was *the* person whom he trusted in things literary. "My relationship to Goethe was peculiar and very tender," Eckermann wrote in March 1844. "It was the relationship of a pupil to his teacher, of a son to his father, of someone in need of culture to someone who had a wealth of it." "Sometimes I only saw him once a week, when I was fortunate enough to have lunch with him—sometimes with several others, sometimes tête-à-tête. But there was no lack of focus to our relationship. I took over the editing of his older papers." Given Eckermann's humility, it can be regarded as true.

But Eckermann's great service lies elsewhere. He knew how to get

Goethe, who was obviously growing more and more taciturn, to talk, even to scintillate; he knew how to reproduce the themes, the problems, the ideas, and the visions that moved Goethe in his old age and in so doing revealed what sort of a cosmos it was in which he was moving. "Eckermann understands best how to extort literary productions from me by the sensual interest that he takes in what has already been achieved and what has already been started." Certainly he was "in Goethe's hands" and Goethe exploited his devotion, but did Eckermann not achieve fame through his *Conversations with Goethe in the Final Years of His Life* that first appeared in 1836, does he not to this very day find his niche in literary history through the almost incalculable number of editions and printings of Goethe's works and is not "Eckermann" even today an indispensable tool for those who work on Goethe, a never-ending source and a magnificent treasure trove? We do not have to agree completely with Nietzsche when he writes in *Human All-Too-Human* that *Conversations* is "the best book" there has ever been, but it is an incontestable fact that this book has to be, and will be, read and reread across the centuries. "Au relire" was Rilke's characteristic farewell.

Chancellor von Müller floats over the collaborators' pyramid more or less freely. Friedrich Theodor Adam Heinrich Müller, raised to the nobility in 1807, a lawyer, a civil servant in the Napoleonic Wars and one whom even Napoleon admired personally, chancellor from 1815 in Weimar, also belonged to Goethe's closest circle of advisers. But his social equality with Goethe meant that he was less a laborer in the Lord's vineyard than a legal adviser and moral comrade-in-arms. He played the latter role, especially in publishing matters, where he tried to strengthen Goethe's skepticism towards publishers, publishing houses, booksellers, and pirates. Even after Goethe's death while acting as executor of his will, Müller's relationship to Cotta remained cool. Thus it is understandable that he probably recorded with a secret joy Goethe's tirade against publishers. His posthumous *Conversations with Goethe,* 1870, are, together with Eckermann's notes, among the most important sources for our knowledge of Goethe's oral pronouncements.

Goethe guided the work of his staff with a loose rein. Fundamentally, he let things take their course and only occasionally interfered to correct something, but in all the preparatory conversations he had reserved for himself the task of structuring the edition. He was absolutely clear that it should not be arranged chronologically, though this had been discussed even in these circles. The edition was to embrace the integral Goethe; old and new were not to be separated but were to appear as an amalgam. His work had not developed chronologically, by stages, but had taken up, simultaneously, past experiences, present events, and visions of the future. "My work is a collective being and it bears the name Goethe," he said near the end of his life. A collective being of this sort cannot be grasped either from the center or from the margins but only as a whole and simultaneously and not as a chronological development. His works, and let us repeat this important statement: "bear witness to a talent that does not develop in stages nor to one that wanders around but to one that branches out on all sides simultaneously from a certain central point and strives for an effect both at a distance and close at hand, deserts forever many a well-trodden path and stays on others for a long time."

But as far as the final authorized edition is concerned, we must also remember the person who really had the last say: Wilhelm Reichel, Cotta's manager and proofreader in the Augsburg printing works where Goethe's works were set and printed. Wilhelm Reichel, a printer from Saxony, had worked for Bertuch from 1803 and went to Stuttgart as Cotta's manager in 1811. At the beginning of 1825 he moved to Cotta's printing works in Augsburg. He was manager, proofreader, and foreman in one, that is, as the responsible person in charge he managed the printing works while being at the same time responsible for the accuracy of the printing, and it was in this capacity that he corresponded with authors as to whether their works were ready to be set. Goethe had known him from Stuttgart, and many of Cotta's letters had contained questions from Reichel. From 1825 onwards he corresponded directly with Goethe and this was one of the reasons why at this time fewer letters passed between Cotta and Goethe. Goethe had great confidence in him, and there were a lot of corrected proofs that Goethe no longer looked at before they were printed; he was often surprised, though, by "improvements," often angered by false corrections. However, for the most part, Goethe thought highly of Reichel's suggestions and his work. "As far as the Herr Reviser's objections and reservations are concerned, these have been handled correctly and I am grateful for his attention to them," he wrote to Cotta on 3 June 1816. Reichel expressed his opinion at length about the layout of the two volumes of poems in the final authorized edition, pointing out different options to Goethe, such as different formulations of titles and half-titles. On the whole, Goethe was "completely" satisfied with Reichel's work, praised his care, gave him medals, and even praised him to Frommann and Boisserée.

The proofreader's work is indispensable even today: the greater the degree to which automated book production withdraws from control by the human eye—even if there are fewer and fewer manuscripts and more and more diskettes—at a certain stage of the production process the proofreader has to supervise the text. The profession is a risky one; it not only demands devotion, but can virtually only be performed by self-sacrifice. The proofreader does not merely exist on the objective basis of a standard handbook of orthography, he must go beyond this and put himself to a great extent into the author's mind-set; to the extent permissible he must put the author's idiosyncrasies, the peculiarities of his grammar, orthography, and punctuation, his consciously personal style, linguistic inventions, and neologisms above the general rules of correct orthography. The proofreader's work is exhausting, nerve-wracking, sacrificial, often torturing, and it is thankless, because he frequently brings down an author's wrath upon his head with his suggestions and corrections and also because his corrections often cost the publisher a lot of money. Hermann Hesse in his *Letter to a Proof Reader* paid homage to the profession but also laid down its limits. I have grateful memories of Frau Dr. Messinger, proofreader for the S. Fischer and Suhrkamp houses in the fifties; she regarded the proofreader as the person who put the finishing touches to the author's work; and I remember many of the proofreaders in our publishing houses without whose painstaking work the authors' manuscripts would not have been ready for the press. But there are few who can pursue such a profession all their lives; their eyes often fail and often their nerves simply go on strike. Goethe's proofreader, Wilhelm Reichel, fared no differently; it is said that in 1836 he became mentally deranged.

This, then, was the staff that Goethe had put together for his final authorized edition: more than a "society of younger and older friends," more than "the assistance of excellent men" as Goethe wrote. It was a competent team that was passionate in its work, and as dedicated as if they were laboring on their own works.

As far as I know there has been no writer before or after Goethe who surrounded himself with a comparably large staff of collaborators and worked so intensively with them. In our century most writers have been loners. Thomas Mann, Rilke, Hesse (to say nothing of Kafka) wrote and published their works without outside help, they even wrote out their manuscripts in longhand, as Martin Walser still does today. Bertolt Brecht is the exception; he seldom wrote, especially in the middle and later years, without collaborators. Above all, it was his work in the theater that was collective. However, this cannot be compared with Goethe's staff that was assembled by the hand of a genius. But whereas nothing was ever final for Brecht—he even said of things that were completed, "Everything needs changing"—if one was to arrive at solutions and keys, Goethe believed that there were clear limits to the amount of discussion and to his capacity for being influenced; in the final analysis he relied on his imagination and insisted on the "secret."

"The Best Decoration"—The Privilege of the Edition   Goethe's letter to Cotta dated 14 January 1824, in which he replied to the latter's excuses about the Viennese reprint, ended in a very Goethean manner with a prospect for the future; he reported that he was once more working on a project that he called "Chronicle." This was an old plan. When he wanted to propose the order in which the contents of the then complete edition should be arranged, he found himself forced to take a "more penetrating look," but he was not successful in doing this in the way he had intended and all that was left for the end of volume 20 was a bare chronological index. However, he never gave up his intention to link the events of his life with the literary works that emanated from them. In the first book of volume 4, "On Art and Antiquity," he had published notes, entitled "Confessions in Abstract Form." Now the "years that he had lived" up till 1824 were to be presented in the *Tages und Jahreshefte*. A presentation of this sort was important to Goethe for more than a decade because, besides systematizing dates and facts in his life, it was also to result in the structure of the forthcoming complete edition, that "norm by which all my papers, especially my correspondence, can be used intelligently and woven into the woof of my life's events." Here Goethe is again stating a clear rejection of an edition arranged on strictly chronological lines. Furthermore it is important for him that all the works that had "already been published should be revised in order to cleanse them of any typographical errors." We can sense the importance that he attached to the structure and the textual form of this new edition, and he not only states the concept but also the manner in which he will realize it with the aid of collaborators. Cotta replies to this important letter, with its prospect of such great significance, on 15 February; he is pleased but reserved. He will "give serious attention" to the plan for the new edition when it is presented. On 30 May,

Goethe tells Cotta how the preparatory work on this edition is progressing. The securing of the posthumous works has reached a "significant point," the archive has been collected in one place; we know from Eckermann that Goethe had had his papers laid out so that they could be prepared with a view to filing them in the large cupboard. They remained in this room until Goethe's death. His son and his assistants were familiar with "the whole and with individual parts . . . each in his own way." He himself worked intensively on what he was now to call "The Chronicle of My Life." This was all done in service of the new edition that was drawing ever closer and that needed to be carefully discussed; he "is careful" too about reflections on the introduction to the different volumes. He wished to present this to Cotta in person, "because the far-reaching significance of these efforts cannot be expressed in words." Cotta does not acknowledge such a significance, or else he is avoiding it. He had visited Goethe on his return from Leipzig in May 1823; the topic of their conversation was the problem of pirated editions; there was no discussion of a new edition. But now Goethe starts to put on the pressure. However, Cotta cannot make up his mind to visit him, he goes instead to Augsburg, to Baden-Baden, to Lake Constance. He is financially interested in steam navigation and takes a trip on a Dutch Rhine steamer which is more modern than those on Lake Constance. He answers Goethe very fleetingly on 14 June 1824 that he hopes to have more free time "from the press of work in our legislature" and says that "Weimar is not so far away that I couldn't hop over if we need to talk face to face." This was a wrong evaluation of the situation. Cotta should have suspected that he had to do more than just "hop over." But no visit took place, no verbal exchange, and Goethe was obviously annoyed. It was at this time that the first talks were taking place about the publication of Goethe's and Schiller's correspondence, a matter that was to bring about a deep rift between the two. It is hard to understand why Cotta did not accede to Goethe's wish for him to come and visit him in Weimar; the fact that in his letters to Goethe he keeps quiet about his many other business dealings is understandable; he cannot and does not wish to show Goethe to what extent he has taken on other activities in addition to publishing. Goethe has therefore to conclude that in such a decisive period for him Cotta is not ready to collaborate in the way he wishes.

Cotta dedicated himself vehemently, with passion and with entrepreneurial, that is foresighted, shrewdness to his financial undertakings. He built printing works and equipped them with the most modern machines, he founded or had shares in paper factories, he acquired great estates and farming properties. Cotta not only owned them, he administered them. He was the first person in Württemberg to do away with the serfdom of his peasants and he fought for equality for the Jews in the country. He converted a monastery in Baden-Baden into the spa hotel Badischer Hof and equipped it with modern baths. He was financially interested in the development of ballooning and steam navigation and was a cofounder and head of the Württemberg Savings Bank: many saw in him a coming Württemberg finance minister. But he also engaged himself in questions of the book trade, as for example at the Congress of Vienna in 1815 where he presented a petition for the protection of authors' and publishers' rights. But his political activity gained the upper hand more and more: in 1815 he was elected representative for the Böblingen district and was involved in drawing up the kingdom's new constitution (that came into effect in 1819). In 1825, at the time when he was having his greatest difficulties with Goethe, he was elected to the Württemberg legislature for the second time and, on 9 December, to the vice-presidency of the Second Chamber. Thus, at this time, Cotta turned his attention more to his financial business and his political ambitions than to his publishing duties—dangerous conduct for a publisher, and for Cotta it was to have explosive results.

Goethe observed Cotta's change of interest, drew his own conclusions from it, and decided to take the safety of his main enterprise into his own hands, that is, to obtain legal privileges for the protection of his works against piracy. Only in this way, as he knew from lifelong experience, was the final tradition of his texts secure; an edition protected in this manner enjoyed a monopoly on the market, was valuable, and the author could expect a large income from it. Goethe informed Cotta of this significant intention in a letter dated 4 April 1825: "We are close to the point where with the common agreement of the revered Federal Convention the privileges of the combined highest authorities could be given to me for the new edition of my works." Goethe had dictated and corrected his short letter twice; the information was to be clear but the lawyer in him knew full well that his application to the Federal Convention was not going to be successful just like that. Cotta, who was clear about the significance of such a privilege, answered him by return mail, saying that "as a publisher I am prepared to do anything that would permit me to carry out, in complete accord with your wishes, what is for me so esteemed an undertaking—one that will crown my bookselling career" and advising Goethe to take "the necessary steps as soon as possible." And he took them.

Goethe's motives are completely clear; he wanted—at great expense, with his own dedication and that of his collaborators—to produce a new edition that was to give the desired form to the texts he intended to be handed down in an order that he would determine. Reprinting, and the consequent possibility of these texts being issued with new typographical errors, was to be forbidden. In the future these texts were to form the basis for all translations, for up till that time foreign editions had also contained errors from pirated versions. A privilege of this sort would secure the edition legally in a manner unknown till then and would create a monopoly. This monopoly would be of advantage to the publisher and, because of it, the author could make greater demands for royalties for "himself and his family." A third important motive was also introduced into the discussion, even if not as a priority. If such a protection were established for *one* author it could also apply to others and could lead to a development that was actually achieved later on, namely, a general copyright law for author and publisher.

Goethe knew the Prussian minister of state and ambassador to the Federal Diet in Frankfurt, Karl Ferdinand Friedrich von Nagler. Both thought highly of each other, as ministers and as men of letters. Goethe told him of his plan to seek such a privilege. Von Nagler assured Goethe of his personal support and with it the support of Prussia. On 2 November 1824 Goethe drafted a preliminary memorandum that he sent to von Nagler. He mentioned his position in contemporary literature, complained of damage from continual piracy that also partially distorted his works, and reminded him further—and this was more than a broad hint—that his works were in accord with "the existing and the desirable good." Goethe asked von Nagler to handle the memorandum confidentially and to examine it first to see whether it could be executed. Von Nagler spoke to his superior, the foreign minister, Count Bernstdorff, who also held Goethe's work in high esteem. Both were of the opinion that though the Federal Diet was not empowered to grant such a privilege, the ambassadors might perhaps make an exception for the "Hero of the German spirit." Von Nagler intervened with Prince Metternich in Vienna and handed him a Prussian memorandum on the subject according to which, "It should be resolved on the basis of Herr von Goethe's present request that he should be granted, as an exception, special privileges free of charge (in view of his outstanding services to German literature)." In this

way both Prussia and Austria were won over, thus creating the best precondi-
tion for Goethe's request, dated 11 January 1825:

Esteemed German Federal Convention!
. . . I . . . lay before the High Federal Convention what follows.

When a seven-year contract that I had entered into with the publishing house of J. C. Cotta in 1815—involving my then extant poetic
and aesthetic works—ran out after its term had expired, we began to
consider a new and enlarged edition that was to include not only the
twenty volumes of the earlier edition but also works that had appeared
individually in the meantime and a number of manuscripts that I had
on hand. It was further desired that the poetic and aesthetic works be
followed by historical, critical, and artistic essays and finally that these
should be followed up by writings dealing with science.

True, in the course of this survey which reviewed the efforts of a
whole lifetime, the wish arose that I should receive, for such a varied
body of work, a proportionate advantage and remuneration that in the
case of German writers generally tend to become attenuated. However,
the question of the means by which a recognized intellectual property
can be preserved for the individual author had arisen shortly after the
invention of printing . . . as there were no general laws governing this.
At the beginning of the sixteenth century imperial letters of protection
gave sufficient security; kings and princes also granted similar rights and
that is the way things have remained until recently.

However, should not the esteemed Federal Convention . . . as a
single body, be inclined to take the same steps that individuals had
formerly had the right to order and determine—rights that they still
have—would not the setting in motion of such an act be of the most
decisive importance for German literature and cultural development?
Would therefore an author who had been active in his fatherland for
so many years, whose pure activity—persisting in harmony with all established and desirable good—stares the man of insight in the face,
express an all too bold wish if he were to ask for himself and his family
such a privilege . . . so that he could both undertake to publish his own
works and also if he were to transfer to a publisher the right to take
mercantile advantage of his intellectual products to extend this legal
protection to him?

I may now say however, without boasting, that during a long lifetime, noble rulers . . . have favored me and honored me with numerous tokens of inestimable kindness, for which reason I dare to hope that those at the highest levels of authority will as a whole be inclined to view benevolently an old and loyal servant and admirer. . . .

I now have the temerity to submit most respectfully the following request:

That I should be granted a privilege by decree of the Confederate Convention for the new complete edition of my works and thus be assured of protection against piracy in all the countries of the Confederation, under threat of confiscation and other punishments that may still be established by future decrees of the Confederation. With the assurance that this will be implemented for me by all the German states and also that I shall, if I apply, be granted, free of charge, privileges by the individual states.

And so I may in conclusion once more urgently commend this matter that is so important both for me and, at the same time, for the whole of German literature, to the Confederate Convention for their gracious consideration and favorable conclusion.

Weimar 11 January 1825

Goethe's approach was now made public. To the general astonishment he did not by any means find everyone in agreement. On the contrary, critics and opponents increased in number and suggested that Goethe had gone too far in his self-estimation and had reached too high; even Goethe's friends were annoyed at his obstinate efforts to gain financial advantages for himself. His emphasis on material goals seemed to them incompatible with the image of the Olympian. In this connection, we can mention Johann Diederich Gries as an example, a man highly esteemed by Goethe, privy councillor in Jena, the translator of Spanish and Italian literature, something which engaged Goethe again and again. In November 1826 Gries wrote to a friend who was an admirer of Goethe's and someone whom Goethe respected: "Boisserée, who spent a long time with Goethe at the beginning of the summer, told me that the latter had hit upon the mad idea of having all the 39 confederate states award him privileges for the new edition of his works. . . . I tried everything, but in vain, to dissuade him from this crazy notion, but his eye-servants and his lick-spittles, Riemer, Eckermann, and their consorts, only encourage him. . . . It is these people who seduce the weak old man into behaving in this way. They bear a heavy burden of responsibility." But it was not only friends who had their doubts about Goethe's procedure. The Württemberg delegate to the Confederate Convention, Herr von Trott, though an admirer of Goethe's work, expressed his regret in his report to the Württemberg government that Goethe, in order to achieve a pecuniary advantage, should desire to receive "an exception to the rule" from the "Confederate Union."

In the detailed discussion about Goethe's request, however, it became clear that the Confederate Convention did not possess the central power that would have made it possible to prevent piracy by the imposition of sanctions. The delegates who wished to spare the meritorious poet an ignominious dismissal of his petition and a strict rejection of his request turned to their respective governments. It is astonishing how quickly these governments gave their consent in the months that followed. Before Goethe learned that the convention could not—for constitutional reasons—accept his petition, he received, as the very first one, the Saxon privilege; it now became clear to him too that it was not the Confederate Convention but the individual governments who had to agree. He was now faced with the decision as to whether he should approach all thirty-nine states. But of these thirty-nine states and free cities, thirty-seven did not demand any further request from Goethe. Only Bavaria and Württemberg continued to express reservations. The grand duke, Carl August, intervened in Munich and Stuttgart and Goethe sent separate petitions to the two governments, who finally agreed. Württemberg, to be sure, only wanted to grant the privilege for a period of twelve years. By the end of 1825 the agreement of all the confederate states had been received; in some cases the period of protection was extended, as Goethe had wished, to fifty years, in some cases it was indefinite. The Austrian privilege document pleased him especially, a parchment, with a seal attached, in a golden case, was how von Nagler registered it, and he informed his minister, so that the Prussian document should not be delivered in a form inferior to this.

It was the Prussian privilege of 23 January 1826 that gave Goethe the greatest pleasure. He had had to wait a long time for it. After the last privileges—those of the four free Imperial cities, Bremen, Frankfurt, Hamburg, and Lübeck—had arrived at the end of 1825, Goethe asked Chancellor von Müller to intervene with the Prussian government. King Frederick William I had signed the document and at Goethe's special request the privilege was published in the "Collection of Laws for the Royal Prussian States": A triumph for Goethe! The privilege was drawn up exactly as he had wished, the period of protection was indefinite, it was valid for the poet and his heirs, and it protected the publisher against pirated versions by placing these under threat of punishment. "I owe the fatherland the greatest thanks for the protection that it has afforded me in connection with my property, namely the edition of my works," Goethe stated, observing that this Prussian privilege was "the best decoration."

Goethe had achieved his goal in what was for him an essential interest. But the whole affair had been very exhausting. On 26 December 1825 he wrote to a friend, "I have scarcely left the house, scarcely left my room; in the course of the past year the privilege affair has kept me in suspense, but now it is as good as over. . . . The publisher of my works also seems to have made up his mind and so next year I can get down to a desirable task."

The receipt of the privilege was the only thing that could make the final authorized edition into what Goethe had in mind. But the torments of this year spent seeking the privilege had made him more experienced, and now perhaps it all seemed a little unworthy to him. From now on he emphasized what he had achieved for other authors rather than for the protection of his own work. Actually from a strictly legal point of view the privileges granted individually by each state should have been set out individually in the final authorized edition. Goethe did not want this, he wanted documentation of his original idea of the privilege being granted by the Confederate Convention, and so for all practical purposes he ignored the actual legal situation. Thus the formally legal, and neither completely false nor completely correct, notice shone forth on the title page: "Under the privileges of protection of the most illustrious German Confederacy." The edition could now be accorded the significance that Goethe and his son August had called, in a letter to Cotta in November 1825, "without boasting, a *National Matter.*"

Almost an Auction: Publishers Try to Oust Cotta The news of the granting of the privilege to the final authorized edition had spread through the publishing world like wildfire and was the sensation of the Jubilate Book Fair in Leipzig at Easter 1825. It had to be clear to everyone who knew the circumstances what a new, complete, and final edition of Goethe's works and the privilege granted to it would mean to a publisher. The "national matter," the "national monument" as Cotta put it in his letter to Goethe of 7 October 1825, was bound, because of the monopoly that it enjoyed, to be a great piece of publishing business above and beyond the prestige that was attached to it—something that could hardly be overestimated. Goethe also saw things in this light and he wanted to be paid for it; the "final return" on his work was to be security for himself, his son, and his grandchildren for years. He therefore accepted with composure the offers from publishers that came tumbling in from Leipzig and other places. He was still in correspondence with Cotta about the edition and he was still not contemplating a breach with Cotta, but on the other hand there were repeated grounds for him to be out of humor. The Viennese piracy had had some long-term consequences, since Goethe had been forced to take into account the lack of royalties; and this and the fact that Cotta had not agreed to visit him and had also treated the question of the edition rather reluctantly, "tepidly," in his letters, annoyed Goethe. He therefore paid more attention to the offers that were arriving than he might otherwise have done and he took his time in coming to a decision. It is true that there is, in the correspondence, no indication that Goethe deliberately spun out the negotiations in order to play one publisher off against another and thus force them to offer the highest possible royalties. There is also no evidence that the disgruntlement between Goethe and Cotta was known to everyone or even that Goethe had publicly considered "entrusting the crowning glory of my life's work" to another publisher. The fundamental certainty of his relationship to Cotta, his "firmly based connection," was only known to a small circle; for the rest, the fact of the new edition, with its receipt of privileges, was probably sufficient reason to arouse great public interest among publishers.

On 4 April 1825 Goethe had informed Cotta that agreement on the question of privileges was "near." "Now who," thus Goethe encouraged his publisher, "could help with advice and action in such a significant, indeed unique, case better than you dear Sir. For this reason I am for the present sending you this preliminary announcement with the request that you let me know what you think about the eventual handling of the affair and thus renew and crown a pleasant relationship that has lasted for so long.

"I have the honor to sign myself with my old trust and fresh hopes."

Cotta assured Goethe immediately that he was "ready for everything," but again he did not come to Weimar. On 7 May he wrote to Goethe that he intended to go to Paris in two weeks' time "with friend Boisserée." Cotta had told Boisserée of Goethe's last letter. Boisserée knew that Goethe had received offers from other publishers and he also told Cotta about them. Since the trip to Paris was to last for two months, Cotta could not be too happy about decisions being made in Weimar and so he pressured Boisserée to spur Goethe on to make a definite decision. Boisserée did this. "Your latest letter," Boisserée wrote to Goethe a week later, "arrived at the same time as Cotta returned from Lake Constance and, acting according to your own sense of things, I thought that I had to mention quite casually as we were talking that you had received several significant offers!—he replied that that was all right as far as he was concerned because in this way one obtained a measure of the market and he would certainly do more than anyone else who was in a position to ensure that the plan would be carried out. Incidentally, he added that he did not yet know what your plan was, he knew neither what you had in mind as to the extent of the work nor the time frame for the work; he had written to you saying that he was ready to come to Weimar in connection with this important matter, but that at the moment he was prevented from so doing by most urgent business.—If it seemed to you to be too long before he could visit you, then he thought that you would send him your plan and some more details so that he could at least state his position provisionally."

Immediately after receiving Boisserée's letter, in his answer dated 20 May 1825, Goethe sent him the plan he had asked for, and it was a pressing and urgent matter for him, as he wanted to receive an answer before Cotta left for Paris. In an enclosure in the letter, he sent Cotta a precise and detailed table of contents for the forty volumes that were planned for the edition "with some notes that will serve to explain things thoroughly"; he would like, he said, "to be able to expect a definitive answer to this as soon as possible." The letter, as always in moments of decision, was laconic, imperative, succinct, and there were two drafts. In the final letter Goethe went further, above all in one point that must have indicated to Cotta how disgruntled Goethe was. Goethe now asked that the "definitive" answer that he wished to get quickly be in writing, and for his part he now ruled out a visit by Cotta. "In order to encourage this I will further add that I will give you the publishing rights for twelve years. I make this however conditional upon the edition's being printed and distributed most rapidly. Considerable offers that I have received from the Leipzig Fair do not permit of any delay and I therefore ask you to tell me straight out what sum you can promise me and my family as the final proceeds of my whole life as a writer. When you look at it closely neither this main point nor any of the subsidiary points make it necessary for us to meet personally or to discuss them face to face; and so for the reasons already mentioned I ask you, before you leave for Paris, to favor me with the courtesy of a reply that will immediately indicate the path I should follow." The letter is written in John's hand, and Goethe added in his own hand the form-greeting "your most obedient" with his signature.

Two further letters were written in this connection on the same day, 20 May 1825, by Goethe himself and by Carl August Böttiger. Goethe for his part turned to Sulpice Boisserée as a mediator. At Boisserée's behest Goethe had sent the table of contents of the forty volumes to Cotta, and now there had to be an end to Cotta's hesitation; he, Goethe, was now awaiting a "definitive first and final offer." The letter is important because on the same day that he is expecting an offer from Cotta he is prepared in his heart, and in the right circumstances, to give up "such a firm relationship" with Cotta. He writes to Boisserée:

> Let me speak forthrightly and confidentially, just between the two of us: I made the offer for a new edition of my works to Herr v. Cotta two years ago; he handled the matter in a dilatory manner, and I accepted that because I still had a lot of work to do on it, so that I can be forgiven if that was the sense in which I felt he had written his last letter.
>
> How easy it is to survey the whole business is shown by the significant offers that I have received from the Leipzig fair from people who had no prior knowledge of the details. This also made it clear that a personal meeting and a face to face discussion were necessary.
>
> Herr v. Cotta who can take in the largest undertakings at a single glance is in a better position than anyone to survey the present business, since he has known the details for years. Therefore, following up on your suggestion, I sent him the detailed plan and am expecting him to respond with a first and final offer as to what sum is going to be paid to the author of this undertaking. I can only hope that he will come to a decision as soon as possible. For the offers that have been made, and which I have promised to keep confidential, are of such a nature that I must either answer them soon or give them up altogether.

You can imagine how painful it would be for me to have to give up so well-founded a relationship, but a quick decision is called for because of my great and often threatened age. Make the best use you can of this, according to your own insights and inclination, since you are in every sense related to both parties.

On the strength of this, Boisserée exercised his influence on Cotta and the latter reacted to Goethe's letter immediately, for he had in the meantime received Böttiger's letter—also written on 20 May. Böttiger, a dubious figure, was closely associated with Cotta. After his retirement Böttiger operated as Cotta's social antenna in Weimar; he hawked gossip, scandal, or at least indiscretions to Cotta's newspapers and it was precisely for this reason and because of his importunity that the controversy with Goethe arose. Böttiger knew the latest mood in Leipzig and Weimar and he communicated it to Cotta in these terms: "Goethe's undertaking—the making of the final biographically ordered edition of all his works—that has been secured by the Federal Diet is the talk of Leipzig. Many booksellers have made him offers. He has answered them all politely but has not rejected them. The last rumor is that they offered him a capital sum of 40,000 thalers. But what he wants above all are continuing royalties for his heirs. What is going to happen?"

Cotta reacted at once. He had now recognized the seriousness of the situation and two days before his departure for Paris he found himself obliged to give a "speedy reply."

According to our last contract I have priority over all other publishers as long as I meet their conditions, I could therefore confine myself to saying that I would meet the highest offer and take it over—but this is not my way of doing business, which leads me rather to say that I would "with pleasure" pay royalties of 10,000 thalers more than the highest offer you receive for the new edition of your works.

Of course I shall see to it that they are printed and distributed as quickly as possible just as I shall always make clear what great store I set by our connection. I may flatter myself that I shall still have and retain priority after twelve years if I meet the same conditions—our departure is set for the day after tomorrow, might I ask you to reply to me in Paris in care of M. Banquier Lafitte et Compagnie.

Opinion can obviously differ about this reaction. One commentator sees in it "a proud answer worthy of a publishing prince." I cannot share this view.

At the beginning and the end of his letter Cotta takes up a legal position, something that is always disadvantageous when dealing with an author; an author wants, as a general rule, to be persuaded about matters of publication and not compelled to do something because of clauses in his contract. The other remark however—that Cotta would "with pleasure" pay 10,000 thalers more than the highest offer—seems to me inappropriate. The offers of the other publishers could have been weighed at this point and Cotta could have entered into a qualitative comparison of the different editions, especially as he had the great advantage of pointing out to Goethe his past experiences with technical production and his staff of proofreaders in Augsburg. The offer of "more" seems to me to be more of an expression of a bad conscience, an exaggerated Grand Mogul gesture, that would serve to calm things down during his two-month absence, but perhaps it was intended in a special way for August von Goethe, who in Cotta's opinion was interested only in money.

Goethe did not send a reply to Paris. On 30 July, the day of his return, Cotta wrote to him, rather as though he had been insulted, that he had asked him to do him the honor of sending a reply to Paris, and he had hoped every day that this request would be fulfilled. "But neither there nor at home, where I arrived today, do I see this hope fulfilled and I may add that this silence is painful to me." He had heard, he said, that Goethe was in good health so "he did not how know to explain to himself why his letter had till now remained totally unanswered. I comfort myself with the fact that your health is not the cause, and since I cannot find the cause in my behavior, it must be chance delays that deprive me of your kind answer." Was it indeed "chance delays" that caused Goethe not to reply? He remembered how—in a complicated financial situation—Goethe liked for moral and practical reasons to use the services of a mediator and he now went along with this: "Unfortunately our dear departed friend, Schiller, who looked after the financial side of our relationship so kindly and so prudently is no longer able to help us. His memory, and all that is so tenderly and beautifully associated with it over a long period, can represent my point of view and will certainly be in a position to remove any misunderstanding, if there should be one." He then added something that Goethe had explicitly rejected. "If you did wish to talk to me I am now free to come to you at any time."

At first Goethe did not respond at all and suggested for his part that the matter should be placed in the hands of a mediator, "and if we have for many years missed that friend who was invaluable to us in so many ways, we do have the good fortune that both of us have found a pure and intimate relationship with an excellent younger man." The "excellent younger man" was Sulpice Boisserée who after some hesitation accepted the delicate mission.

Of course in the months immediately preceding, and at the time when Cotta was in Paris, certain changes had taken place in Goethe's household. They were occasioned on the one hand by the fact that he was introducing his son August more and more into the "commercial" negotiations and on the other by the fact that his ill humor vis-à-vis Cotta made him consider a possible change of publisher. The offers that reached him after the Easter Fair played their part in this. Goethe developed numerous drafts for negotiations; some he dictated in his own name, some in a form that August could sign.

The idea of publishing the work himself also played a part in these considerations. The idea was not a new one to Goethe; he even mentioned the idea of publishing the work himself in a petition to the German Confederate Convention before he mentioned going to a publisher. The new impetus towards self-publication came from Johann Wilhelm Hoffmann, the court bookseller in Weimar. He had taken over the publishing house in 1802; Goethe knew it well and it was probably his main supplier of books. Later on Hoffmann was associated more with Goethe's son August, and it was to him that he expressed his resentment of Cotta who, he said, asked prices that were too high, whose books were of poor quality ("tastelessly thrown together and full of typographical errors"), and who had made the ominous arrangement for the Viennese reprint at Goethe's expense. He wrote to August on 25 April 1825, while discussions between Goethe and Cotta were underway, that the idea of petitioning for the privilege must have come from Cotta, who "wanted to add several hundreds of thousands to his other millions." August was all too ready to listen to this sort of thing; he repeatedly mentioned Cotta's wealth and repeated the suspicion, voiced by those who envied Cotta, that he made his profits at the expense of his authors. It was alleged that he was aiming at making huge profits with his Schiller edition. Hoffmann mentioned a sum of 400,000 thalers and tried to persuade Goethe that he should make such a profit himself; but Goethe finally—probably recalling his experiences with a similar undertaking long before—gave up the idea. He thought highly of Hoffmann as a bookseller, but the latter had no experience as a publisher and a forty-volume edition could not be realized by a nonprofessional either in production, or in the organization of distribution, sales, advertising, and the press. One has to have seen the fascicle "Booksellers' Offers" in Goethe's files on publishing in the Goethe-Schiller Archives in Weimar! It was certainly put together by a clerk or a secretary, but the papers are presumably arranged in the way Goethe received them and read them. He received thirty-six offers for the publication of the edition. One can imagine that they impressed him, but one can also imagine that they made all the negotiations more difficult for him and that it must have been hard for him to come to a decision in the course of these weeks and months. Goethe scholars have analyzed these "Booksellers' Offers" and summarized them; Goethe himself had conducted negotiations personally with the brothers Brockhaus and given them the greatest chance; preliminary negotiations were also conducted with Joseph Max in Breslau and with the publisher Georg Andreas Reimer in Berlin. Shortly after sending his letter to Cotta on 20 May, Goethe received nine offers; by the end of the year there were thirteen more, and the remainder arrived at the beginning of 1826. The publishers are listed according to the royalties that they offered:

Hahn Hanover, in common with other publishers	118,000 thalers
Heyer, Giessen	85,000 thalers
Schlesinger, Berlin	60,000 thalers
Brothers Brockhaus	50,000 thalers
later increased to	70,000 thalers
Max, Breslau	30,000 thalers
Hennings, Gotha	30,000 thalers
Greiner, Graz	ca.17,000 thalers

The following publishers made offers without offering any royalties: Arnold, Dresden; Baumgärtner, Leipzig; Fleischer, Leipzig; Gleditsch, Leipzig; Hermann, Frankfurt; Leske, Darmstadt; Reimer, Berlin; Sauerländer, Aarau; Varrentrapp, Frankfurt; Wallishauser, Vienna; Wesché, Frankfurt. To some extent outside the publishing competition, the Bureau of *The Korrespondenzblatt for Merchants* came up with an offer of 200,000 thalers.

What must Goethe have thought of all this? There had not been such a process—carried on in full view of the public—in the history of literature and publishing for a long time. Goethe must have been concerned that his work, "the final sum," should be handed down as true to the original as possible. He knew that the whole effect of the work at home and abroad, all the succeeding publications that would be based on it, the individual editions, the anthologies, translations, the increasingly extensive secondary literature, the immense and growing Goethe research, all of this would depend on this edition, but that the other "final sum" for "him and his family" was also dependent upon it. And it was clear to him that he himself was the one called upon to make a decision, for no one, neither his son August nor his advisers on his staff, could shoulder the burden for him. We can agree that the thirty-six offers of publication constitute "almost an auction" and it demonstrates to Goethe, to his satisfaction, the broad area of his recognition, the far-flung Goethe-empire that he had built up. It is larger than the German Confederacy and more lasting."

Germany Asks: Will Cotta Publish Goethe? The negotiations between Goethe, Boisserée, and Cotta continued, hampered again and again by difficulties. Goethe had received a manuscript by an author and sent it to Cotta, who only reacted when he received a reminder, at which point he returned the manuscript to the author saying that it was not suitable for his firm; the author complained to Goethe and Goethe was annoyed that something he had recommended should be treated in such a cavalier fashion by Cotta; the manuscript was accepted by another publisher and the author then had the nerve to ask Goethe for compensation because the manuscript had lain too long at Cotta's.

Goethe was often tired of the negotiations. He hoped that his son August could take them over and had constantly to be reminded that August was not interested in which firm would be best for the edition but exclusively in who would offer the highest royalties for it. Ludwig Friedrich Froriep, an informer for Cotta, told him, "The success of your edition of Schiller's works seems to have made a great impression on G.—the son more than the father. After what happened at and what was done by the Confederate Diet to secure property rights in the final edition of G's works, G. is mainly involved with the idea and the preparation of the edition. G., the father, continues to be well-disposed to you, this is less the case with the son and he has the greatest (the decisive!) influence upon his father. . . . As you know, when G. is satisfied or dissatisfied he expresses himself less in definite words than in hints and often by mimetic signs. He is still well disposed to you, but—."

Cotta, overburdened with other work, tied up in political dealings, hesitated for a long time, too long a time. And so it was probably Froriep's remark, "He is well disposed to you, but . . . ," that caused him to make an offer which he presented in a "Plan and Suggestion" (on 27 August 1825):

> In offering you, in my earlier letter written before my departure for Paris, royalties of 10,000 Reichthalers more than anyone else for your collected works, protected against any pirated versions, I wished to show that I regarded our relationship as not being based merely on contracts, but rather I wanted to show you that I value it above all else—this offer of 10,000 thalers more has now risen to 60,000 in the face of offers by other people, and your esteemed son wished this to rise to 100,000. This, and perhaps more, is possible depending on the extent of the public's participation.
>
> My proposal is therefore: to fix 60,000 as the basic royalty and, for every additional 10,000 subscribers over 20,000, to add a further 20,000 thalers, so that 60,000 is fixed and then if 30,000 people subscribe it will be 80,000 thalers, then if 40,000 it will be 100,000, if 50,000 then 120,000 etc. etc. In this way the royalty will increase according to the participation of the public, without being entirely dependent upon it and, since we could establish one year as the period during which subscriptions would be received, we should be able very soon to see what the situation is.
>
> The price would have to be very reasonable, about 14–16 thalers for the 40 volumes so as to get as many subscribers as possible.
>
> I flatter myself that with this plan I have also met your son's expectations as well; in any case I can say on my own behalf that it arose only out of the immutable conviction of my great reverence for you, out of the most delicate respect for our relationship that has lasted so long and is so dear to me and out of the great value that I set upon the continuation of the same.

Goethe, obviously relieved, confirmed this "declaration" on 2 September hoping that it might now become the basis for the next negotiations. Goethe signed his letter, "with confidence." And he added that he was writing this in great haste on the eve of our "jubilee that lies urgently and pleasingly before us."

Grand Duke Carl August celebrated the fiftieth anniversary of his accession on 3 September 1825 and Goethe too was preparing himself for 7 November, the day on which his own fifty years in office were to be cele-brated—Goethe had entered the Weimar civil service on 6 November 1776. At bottom Goethe wished to see in the festive mood of these jubilee celebra-tions the final end of his whole publishing affair. But the piece of business was not yet perfect.

On the same day that Goethe wanted to celebrate the completion of the matter, he had a conversation with his son August who was now to send a draft contract to Cotta. August then also wrote to Cotta on 16 September, "I have asked my father's permission to send the enclosed and take this opportunity to express to you how very pleased I am that a relationship that has lasted for so long should be extended to include me and my family; the more significantly and the more securely it is introduced for the future, the more valuable it must be to me and I may assure you that I acknowledge it in its totality."

The "enclosed" were a preliminary draft of a contract and two further enclosures that concerned technical matters and matters relating to the privi-lege. The draft contract contained, in 16 points, the matters relating to the "new" edition. The question of the extension of the contract and the question of the calculation of the number of subscribers and the number of copies sold immediately became ticklish and was to remain so in the future. Enclosure A contained a demand for a high quality of typography, questions as to the size of the printing of the individual parts and the deadline for their appearance, questions as to the deadline for the delivery of manuscripts and a demand that the greatest attention be paid to proofreading. Goethe had already set up his staff of workers, now Cotta was to do the same: "it would be desirable that a central position be occupied by a proven literary figure to whom the revised master copy could be sent and with whom one could consult about unforeseen problems." In Enclosure B the receipt of privileges is again men-tioned and Goethe's concern as to "how the whole process of negotiation and the award of privileges were to be made public in print." It was important to Goethe that the negotiations with the Confederate Diet be made public, and so he suggested that the negotiations about privileges together with the names of the subscribers "be presented to the public in a small preliminary volume." Goethe sent the papers to Cotta on 19 September.

Cotta answered Goethe's letter about the contract on 7 October. He agreed to all the points, except that in the clause about negotiations for extending the contract he would like to see included his "right of first refusal under the same conditions." There was agreement about technical matters (in fact Cotta set up the proofreading staff that Goethe had wished for in Augsburg). At the same time Cotta wrote to August von Goethe and responded to him about his future expectations, "Be assured that the more significant the newly established bond is for the present and will be for the future, the more my efforts will be directed to demonstrate in every way that I regard my having entered into this relationship as one of the most important events of my life and that every step I take must prove the deep respect and the high esteem in which I hold your father."

The reply from the Goethes, father and son, was delayed. Goethe had been occupied with the fiftieth anniversary celebrations so that it was not until 20 November that he returned to those points that were, at a later date, to be a constant source of annoyance and food for constant skepticism: how is the author to be kept informed of the number of subscribers and of the sale of individual copies? We have to understand the insistence upon this point, for a further overall royalty depended on the number of subscriptions and on the sale of individual copies. But how could an overall view be achieved? In the same letter he mentioned an irregularity that makes clear why this question was so important: Cotta was producing an individual edition of *Faust* that was relatively expensive with a retail price of 1 thaler 10 groschen (Hoffmann the bookseller had informed Goethe of this price and remarked on the quality of the edition—"blotting paper!") and Cotta had neglected to send Goethe any author's copies. The further demand now was that the edition should be presented in two versions; father and son were of the opinion—seizing on Cotta's concept of a "National Monument"—that the new edition might be regarded as a *"National Matter."* It was therefore not only to appear as a pocket edition but also as a handsomely bound octavo edition. Incidentally Goethe insisted that it was now time to bring matters to a head, "since one scarcely knows how to escape from increased offers, some even with support from the highest quarters." (Hoffmann the bookseller had informed Goethe that Grand Duke Carl August supported his offer, but there is no written evidence of this.) Cotta replied by return of post. He promised Goethe that he would introduce a special accounting in his bookkeeping so that subscribers could be registered and the sale of individual copies could be settled with the author. True, he adopted an odd position with regard to the *Faust* edition that Goethe had found fault with:

he had at his disposal, and no one doubted this, the right to reprint and had, because the edition was to be constantly available, printed only a small edition as a precaution: the relatively high price derived from calculations based on this small edition. This is not a valid argument since, in the case of *Faust*, Cotta could presumably have printed from the existing lead type. But then as confirmation of his innocence he gave an explanation that he would have done better to have omitted: Had he wished to deceive, he wrote to Goethe, the new date of publication—1825—would not have appeared as the imprint, "that could easily have been left as it was, if it were possible that anything in my dealings could have given rise to even the slightest appearance of dishonesty." What sort of deception is forced upon an author here? No publisher should argue like this and certainly not in the face of a skeptical author, and not a publisher like Cotta who, as a "meticulous businessman," would certainly not wish to give an appearance of conscious dishonesty. But it is precisely the argument he uses in this context that shows how much he was influenced by the continuing criticism of his colleagues and by his competitors' policy of making offers to Goethe. Cotta concludes his letter with a suitably melancholy reference; he is delighted at Goethe's celebration of his fifty years in office, he himself had spent thirty-eight years in the book trade "and if I may be allowed to speak on my own behalf, my honest efforts have not failed to have a great deal of beneficent effect and it is this that compensates me for a lot of unpleasantness; nevertheless it is often hard for me to continue along this path that brings in its wake so much that is offensive to my delicacy of feeling."

The following letter of 21 December, signed by both the Goethes, was certainly offensive to Cotta's delicacy of feeling. Goethe and his son August had discussed this letter in great detail, as is evidenced by a diary entry. Once again there is a strong hint about the many offers that have "recently come back with such urgency and become so significant that even if they do not entirely conform with our initial view they come very close to it." This was the time when the offer of 150,000 thalers had arrived from the bookseller Hahn in Hanover, and no less a personage than Chancellor von Müller was in favor of this competition. Supposedly, the two Goethes said in their letter to Cotta, it would be very easy to sell as many as 40,000 copies, "if they are presented to the public in a suitable manner." And for this reason a contract should be drawn up with this figure in mind, so as "to see the royalty of 100,000 Saxon thalers paid off by definitely stated deadlines." This was followed by the statement that the edition should be completed in four years, with two installments a year, each installment of five volumes, that the author would obligate himself to deliver in succession.

The letter emphasized once more the importance of announcements that contained what the author had to say about this. But then there was a turn of phrase that must have appeared to Cotta like biting ridicule if not scorn; three years before the expiration of the contract Goethe would like to negotiate an extension; if agreement could not be reached, the author must then be free to "entrust his future rights" not just to Cotta but also to those who "offered more or less." The reason he follows up with is truly double-tongued, and is given in full view of the fact that the original demand for 100,000 thalers is now about to be repeated: "For in this case, as we have seen on this occasion, it cannot simply be a matter of more or less, but of the trust that the publishing firm inspires; just as this time, in accordance with our earliest views, we have placed it, with complete conviction, in your own good hands." Cotta could suspect from the final statement—"that the present settlement might also serve to reassure our family situation"—that August von Goethe had had his way in formulating this new demand and he was deeply hurt at how little "trust" had been placed in him and his firm. Now he, for his part, relapsed into silence vis-à-vis Goethe, nor would he let himself be forced into making any public announcement, not even when Böttiger provoked him on 21 October 1825 with the question: "The whole of Germany is now asking will Cotta publish the highly favored Goethe?"

It is true that, in Sulpice Boisserée, Cotta had a partner who, in this situation, passed the test with flying colors. Boisserée let Goethe know quite clearly how outraged he was at Goethe's last letter to the publisher; it was unrealistic of Goethe to use 40,000 volumes as a basis (something that subsequently proved true—scarcely 14,000 copies were sold in Goethe's lifetime), besides which Cotta was insulted by Goethe's lack of trust and by his not telling him how high the offers were that he, Cotta, was ready to exceed by 10,000 thalers. Boisserée could also tell Goethe something else that the latter had probably repressed; in the case of the complete edition's being entrusted to another publisher, the new publisher could sell the complete edition as a whole, but he could not sell separately those works that were under contract to Cotta. Goethe, it is true, thought that he could invalidate these arguments, above all he pointed to certain disappointments that he had experienced in the course of the years that he had been with Cotta. But Boisserée insisted.

He advised Goethe not to stretch the bow of his demands too taut; in the final analysis, Cotta could assert his rights of first refusal from the old contract and insist upon his offer to pay 10,000 thalers more; Cotta had been sensitive enough not to mention this for a long time. This did not fail to have an effect on Goethe and we can now see that he is having a change of heart. He once again felt himself more attracted to the old relationship with Cotta, and in his letter to Boisserée on 12 January 1826 he divulged his "decided preference for the relationship with Herr von Cotta." He probably also suspected that through his son August he had gone too far with his demands and had been too hesitant to show his trust. August was under the influence of Hoffmann, who was part of the competition and who saw this as the chance of a lifetime. Goethe now wanted, as he wrote to Boisserée, to let bygones be bygones and in two letters (28 December 1825 and 3 January 1826) he asked Boisserée to come to an agreement with Cotta in a conciliatory manner, but his skepticism came to the fore once again. When he was discussing the final text of the contract with Boisserée he complained in harsh words of what Cotta had done to him.

> However let me state the chief annoyance that prevails in these negotiations: it is this—that the publisher knows at any given moment what is profitable for him and his family, while the author is totally in the dark about it. For where can he learn—given the totally lawless situation of the German book trade—what is his by right and what is traditional, and what booksellers forgive one another by other arrangements and what liberties they take with authors. . . . You have, as a mediator should, faithfully reported the arguments that Herr v. Cotta makes against us; however if we openly and clearly give voice to the counterarguments with which we think we can invalidate his, then we find ourselves in the unpleasant situation of bringing up the past, which we would prefer, as we are talking of the renewal of a close and earlier relationship, to forget.
>
> Perhaps we shall also achieve our object without having to pester you with such an unpleasant narration of the facts.

But Boisserée was already far advanced in his negotiations with Cotta. At the end of January 1826 he was able to tell Goethe that, with the exception of the duration of the contract, Cotta agreed to all the other points just as

Boisserée had discussed them with Goethe; Cotta wanted the duration of the contract set at twelve years after the appearance of the last parts. Cotta expressed his readiness to publish the posthumous works, in addition to the forty volumes, under the same conditions. In his accompanying letter of 23 January 1826 Boisserée comes down decisively on Cotta's side and urges Goethe to come to an agreement with Cotta, for the latter had now abandoned his position, his "increased offer" of 10,000 thalers:

> During the multifarious negotiations over your final and increased demands it has become clear to me that, up to this point, Cotta has only been kept from taking this unpleasant step because of his really deeply rooted esteem for you, and now that we have arrived at the final stage I consider it my sacred duty to draw your attention to this. It is precisely the personal interest that Cotta takes in such an *important piece of business* that gives him, I think, just as much right to expect you to continue the friendly relationship with him as it is desirable, indeed necessary, from the other point of view that you should not let your happy old age be clouded by disagreeable things.—
>
> May I, accordingly, express the hope that you will now settle this business: I ask you in order to efface the impression of the recent negotiations and in order to establish the new relationship with your son on a better footing, to treat Cotta with complete confidence, tell him what the higher offers are and also show him a personal friendliness.

Goethe allowed himself to be persuaded. He regarded this letter as "bringing the decision closer." On 30 January 1826, that is, before the contract was signed, Goethe told Boisserée of his concurrence, which was such a relief to him, in the following laconic statement:

> May your word be Yes! Yes!
> All right Yes! and Amen!
> More soon.

Boisserée was able to record in his diary on 7 February: "Letter from Goethe, very enthusiastic at my having put an end to his torment and sorrow." After this everything proceeded very quickly. Goethe arranged the duration of the contract in accordance with Cotta's wishes. A final text was now drawn up on the basis of the first draft of the contract. It kept the sum of 60,000 as the contractual sum to be paid, and Goethe now asked for a further payment of 5,000 thalers in view of the other offers that Boisserée was now able to report to Cotta (he probably only made this rather modest demand as a way of saving face vis-à-vis his son). All the other points remained as they had been mentioned earlier. The question of complimentary copies was put in concrete terms; a double system of bookkeeping, the details of which were to be worked out, was to take over the control of sales; the forty volumes were to appear over four years, two batches of five volumes in each year, royalties to be due in every case after the delivery of the batch to the fair.

The draft of the contract was signed by Goethe on 3 February 1826 and by Cotta on 14 February, the definitive contract on 3 and 20 March. On the day the draft contract was signed, 3 February, Goethe once again took stock and in a letter to Cotta developed perspectives for the present and the future:

> Since the calm to which our spirit aspires cannot be expressed in words and symbols, please let me say to your Honor in general what is the most important thing; for the first time in years I feel in these moments a true satisfaction now that I am certain that the results of my literary activity are placed in your hands; more valid evidence of mutual trust could not be given.
>
> Step by step it will become evident that I have no other concern than that of completing these products of my life to the honor and advantage of us both. If you act in the same sense then there is probably no question but that we shall bring about something that is valuable and worthy. I close by commending myself and my son to further benevolent cooperation.

On the same day Goethe thanked Boisserée for his self-sacrificing services as a mediator: "What would I not promise, my dearest sir, if I could talk to you for an hour! For how shall pen and paper suffice! I have to make use of a mythological metaphor: You seem to me like Hercules who comes to the help of Atlas, of Prometheus. If you knew what I have suffered this year, you would not find such figures exaggerated."

The negotiations had lasted a year; it had been a hard struggle and it had affected, indeed shattered, the mature relationship between Goethe and Cotta. But in the end Cotta was able to garner Goethe's "most important matter" into his publishing barn. In his letter of 14 February he was unable to express in words how much Goethe's letter of 3 February had touched and moved him. "What I could never doubt has been confirmed by this;

your noble, beautiful sense has here too seized upon what is right and that is something that can give us all satisfaction in such a delicate relationship. My inmost, most hearty thanks for that. My very melancholy and agitated spirits have been lifted up again by this process and as I now address myself to this affair with joy and pleasure, so all my efforts will be to conduct it and bring it to fruition with dignity and to the honor and advantage of us both." Thus it was clear who was going to be the publisher of the "highly favored Goethe" now—and in the future. Meanwhile, the agreement and the conclusion of the contract had hardly become publicly known before envious people and opponents awoke once more. These were booksellers who complained to Goethe that Cotta was unreliable in carrying out his promises with regard to deadlines for delivery and in the quality of his printing; people were afraid that the retail price would be too high or that there would be changes in it as the edition was in the process of appearing. Anonymous letters reached Goethe saying that he had given Cotta the edition without taking proper care, something which, given the course of events, it is hard to maintain. Goethe was, it is true, irked once more and this moved him to make a critical remark about the whole German book trade in a letter to his friend Carl Friedrich Zelter on 26 August 1826: "Gusts of wind like this are good as they increasingly clear up the gloominess of the German book trade, lift the blanket beneath which authors and public are both betrayed and under which the Sosii carry on their lucrative game. The empire is now divided against itself and we will see that we gain an advantage from this."

The letters he received served to warn Goethe that he had to take the presentation of his edition to the public seriously. For this reason his attention was drawn to all of the publisher's advertising projects. He himself drafted an "Announcement of Goethe's Final Edition of His Complete Works." Once again he came up with a precise table of contents for the whole forty volumes.

The first batch of the edition, containing five volumes, appeared for the Easter Fair in 1827: *Goethe's Works. Complete final edition. First (to 40th) volume. Protected by the privileges of the most serene German Confederacy. J.C. Cotta Stuttgart and Tübingen 1827–1830.* The final batch of the pocket edition appeared in December 1829, the final batch of the octavo edition in March 1831.

Could Cotta, now that he had brought this important "national matter" into his publishing house, relax? His rights would never be disputed, and after Goethe's death the edition would be expanded by the inclusion of the posthumous works; fifteen volumes of these appeared in 1833, among them *Faust,* Part II, and the fourth volume of *Literature and Truth;* the edition was completed in 1842 by five supplemental volumes, so that the final authorized edition consists of sixty volumes.

Nevertheless there were repeated grounds for disputes between Cotta and Goethe while the edition was in production. At the very outset there was a cause for annoyance because the announcements in the advertisements that appeared both in the daily newspapers and as separate publications appeared too late. Booksellers' demands for discounts were a constant stumbling block and Cotta wished to meet them generously; thus the booksellers received additional complimentary copies when they had sold a certain number of copies that had already been ordered and the author received no royalties on these complimentary copies. Goethe had agreed in the contract that one complimentary copy be given for every ten copies sold (incidentally this corresponds to the present practice of an allowance of 11/10 copies). But Cotta and Boisserée pressed him to make much greater concessions, at least until the introduction of subscriptions; the idea now was that one complimentary copy should be given for every four copies sold. After receiving this advice and influenced by the booksellers' protests, Goethe accepted this extreme arrangement, perhaps also because he saw that Cotta really had to fight against the booksellers, for the number of voices raised in criticism increased, as Cotta told Goethe: "Envy has drawn the majority of my enemies together, but there is hardly one who would take my place if he knew the burden I bear and the efforts I make and what for. People think I am wealthy, very wealthy, yet it is possible that I shall die poor at least in relation to this view—for who knows the sacrifices I have made for art and science and am still making! Who is aware of my losses, suffered mostly in the spirit of the most charitable effort, an effort that I am permitted to mention because I regard it as my duty." A further point of contention was that the publisher could not keep the deadlines that had been announced for the delivery of the individual batches; Goethe was constantly hearing that the publisher "had broken his word" although Cotta himself had told Goethe that the deliveries were on time. And once again Goethe was in a bad mood. At this time there are again signs that things were falling apart in Goethe's relationship to Cotta, this time on account of the publication of the Goethe-Schiller correspondence.

Difficulties arose in July 1827 while the work was being produced. Reichel, the proofreader in Augsburg, had now made his "final" mark upon the final authorized edition by rearranging the order of the writings in one of the volumes, with the result that there were fewer signatures, and he did this without informing Goethe. The latter complained, justifiably, that it was impossible for such "a significant decision" to have been made without his being informed. Cotta apologized, told Goethe that he was sorry, and asked him sincerely to reply quickly and forgive him. Goethe kept quiet.

As early as April, Cotta had learned of a pirated edition of Goethe's works in Gotha within the framework of the undertaking of a "Miniature Library of German Classics." He called upon Goethe to proceed against it: "If the Gotha reprint is not suppressed, then the German book trade will have been dealt a most mortal blow—I can prove this and it is not the booksellers but the authors who are bothered by this." Goethe refused to become involved in the matter and maintained his silence. Then, later, on 24 October 1827 he explained his behavior to Cotta:

> I have always preferred to remain silent than to respond when differences arise between friends, or relatives and associates, for in such cases everyone more or less stands pat on his own opinion and in this way new differences generally arise out of the statements people make, and the misunderstandings become more involved instead of being cleared up. On the contrary, I have found that *time* is the most reliable mediator; in the course of time actions develop and these are the only valid language that can be used between friends to express the true relationship. In the present case, may I assure you that had I been able to foresee that you would take to heart and regard as a reproach the statement that the cooperation of a living author in producing an edition of his works would be useful, I would have gladly refrained from making it, and it was for that reason that I wished to confer with you before-hand. I was long convinced that unfavorable circumstances produced the shortcomings in the edition of Schiller that has been so bitterly attacked.

But whatever kind of difficulties there were, in the end Goethe and Cotta worked together on the realization and production of the edition. True there was a long hiatus in communication between the two men in 1827 and 1828, especially as a result of the difficult negotiations on the Goethe-Schiller correspondence. However, Goethe was able to report to his son August on 9 September 1828 that Cotta had taken the opportunity "of sending a letter of conciliation. I have of course answered him kindly, decently, and diplomatically." The letter that Goethe wrote to Cotta a day later from Castle Dornburg does not seem to me all that decent and diplomatic; on the contrary his relationship with Cotta "emerged significantly" because of the death of the Grand Duke Carl August:

> Your Honor's
> kind letter reaches me at the moment when an irreparable loss reminds me that I should look round and take note of what is left on this earth that is of value to me. When I do this, my relationship to your Honor emerges significantly and I have to congratulate myself that I see a matter that is bound up with my own and my family's welfare entrusted to the hands of a man who pursues the most noble ends with resolution and who has earned for himself, both by his skill and his honesty, universal repute and trust.
>
> Accordingly, my most earnest wish must remain that our mutual relationship be kept clear and pure so that we may recall with confidence those beautiful days when we celebrated the beginning of a relationship—under the eye of, and with the loyal participation of, a friend who died too early—that was to last so long and bring us both such prosperity.

The publisher could certainly agree with a view like this that arches over the relationship from the beginning to the present and sums it up over decades. Cotta had achieved what had been his highest aim; he had in his house the edition that Goethe had called "the most important thing of my life" and in this way he took care of all of Goethe's work. He was Goethe's publisher.

Cotta: Goethe's Publisher, 1825–1832

ஒ୨୧ை

"I wouldn't know
what to do with
eternal blessedness if
it did not offer me
new tasks and
difficulties to
overcome"

So COTTA HAD DONE IT; he was, apart from a few rights that a few other publishers could still claim for individual works, Goethe's only legal publisher, and this he remained until Goethe's death. His firm retained the publishing rights until 1867, when "perpetual publishing rights" were rescinded and thirty years was established as the duration of copyright protection.

In the last years of their lives the association between Goethe and Cotta proved to be different from what it had been previously. Goethe was busy preparing parts for the final authorized edition; the editing and negotiations for the publication of his correspondence with Schiller proceeded laboriously; and he had to grapple with the thankless task of "composing" the *Journeyman Years* afresh from an "unfinished" version of 1821. Goethe called his principle for revising the work "dissolving the little work from scratch and building it up again." The drafts of the composition that are published in the Weimar Edition—there are no less than 50!—show how difficult this work turned out to be for him. We read in the story that is integrated into the novel *The Man of Fifty* that a "great deal of mess" was necessary to get to "the clean copy." The way he worked is astonishing, his ability to concentrate a phenomenon. His writing at this time became more and more exclusively dictation. The actual process of this dictation has still not been investigated, perhaps it is no longer possible to do so. We do have an account by Schuchardt, one of Goethe's assistants, who tells of his cooperation with Goethe on *The Journeyman Years* and of Goethe's method of dictation. "He did this with a sureness and fluency that many would only be capable of from a printed book. If this had taken place quietly and without outside disturbances I would hardly have paid attention to it, but in between came the barber, the hairdresser . . . the clerk, all of whom had permission to enter without being announced . . . As a hearty 'Come in!' rang out in reply to a knock, I finished the last sentence and waited until the person left again. Then I repeated as much as seemed necessary to me for the context, and the dictation continued until the next interruption, as though nothing had happened. This was really too much for me and I looked all round the room to see whether there wasn't a book, a draft, an outline that Goethe was looking at as he passed (for during dictation he kept walking round and round the table and the writer) but I was never able to discover the slightest thing."

Goethe used this method of "free" dictation only part of the time. Diaries and writings left to posterity are evidence that he liked to work from drafts and detailed plans that he called "schemata." He often worked out, the day or evening previously, something that was to be the basis of his dictation on the following day.

Goethe's great task at this time, his second "chief business," was the completion of *Faust,* and it is a miracle that this was possible given the advanced age of the author and his changeable state of health. Goethe completed *Faust,* Part II on 22 July 1831; he put away the manuscript that was only published in the posthumous volumes of the final authorized edition. He is supposed to have said to Chancellor von Müller that "he wouldn't know what to do with eternal blessedness if it did not offer me new tasks and difficulties to overcome."

Close acquaintances were dying all round him, the Grand Duke Carl August, the Grand Duchess Louise, poets of his own generation, Schiller and Wieland before him, even the next generation—Byron, Mozart, Schubert, and Weber all died before him. It was time "they went," he confided to Eckermann, indeed they had to be "ruined" so that "other people would be left with something to do in this world that is destined to last for a long time." A macabre reflection.

Charlotte von Stein died on 6 January 1827 at the age of eighty-four. She knew what Goethe thought about death and funerals and so she expressly stated in her will that her funeral procession should not pass Goethe's house. Goethe's son August died on 26 October 1830 in Rome. Chancellor von Müller, who brought Goethe the news two weeks later, noted that "he received it [the news] with great composure and resignation. 'Non ignoravi, me mortalem genuisse' ('I am not unaware that I sired a mortal'), he cried as his eyes filled with tears." Throughout his life August's relationship to his father had been that of the "drama of the talented child." He was, and remained, the son who owed all his posts and advantages to his father and who could never work himself up to a position higher than that of a mid-level civil servant. Symptomatic of his situation—certainly not unusual at that time—seems to me to be the book that his father had given him; not an empty sketchbook in which the son could have made his own entries (he got one of those too) but a family album in which he was to enter other people's sayings. True, there was already one entry to be read in the book that Fichte addressed to him: "The nation has made great demands of you, unique son of the unique man of our age. Count me then among those who will watch most attentively to see whether you will educate yourself to fill your father's place one day."[1] No wonder August could not develop, that as a young man he took to alcohol and dissipation; he did little to oppose his fate, [speaking out only once, in Ottilie's periodical "Chaos": "I no longer want to be led by the reins / as I have been up till now / I'd rather stand on the edge of the abyss / and free myself from every bond." August died of a stroke in the night of 26/27 October 1830. He was buried in the cemetery at the Pyramid of Cestius. Goethe erected a gravestone and decided on the inscription: "patri antevertens" ("preceding his father"). Whatever else his death may have meant to Goethe (he later recapitulated in summary form the last weeks of his son's life, in a letter to Zelter on 23 February 1831), he now had to give up the hope that his son would be able to support him in negotiations with his publisher about his posthumous works. "Expect trials to the end!" Goethe wrote to Zelter on 21 November 1830:

> What is actually strange and significant about this trial is that all the burdens that I thought I could slough off and hand over at once and in the new year to a younger person I must now go on bearing and with even greater difficulty.
>
> It is here alone that the great concept of duty can keep us going. Nothing bothers me except keeping my physical balance, everything else will follow. The body must, the spirit will, and the person who sees the most necessary path prescribed for his wishes does not need to think things over very much.

When Goethe wrote this astonishingly cool and objective letter to Zelter he had been thinking for five years of editing his correspondence with his great friend Schiller. Perhaps this is why when talking to Zelter he always tried to survey the whole and strike a balance.

At the end of November 1830 Goethe suffered a severe hemorrhage, but he had no thought of dying, of death. He joked forcefully about dying: Ninon de Lenclos had lived till ninety, "after having in her eighties given pleasure to, and driven to despair, hundreds of lovers." He simply tried to banish death. Death was for him a transition. He believed in a continuation; the proud statement that Eckermann noted on 4 February 1829 is evidence of this: "The conviction of our continuance comes to me from the concept of activity; for if I go on working without rest until my end, then Nature is bound to show me another form of being, if my spirit cannot endure the present one."

Goethe, then, had his two main pieces of business, the edition of his works and *Faust,* and he concentrated on them with astonishing intensity. For him, Cotta was in 1807, from 1816 to 1822, and now from 1825 *his* publisher. But Goethe was not Cotta's only author. Such a fact alone is often the source of misunderstandings, annoyance, arguments, quarrels, and perhaps even the cause of an author's changing to another publisher, where of course the same situation obtains. Martin Walser has expressed this from a contemporary point of view; the author has *one* publisher whom he values, whom he trusts, to whom he can feel linked in friendship, indeed whom he on occasion even loves. But he then has to discover that his publisher does not have just one but many authors, a "harem of authors," and it is this situation, according to Walser, with which the author has to come to terms.

Cotta was acting out of self-interest when he set out to win Schiller and Goethe over to his firm. Both were *the* great authors of their time. Cotta "won" Schiller by expressing his friendship for him and by generous gifts of money to him and his family; he secured Goethe by his readiness to publish all his works and pay royalties that were, in the final analysis and taken as a whole, unique in the history of literature. He committed himself to both of them, however, because he was willing to take care of their works in their totality, to present their whole intellectual physiognomy to the public and also to publish their individual works even if from the outset these represented a loss. He never ceased to bring the works of his authors on to the market by all the means at his disposal. Beyond this, however, Cotta made further investments in them by publishing cost-intensive and failing journals, the *Propyläen,* with its issues on "Art and Antiquity" or "On Science with Special Emphasis upon Morphology" that were intended to increase Goethe's popularity. In the course of all this he discovered that Goethe, for his part, would not accept invitations to collaborate on the Cotta journals, the daily papers, the *Morgenblatt für gebildete Stände* that he founded in 1807 and valued so highly, nor on his various calendars; indeed he often did not respond to the requests at all. Cotta took all of this, in the truest sense of the words, "into account." He was sure of other returns. Goethe and Schiller, the fixed stars, he calculated correctly—and this is the way literary publishers calculate in the twentieth century, at least up to the present—would bring other authors in their wake, and so Cotta succeeded, at one time or another, in binding most of the important authors of the day to his firm.

Furthermore, when the contractual situation with Goethe had been cleared up, and Cotta was his sole publisher, he continued his other activities. In mid-February 1807 he moved his Stuttgart Cartographic Institute to Munich; on 1 January 1828 Cotta founded a daily paper *Das Ausland* ("Abroad") and on 1 January 1829 the political newspaper *Das Inland* ("At Home") that lasted until June 1831. In the course of these years he also founded the paper mill König, Cotta & Bauer, outside Würzburg. In between he also traveled as a member of the Württemberg diet through the various lands of the confederacy, especially to Berlin, for customs negotiations. His standard of living, his purchase of estates and houses, his shares in business undertakings gave the public the impression of great wealth. People begrudge a publisher this; all too often he was accused of drinking champagne out of the skulls of authors who had starved to death. The by no means small band of critical opponents, who were always ready to speak out in public, grew. But Cotta did not allow himself to be put off by them. The extent of his activity is astonishing but the exertions required by the business often weakened him and made him ill.

Small wonder that the relationship to his author Goethe changed fundamentally. While it had previously been a matter of pride for him to read proof himself, to write statements out in longhand, and to concern himself down to the last detail with Goethe's wishes, he now left the technical questions of the production and arrangement of the edition to his collaborators Lebret and Reichel; Cotta's son Georg also intervened on occasion in the correspondence. True, Cotta also got involved when there were delicate matters to discuss and difficult problems to solve. Difficult problems arise mostly where they are least expected. The edition of the correspondence between Schiller and Goethe seemed to be a perfectly clear and normal proceeding. But it was precisely out of this that unexpected difficulties arose because of the sensitivity of the authors involved. There are simply "many links" that need to be taken into account "between the conscious and unconscious" when dealing with artistic genius, as Goethe wrote in his last letter to Wilhelm von Humboldt on 17 March 1832.

The Epistolary Conversation between Goethe and Schiller Cotta was the first person to come up with the idea of publishing the letters exchanged by Goethe and Schiller. He had already spoken about it with Caroline von Wolzogen shortly after Schiller's death. Now, on 19 December 1806, he turned to Goethe and spoke up on behalf of the *Morgenblatt für gebildete Stände* that was so important to him: "apart from political things it embraces everything, and your intellect contains so infinitely many things which it would greatly delight the public to brush up against." He thought that some of Goethe's and Schiller's letters would please the public: "A few of the letters exchanged between you and Schiller would be a great gift to me." He had to wait for this great gift.

Seventeen years later Cotta learned from Goethe, that he, Goethe, was reading Schiller's letters: "For in recent weeks," he wrote on 11 June 1823, "I have assembled and arranged all the letters from Schiller that he wrote between the years 1794 and 1805—something that I consider as perhaps the greatest treasure I possess—from his first invitation to *Die Horen* to a few days before his death." Goethe began the compilation in the summer of 1823. But he had already come upon Schiller's letters in 1822. In June 1822 he had asked Schiller's widow Charlotte to give him back his own letters. At first Charlotte was willing to do this, but apparently under the influence of her sister Caroline, who had always thought that her brother-in-law's image was diminished by the rivalry with Goethe, she hesitated to accede to the request. Goethe made a mistake by offering to buy back the letters for a small sum; it was precisely this that strengthened the two women in denying his request. Goethe had told von Humboldt of his enthusiastic reading of Schiller's letters. "There is some sort of trouble between Schiller's widow and Goethe about Schiller's and Goethe's letters," Humboldt writes in a letter to his wife on 12 November 1823: "Schiller's widow, however, would like, and justifiably so, not to give up the advantage that her children might derive from these letters. So she is keeping Goethe's letters back and has rejected a few suggestions on Goethe's part for buying them back for a small sum."

Goethe continued with his reading and now wished to publish a few of Schiller's letters; he wrote to Caroline von Wolzogen on 22 March 1824: "The letters testify to a noble, pure, joyous, innocent relationship and would be the right thing to enhance the public's wishes and the publisher's interest." In fact Goethe could be convinced of the substance of these letters and at the same time be certain that they documented the human and intellectual phenomenon of a unique bond between partners and friends. In the context of the advance copies of the Schiller letters Goethe wrote of friendship: "Friendship can only be generated in practical fashion and survive in practice. Affection, even love, does not help friendship. True, active productive friendship consists in our keeping step in life, that my friend approves of the steps I take, and that I approve of his, and that we go on together unshakably, however different our ways of thought and life may be in other respects." Friendship cannot be characterized better, and one understands the saying "lost without a guardian angel," but lost too without friends. A selection of twenty-seven of Schiller's letters was printed in 1824 in number 1 of volume 5 of "On Art and Antiquity."

There are many entries in the diaries for 1823 and 1824 that confirm the fact that Goethe was reading Schiller's letters intensively at this time. But Charlotte von Schiller still continued to refuse to give up Goethe's letters; she possessed the originals and there were no copies. Goethe talked to Humboldt, who was in Weimar at the time, about the legal situation. At that time there was no regulation of the rights of ownership and publication of letters. Today the whole matter is subject to law. Letters, as property, belong to the recipient and not the writer or sender; publication and exploitation rights remain the property of the writer or his heirs. If we apply this principle to the case in point, then the letters that Schiller sent to Goethe were Goethe's property, but only Schiller's family could have decided about the publication rights, and, vice versa, Goethe's letters were the property of Schiller's heirs but only Goethe could decide about their publication. Humboldt was of the opinion that Schiller's letters were the family's property and only the family could decide about their publication. In this legally fluid situation, Humboldt made an advance: He wrote to his wife, "By giving Goethe my letters from Schiller, but in asking him to give them to Schiller's widow when he had read them and by thus indirectly indicating to him that letters written by Schiller could justly be considered the property of the children, I have set the matter in motion again."

"The setting in motion again" consisted in Goethe's and Schiller's heirs looking upon Humboldt as a mediator. Humboldt accepted: whether mediation would succeed was still in doubt, for although Goethe and Frau von Schiller "love and respect each other, they both stand fast by their opinions." Goethe and Caroline, Humboldt observed, "have actually drifted apart and she sometimes judges his character and behavior with a severity that is painful. On the other hand it is true that he has not acted well towards Schiller's children."[2] Humboldt took up his conversations with the Schiller family. As a result, Goethe received a letter from Caroline von Wolzogen dated 21 March 1824: The Schiller family agreed to publication, although Cotta as "a man of honor and a friend" was to be involved, and he would certainly pay "a significant sum for this remarkable correspondence." All royalties accruing from the publication were to be divided equally between Goethe and the Schiller family. If Goethe were in agreement with this he would receive his own letters back and could dispose of Schiller's letters as freely as though they were his own property. She closed her letter, "With the same confidence that Schiller bore you in his soul, the matter now lies in your hands. I know the way in which he would have been thinking if he had been acting on behalf of your family and I feel that you cannot act otherwise."

Goethe agreed to the letter—he could hardly have wished for more—and certainly Humboldt would have encouraged him to accept the offer. Goethe did this in his well-known way. He drafted a "decree"[3] that he sent to the Schiller family with the request to forward it Cotta, in "whatever form they liked" after they had looked at it and agreed on it.

The document reveals a definite intention to publish the correspondence and also the important fact that Goethe himself wanted to assume the responsibility for the editing. All the royalties arising from sales were to be divided equally. The things that still remained to be discussed were the term of the contract and a second, cheap pocket edition. What might Goethe have meant by his concluding sentence, "This is without prejudice to the settlement of further details"? Given his prior experience, Cotta must have been disturbed at the idea of the "settlement of further details."

At this point Goethe still did not know when, and if, his own letters would be available. Caroline too was energetically playing the game of inducing Cotta to give higher royalties. Frau von Schiller sent Cotta the so-called "decree" on 26 March and wrote to him:

> After negotiations that were initiated last November by Herr von Goethe through the good offices of Herr von Humboldt and continued by my sister about the publication of the correspondence that has been so long under discussion, I enclose a statement by Goethe resulting from this. If you accept this offer and send us half the royalties as is guaranteed for participation in future editions, we shall immediately give him the letters.

Cotta recognized the importance of the matter and wanted to see Goethe and talk with him personally, but had to confess in a letter dated 8 May 1824, "I can scarcely find a moment to write a few lines, let alone undertake a visit. Frau von Schiller has sent me the good news that the correspondence between you and Schiller will now be published by me; I cannot tell you how pleased I am by this and how excited I am at the prospect of it. Frau von Schiller will have informed you that I accepted the proposed conditions immediately, and will have told you of my added wish that eventually I might, if possible, own the originals as a dear and rare monument for my descendants, I am sure you will agree to the fulfillment of my wish." The idea of wanting to own the originals of a correspondence as a monument for one's descendants is a very strange notion. The publisher's argument should have been presented differently. He wished personally to gain a picture of the authenticity of the project, check the accuracy of the transcription, and perhaps read those passages of the correspondence that Goethe did not want to publish immediately. He could also have appealed to Goethe's attitude to all originals; for Goethe, the great collector of original documents, the external was always an expression of the inner as far as he was concerned. But Goethe, and this could have been foreseen, could not agree to Cotta's idea; he had far-reaching thoughts on the matter. The correspondence in its original form was to be kept secret for twenty-five years (he already had Frau von Schiller's agreement to this). It is easy to see the reason why; living persons who are mentioned critically or even insulted in the letters were to be protected.[4]

Cotta had informed Frau von Schiller that he agreed to publish the correspondence and had asked her to put the originals at his disposal. Quite independent of Goethe, however, Frau von Schiller hesitated; she asked Goethe to provide arguments for her refusal. Goethe helped her and drafted the outline of a reply for her:

> You should write to Herr Cotta in the following vein: Since, dear Sir, you have expressed your readiness to accept the publication that we have suggested, I have immediately given Goethe's letters to the Minister of State who is going to begin editing them at once and will make a fair copy. We are both delighted to have the opportunity of renewing earlier relations.
>
> We do have a number of objections, however, to handing over the original manuscripts after the completion of the printing, and only in the course of editing can we determine to what extent this will be possible.
>
> Whatever else remains to be settled in this matter, please have the goodness to negotiate with the Minister of State with whom we shall be in touch at all times, and we shall not hesitate to give our assent to what has been agreed.

Frau von Schiller accepted this draft, altered it slightly, added a greeting and sent it to Cotta on 16 April. Cotta agreed with the decision. We read in Goethe's diary for 10 April, "My letters to Schiller arrived from the Frau Hofrätin. I sorted them out at once and put them in order and was busy with them till well into the night." And the project engaged him further. By the end of May he had looked through half the letters. The editing of his correspondence with Schiller, so he wrote to Cotta on 30 May 1824, was a significant and, in many senses, a pleasing business; taken altogether, his and Schiller's letters expressed "the deepest secrets of friendship," but he had underestimated the editorial work and there was a lot to consider. Here Goethe learned by experience what is known to every editor to this day: there is nothing as complicated as editing letters. The editor must show concern for living persons, he must reckon with possible protests where intimate details are involved, names and places must be spelled correctly, factual information must be checked, dates verified, unclear passages explained, apparent mistakes and misunderstandings must be eliminated, quotations must be checked, and a lot more.

Goethe was reading Schiller's letters continuously in the years between

1824 and 1826 and he reread his own as well. There was discussion in the circle around him as to whether they should not think about a separate edition of Goethe's letters to Schiller. But Goethe was opposed to the idea of a separate volume. He wanted the *exchange* of letters that was based on the exchange of ideas; and he esteemed Schiller's letters more highly than his own. "The latter are certainly very necessary for enlightenment and enlivenment," he wrote, "but in their inner and independent value they are no match for Schiller's letters; he was more inclined to reflect upon persons and writings than I was, and his very free epistolary statements are invaluable as unconditional and spontaneous outpourings." Goethe said at the beginning of his relationship with Schiller that Schiller meant "a second youth" to him, and now he recapitulated everything—the struggle over the *Xenien,* the different phases of the dialogue about *Wilhelm Meister;* it was precisely at this point that differences between his poetics and Schiller's are made clear. Schiller was the man for great theoretical reflection, while Goethe writes of *Wilhelm Meister* (in 1814) that "he had written this little work, like my other things, as a sleepwalker." The dialectic of reflection and shaping, of consciousness and unconsciousness had become clear to him in his correspondence with Schiller. This was something that occupied Goethe throughout his life, and in his last letter to Wilhelm von Humboldt, on 17 March 1832—a letter that reads almost like a last will and testament—he speaks of the "manifold interactions" that exist in the artistic genius "between the conscious and the unconscious": "Consciousness and unconsciousness will act like a letter and an envelope, a simile that I very much like to use."

How deeply the workshop conversations about *Faust* and *Wallenstein* must have affected Goethe. He had pondered for a long time about making some sort of comment upon the change that took place in the correspondence after Schiller moved to Weimar in December 1799, but he decided not to. He also finally decided not to fill in the gaps with a "narrative." It would understandably have been hard for him to write such a commentary and narrative, for then he would have had to go even more deeply than in the letters into the differences that existed between him and Schiller on many objective and poetical questions. The fundamental difference had come to light in that very first conversation on Goethe's *Metamorphosis of Plants,* in which Schiller called Goethe's thesis not an experience but a mere idea; it is astonishing that a friendly relationship could have evolved in spite of such fundamental differences. Goethe's creative method, his *méthodos,* his "pursuit," was not so much criticized by Schiller as challenged. Later he formulated his fundamental art historical view and this was aimed at Schiller. It makes a great difference whether a poet seeks the particular in the general or the general in the particular; allegory derives from the former, where the particular only functions as an example of the general; the latter however is actually the nature of poesy, which expresses a particular without thinking of the general or indicating it: whoever seizes upon this particular also receives the general with it but is not conscious that he is doing so or at least he only becomes conscious of it late in the process. This "great difference" is a fundamental difference in the way the poet looks at the world. Once again: it is astonishing that in spite of this deep division the relationship endured and remained productive.

This proved completely true in another case; Goethe had a clear conception of "the nature of poetry," of the dialectic between reflection and shaping, between conscious and unconscious creation that was in complete contradiction to Schiller's. Schiller was clear about his own relationship to German idealism and he hoped too to profit from Goethe. The epistolary exchange about the rewriting of Schiller's ballad "The Cranes of Ibicus" is extremely characteristic of this. Schiller learns from Goethe that cranes fly in flocks and he at once introduces this into a new version of the ballad. On the other hand Goethe is impressed by the extent to which Schiller chances upon concrete experience from a theoretical starting point. Goethe understands this with a certain admiration at a later date when he writes to Schiller, while on his Rhine trip, that the motion of the water at the falls of the Rhine in Schaffhausen was just like that of Schiller's description in the ballad "The Diver." Schiller comments, "I was unable to observe this natural event except in a water-mill, but my detailed study of Homer's description of Charybdis may have kept me close to Nature." Idea or observation, conscious or unconscious, this basic problem of the creative process is the great theme of the correspondence, and this theme has a perspective that endures to the present day. Goethe's *Theory of Color* was characterized by observation; in the epistolary conversation it too is discussed and it is fascinating to read how Goethe's empiricism encounters Schiller's speculative intellect. Goethe's opponent in his theory of physics and in mathematics was Newton: Goethe suffered defeat, Newton's theories prevailed and this is the sense in which the whole of physics has developed up to the present. Yet today modern physics is once more confronted with the question of the evaluation of theory and observation.

The second great theme that runs through the correspondence is the problem of form. Goethe and Schiller both agree on the starting point; antiquity is the example that cannot be excelled, and research into the poetic laws established at that time and their application to the material and contents of contemporary poetry remain essential. There is a wide-ranging discussion of reflections on the theory of genre in this correspondence; whole schools of literature in succeeding ages are based on these statements. Goethe accepts Schiller's criticism of *Wilhelm Meister* that the novel "lacks a certain poetic boldness, because as a novel it is always trying to please the mind." On the other hand Schiller praises *Hermann and Dorothea,* where nothing of Goethe's spirit is lacking, "the work leads him into a divine world of poetry." Goethe agrees with this. He hopes that "a pure form helps"; *Wilhelm Meister* does not have that, so "we will have to wait and see what genius will bestow on us in the autumn of our life." When he resumes work on *Faust* he departs from the high formal demands that Schiller made, when he writes that he "takes things more easily in creating this barbarous composition and intends only to touch upon the highest demands rather than fulfill them." But Goethe and Schiller were great in that they could regard such fundamental differences over form as characteristic of one another and could accept it. What is particularly astonishing in this relationship between two authors is the extent to which they trusted each other and were always open to the concerns of the other. Observing the relationship between authors who are often only concerned with their own affairs and are prejudiced against what others do, we can safely say that this was a unique occurrence.

In his lecture "My Schiller" in which he sets Goethe off polemically against Schiller, Martin Walser states that it was in the last years, in particular, that the relationship between Schiller and Goethe flourished and that these years passed "productively." "If things had gone as well with them as they did in the second half of the 1790's then it would have been advisable to publish Goethe and Schiller in the same way as the Marx-Engels edition."

On 20 July 1824 Goethe had looked through the correspondece with Schiller up to the end of 1796 and, as he writes, "recognized over and over again the significance of the whole." This significance lay for him in the fact that private documents of two writers who together created the classical period of German literature were now assembled and merged; this would create "a unique objective document and the correspondence itself could develop into a classical work."

In December 1824 John, the secretary, began to copy the Schiller portion of the correspondence; Goethe's letters were copied later. Goethe was busy with the correspondence throughout the year; he checked the copies, made "insertions," and "arranged and finally corrected the letters."

What did he "correct"? Hints as to Goethe's method of editing are given by his insertions and by comparing the printed texts with the original letters, something that was first done by Wilhelm Vollmer, the editor of the Schiller-Cotta correspondence. Goethe saw that he would have to omit very few letters and that fewer cuts were necessary to protect the rights of individuals than had at first been thought. This "protection" was more of a moral appraisal for at that time there was as yet no legal obligation to preserve individual rights.

It is also certain that Goethe as an editor had never intended to embellish anything nor change anything that affected the personal or literary relationship between the two. He did not attempt any adumbration and certainly no canonization—that was left to later Goethe research. Goethe stood by the differences, the ambiguities and the contradictions; he and Schiller were "intellectual antipodes" between which, as he found in the essay "Happy Event," "the gap is greater than the diameter of the earth." And yet they remained invaluable partners for one another, each of them a major literary power.

The fact that the preparation of a manuscript that was ready for the press did not progress as rapidly as Goethe had always assumed it would was the result of his work on "major pieces of business," the final authorized edition and the continuation of *Faust,* but also of the fact that the importance of the correspondence became more and more clear to him and as a result he became much more scrupulous about which letters to include. He had to consider how "political" these letters could be and how they would be read at court—to say nothing about the increasing number of his adversaries. Meanwhile Schiller's heirs were exerting pressure because of the royalties they were owed. In a letter to Caroline von Wolzogen of 10 July 1825, Goethe suggested that he make a prepayment of 2,000 thalers out of his own pocket, the sum to be due on Michaelmas Day (29 September); and again he reaffirmed that all the royalties deriving from the publication, "according to the old and steadfast friendship," were to be divided fifty-fifty and he had his son August confirm the agreement. August signed the letter "as son committing myself to all the above." Oddly enough Goethe did not make the payment; we do not know the reason and he gave no further explanation to the Schiller family as to why. The family became restless and finally grew angry. Schiller's son, Friedrich Wilhelm Ernst, a lawyer and since 1824 active at the Court of Appeal in Cologne, took it upon himself to remind Goethe about the payment. He did this *suaviter in modo, fortiter in re* in his letter of 22 March 1826 in which he indirectly accused Goethe of breach of contract and asked for the promised payment. It remains inexplicable why Goethe did not even then make the payment. It is hardly thinkable that he should not have been in a financial position to do so, since he had received a payment of 5,000 thalers from Cotta in February 1826 for the additional money negotiated for signing the contract for the final authorized edition. He did not want to pay. A week later, he informed Ernst von Schiller that the editing would be finished in a few months and the manuscript would thus be ready for the press; for this reason he felt (a strange conclusion) that he was no longer bound by the previous year's arrangement. But once again Goethe had underestimated the extent of the editorial work, and the deadline for completion that he had foreseen could not be kept.

It was only after a pause of almost two years that Goethe once more took up with Cotta the matter of the correspondence; on 26 August 1826 he sent him the important news: "After Frau von Schiller's death the edition of my correspondence with her children's late father is once more the subject of conversation. The manuscript is completely ready for presentation."

How did Goethe succeed in having the manuscript completely ready for the press in August 1826? In the preceding months he had—perhaps already influenced by his reading of his and Schiller's letters—finished a work related to his *Faust* that was of cardinal importance to him (and to which we shall return). Now he was free to finish the manuscript of the correspondence.

Schiller's heirs still received no news from Goethe. When Ernst von Schiller had not heard either from Goethe or from Cotta within two months, he decided to go to Weimar to see Goethe—"the matter is so flagrant that I believe that Goethe will be ashamed and will pay"; if not, he would take legal steps. But Goethe was not ashamed—and neither did he pay. So Ernst met with Goethe's son August, with whom he was friends, who told him of his father's editorial labors and the large expenses involved in the edition: from his father's point of view his offer was an accommodation to the family but it was not legally binding. In a subsequent conversation with Goethe Ernst gave up his demand. Goethe reports this agreement and also that he had "corrected other earlier things." Both of them were working on a "decree" for Cotta. This decree was based on Cotta's earlier promises of royalties, 2,000 thalers per volume, and if the correspondence were to appear in a pocket edition 4,000 thalers. The 970 original pieces of the correspondence were packed in a box in the presence of Ernst von Schiller, sealed and wrapped in waxed cloth and handed over to the Weimar government for "the prince's privy purse" with instructions to preserve the package of letters "in scrinio principis" until 1850, after which both heirs could dispose of it as they saw fit. The two, Goethe and Ernst von Schiller, signed the decree. Ernst von Schiller expressed his "respectful" thanks. Cotta had been in Berlin for negotiations on questions of customs duty and was now journeying back to Munich via Weimar. "At the same time on my own behalf and on behalf of my brothers and my sister whom I have already mentioned, I take this opportunity to inform His Excellency, Minister von Goethe, most respectfully that we recognize to its full extent the extraordinary amount of work that His Excellency has put into the editing of the von Goethe-Schiller correspondence and that we feel the most heartfelt thanks for the loving way in which His Excellency has acted for us in this common matter, and I offer His Excellency this thanks in the name of myself and my brothers and sister." Goethe enclosed with the sealed package a sort of balance sheet of the edition, according to which "a clean manuscript, in five folio volumes," would contain "in complete form, the whole of the two friends' correspondence written in the years 1794 to 1805."

However, the manuscript did not go direct to Cotta but, on 31 December 1826, to Sulpice Boisserée, who was once more to assume the role of mediator. Boisserée knew that Cotta was urgently awaiting news and was indeed indignant about the fact that for a long time it was only through him (Boisserée) that he had news of the progress of the edition. Boisserée implored Goethe to write to Cotta personally: "Please refer to the fact that by then I should have handed over the documents and say something nice to him as to why you sent the documents through me etc." Goethe followed his advice and in his letter of 26 January 1827 he expressed the hope that Cotta would "have a pleasant and quiet time," "when you open this." Then with a sly dig that would embarrass Cotta, rouse his conscience, and, indeed, induce a feeling of guilt, he gave his reasons for involving Boisserée so frequently. "I always have to think of you at home, or on a trip, involved in the most important business, and I am reluctant to bother you with anything that is not an urgent necessity. Our Boisserée's mediation puts my mind at rest and I send him a lot of things that he presents to you at the appropriate time." Then he comes to the point: "A few days ago I sent friend Boisserée what Ernst von Schiller and I worked out the last time he was here. Our proposals are in accordance with our earlier agreement and I may say that the mass of manuscripts as it exists makes a splendid cornerstone that will support and hold together mine and Schiller's works. The concept that we both wished for, the way we formed each other, how we furthered one another, what got in our way, and how far we prospered in our efforts and why we got no further will all become clearer and must serve as a guiding light to those who are also aspiring."

For the rest, Goethe asks that the second part of the agreed royalties for the final authorized edition be paid in the second half of March. Cotta's reply of 3 March 1827 was delayed and somewhat reluctant. Boisserée was away and he would have to wait for his return, the date of which he did not know. He agrees expressly to Goethe's wish for a somewhat advanced payment of royalties, saying that he had planned it for the Easter Fair (interim payments involved "significant bank charges"). Unfortunately Cotta had good reason to state this in such detail. He had had to raise loans to finance not only editions of Goethe but also of Schiller and Herder, and these now began to be burdensome to him and cause him difficulties especially with his son.[5]

Goethe reminded him in March about the correspondence project: "The Schiller correspondence is ready to be packed up when the detailed declaration is ready" and again, not without artfulness vis-à-vis the publisher who was certainly in no way guilty of the delay, he mentions that the speedy appearance of the correspondence "would exert a great influence on the editions of the works of the two friends."

In the following weeks and months, Cotta's communication with Goethe and his son August is restricted entirely to booksellers' complaints about the delay in delivering the Schiller edition; about the poor quality of the production; about the vexed question of the unaccounted for "job copies" of the final authorized edition and about the announcements of the pocket edition that were either delayed or inadequately executed; and not least about the discussion of accounting for the fees to be paid. It was not until 31 October that Cotta returned to the correspondence though, it is true, with a disarming confession. He asks Goethe when they can start setting and printing the correspondence, he asks about the arrangement of the edition and tells him of the idea he has for producing an octavo edition after the pattern of *Literature and Truth*. But then Cotta tries to be especially clever: he had not yet agreed to the demand for 4,000 thalers in royalties for the pocket edition of the correspondence and in order not to have to accept this as a fait accompli he first mentions an earlier agreement "that I corrected with the late Frau von Schiller from the financial point of view." But first he has to make what is for a publisher a most regrettable confession, he "cannot" find the "instrument, that is, the agreement which has probably been mislaid among some other papers as a result of my travels hither and thither." Goethe knew nothing of an agreement between Frau von Schiller and Cotta, Cotta had never mentioned such a thing nor had Ernst von Schiller said anything about it in their extended conversations. Was he being deceived by one side or the other? Did he fear that the "decree" that had been passed on by Boisserée might also disappear among Cotta's papers?

Goethe started another correspondence with Boisserée in connection with Cotta's letter. Boisserée had already written to him that "friend Cotta is once more up to the ears in . . . business which is very confused this time," that he agreed to the royalties for the octavo edition but was not of the opinion that they could start typesetting at once. Goethe waited, but on 11 November he brought Boisserée in; "Herr von Cotta is making noises about the Schiller correspondence once more, but without the determination that is so necessary in such cases. . . . I will write to him about this in greater detail soon and I also wish to do his bidding in this matter because he must be in the best position to know how something of this sort is to be tackled and how it can progress." In fact Cotta did lack the "necessary determination," he hesitated. He thought, as many publishers do today, that letters do not as a rule sell very well, besides which the manuscript was unusually extensive and the production of such a volume of letters was very cost-intensive and laborious.

It is Goethe who resumes the correspondence while expressing a particular wish. His very self-willed letter of 17 December 1827 angered Cotta; indeed it gave rise to vehement discord and a violent interruption of his relationship with Goethe. Goethe believes that "this strange manuscript as it lies in front of me is of the greatest importance; it will, in a moment, satisfy people's curiosity and furthermore it will continue to be most effective from a literary, philosophical, and aesthetic point of view as well as from many others." Then Goethe reminded him of the "essay" that Boisserée had sent to Cotta in January. "Your agreement to the proposals that have been made will immediately set the matter on the right track. . . . The manuscript is far, far larger than I had ever imagined." After this came the passage that pierced Cotta to the core of his publishing heart, that shocked and enraged his contemporaries:

> I am enclosing a few pages so that you can see for yourself and note that . . . probably 5 or 6 decent octavo volumes will be filled.
>
> You will agree to my not sending the manuscript without a prior conclusion of the negotiations, when you observe that I am responsible to Schiller's heirs, among whom there are two females and that I have therefore to be prepared for any eventuality . . . . and I would—after not only being satisfied for myself but also assured on their part—mail the box that has already been packed for a long time thus finally bringing to a close a matter that has cost me a lot of trouble, worry and expense.
>
> For I will only confess that a good-natured folly when I took over the honorary editorship cost me an incalculable amount of time and not a small loss of money.

The stumbling block was the sentence "my not sending the manuscript without a prior conclusion of the negotiations." I must confess that I cannot share Cotta's, nor the public's, ensuing outrage over this. Cotta knew of course what he wanted to gain by his contract and what payments he was making. Goethe had indeed reprinted letters by Schiller in *On Art and Antiquity* and had given Cotta examples of letters from them both. And finally it was after all a question of texts by Schiller and Goethe, "prime writers" as Cotta himself liked to describe them. Did Cotta not recall that Goethe occasionally played games like this with publishers? Vieweg too had had to offer and pay royalties before he was able to read the text of *Hermann and Dorothea*. As much as I respect the publishing principle of knowing precisely what one is trying to obtain for the firm, in this case Cotta must have known, and he did know, what it was all about. He took an astonishingly long time over his answer; he did not write to Goethe until 11 February 1828, almost two months later. "I will not try to describe the impression that your letter made upon my spirits that were already melancholy enough without this, suffice it to say that it was the cornerstone of a very trying year."

The year 1827 had been a hard one for Cotta. The financial difficulties that we have already mentioned as well as the collection of outstanding debts from bookstores led to complaints and quarrels and even affairs of honor. Cotta had long-winded arguments with Herder's heirs. Piracy and censorship in his own papers posed great problems for him. But then he discusses in the letter what he regarded as the real insult. "A manuscript by prime authors is offered to me for 8,000 thalers—I am not allowed to look at it as only after I have paid this sum will the manuscript be despatched." Of course in the case of works by established masters he will make an exception to the rule of seeing something first before buying it and paying for it. "But what if there is trust on the one side while the other expresses a mistrust that is unusual in nature?" This is for him "the most painful experience." And then he lists what he has agreed to and what he has accepted in the more than thirty-year relationship and the way in which he has most conscientiously fulfilled these obligations. He had always done his part, especially when he thought of his kindness to the Schiller heirs "among whom there are two females," and he mentions that the family had already received 5,026 thalers, that is, 1,026 more than their share. He concludes: "Please let your inmost voice respond to this cry from my heart—for in spite of all my troubles I cannot and will not dismiss the thought that it was not your heart that was talking in your letter." With the letter he enclosed the documents that he had exchanged with Charlotte von Schiller and her sister Caroline von Wolzogen. However, these letters did not make Goethe happy, on the contrary this news of the negotiations with the Schiller heirs (of which he had known nothing and that Ernst von Schiller had not reported to him) made him extremely angry; he was not ready to reply and kept silent for a long time.

Boisserée excused Cotta, "who had experienced a lot of unpleasantness recently." But when he sent him a definite proposal for a contract, Cotta answered Boisserée, saying that he was in agreement with the additions: "The thought of sparing you annoyance puts me beyond all the unpleasantness that is necessarily associated with mediating between two persons both of whom feel that they have been insulted." On 8 March 1828, the contract for the *Correspondence between Schiller and Goethe* was legally signed. It must have annoyed Goethe that Cotta returned to the question of the 4,000 thaler payment to the Schiller heirs after the contract had been signed. Goethe did not reply again. Goethe's angry outburst—already mentioned and often quoted—on 21 May 1828, "Booksellers are all fiends!" can be understood in the light of this mood.

Cotta, however, found Goethe's silence oppressive and so he took

Goethe's birthday as the occasion for renewing the relationship, writing that he was minded "on this festive day to express my feelings towards you and the pain that your long silence has caused me"; he wrote that he was also sure that what had insulted him so deeply had not originated with Goethe. After Goethe had replied "kindly and diplomatically," Cotta reacted in two ways; one was to intensify the process of the production of the correspondence and the second was for him finally to announce that he would visit Goethe.

After this visit there was no need for further correspondence about the letters, production was under way and there were no further problems. Goethe could report on 30 November that the first volume of the correspondence was in his hands, the second volume followed in the same month, and one year later the other four volumes; thus *The Correspondence between Schiller and Goethe in the Years 1794 to 1805 in Six Volumes* had appeared and was available to the public. Goethe had intended to dedicate the first volume to the Bavarian king Ludwig I, who had conferred distinction on Goethe by sending his court painter to Weimar to paint the author's portrait. Though it did not appear until it was included in the final volume, the dedication brought the king true joy.

There is no question but that with this work Goethe created, even from their private statements, an objectively classical work both for himself and for Schiller—a unique document. They were ahead of their time in the theory of art, in the way they integrated the development of philosophy and aesthetics from Kant to Hegel. Their theory was never insipid, it was always linked, like the letter and the envelope, with the conditions of artistic creative practice. Understandably, there was an immanent contradiction within this relationship, as there had to be; that the "friendship" arose in spite of this, the friendship that "created in practice acquires its temporal extent in practice," is among the greatest human accomplishments of the two writers. Friendship here also means "that we keep in step with one another in life." Goethe and Schiller never allowed themselves to be divided, not even in statements to third parties. Schiller confessed that it was not only Goethe's great intellectual advantages that bound him to him: "If, as a person, he was not of more value to me than anyone I have ever met, then I would only admire his genius from afar. I may truly say that in the six years that I lived with him I never once doubted his character. There is a noble truth and probity in his nature and the greatest seriousness about what is right and good, and it is for this reason that gossips, hypocrites, and swindlers always felt ill at ease in his presence. They hated him because he despised so heartily what was flat and insipid in life and science and detested false appearances, and thus he is bound to incur many people's displeasure in the present bourgeois and literary world."

Goethe experienced a few more reactions to the publication of the correspondence. One writer made fun of it, saying that by its publication Goethe had made the whole world privy to the miseries of the private life of both authors, and readers were bored with "visiting cards and menus." But where are such "miseries" to be found in the correspondence? Grabbe was mistaken. The first critical evaluation of the correspondence states, "Nothing else furnishes . . . the initiated and those wishing to be initiated, younger writers to a man, and especially the struggling poet, with such rich, deep, ennobling, and attractive instruction and exemplification."

Goethe research has in part sustained this sacral exaggeration of the "Dioscurian pair" which, as an essay of 1847 observes, "we have already grown accustomed to look at in our literary firmament." It was left to G. G. Gervinus,[6] the originator of the critical writing of literary history, in his work on *The Goethe Correspondence* to sound more critical notes. "The world has perhaps never seen two people, who differed so completely—from every point of view—in such a strange relationship."

"Booksellers are all fiends" So Cotta had passed the tests imposed on him by the Goethe-Schiller correspondence, but he was constantly faced with new tasks that produced new difficulties. Time and again he had to involve himself in day-to-day events as, for example, in the matter of frequently recurring rumors about pirated versions and the constant hue and cry about job copies that bore no royalties.

Cotta and Goethe finally met again in 1828 after a five-and-a-half-year hiatus. The publisher arrived at Goethe's home with his second wife on 27 September 1828. Goethe had stated that Cotta only visited him when he was undertaking a journey for different purposes, that he had never come to Weimar simply to see him. But Cotta was lucky, Goethe liked his new wife exceptionally well: "The presence of your new wife," Goethe wrote, "left the most pleasant impression on us and we often delight in the memory of having personally done the honors to such an esteemed couple. If you remember us in the same way then the relationship that has lasted so long, and that is so important, can only become even more beautiful and a mutual advantage will be ennobled by the most worthy feelings of mutual trust." Cotta expressed his thanks fulsomely for his reception; he was delighted and moved, he said, "by your most kind and friendly reception, for the never to be forgotten hours that you spent with us and for the youthful power and liveliness of your conversation which bore testimony to your so highly valued well-being. . . . We were once again in Weimar in your animating presence!" One is tempted on reading these letters to think that the relationship between author and publisher could not be better, could not be more hearty ("a mutual advantage will be ennobled by the most worthy feelings of mutual trust"), and yet in every author-publisher relationship that develops along the lines of friendship there is always a kernel of uncertainty, of doubt, perhaps even of mistrust. From the author's point of view the publisher disposes of a power whose decisions affect the author's very existence. In Goethe's case a sort of mistrust continued to smoulder, and for this reason he was able, in his spontaneous and direct manner, to come to surprising judgments. While the forty volumes were being produced, Goethe complained about every delay, though these were unavoidable in view of the unstable circumstances of the day that were, for the majority of small German states with their different constitutions, their different legal codes, their censorship regulations and postal arrangements, the result of the Napoleonic Wars. The processes of proofreading, with its delays and losses between the changing printing works and Weimar, were nerve-racking. Only in this way can we explain why so shortly after the announcement that the relationship "could only become more beautiful" another anathema was pronounced; when a signature that had been expected did not arrive Goethe was reported by Chancellor von Müller to have said, "Booksellers are all fiends, there must be a special hell for them." It was a spontaneous remark made on a walk. Goethe never returned to it, did not record it; it was certainly not his intention that it should be published.

Cotta wrote to Goethe on 13 November 1828 that he had to go to Berlin again for a month; but this time he did not visit Weimar either on the journey there or on the way back. Goethe noted this carefully and he let nothing stand in the way of his reading Cotta a lesson on 30 November, a lesson it is true that he labeled "an observation." "Let me now make an important observation that I am driven to by your recently desired presence. Men who are joined by such important vital considerations should not delay meeting personally and discussing things face to face. Distance alienates kindred spirits, take it how you will; a moment in one another's presence lifts all the mists that all too easily increase and intensify with distance." That was clear. Even today a publisher must take this admonition to heart vis-à-vis his authors, even today a face-to-face conversation is to be preferred to all the letters and telephone calls. Goethe returns again and again to the desirability of a personal interchange. Several months later he closes a letter with, "saving a lot of other things for the personal meeting for which I stand in hope." Goethe wanted to hand over to Cotta his poetic dedication to the king of Bavaria of the Goethe-Schiller correspondence; now he sends Cotta the work that had been occupying him, alongside the *Journeyman Years* and *Faust,* his defense of his writings on the *Metamorphosis of Plants.* A botanical work that had appeared in Paris in 1827 inspired him to translate into French, with the help of his friend Soret, a chapter of his own work, and for this purpose he engaged in new botanical researches and wanted to present, more or less "in its final version," his morphological position. Since this work was very important to Goethe, Cotta acceded to his wish and published the work *Essay on the Metamorphosis of Plants/Essai sur la métamorphose des plantes* in a bilingual edition of 1,400 copies: it was a publication that certainly did not have a market of this size. Goethe demanded 1,000 thalers, but Cotta reduced it to 500.

The desired meeting took place on 2 June 1829; Cotta later expressed his thanks for the visit, the "enjoyable and wonderful day that you gave us." Though he had to tell Goethe that he had fallen seriously ill after his return, he was however recovering and at once plunged back into his varied occupations. But in spite of that he wanted to send Goethe a greeting on the occasion of an enclosure that he had been asked for; the enclosure contained a survey of the subscribers to the 14,684 copies of the pocket edition that had been sold up till then (853 copies of the octavo edition had been sold), with pages of details about the bookshops that had subscribed. Goethe did not react, the figures could scarcely have pleased him. In a later reckoning, the number of copies on which royalties were paid was further reduced, because the job copies had not been agreed on with the author. A short while later Cotta's son George wrote to Goethe; his son, Cotta's grandson, had been born on 28 August, on Goethe's birthday, and he asked Goethe to be godfather. Goethe did not go to Stuttgart but he did agree to be the child's godfather.

In the meantime there were suspicions about another pirated edition. Two booksellers in Hamburg announced a new Goethe edition without naming a publisher and with very precise editorial information from which it could be concluded that the work in question embraced sixty volumes. The whole thing was speedily cleared up; both booksellers were referring to the Cotta edition, and the source of the rumor was "an error" according to an attorney whom Cotta had employed. In spite of the speedy clarification the correspondence on the subject dragged on until well into the year 1831. The very fact that, in spite of the publicly acknowledged privilege proceedings, it was still possible for there to be illegal editions depressed Goethe. Again he was enveloped in silence for a long time. On 16 June 1831, he wrote to Cotta. He talked about "the misadventures that had befallen him in the previous year" that had "involved a complete change in his way of life." But he was confident that "in all this as in other things, I shall continue to exert a modest influence."

"The main business" Peter Huchel, who lived in Staufen im Breisgau from 1972 until his death, would smile ambiguously when he was asked if his poem "The Stranger" was based on Johann Faust. Erhart Kästner, who also lived in Staufen for many years, devoted some studies to the scholar and astrologer, the arch-practitioner of black magic, the contemporary of the humanists, of Luther, and of the Peasants' Revolt. Georg Zabel (Georgius Sabellius Faustus) was probably born in Staufen around 1540; the "impudent unscrupulous rogue" adopted the name "Faustus"—"the favored one"—later on. The first consistent representation of the life of Dr. Faust appeared in 1587, printed by the Frankfurt bookseller Johann Spiess: *The History of Dr. Johann Faust, the notorious magician and practitioner of the black arts / how he pledged himself to the devil for a fixed period / how he had as a result some strange adventures, arranged and carried out by himself / until he finally received his well-deserved reward.* Here Faust already makes his pact with the devil, and Mephistopheles, the famulus Wagner, and Helen all figure in the story. Goethe did not know the *History*. He borrowed it on 18 February 1801 from the duke's library in Weimar. But already as a child, Goethe had gained his first impressions of the Faust material from other sources, popular versions. The *History* had been translated into English shortly after its appearance and in 1588 Christopher Marlowe used it as the

basis of his *Tragical History of Dr. Faustus*. The German material returned to its homeland by way of this extremely successful play and became a folk play. Goethe had seen it as a puppet play and recorded the impression both in *Poetry and Truth* and in *Wilhelm Meister's Theatrical Mission*. Thus we read in *Poetry and Truth* that it was in Leipzig that the Faust legend took definitive hold on him. The young Goethe wanted to know what "held the world together at its core" and so he studied mystical cabalistic writings, astrology, the works of Paracelsus and Swedenborg, and he read Gottfried Arnold's *Unbiased History of the Church and Heresy*. Goethe recognized in *Poetry and Truth* that "his [Arnold's] views agree very much with my own and what particularly delighted me in his work was that I gained a more favorable opinion of many heretics who had previously been represented to me as crazy or godless." Faust, the ally of the devil, grew upon Goethe. In Book 5 of *Poetry and Truth*, he writes about a young girl he had met when he was fourteen years old: "This young girl's figure followed me from that moment on everywhere I went; it was the first lasting impression that a female being had made upon me. . . . since I could neither find, nor wished to seek, an excuse to see her at home I went to church out of love for her and had quickly discovered where she sat: and so throughout the long Protestant service I could feast my eyes upon her. I did not have the courage to speak to her as she left and I was delighted when it seemed as though she had seen me and nodded in response to a greeting" (Faust was to meet Margaret in front of the cathedral). Many people have an experience of this sort, and this one followed Goethe all his life. He also incorporated this experience into his "poetic confession."

After having had to analyze the amount of punishment meted out to female infanticides for his doctoral thesis in Strassburg, he was a witness in Frankfurt to a trial that ended with the execution of a female infanticide in January 1772. Copies of the records of the trial were found in Goethe's father's house.[7] We know that the famous passage in *Poetry and Truth*, one that Goethe constantly referred to, is about this female infanticide. He worked on individual scenes from 1773 till 1775.

Goethe had been in Weimar for just four weeks when a visitor to his house reported, on December 1775, "Goethe read from his half-finished 'Faust' one afternoon. The duchesses were powerfully moved at some of the scenes." There were further such readings; Wieland was present in Frankfurt on Goethe's birthday in 1781 when a Chinese shadow play was performed in which Iphigenia and Faust appeared. "Of course there was no talk of "half-finished." We should know nothing of this Weimar "Faust" if it were not for the fact that a lady-in-waiting, moved by Goethe's reading, had asked him for the manuscript and made a copy of it. The original is lost, but the copy, which was discovered in 1887, transmits the early text that we know as the "Urfaust."

"Faust. A Fragment"

Goethe did no work on *Faust* for his first ten years in Weimar, and other great works like *Egmont, Iphigenia, Tasso,* and the novel *Wilhelm Meister* remained incomplete. Personal events, but above all his official duties, the failure of political reforms that were to have lifted or at least mitigated the backwardness of the dukedom of Saxe-Weimar—all these experiences could not to be introduced into the plan for *Faust.* On 2 September 1786 he signed a contract with Göschen for the edition of his works for which *Faust* was earmarked as a "fragment." For many authors, publishing contracts of this sort may be only of a formal character, but a contract is a contract; it has been signed and efforts must be made to fulfill it. In any case this contract with Göschen was the decisive impetus for resumption of work on *Faust.* Goethe set off on his Italian journey in the autumn and there he hoped to rediscover his poetic productivity, hoped for a "second birthday, a true re-birth from the day I set foot in Rome." He changed the announcement of his works for the Göschen edition, and fragmentary writings were earmarked for appearance in the four volumes. *Iphigenia* and *Egmont* were now complete. "I shall work on *Faust* last of all," he wrote to Duke Carl August in December 1787, "when I have everything else behind me. In order to compete the play I shall have to pull myself together in a very special way. I must draw a magic circle around myself and may a favorable fortune give me the perseverance to do this." Goethe tried repeatedly to draw this magic circle in Rome. In the March correspondence of the "Second Roman Sojourn" he reported on 1 March 1788: "First, the plan for 'Faust' was made and I hope the operation will be successful. Of course it is one thing to write the play now and another to write it fifteen years ago, but I think it will lose nothing in the process especially as I now think that I have picked up the thread again. I also feel confident about the tone of the whole thing; I have already written a new scene and if I were to fumigate the paper I would think that no one would find anything left of the old ones. Since my long rest and absence have totally restored me to the level of my former life, it is remarkable how like myself I am and how little my inner self has suffered from the years and from events. When I see the old manuscript in front of me it often provides me with food for thought. It is still the first, indeed the main scenes were written without a draft, and now it is so yellowed with time, so ragged (the sections were never bound), so brittle and crumpled at the edges, that it really looks like the fragment of an ancient codex, so that I now have to set myself back into a period that I have lived through myself just as then I removed myself into an earlier world by thought and guesswork."

In the garden of the Villa Borghese he managed to work out a "Nordic scene," the "Witches' Kitchen," and this marked the beginning of a new treatment of his material. He wrote in five-feet rhymed iambics, the meter that later came to be identified with German classicism. And Goethe solved another formal problem in this scene: it was still unclear how Faust, already on in years, could woo Gretchen as though he were a youth; now Mephistopheles bewitches and rejuvenates him with the witches' potion. But in spite of all his efforts Goethe cannot complete *Faust* in Italy. "Lila is finished, Jery too, my small poems will soon all be compiled," he reported to the duke on 28 March 1788, "then, next winter, *Faust* remains to be written, for which I feel a special inclination. May I succeed only half as well as I wish and hope!" But he did not succeed, and the return to Weimar, the necessary process of accustoming himself to new circumstances and personal difficulties, prevented him from continuing the work. On 5 July 1789 he had to confess to Carl August, "I will have to publish *Faust* as a fragment for more than one reason." True, he tried to arrange the fragment in a sensible order. "I have been well and have worked hard," he wrote to Carl August on 5 November 1789. "Faust is fragmented, that is to say laid aside in its present form. Mitteldorf is copying it. A stranger draft was probably never submitted to him before. It is really strange to see all these lunacies written by the hand that is otherwise accustomed to submitting '*steadfastness, love and loyalty*' to us." We can extrapolate a certain distancing from this "fragmentation" from these lines, and Johann Martin Mitteldorf, Goethe's clerk and private registrar in Weimar, must indeed have been surprised by the "plan." The Goethe of 1790 was a different man from the one who had picked up the "Faust" material in the 70s. The former felt himself isolated and misunderstood: "no one understood my language." But now events in France meant "a new epoch in world history" for him, and thus it was clear that the Faust material could not be further developed at the time. It remained a fragment.

In January 1790 he sent *Faust* to Göschen. The first edition of *Faust* was ready that summer—two years after he had promised it: "*Goethe's Works. First to eighth volume. Leipzig, George Joachim Göschen. 1787–1790. Seventh Volume, Faust, a Fragment. Jery and Bätely. Wit, Cunning and Revenge, 1790.*" However, *Faust a Fragment* was also published separately by Göschen in 1790: "*Faust a Fragment. By Goethe. Authentic Edition.*" Numerous pirated versions were tossed on to the market, many on better paper than Göschen's original editions, but most of them with more typographical errors than the "authentic" edition.

It was only to be expected that *Faust* as a fragment aroused some misunderstanding even among Goethe's friends. Goethe maintained that no one in the whole nation understood his language, but that was not the case. A review said: "Germany's greatest writer, who knew how to aspire to the refinement of Greek taste and the regularity of Greek art in his 'Iphigenia,' presents us in this part with a masterpiece in a quite different style, but which bears just as unmistakably the great characteristics of genius: if Goethe had written nothing else this alone would make his name immortal; [it has] to be admitted, here is the German Shakespeare."[8] Another review ended "After reading the whole we still have one more wish; Oh! that 'Faust' were not a fragment."

"The First Part of the Tragedy" 1797–1801

It was the "happy event," the friendly partner-like relationship between Goethe and Schiller that was to get Goethe moving on the "Faust" material again. Schiller took the fragmentation of *Faust* as the occasion for his important impulse of 29 November 1794: "I would read the as yet unprinted fragments of your 'Faust' no less eagerly for I confess to you that what I have read of this play is for me the torso of Hercules. There is a force and an abundance of genius in these scenes, and I would like to pursue as far as possible the great and bold nature that breathes in them." But Goethe was unable to accede to this wish, he replied to Schiller. "I can tell you nothing about *Faust* at the moment, I do not have the courage to undo the packet that contains it. I could not copy it without working on it and I have not the courage to do so. If in the future there is anything that can make it possible, it will certainly be your interest." And Schiller really did not give way, he constantly raised his "intercession for 'Faust.'" But Goethe kept quiet about the matter for years. On 21 June 1797, over two years later, he complained to Schiller that his situation "gave him little about which to rejoice at the moment." But on the day after, 22 June, he informed Schiller unexpectedly and openly:

> As it is very necessary in my present restless situation for me to find myself something to do, I have decided to go to my Faust and if not finish it, at least bring it a long way further along. I shall do this as I break up what is printed and amalgamate it, in great masses, with what is already finished or in my mind and thus prepare more closely the execution of the plan that is actually nothing more than an idea. Now I have once again undertaken the idea and its representation and I am to some extent at one with myself. But now I would wish you to be kind enough to think the matter through when you have a sleepless night and to tell me what demands you would make on the whole thing, and thus—as a true prophet—relate and interpret my own dreams for me.
>
> As the different parts of this poem, depending on their mood, can be treated separately if they are only subordinated to the spirit and tone of the whole, as in any case the whole work is subjective, I can work on it at isolated moments and thus I am now also in a position to get something done.

One day later, he has already written a "Detailed scheme for Faust." Goethe seems to downplay his work up to that point as "subjective," but it is astonishing how he develops it especially in his discussions with Schiller. The latter criticized the loose structure of the fragment and the lack of bridges between scenes. Schiller certainly had no direct part in the development of the form, but his objections force Goethe to clarify his thoughts about the structure of the whole. He now has to bring Faust to the Emperor's court, in order to be able to join him with Helen, and, as an unavoidable part of the material, the pact with the devil has to be concluded and the decision made as to whether this companionship shall lead, as in the folk books, to hell or to salvation and redemption from evil. It is only now that the Faust figure becomes clearer in the sense of the drama of the human race, its position between God and the Devil, the symbol of a sinful humanity, but a humanity which finally seeks to be redeemed and will finally enjoy the grace and the redemption it longs for.

In July 1799 Goethe hoped that the *Faust* scenes would grow out of the ground like a huge "family of sponges," but then there was another long break. Schiller wrote to Cotta on 24 March 1800 and asked him to invite Goethe to finish *Faust* by making him a tempting offer. Cotta reacted by offering Goethe 4,000 gulden for *Faust* and added, "please have the goodness to accept my liberality!" Goethe allowed himself be moved by this external stimulus and took up work on *Faust* again. "Cotta's liberality," he wrote to Schiller, "is very pleasant. I have a letter from him about *Faust* that you are probably responsible for, I must thank you for this. For really, as a result of this enticement, I have once more taken up and thought through the work today." The fruit of this thinking through is the final division of the work into two parts and the decision to have a fifth act, the first version of which Goethe probably even wrote at this time. However Goethe was mainly engaged on the third act, in which Helen appears and releases Faust from "Nordic" medieval barbarism. Goethe's diary bears witness of his continuing work on *Faust* until 7 April 1801, but then the work comes to a halt once more. Goethe fell ill. Schiller wrote resignedly to Cotta on 10 December 1801: "You ask me about Goethe and his works. Alas, since his illness he has done no more work nor does he seem to be making any plans to do so. Although he has marvellous outlines and drafts of works, I fear that nothing more will happen unless there is a great change in him.

"He is too little the master of his mood, his melancholy makes him indecisive and he distracts himself too much with all the amateur activities that he engages in in connection with scientific things. . . . I almost despair of his ever finishing his Faust." Schiller was not to live to see it completed.

It was not until five months after Schiller's death that the topic of Faust cropped up again in the correspondence between Goethe and Cotta. Goethe had agreed with the publisher on a thirteen-volume edition of his works, and Cotta insisted, as Göschen had before him, on a new revision and an expansion. "I am still not sure in my own mind what I am going to include in the fourth volume," he wrote to Cotta on 30 September 1805. "If it is at all possible I shall come on to the scene straightaway with 'Faust.' He and the other woodcut-like jests make a good whole and would serve to arouse a livelier interest in the first batch of volumes. Tell me the latest date by which you must receive the fourth volume so that I can more or less estimate what I have to do." Cotta misunderstands what he means by "woodcut-like" and asks Goethe for drawings for the woodcuts, but in his letter of 25 November 1805 Goethe refuses him.

"Faust with Riemer" appears frequently as an entry in Goethe's diary in spring 1806; he writes the "Prologue in Heaven." He is stimulated by and adopts a lot of motifs from the Book of Job, and the prologue now presents the overall framework within which the action of the whole play will take place. It can be summed up in the two statements: "Man errs as long as he continues to aspire" and "A good man in his obscure ways is well aware of the right path."[9]

This is also the period when he wrote the first lines of the Helen tragedy, but they are not included in the complete edition at this time. Goethe notes that the final version of *Faust* is now going to the printer. When Cotta visited Goethe in Weimar on his way home from the Leipzig book fair on 25 April 1806, he was able to accept the manuscript personally. Because of the events of the war, and especially Germany's occupation by Napoleonic troops, the printing was delayed until the Easter Fair in 1808; *Faust* then appeared as volume eight in the framework of the thirteen-volume complete edition. At the same time, Cotta published an individual edition: "*Faust.* A Tragedy by Goethe. Tübingen 1808." The work immediately aspired to a central position in literary criticism, which praised it on the one hand and criticized and polemicized it on the other. On the whole, the summary that Goethe gave Eckermann on 3 January 1830 is apposite. He had just received the latest French translation of *Faust* by Gérard de Nerval; "strange thoughts" went through his head, "when I think that this book now exists in a language in which fifty years ago Voltaire was sovereign." He says that Voltaire was very important to him and that the extent of this influence is not clearly enough stated in his autobiography; also, what is certainly not clear is what it cost him to protect himself against these influences. Goethe then continues, "But Faust is something that cannot be measured, and every attempt to bring him nearer to the understanding is in vain. People must also remember that the first part emerged from the individual's somewhat gloomy situation. But this gloominess stimulates man and he labors away at it just as he does at all insoluble problems."

The final version of Part One appeared in the twentieth volume of the final authorized edition.

"The Tragedy, Part Two." 1808–1831

Even as the first part was appearing in May 1808 Goethe was working with Riemer on the sequel, but then the *Faust* poem once more receded almost entirely into the background. There were other projects to be completed,

The Elective Affinities (1809), *The Theory of Color* (1810), and after 1811 he was working on his autobiography. In October 1816, true to his dictum that an autobiography was there to "fill in the gaps of an author's life," he dictated for this work his table of contents for *Faust,* Part Two, that is, "the action of the first to fourth acts according to the older plan." Faust becomes a wealthy man, he grows old, and "what else happens will emerge when in the future we collect all these fragments—or rather the passages that have been worked out as scattered pieces—of the second part and in this way salvage something that will be of interest to readers."

"Goethe's renewed work on *Faust II* arose out of his work on *Poetry and Truth,* Part IV, and on the *Chronicle of My Life* (in the 'final edition' Goethe wanted to round off his complete autobiographical works and complete them, but he did not succeed in doing this). He takes up the work on *Faust II* as early as February 1825. This is the day on which—in conjunction with his work on Book 18 of *Literature and Truth*—Goethe picks up the old 1816 plan for *Faust.* For the next few years his work on *Faust II* (initially on the Helen act, Act 3) supplants his interest in *Literature and Truth,* IV. The first phase of the work lasts from 26 February to the beginning of April; the second phase begins on 12 March 1826 with his reading from Faust (Helen act) to Eckermann and probably results in part from his intention to publish the Helen act from *Faust II,* before the publication of the whole work in the fourth volume of the final edition, true to his intention of making every batch of volumes in the edition more significant by the addition of new works. The prepublication of the beginning of Act I, in volume 12, arises out of the same intention and it is possible that the new phase of work on *Faust II* that begins in December 1829 (the writing of the end of Acts I and II) resulted from Goethe's intention to continue the prepublication of scenes from *Faust II* in the seventh batch of volumes."[10]

Once again, for the third time, it is possible that it was an impulse from the publisher as well as Goethe's conceptual ideas about the edition that caused him to busy himself with *Faust.* It is here that the degree to which the writing of individual works is linked with work on the final authorized edition becomes especially clear.

Goethe scholars have carried out detailed research on his plans for work on *Faust,* especially in the period from 11 April until 24 June 1826. Goethe has now changed his way of working. Previously he had dictated or written the scenes rapidly and spontaneously, now he makes very careful sketches, thinks them over during the day, the evening, and the night, so that on the following morning he can round them out as he dictates. His friend Zelter is drawn more and more intensively into the literary discussion. Goethe often supposes that the new things he is inventing will be alien to his contemporaries and the thought torments him. He writes on 3 June: "So I can confide in you that in order to give a proper weight to the first set of volumes in my new edition I have resumed preliminary work on a significant piece of writing that I have not looked at since Schiller's death—not to expand it but to contract it—and which without the present stimulus would probably have remained *in limbo patrum* [Abraham's Bosom]. True it is the type of work that will make inroads into the most modern literature but also one that no one, no matter who, may have any idea of. I hope to see great confusion caused by it, as it is intended to smooth over a quarrel."

Goethe's idea was that the Helen passage, both by its content as well as its special form, was to smooth over the quarrel between Classicism and Romanticism; for this reason it was entitled *Helen. Classical-Romantic Phantasmagoria.* At this time Goethe thought that it might be produced, and for this reason he kept emphasizing the importance of the Helen act. Eckermann also maintained that Goethe's view was that "culture in Germany was now at such a high level that such a production would not long remain misunderstood and without effect." Goethe was not wrong, and we can see that the act is effective right down to the present day.[11]

In order to dispel the confusion of which he was afraid, Goethe wrote an "announcement" in June that was to explain, by means of a commentary, the relationship between the first and second parts. "Helen, classical-romantic phantasmagoria. Entr'acte for *Faust.*" However, the announcement was not published. Goethe continued to work on *Helen* until 24 June, the date generally accepted as the one on which the Helen scene was finished. In a fragment of a letter to an anonymous correspondent he makes an interesting statement:

> More about Helen soon, the work is finished and is as strange and problematic a piece as I have ever written. Perhaps we shall make some more of it known in the next six months. The most remarkable thing about this play is that without changing its locus it covers exactly three thousand years, it observes meticulously the unity of action and place, but allows the third (time) to pass as in a phantasmagoria.

Goethe had asked Zelter to visit him in Weimar in the summer. Zelter arrived on 7 July 1826, and, according to Goethe, "Professor Zelter read Helen to himself. . . . (He) stayed with me and read the beginning of Helen aloud." After Zelter had finished reading the Helen scene, Eckermann received it, finishing it on 8 August. Both of them discussed with Goethe details that needed changing. Five days later, Schuchardt began making a fair copy of the manuscript from the different bits and pieces. The manuscript went to Cotta to be printed on 26 January 1827; it has been preserved and has proof marks by Goethe, Riemer, Eckermann, and Göttling. But the Helen complex continued to occupy Goethe, as we learn from his letters, most specifically the letter to Wilhelm von Humboldt on 22 October 1826.

> I spent the whole summer at home and continued working without interruption on the edition of my writings. Do you still remember perhaps, my dear friend, a dramatic *Helen* that was to appear in the second part of *Faust*? I see from Schiller's letters in the early years of the century that I showed him the beginning and also that he loyally recommended that I go on with it. It is one of my oldest ideas, it is based on the puppet play tradition where Faust makes Mephistopheles procure Helen for him. I have continued to work on it from time to time but the play could not be finished except in the fullness of time, as it embraces 3,000 years, from the collapse of Troy to the capture of Missolonghi. This can be considered an age in the highest sense of the word; the unity of place and action are, however, most punctiliously observed in the usual way. It appears under the title:
>
>
>
> Helen
>
> Classical-Romantic
>
> Phantasmagoria
>
> Entr'acte for *Faust*
>
>
>
> True, that doesn't say much, but yet it's enough, I hope, to call your attention in more lively fashion to the edition of my works that I intend to bring out at Easter.

Goethe added to the "announcement" about Helen on 17 December so as to bridge to some extent the "gap between the well-known and lamentable end of the first part and the entrance of a heroic Greek woman." He sent these "antecedents" to Humboldt, who however, like Eckermann, advised him against publishing them. Both of them feared that Goethe might lose interest in completing the work once he had announced his intention. Once Goethe had the manuscript in front of him ready for setting he wrote to Reichel, the manager of the printing works in Augsburg, about the typography of the text, particularly with a view to establishing a successful typographical form for the changing meters, for the different lengths of strophe, and for the overlapping of one meter with another. When the text appeared in 1827 in volume 4 of the final authorized edition (it was separate and not integrated into the drama—not until 1832 in the first volume of the posthumous works did the Helen act become a part of the drama itself) he expressed himself satisfied with the composition and the printing. Then in *On Art and Antiquity* there appeared a very much shorter version of the "announcement": *Helen Entr'acte in "Faust."*

In spring 1827 Goethe continued work on the scenes at the "Imperial Court" and they were completed at the end of 1827. From July onwards, work on the "main business" went ahead swimmingly. On 15 January 1828, he writes that "he feels he has come closer to the completion of work on *Faust.*" After Goethe had "arranged" the first act "according to the fair copy and his draft," he sent 31 folio sheets, written out by his secretary John, to Cotta's Augsburg printing works. Reichel received separate typographical instructions a week later, in which Goethe left the clarification of "ambiguous cases" entirely to Reichel's discretion. He thanked him for the fact that "the division of the different types of poetry . . . has once more turned out to be successful, for which I again have to express my best thanks to you for your care and attention." *Faust Part Two* appeared at Easter 1828 as volume 12 of the final authorized edition. An octavo edition followed in 1829. Both editions contain the note "to be continued"—Goethe worked on this continuation but it did not appear in his lifetime.

Continuing Work on Faust to March 1832 (The "Pocket Edition") Goethe, conscious that time was growing shorter for him, continually took up the *Faust* "papers," but it was hard work for him; at best he would write one page a day. He felt, as he said to Eckermann, "confused . . . by the grimaces of everyday life." Grand Duke August died on 14 June 1828. He had visited Goethe for the last time on 28 May to say farewell to him before setting out on a journey to Berlin; he died on that journey. The days in Weimar were filled with funeral and memorial ceremonies. Goethe fled to Dornburg on 7 July and he wrote to Zelter from there on 26 July:

> The hopes that I had of giving you the continuation of *Faust* at Michaelmas have been dashed by this event. If this thing is not continually high-spirited, if it does not make the reader want to stretch himself beyond his powers, then it is valueless . . . .
>
> The beginning of the second act is successfully completed, I want to say this in all modesty because we would not write if it were not already written. Now it is a matter of the end of Act One that has been sketched out down to the last detail and, if it weren't for this calamity, would already have been put into pleasing rhymes. But we have to leave this to the days ahead.

"The days ahead"—the fewer and fewer years left to him. On 18/19 July 1829 he was able to inform Zelter of the approaching completion: "The fact that you revert to *Faust* Part Two pleases me a lot; it will inspire me to put aside a lot of other things and at least complete the most essential things in connection with this as soon as possible. The ending is as good as written, and much that is important in the passages in between is also completed, and if the higher authorities would only arrest me and confine me to a lofty fortress for three months then there would not be much left. I have everything so clearly in my mind that I am often uncomfortable about it."

However, the "lofty fortress" did not happen, nothing emerged from three months of concentration since in Weimar in August 1829—at first contrary to Goethe's wishes—*Faust I* was produced and he had to think about how to represent certain figures and, as he put it, "phenomena" on the stage, how to make them "comprehensible."

In December he was able to resume work on *Faust II* full of determination. He felt that he did not have much time left to him. On 27 December he read Eckermann the scene about paper money, on 30 December the scenes "Gloomy Gallery" and "Castle Hall," and on 10 January 1830 the scene where "Faust goes to the Mothers." Eckermann, "strangely moved," asked for additional explanations. Goethe replied, "I cannot tell you any more than I found in Plutarch, which is that in Greek antiquity people spoke of the *Mothers* as of divinities. This is all that I owe to tradition, the rest is my own invention."

Goethe worked on indefatigably. Eckermann has stated that Goethe was working on the "Classical Walpurgis night" in January. The content and draft of this play within a play were written by Goethe as a counterpart to the Walpurgis night in the first part. Faust, who "wants to bring Helen back to life," is led by Mephistopheles to the gates of Hades. In a magic circle in the Walpurgis night apparition, Nature and Intellect are joined and the three thousand years of this phantasmagorical time are all mixed up together. Faust is searching for Helen; Faust finds what he is looking for. Mephistopheles, the enemy of life, becomes the ugly one: Goethe evokes Creation with his references to Neptunism and Vulcanism, until he finally expresses everything in the "miracle" of the union of water and fire, the union of all the elements: life and the spirit are united here.

In the following months, too, Goethe's continuing involvement with the "main business" is documented in detail; he thanks Eckermann, who "is the person who can best extort literary productions from me." Eckermann preserves Goethe's statements for the record: "It is not good for human beings to be alone . . . and especially not to work alone; rather they have need of sympathy and inspiration if they are to make a success of something. I thank Schiller for the 'Achilleis' and many of my ballads that he urged me to write, and you can take the credit if I finish the second part of *Faust*. I have told you often enough, but I have to repeat it so that you are aware of it." And he went on working. On 25 June he wrote to his son August in Italy: "Tell Eckermann [who was traveling with August] that the Walpurgis Night is completely finished and as to what is still needed. I have good hopes." This completed the second act. The completion of the "Walpurgis Night" meant that Goethe had integrated the Helen material into the overall *Faust* drama. The manuscript grew and grew, but now the thought was firmly fixed in Goethe's mind that he did not want to publish what he was writing at the time—his "best." In talking to Chancellor von Müller, his executor, he reverted to Voltaire who, he said, had made a mistake in releasing his new drama *Irene* for production in 1778: "Voltaire, one of the greatest of minds, was weak enough in his old age to allow another tragedy by him to be performed. I on the other hand am becoming more and more inclined to secrete the best that I have written and may yet write."

When, at this time, Cotta's wife once more asked Goethe for a contribution to the *Ladies Calendar,* he refused and added in a postscript to a letter to Cotta on 9 July 1830, "I must ask your pardon, which I hope the more readily to receive, as an attempt at the present time to produce something suitably significant would certainly not succeed."

Is it modesty, is it caution, is it the wisdom of age that makes him not want to publish what he is working on? This is the time at which he writes the short verse in the *Zahme Xenien* that has been preserved in *Scherz und Ernst:* "Is that sensible and right? / Do you want to insult friend and foe! / I have no longer any interest in adults, / Now I have to think of my grandchildren." There are only a few writers who have thought and acted like Goethe in this connection. Joyce left no posthumous works behind. Proust went on writing to the last year of his life; he was still working on the proofs of his works on his deathbed. Samuel Beckett wanted to determine personally which of his works were to be published. Kafka arranged for his manuscripts to be destroyed but his literary executor did not carry out his wishes. Robert Musil's "failure" in writing his novel *The Man Without Qualities* was anything but "voluntary"; at the end of his life he published a volume *Posthumous While Still Alive* and gave his reasons for the title in a foreword, saying that "readers have a pardonable weakness for a writer who calls upon them for the last time."

But Goethe wanted to think of his "grandchildren," of people in the future. And so he went on immediately with what was "still needed," Act 4 and the missing beginning of Act 5. After an illness that put him, as Eckermann says, "not far from death," Goethe resumed intensive work in December. He staked everything on one card, finishing Act 5; he seemed to have given up hope of Act 4. On 17 December he notes "Completion of *Faust,* and fair copy," and on 4 January 1831 he confided in Zelter: "The first two acts of *Faust* are finished. Perhaps Cardinal *von Este's* exclamation with which he thought to honor Ariosto would be in place here. Enough! Helen appears without more ado at the beginning of the third act, not as a figure in an entr'acte, but as a heroine. The progress of this third part is well known, to what extent the gods will help me with the fourth act remains to be seen. . . . I would like to read through the second part of Faust once more in the proper order, from the beginning to the bacchanalia. But I protect myself from such things; in the future, others who can come to it with fresh voices may do so and they will have suggestions." After a short break while he put papers in order and wrote his will, Goethe took up Act 5 again in April. The entries in his diary confirm that the eighty-one-year-old was working indefatigably, and he finally succeeded in finishing the beginning of Act 5. "The intention of these scenes too," he confessed to Eckermann on 2 May 1831, "is over thirty years old, it was of such importance that I did not lose interest in it, but so hard to carry out that I was afraid of it."

After that, Act 5 was finished, and there were a few very minor alterations left to be made. On 6 June 1831 Eckermann records a very important conversation. Goethe had shown him the beginning of Act 5 that had long been lacking. The two then talked about *Faust*. Goethe's intentions were that "he should be exactly a hundred years old" and was to be saved; Goethe was considering how to represent all this. Then they talked about the ending and he drew Eckermann's attention to the lines: "The noble limb of the spirit world is saved from evil; whoever goes on striving we can save." "The key to Faust's salvation is contained in these lines," said Goethe. "In Faust himself there is an ever higher and purer activity until the end, and from above the eternal love that comes to his aid. This is in complete harmony with our religious notions according to which we are saved not merely through our own strength but by the divine grace that is added to it."

The first news of Goethe's work on Act 4 comes from Eckermann. Goethe notes in his diary on 12 February 1831 the sentence that could almost serve as his motto in the months that remained to him: "The main work heartily and courageously attacked." According to Eckermann Goethe said, "As you know I had long had in mind *what* was to happen; it was simply with the *how* that I was not completely satisfied, and now I am glad that I have had some constructive thoughts. I shall think through the whole gap from Helen to the completed fifth act and write it down in an extensive plan so that I can then work on and execute the passages that attract me initially with complete pleasure and certainty." Goethe always had intended to outline the individual pieces clearly while leaving the whole obscure: and he continues, in a conversation with Eckermann, "with a composition of this sort it is merely a matter of the individual masses being significant and clear while the whole remains incommensurable, simply because—like an unsolved problem—it attracts people's attention again and again."

Goethe had the manuscript of the second part rebound at this time, with blank paper inserted at the place where the fourth act still had to be written; "there is no question," he confided to Eckermann, "that the completed thing attracts and lures me on to finish what still has to be done. There is more in such sensual things than we think and we have to help the spiritual with all sorts of arts." His remark on 2 May 1831 is a reference to this help: "Thanks to a number of arts I am underway again and if fortune is favorable I shall write Act 4 straight through." He knew that he had a lot of "thinking exercises" to perform; the first part, in his view, offered "subjective material" but in the second part he wanted to have a "higher, broader, lighter, less passionate world, and anyone who had not looked around a bit and had some experience will not know how to come to terms with it." Goethe wanted to settle the quarrel between classicism and romanticism, and of course he could not have invented the relationship between Helen and Faust until he had managed to harmonize his view of antiquity with his view of the Middle Ages. On 6 March 1830 he prophesied to Frédéric Jean Soret that "important things" would be readying themselves in Paris. "We are on the eve of a great explosion." It took place during the July Revolution in Paris; King Charles X had to abdicate. Perhaps it is in this context that we have to understand Faust's view of the state, his sovereign view of a free people on free territory. Faust's worldwide plans for colonies linked with the heroic struggle of man against the forces of nature, the ideas about colonization at the end the play, could have had their origin in Goethe's experience of the terrible inundations on the North Sea coast in the winter of 1824/25.

May and June became productive months for Goethe. Again and again we come across the words "Poetic material." He is able to report to his friend Zelter on the progress of the work. On 1 June 1831 he assures him, "It is no small thing at the age of eighty-two to portray, outside of oneself, what one planned at the age of twenty and to clothe an inner skeleton of this sort with sinews and inner and outer flesh and also perhaps throw a few folds of a cloak around the finished product so that everything remains an obvious secret that will go on delighting people and giving them something to do. . . . Since the beginning of the year I have achieved a lot that I can consider successful because I, at least, do not know how to do it better. Take this as an announcement of the same legacy." In July he set himself the goal of having the work on *Faust* finished by his birthday. On 21 July the diary records "Completion of main business," and a day later, "The main business achieved. Final fair copy. All fair copies bound." The last part that he wrote is the investiture scene. This is the conclusion of the arc of his life. As a boy he had been present at the imperial coronation in Frankfurt and had become interested in the institution of the empire. On 14 July 1831, he borrowed from the library in Weimar the book that he had studied as a boy, *New Interpretations of the Golden Bull,* and he used many of the details for his work.

At this time, however, his resolve not to publish the most recently written parts and to seal them up for posterity became stronger. Friedrich Christoph

Förster, the publisher, visited Goethe just before his birthday in August 1831. He records: "On my last visit, two large folio volumes containing manuscripts were lying on his desk, and, pointing to these, he said, 'the second part of Faust lies here sealed with seven seals; but only when I am no longer in a position to do so can others lay a hand on it.'"

But in September he was still working on the text. "The whole thing is in front of me," he wrote to Zelter on 4 September 1831, "and I have only a few small things to correct. So I will seal it and then it can increase the specific gravity of my ensuing volumes whatever happens to it." September must have seen the sealing up of the fair copy, the manuscript that contains the whole of the second part; the folio volume contains 187 written pages. On the cover is the title: "Faust. Second Part, 1831." Act 3 was copied by Johann Christian Schuchardt, everything else by Johann John.

He felt that he had constantly to defend this sealing up vis-à-vis his friends. Thus on 1 December 1831 he writes to Wilhelm von Humboldt: "I now had to take heart and seal up the bound copy in which what has been printed and what is not yet printed are interspersed so that I shall not be tempted to work further on it in certain places; though I do indeed regret that I cannot communicate it to my dearest friends, something the writer does so gladly." On 24 November, writing to Boisserée, "When I sealed up my completed *Faust* I was not really happy; for it did occur to me that my most valued friends, who in general agreed with me, would not very soon have the pleasure of spending a few enjoyable hours with these seriously intended jests and, of becoming aware, in the process, of what has been going around in my head and my mind for many years until it finally took on this form. . . . However my comfort is that precisely those with whom I must be concerned are all younger than I am and will in due time enjoy what I have prepared and saved for them in memory of me."

Goethe did not keep to his resolution. He opened the sealed manuscript in January 1832 to read to his daughter-in-law Ottilie from it on two occasions. In the process precisely what he had feared happened—"possibly continuing the work in certain places." On 17 January his diary says, "added a few things I noticed in *Faust*. John made a fair copy." On 18 January, "rewrote a few things." On 19 January, "Various fair copies." On 24 January, "New stimulus for *Faust* in the direction of a more extensive execution of the main themes that I had handled too laconically so as to get finished. Fair copies by John."

Goethe's last letters show what this conclusion meant to him. He knew what he had achieved, he knew that his contemporaries would have difficulty in understanding his "main business" simply because it was not complete and because it made too many demands upon the reader. But he was also sure that there would be readers who, in the course of the years, of decades or even more, would accept his work, understand it, and value it. He clung to this hope even when the first reactions were not exactly encouraging. At this time the voices had grown much more critical, but Goethe had scarcely paid attention to them; the only criticism he still read was Karl Ernst Schubarth's, the principal of the high school in Hirschberg. The latter had sent Goethe his lecture "On Goethe's Faust" that began by expressing the opinion that he, Schubarth, did not consider *Faust* the "main work, the peak, the crown." This is the sort of mistake a critic can make.

It was only after Goethe's death and in accordance with his wishes that his "integral fair copy" appeared: "*Goethe's Works*. Complete and final edition. Volume 41. Goethe's posthumous works. Volume One. Stuttgart and Tübingen. 1832./*Faust*. Second Part of the Tragedy in Five Acts." The first edition appeared in 1832, again in crown octavo as a pocket edition; the regular octavo edition appeared in 1833. The title contains the note: "Finished in Summer 1831."

Goethe's fragmentary method of working that combined his old and new areas of life, experience, and knowledge, his cry "Thus Poetry commands!" certainly had consequences for the 1832 edition of *Faust*. The text that was supervised by Riemer and Eckermann has no sort of valid, or even final, form; it contains many errors and unfortunately some editorial highhandedness as well. The consequences can be felt right down to the Weimar edition that presents the whole of the material known at that time with such a lack of clarity that only the connoisseur has access to the text. Erich Schmidt took as a basis for the text of *Faust II* only Act 1 and Act 3, the publication of which was authorized by Goethe himself, and only admitted the main manuscript for the rest. Thus Goethe's work as a writer and editor, something that he had developed in his "long and actively reflective life" continued to have an effect.

Goethe now had to struggle with his health in order to produce his letters as well as his works. The last entry in his diary reads: "16 March. Weimar. Spent the whole day in bed because I did not feel well." But then on 17 March he wrote this letter to Humboldt:

It is more than sixty years that the concept of *Faust* has lain before me in youthful clarity, though the whole sequence of the work was less detailed. I have always allowed the intent to be my gentle companion and I have only worked out individually the passages that are the most interesting to me and have joined these to the rest by an equivalent interest, so that in the second part gaps still remained. Thus it is at this point that there emerged the great difficulty of achieving, by intention and character, what actually should only by rights be the purview of a freely active nature. But it would not be good if it were not possible, after such a long and actively reflective life, and I cannot fear that people will distinguish what is older from what is more recent, the later from the earlier, that we are anxious to present to future readers for their well-disposed understanding.

There is absolutely no question but that it would afford me endless pleasure if I could in my lifetime dedicate and communicate these very seriously intended jests to my valued and widely dispersed friends—to whom I am utterly grateful—and receive their responses to them. The day however is truly so absurd and confused that I am convinced that my honest and long-lasting efforts in the service of this strange structure would be badly rewarded and beached and lie there like a wreck in ruins and would be covered over at first by the sands of time. A confused doctrine for confused action rules over the world and I have nothing more urgent to do than where possible to intensify what lies in me and what remains to me and to restrain my peculiarities, just as you, my worthy friend, also manage to do in your castle.

What an achievement for a writer to complete unusually, uniquely, a work that takes more than a lifetime in the writing; "long-lasting" is a powerful exaggeration. Above and beyond this he succeeded in publishing the greater part of his work and in arranging and preparing the rest for posthumous publication. And it is not only his "main business," it is his magnum opus, one of the greatest works known to world literature.

What did it earn Goethe during his lifetime? The sales of the complete edition and the individual editions were quite moderate. The balance sheet bore no signs of success. Now, it is also true that Goethe was not a good promoter of his drama. Basically he did not really believe in the theatrical effectiveness of his *Faust* "as it is." He wrote on 1 May 1815 to the theater manager, Count Brühl, who proposed producing it in Berlin, "It [Faust] is

far too removed from a theatrical idea." The only performance worth mentioning, the German premiere of the first part, took place on 29 January
1829 in the Court Theater in Brunswick. The undertaking was successful
and had the effect that, on the occasion of Goethe's eightieth birthday, other
German theaters in Hanover, Bremen, Dresden, Frankfurt am Main, and
Leipzig produced the play. Finally, the theatre in Weimar went into action
and played *Faust* on 29 August 1829. Goethe had taken part in the preparations but was not present at the first night. He says in his diary for 29 August,
"Alone in the evening. Performance of *Faust* in the theater." No further
comment. Did Goethe not wish to observe success or failure, or was he
disappointed that during the period of preparation the censor had intervened
in Minister Goethe's work? At that time there was no possibility of a textually
accurate performance of the sort that authors and theatrical publishers demand today. The censor rewrote: "breast to breast" had to be replaced by
"glance to glance" and "garter" had to be replaced by "bracelet." But outside
Weimar the censors intervened more energetically. In otherwise liberal, Protestant Saxony the name of Luther might not be mentioned in the "Song of
the Rat"; in Catholic Vienna "priest" could not rhyme with "beast" and the
actor playing Faust had to substitute the new rhyme "rains" and "hollow
brains"—Goethe himself was thus not able to see a decent production of
his *Faust* on the stage.

The effect of the *Faust* poems on his contemporaries was of a very diverse
nature. When the *Faust* fragment first appeared in 1790 the reviewers did
not know what to make of the text. In addition there was the defeat of
Prussia and the French occupation. True, Goethe found that his circle of
friends paid attention to the work; Karl Friedrich von Reinhard, Charlotte
Schiller, and Zelter praised the work. Christoph Martin Wieland, however,
reached the false conclusion, "You see that at the moment you only have to
be daring in order to succeed." Wieland ends his letter: "In spite of all this
I fear that our friend Goethe has hurt himself more with this piece of daring
than his bitterest enemy could ever do, and his publisher will be the only
one who will feel good about it." Another friend was also not in agreement
with the text as it was, but he was of the opinion that before the play was
finished it would not be possible to reach a just verdict. Franz Grillparzer,
the Austrian dramatist, again was "moved"; he read it twice and many of
the scenes set his "imagination afire, tore my soul open away from Schiller's
rough, grotesque sketches and confirmed my love for Goethe."

When Goethe published the Helen poem, the third act of *Faust Part 2,* in 1827, criticism was more favorable. But above all it was foreign newspapers that emphasized the importance of the text. Goethe mentioned three reviews: that of the Russian literary historian Stepan Petrovitsch Schewireff; of the Frenchman Jean-Jacques Ampère, who published a review in the periodical *Le Globe;* and of Thomas Carlyle in the Edinburgh periodical *The Foreign Review.* Goethe wrote of these reviews in "On Art and Antiquity": "Here the Scot tries to penetrate the work, the Frenchman to understand it, and the Russian to take it for his own. And so Messrs Carlyle, Ampère, and Schewireff, without any sort of consultation, had completely executed all possible categories of participation in a product of art or nature. Let us leave to our benevolent friends whatever more there is to argue about in this. Taking notice of and pointing out the interweaving of the threefold effort that can never really be differentiated, they will take the desired opportunity of explaining to us the most manifold aesthetic effects." On the whole, then, Goethe could not be pleased with the reception of his *Faust.* It was, however, clear to him that his contemporaries were bound to have difficulties with the text. He did not live to experience the fact that the part of *Faust* that was published posthumously met more or less with a lack of understanding on the part of contemporaries.

Part One it is true continued to have an effect upon at least two minds. Hegel praised the text as the great German national poem and, as he wrote in his *Lectures on Aesthetics,* the "absolute philosophical tragedy in which, on the one hand, the lack of satisfaction in science, on the other the vitality of worldly life and pleasure, and altogether the tragically attempted mediation of subjective knowledge and striving with the absolute in its essence and appearance gives a breadth of content of a sort that no other dramatic poet has dared to attempt in one and the same work." Heinrich Heine was also moved by the poem, seeing Faust as the symbol of national development. In his *Romantic School* we read: "the German people is itself that learned Doctor Faust, it is itself that spiritualist who has finally understood, through the intellect, the insufficiency of that intellect and demands material pleasures and gives the flesh back its just deserts. . . . But it will be some time before what has been so profoundly foretold in the poem is fulfilled in the German people, before they perceive through the intellect the usurpations of the intellect and vindicate the rights of the flesh. That will be the revolution, the great daughter of the Reformation." And so it was left to succeeding decades and the next century to explore and expound the meaning of the work and to lay bare parts of that "inner skeleton" of which he wrote, as we have said, to Zelter that it was not easy "to clothe an inner skeleton of this sort with sinews and inner and outer flesh and also perhaps to throw a few folds of a cloak around the finished product so that everything remains an obvious secret that will go on delighting people and giving them something to do." Here Goethe was perfectly right, scholars and readers are still puzzling over the "obvious puzzle" even today. Perhaps those who are professionally involved in this solution should be resigned. There will always be things that will, in the final analysis, be inaccessible to the scholar committed to rationality, but they should go on pleasing readers and giving them something to do. Goethe himself called *Faust* a tragedy, and truly this play is the tragedy of man in the world; it embraces his past and present, his future and his eternity. Thus this work is the tragedy of being human, the tragedy of the person of whom the Lord says in the prologue—and not by chance—"Man errs as long as he continues to strive." In spite of this observation, Goethe affirms life in his old age: "No matter what, life is good." And, still in command of his situation, the author also looks back: six months before his death he writes: "There it is, whatever has come of it. And if it does still contain enough problems and by no means explains everything, it will please those who understand expression, hint, and gentle suggestion."

"I try to employ every good moment to be of value to those who partake of me to the very end" The extremely complex and protracted Part Two of *Faust* was completed in summer 1831. In June of the same year Goethe was able to finish work on the German-French edition of *Essay on the Metamorphosis of Plants*. Fromman had finally sent him the proof sheets. This work was also not easy for him. Fromman had already told Cotta in February 1831, "How strong the book will be, I cannot tell you, any more than I can tell you when it will be finished." It was only in March and April that Goethe started work on the manuscript, again with Frédéric Soret. However at the end of April he was able to give Sulpice Boisserée the good news that he had succeeded in finishing it: "Actually with this part a great burden is lifted from me that people will not recognize in the fifteen signatures. To be involved with the printing since June of last year and to have to work through and carry out such a thing with all the attendant vicissitudes was no small thing for me." The work

appeared in the middle of June 1831; it was to be the last work that Goethe himself saw through the press. He could not complete the other "work" on which he was working, the collection, sorting, and editing of his correspondence with Zelter: he entrusted this work to Riemer. On 6 June, when Goethe showed Eckermann the beginning of Act 5 of *Faust II,* he said, "By the way, you will admit that the conclusion where the soul that has been saved ascends was very hard to do and that I could easily have lost myself in vagueness in dealing with such supernatural things if I had not given my poetic intentions a benevolently restricted form and firmness by means of the clearly defined Christian-ecclesiastical figures and ideas." Although he continued making minor changes into September, Goethe considered *Faust* completed by 22 July 1831. When Eckermann came to lunch a few days later, he found Goethe "extremely happy": "I can now look upon the rest of my life as a pure gift and, fundamentally, it does not now matter whether I do anything, or what I do."

But life is not a matter of indifference to him. Goethe has completed his "main business." Having succeeded, he can now feel free to live for himself and for others. His message to Cotta on 16 June 1831 can be seen as the expression of this attitude:

> While I now hope with this intimate confession to excuse and make up for many a delay and a long silence, I will also assure you that my honest wish is that the venerable couple's later years may be spared external misery in such a manner that the inner vitality will remain powerful enough to continue to be active in such a diverse and multifaceted manner. In spite of this the years take away what they previously gave us; if now the external world wishes to take away its portion then we shall at the end stand there all too naked and helpless.
>
> But do not let it end despondently but rather with the assurance; that I seek to employ every good moment in order to be of value to those who partake of me to the very end.
>
> Sincerely and faithfully.

Cotta was understandably pleased with such a message. He answered on 10 July with a confession: "I seek daily, as I feel the force of the years, to reduce the circle in which I operate and have already taken many a serious step in this direction. However it is not my intention to retire; on the contrary, I hope to maintain a suitable circle of business acquaintances and to move courageously within it as long as I am granted the opportunity. But *courage* belongs to our time, one that has to be called for everyone a serious time, and for many a stern, testing time."

Both had to withstand tests. Succeeding letters from Goethe and Cotta come at the end of a relationship between author and publisher that had lasted for more than a generation. Cotta sends Goethe birthday greetings on 22 August 1831: "the celebration that we hold at this time is truly doubly blessed; it is not merely a celebration of what has been preserved for us but of what has been given to us again, and the vision of such a wise guidance by providence strengthens our courage and faith to proceed in the serious times in which we live; and so, honored, worthy man, your life exerts a beneficent influence on your friends and contemporaries, on all sides and in every way, and your fate—to be for so many the chosen one—is fortunate and enviable." And Goethe sends his thanks in friendly fashion; he knows, he says, "that a relationship that has lasted so many years can be recognized by its blossoms and its ripened fruits whereas many others who were living and striving by my side had already had to set themselves a more limited goal. If your inclination has up to now remained unchanged then I may hope for the future to commend myself and my family to you in the best manner possible. Since there is no need of assurance that my thoughts and feelings always remain the same and that it gives me the greatest pleasure to be able to sign myself in all honesty the dedicated friend and servant of the esteemed pair. . . ."

The last news from the House of Cotta is the fulfillment of a "sad duty": George and Sophie Cotta tell Goethe of the death of their son Johann Erlbad Aurel, Goethe's godchild. Whether Goethe was alive to receive the news is uncertain.

Goethe dies in Weimar on 22 March 1832. He had completed his life as "a work of art," garnered the fruits of his "artistic truth" into the barn. The first of twenty volumes of *Goethe's Posthumous Works* was published by Cotta in December 1832. On 29 December, in the same year, Johann Friedrich Cotta died in Stuttgart.

Notes

Introduction

1. Bertolt Brecht put this important cultural insight into the mouth of his hero Galileo, more as a passing remark (*Leben des Galilei,* in *Werke,* "Grosse kommentierte Berliner und Frankfurter Ausgabe," vol. 5 [Berlin and Frankfurt am Main 1988]), p. 282. I know of no more beautiful and at the same time apposite definition of the book than this paradoxical combination of "consecrated" and "commodity." The paradox exists as long as books have existed: every writer, publisher, bookseller knows it. I have quoted this aside of Brecht's in many of my works and lectures and certainly ascribed a different meaning to them from that which Galileo had in mind.

2. Letter to Johann Jakob von Willemer, 22 December 1820.

3. The passage in the conversations with Eckermann (*Conversations with Goethe in the Last Years of His Life*) runs, "A German author, a German martyr!—Yes, my friend! And you will find it no different. And I am scarcely in a position to complain; none of the others had it any better, for most of them it was worse, and it was just the same in France and England as it was here at home." In the *Horen* he writes, under the title "Literary Sansculottism": "Thus the German writer finds himself at the age when concern for his living, his family, forces him to look beyond himself, and at which with the most melancholy feelings, he has to undertake work that he does not respect in order to acquire the means to be allowed to produce that which his trained mind seeks to make its sole concern."

4. Goethe, *Poetry and Truth,* translated by John Oxenford (Chicago: University of Chicago Press, 1974), p.355. All subsequent quotations from *Poetry and Truth* are from this edition unless otherwise stated. They are cited as Oxenford.

5. Oxenford, p.219

6. Figures about monetary income, as such, do not tell us much. Only the purchasing power of the currency at a given time can reveal the actual level of the value of such income. It is hard to draw comparisons between the value of money at different times, since many aspects have to be taken into account, the valency of which cannot always be determined. Thus we can only approximate.

If Johann Caspar Goethe earned 2,700 guilders (excluding rents) in the 1780s from the estate that his father left him, then the first salary that Goethe drew, from January to June 1776 paid out of Duke Carl August's privy purse, does not seem extraordinarily meager. The Saxon thaler at this time was worth somewhat less then two Frankfurt guilders (1 : 1.77). In addition, Goethe received free board and the furnished garden house on the Ilm.

If, like Richard Wittmann ("Die Buchhändler sind alle des Teufels' Goethe und seine Verleger," in *Börsenblatt* (27–30 March 1982), pp. 821–25, or Ulrich Küntzel *Die Finanzen großer Männer* (Berlin and Vienna, 1984), we set the value of the thaler at roughly DM 40 (in 1990 terms), then Goethe had an income of approximately DM 24,000 for the first half of 1776. This would be the equivalent of a gross monthly income of DM 4,000 (approximately U.S. $2,200 at 1990 rates of exchange).

Now it is true that taxes were far less and purchasing power was much greater. For example, the price of a book was, on average, 20 groschen (24 groschen = 1 thaler) in the 1780s.

7. In order to reach a proper estimation of Goethe's assets at this time, we also have to take into account the value of the real estate (about 5,000 thalers), as well as the value of his immense art collection on which, for a period of sixty years, he is thought to have spent at least 100 ducats per annum (catalogue of the exhibition, *Kostbarkeiten aus Goethes Kunstsammlung,* 12 May–21 June 1987, p.4). In order to assess the monetary value with some historical accuracy, a number of comparisons would be necessary: for example, if a student's annual expenses were at the time, for example, 500 guilders, in 1985 the average annual costs for a student were DM 10,000. Thus one could reckon a guilder as being worth DM 20. Again a guilder "was divided into 16 groschen, for which in 1789 Schiller . . . in Jena could eat eight midday meals, twice as many as he would have bought in Weimar for the same sum" (Ulrich Karthaus, "Friedrich Schiller," in *Genie und Geld. Vom Auskommen deutscher Schriftsteller*, edited by Karl Corino, [Reinbek, 1991], p. 153: in the same work, Volker Bohn writes about Goethe's income, pp. 140–50).

8. Oxenford, p. 141.

Chapter One

1. Letter to Friedrich Heinrich Jacobi, 21 August 1774 *(Goethes Briefe. Hamburger Ausgabe in 4 Bänden,* edited by Karl Robert Mandelkow and Bodo Morawe [Hamburg, 1962 (actually 1961)–1967, vol. 4; Munich, 1988, vol. 1; Munich, 1988, vols. 2–4]). Cited hereafter as *HA.*

2. Oxenford, p. 201.

3. To Friedrich Oeser, who had not liked his poems.

4. Abbé Charles Batteux (1730–80), French literary critic, member of several French academies, tried to establish binding categories for the production and evaluation of works of art. In his poetics of imitation, the theory of mimesis, he dominated European Enlightenment poetics and also gained a great deal of influence on German literary aesthetics, especially on Gottsched, particularly with his *Traité sur les Beaux-Arts réduits à un même principe.* Lyric poetry—as an imitation of feelings—was raised by Batteux to become a paradigm of poetry. Johann Adolf Schlegel published a

German translation in 1751, *The Limitation of the Beaux-Arts to a Single Principle;* Goethe's father had a copy of the 1759 edition in his library.

5. *Positiones juris quas auspice deo inclyti jureconsultorum ordinis consensu pro licentia summos in utroque jure honores rite consequendi in alma Argentinensi die VI. augusti MDCCLXXI. h.l.q.c. publice defendet Joannes Wolfgang Goethe Moeno-Francofurtensis. Argentorati ex Officina Johannis Henrici Heitzii, Universit. Typographi.*

Johann Ulrich Metzger wrote of Goethe's dissertation, from Strassburg on 7 August 1771 to Privy Councillor Friedrich Dominikus Ring in Karlsruhe, "I'm also mentioning a novelty that lets you see that our faculty is administered just as well as any other. We have a student here called Goethe from Frankfurt am Main, who, as they say, has been in Göttingen and Leipzig and was a very good student. This young man is puffed up with his knowledge but especially by some of the malice of Herr Voltaire, and wanted to write a thesis entitled *Jesus autor et judex sacrorum*. In which among other things he suggests that Jesus was not the founder of our religion but that some other scholars had created it in his name. The Christian religion is nothing more than a healthy system of politics etc., etc. However people were good enough to forbid him to publish his masterpiece. Whereupon, in order to show his disgust, he submitted the simplest of all theses, e.g., *jus naturae est quod omnia animalia decuit*. People derided him and he was finished" (letter, originally in French, *Jahrbuch der Goethe Gesellschaft,* 23 [1902], pp. 218f.). Metzger is however rather an unreliable witness (cf. E. Genton, *Goethes Strassburger Promotion,* [Basel], 1971) and—contrary to the traditional view of Goethe scholarship—he was not a professor of law but a law student. The proceedings of the Strassburg Faculty of Law for 6 August 1771 also notes the contrary, *Dissertationem inauguralem Positiones Juris exhibentem cum applausu defendit Dominus Joh. Wolfgang Goethe, Moeno-Francofurtanus,* and this corresponds to Goethe's own account in *Poetry and Truth.* (Pointed out by Valentin Koerner.)

6. Cf. Wolfgang Ungern-Sternberg, *Schriftsteller und Literarischer Markt,* in *Hansers Sozialgeschichte der deutschen Literatur,* vol. 3 (Munich, 1980), pp. 133–85, especially 151–55, and of course, Johann Goldfriedrich, *Geschichte des deutschen Buchhandels,* 3 vols. (and an index vol.) (Leipzig, 1908–13[92]), vol. 3, pp. 187, 204ff. According to the publisher Franz Josef Eckebrecht, there were in 1779 twenty net booksellers; in 1791 there were, among the total of 398 publishing booksellers, 29 pure publishers represented at the Leipzig fair (cf. Hans Widmann, *Geschichte des Buchhandels* (Wiesbaden, 1975), pp. 104ff). In the 90s the retail book trade began in general to separate from the publishers (cf. Hans Gerth, *Bürgerliche Intelligenz um 1800. Zur Soziologie des deutschen Frühliberalismus,* ed. Ulrich Herrmann [Göttingen, 1976], p. 100).

7. Ungern-Sternberg, *Schriftsteller,* p. 173.

8. *Goethe. Berliner Ausgabe,* ed. (Akademie Verlag), Lektorat Deutsches Erbe unter der Leitung von Siegfried Seidel, 22 vols. and 1 supplemental vol. (Berlin and Weimar, 1956–78 [so-called "Berlin Edition," referred to hereafter as *BA*]), vol. 7, p. 835. Justus Moser, "On the Rule of Force," *Osnabrückisches Intelligenzblätter,* April 1770.

9. Letter to his friend Johann Daniel Salzmann, 28 November 1771.

10. Letter to J. G. Ch. Kestner, 1 February 1773.

11. Dieter Breuer, *Geschichte der literarischen Zensur in Deutschland* (Heidelberg, 1982), p. 143. On censorship in the eighteenth century compare also, inter alia, the works of Heinrich Herbert Houben, especially *Verbotene Literatur,* 2 vols. (Berlin 1920; Bremen, 1928); and *Der ewige Zensor* (Kronberg, 1978).

12. Oxenford II, 139–40.

13. Walter Benjamin continues: "In 'The Sorrows of Werther' the bourgeoisie of the day found its pathology clear-sightedly and at the same time flatteringly portrayed in a way similar to that in which today's does in Freudian theory. Goethe wove his unhappy love affair with Lotte Buff, a friend's fiancée, into the amorous adventures of a young man-of-letters of his day whose suicide had attracted attention. The weltschmerz of the epoch develops in all its nuances in Werther's moods. Werther is not only the unhappy lover, who finds in the violence of his emotions ways to Nature that no lover had sought since Rousseau's *La nouvelle Héloïse,* he is also the bourgeois whose pride is wounded by the barriers of class and who, in the name of human rights, in the name of the creature himself, demands recognition. In Werther Goethe gives voice to the revolutionary element in his youth for the last time for many years." From: "Enzyklopädieartikel," in Walter Benjamin, *Gesammelte Schriften,* ed. Rolf Tiedemann, vol. 2/2 (Frankfurt am Main, 1977), pp. 703ff.

14. *Werther* still has an effect in our own time. The bicentennial celebration in 1974 was observed by publications and essays. In Ulrich Plentzdorf's story *The New Sorrows of the Young W.,* the main character, Edgar Wibeau, is reading Goethe's novel and sees his own situation reflected in Werther's. As the one example in recent German literature that derives from the Werther tradition, the paperback edition of the story had sold a million copies ten years after its initial publication. Ulrich Plentzdorf, *Die neuen Leiden des jungen W.* (Frankfurt am Main, 1973; English-language edition, *The New sufferings of Young W.,* translated by Kenneth P. Wilcox [Frederick Ungar, New York, 1979]). See *Plenzdorfs Neue Leiden des Jungen W.,* edited Peter J. Brenner (Frankfurt am Main, 1982). On the history of the work's influence in general, see *Zeitgenössische Rezensionen und Urteile über Goethes "Götz" und "Werther"* (Berlin 1935) and Georg Jäger, "Die Wertherwirkung. Ein rezeptionsästhetischer Modellfall," in *Historizität in Sprach-und Literaturwissenschaft,* ed. Walter Müller (Munich: Seidel, 1974), pp. 389–409, and Georg Jäger, *Die Leiden des alten und neuen Werther. Kommentare, Abhandlungen, Materialien* (Munich, 1984).

15. Hans Blumenberg's "Epigonenwallfahrt" (in *Akzente* 37 [1990], 272–82) can only be read, like so many of his works, with pleasure and profit. Immermann, the author of the novel *Die Epigonen,* journeyed to Weimar in 1837. He wished, according to Blumenberg, to put paid to the suspicion that Goethe's memory was a handicap for the epigones. Immermann's diaries are evidence in support of Blumenberg's view that he was "an instructive energizing force for the decade after the death of Goethe." He met the "three protectors of the unpublished works" in Weimar— Eckermann, Riemer, and Müller; the last mentioned, he says, was regarded for his part as a "bucket that drew from the well of society" and who preserved the "local

treasure trove of anecdotes from Goethe's sphere of life" while on the other hand maintaining a "canonical rigidity . . . about anything remotely connected with Goethe." Blumenberg refuses to express admiration for anyone in charge of an author's unpublished works: "work in the shadow of the dead, that withholds and distributes, cannot expect any respect." Immermann discovered that "the supporters of the cult of the dead man in Weimar" live "off the vitality of the cult figure"; "the emanation of 'an abundance of the most brilliant light' issues from life and death, not even from the works at the very place of their origin." Blumenberg quotes Immermann, Gutzkow, and the philosopher Friedrich Victor Plessing: "Werther on his appearance in Germany did not in the least arouse—as he has been charged with—a sickness, a fever, but only discovered the malady that lay hidden in young minds." But even if *Werther* only gave form to sentimentality, it would still be an achievement that is larger than life. It is true that Immermann finds the so-called solution in *Faust II* "actually silly." Goethe's legacy could not, in Blumenberg's view, have been more harshly attacked, and he asks, "Are you still an 'epigone' if you can stand on your own two feet like this?" In my opinion, absolutely.

16. Letter to C.F. Weisse.

17. (1) Letter from Heinse (13 October 1774), in *Goethe in vertraulichen Briefen seiner Zeitgenossen,* collected by Wilhelm Bode, new edition, Regine Otto and Paul-Gerhard Wenzlaff, 3 vols., 2d edition (Munich 1982; originally Berlin and Weimar, 1979), vol. 1, p. 69.

(2) August Bürger, letter (August 1775) to Johanna Fahlmer, *WA,* 4:2, 284.

18. *Der junge Goethe,* ed. Hanna Fischer-Lamberg, revised, 3d edition, 5 vols. (and 1 index volume) (Berlin and New York, 1963–74), p. 263.

19. Johann Goldfriedrich, *Geschichte des Deutschen Buchhandels,* 3 vols.(and 1 index vol.) (Leipzig, 1908–13 [1923]).

20. Oxenford II, pp. 312f.

Chapter Two

1. Viscount Goschen originally wrote his grandfather's biography in English (*The Life and Times of Georg Joachim Göschen, Publisher and Printer of Leipzig,* 2 vols. (London, New York, 1903) and the text cited here is from that work. The German edition is somewhat different, though essentially the same, as he notes in the foreword to the German version (*Das Leben Georg Joachim Göschens von seinem Enkel Viscount Goschen,* revised by the author, translated by Th.A. Fischer, 2 vols. (Leipzig: G.J. Göschen'sche Verlagsbuchhandlung, 1905). He was unable to write a German version "because he lacked the ability as a writer." But he was "inspired by the warm desire . . . to depict, with his own pen and with the affectionate devotion of an heir, the fate, the character, and the total personality of his grandfather." The German version took note of critical remarks made by English reviewers about the original edition. The source material is cited reliably, and the presentation of the facts of Göschen's forty-three-year-long publishing activity is well-founded. However, a

certain caution has to be observed in accepting the judgments, especially those about the attitude of authors towards Göschen. Viscount Goschen wrote his work and judged events from his grandfather's perspective and he tried to justify his grandfather's actions and decisions from his point of view.

2. Goschen, vol. 1, p. 140.

3. Quoted from *Johann Wolfgang Goethe. Sämtliche Werke. Briefe, Tagebücher und Gespräche,* 40 vols. (Frankfurt am Main 1983–), (*Bibliothek deutscher Klassiker*), called the Frankfurt edition (*FA*), I, 1, 268.

4. Letter to Carl August, 31 December 1783.

5. "If we were twenty years younger . . . we would sail to North America" (to Freiherr von Müller, 10 May 1819). "What would have happened if I had gone with a few friends to America thirty years ago . . . ?" (to Sulpice Boisserée, 2 August 1819). Then there is the famous passage from *Wilhelm Meisters Lehrjahre:* "I shall return and, in the midst of my family, in my house or my orchard, I shall say, 'here or nowhere is America!' " (*Johann Wolfgang Goethe. Sämtliche Werke nach Epochen seines Schaffens. Münchner Ausgabe,* 21 vols. (in 26), ed. Karl Richter, Herbert G. Göpfert, Norbert Miller, and Gerhard Sauder, Munich 1985–), commonly called the Munich Edition (*MA*), 5, 433.

6. Letter to Philipp Christoph Kayser, 14 June 1782.

7. K. R. Eissler, *Goethe, a Psychoanalytical Study, 1775–1786.* It is strange that this study claimed little attention until 1986. I read the first volume without profiting a great deal. The central theme is Goethe's relationship with his sister Cornelia. Eissler would like to make this brotherly love, burdened as it was with incest taboo, possessive claims, and feelings of guilt, the key to Goethe's love-life, and sees in it the reason for his falling in love so frequently with women who were sexually taboo, and whom he could not possibly marry. He even regards it as the origin of Goethe's literary activity. He characterizes the relationship to Frau von Stein as that of a "patient-analyst situation." Without mincing words he describes it as "asexual" and "frigid." He always compares her to Cornelia: both, according to Eissler, had had the same difficulties with their spouses—how does Eissler know this? And how does he know that the thirty-eight-year-old was first able to overcome his impotence in Rome and have his first sexual relationship there? Eissler is also not afraid of terrible puns: Goethe goes to Italy (*"gen Italien"* = *"Genitalien"* ["genitalia"]). Things do not deserve to be treated as voyeuristically as this. I have reservations every time Eissler makes a firm judgment. Goethe wrote to Frau von Stein of New Year's Day 1778, "I would so like to send you something for the New Year and I can find nothing. I was tempted to send a lock of my hair and had already tied it up, when it occurred to me that this tuft would have no magic for you" (*WA,* 4: 3, 204). Eissler sees this as a castration element that runs through the whole relationship to Frau von Stein. He sees *Iphigenia* as part of an "autoplastic process." *Iphigenie* was a grandiose wish-fulfillment, on the one hand the salvation of a man hounded by the Furies because of the sister he thought he had lost and, on the other, "No doubt this great composition was created under the sign of rivalry with a friend (the Duke) who had

begotten a child" (1: 340). It also seems rather far-fetched to assume that there were homosexual relations between the duke and Goethe and to conclude that because they both admired Cornelia Schröter that it was precisely this "friendship that gave them the opportunity to enjoy sublimated homosexuality in both its active and passive form without feelings of guilt." But to be fair, Eissler does not simply construct a "case." He does not, like many positivist literary scholars, pay attention only to biographical facts, but looks for the connection between biography, disposition, correspondence, and literary works, in order to reveal the creative process. In the process he is candid enough to record what is special and what cannot be explained: "The magnificent qualities that we come across in all the phenomena of his existence. . . ." Nevertheless at the conclusion of the investigation he comes to "the result" that a particular property of genius that we find in certain people must be regarded as a sort of psychopathology. This reflects my own experience as a publisher.

8. *Misel* is the Alsatian diminutive for *Mus* (mouse) and is a term of affection for a pretty young girl.

9. The whole passage reads: "But writing letters means baring yourself to ghosts and they await this eagerly. Written kisses do not reach their destination but are drunk up by ghosts en route. This nourishment makes them increase in an unheard of manner" (Franz Kafka, *Briefe an Milena* [Frankfurt am Main, 1966], p. 199).

10. Goethe was in Berlin from 15 to 20 May 1778. Thus Walter Benjamin was wrong when he wrote, "So he never set foot in Berlin." With regard to Benjamin's view, we can understand the statement. He had been given the "curious task," as he wrote to Gershom Sholem, of writing an article on Goethe for the "Great Russian Encyclopedia from the standpoint of Marxist doctrine." Benjamin was right when he said that all his life Goethe disliked large cities, never setting foot in Paris or, as Benjamin believed, Berlin, "for in the whole of Europe the bourgeois revolution was dependent on cities." True, Benjamin wonders, in his letter to Sholem, about a "Marxist" view of Goethe: "I have to decide for myself what such a treatment consists of and what it teaches. If 'literary history' in the strictest sense has as little reality from the Marxist point of view (as I am very much inclined to assume) as it does from any other reasoned point of view, this does not preclude that my attempt to treat a subject from such a perspective, a subject I would not otherwise treat, may result in something interesting enough to be safely rejected by the editorial board, if worst comes to worst" (from *The Correspondence of Walter Benjamin, 1910—1940,* edited and annotated by Gershom Sholem and Theodor W. Adorno, translated by Manfred R. Jacobson and Evelyn M. Jacobson [Chicago: University of Chicago Press, 1994], p. 302). The writing of the article dragged on for a long time from the date it was commissioned in February 1926; Benjamin did not complete it until October 1928. When the article appeared in the encyclopedia, it was no longer possible to recognize Walter Benjamin as its author. Rolf Tiedemann has calculated that only 12 percent of the printed Russian version parallels the manuscript by Benjamin (see Tiedemann's notes in: Walter Benjamin, *Gesammelte Schriften* 2/3 [Frankfurt am Main, 1977], pp. 1465ff).

11. Letter from Chancellor von Müller to Count Richard, 15 January 1827; see Ernst Grumach, *Müller: Kanzler von Müller. Unterhaltungen mit Goethe.* Kritische Ausgabe, besorgt v. Ernst Grumach (Weimar 1956), p. 334.

12. *FA* I, 14, 842. Goethe mentions this saying in connection with his definition of the demonic: "But what appears to be most frightful is the demonic, when it emerges overwhelmingly in one individual. In the course of my life I have often been able to observe many people of this sort, some close at hand, some at a distance. They are not always the most excellent people, whether as to intellect or talent, and they seldom recommend themselves by their goodness of heart; but an enormous power emanates from them, they exercise an unbelievable force over all creatures, even over the elements. . . . They seldom or never find contemporaries who are their equal and they are unconquerable except by the universe itself with which they have begun their struggle; and it is from such observations that that strange but terrible saying may have emerged: nemo contra deum nisi deus ipse." In contrast to the first three parts of *Poetry and Truth,* the fourth part that appeared posthumously in 1833 has no motto. The editors, Eckermann, Riemer, and Chancellor von Müller, wanted to add the motto and Riemer remembered that this was Goethe's idea as well. According to Riemer's record, Goethe had noted the saying in the form, "Nihil contra deum, nisi deus ipse [Nothing against God unless it is God himself]" and had suggested a different translation from the literal one: "A god can only be balanced by a god." According to Riemer's diary for 3 July 1810 Goethe said of this: "A splendid dictum, of infinite use. God always meets himself: God in man, himself again in man."

13. Richard Friedenthal, *Goethe. Sein Leben und Seine Zeit* (Munich: 1963), p. 262.

14. Julius Petersen edited for the Insel Verlag in 1907 a three-volume edition of *Goethe's Letters to Charlotte von Stein.* The introduction begins: "The noble goddess of the poem 'Dedication' that decorates the entrance to Goethe's works, is the transformed image of an earthly woman who, like no other, purified and ennobled the poet's life and works. It is Charlotte von Stein who cooled the brow of the passion-torn Stürmer und Dränger and poured the purest balsam into his life's wounds; she made him see himself clearly and made him at peace with the world, and he received from her the inspiration for his most noble style; the veil of poetry from the hand of truth" (p.vii).

15. *The Secrets (Die Geheimnisse)* (*WA,* 116, 169–83) is a fragment of a poetic epic written in 1784 and 1785. Goethe wrote to Frau von Stein on 8 August 1784: "I am sending you something, by Herder, that I have written for you two" (*WA* IV,6 334); "you two" were Frau von Stein and Herder. Only forty strophes were completed by 28 March 1785. "The undertaking is too immense for my situation, meanwhile I shall go on and see how far I get" (to Knebel; *WA*, IV, 7, 33). *The Secrets* was to represent a religious fraternity, in which twelve knights symbolize the twelve religions. However, Goethe got no further. He finally gave up writing it and published the fragment in 1789. Apparently both Herder's ideas as well as the idea of Frau von

Stein were too clear to him. Wilhelm von Humboldt got to know of the text on the occasion of a reading in Dalberg's house in Erfurt. When he climbed Mount Montserrat, he remembered *The Secrets.* And now Goethe took up this image of the mountain. In an essay in Cotta's *"Morgenblatt für gebildete Stände"* (No. 102, 72, April 1816) he wrote, at the suggestion of a student group from Königsberg, that he wanted to guide the reader "through a sort of ideal Montserrat" (Johann Wolfgang Goethe, *Schriften zur Literatur,* edited by the Academy of Sciences of the German Democratic Republic, 7 vols. [Berlin 1970–1982], 3: 314f.). The monks who live on the mountain are gathered round one man called "Humanus"; this "mediator" is to show "that every particular religion reaches a point of its highest fruition, in which it approaches that superior leader and mediator, and in fact unites with him" (ibid., 16).

16. *Göthes Briefe an Frau von Stein aus den Jahren 1776–1826,* ed. Adolf Schöll (Weimar, n.d.). The 1,700 letters or notes sent from one house to the other by messengers, the poems that lay between letters and notes, all these papers were thrown into disorder when the Steins' house was plundered in 1806. Charlotte had bequeathed them to her son Fritz, he had bequeathed them to his nephew, Karl von Stein, who bequeathed them, in his turn, to the grand duchess of Saxony. Most of the letters were unknown to contemporaries, as was the degree of Goethe's relationship to Frau von Stein; Goethe himself, who openly and unreservedly stood at her side, nevertheless veiled his relationship to her from his contemporaries: there are no records of statements about Frau von Stein to Eckermann or any of his other interlocutors. It was only in 1886, after philological studies by Wilhelm Fielitz, Heinrich Düntzer, and Julius Wahle, that Erich Schmidt edited the texts in the fourth section of the Weimar Edition. Julius Petersen's three-volume edition for the Insel Verlag in 1907 (it is not this edition but a later one from 1923 that is mentioned in the bibliographies) was the first popular edition of the letters.

17. Werner Schmidt in his commentary on Friedrich Justin Bertuch, *Bilderbuch für Kinder,* facsimile edition, 1977 (Edition Leipzig and Insel Verlag), vol. 3.

18. For many authors proofreading is a torture. The text has left the familiar manuscript form, has been alienated by different characters, and is often hard to read on the proof-sheets. The first detachment of the text from the author has taken place. Once when I was talking to Heiner Müller about Goethe's reluctance, indeed his refusal, to read proof of his own text, he said something surprising. He too had a similar reluctance, but he simply had to read proof, as he had no Herder to do it for him. In Goethe's case, according to Müller, his reluctance to read proof, to see his text solidified in characters, as a sort of corpse, was like his reluctance to attend funerals. In point of fact, Goethe would not go to funerals. As he says in the Prologue in Heaven, in *Faust,* Part One: "I am not at home for a corpse, to me it is like a cat and a mouse."

19. See *WA,* I, 19, 331. Whether the editors of newer editions should take the first or second version as the basis of the text will remain a problem that can scarcely be solved. How shall we proceed today—must we use an older form or a more modern one? Goethe changed the form of *"ahnden"*(1787) to the more modern one

of *"ahnen"* which he used later in Weimar; again the modern reader will perhaps appreciate the effort an editor has to make in choosing between *"heurathen," "heuraten,"* and *"heiraten."*

20. This was the "Duden" or orthographic authority of the eighteenth century, *Vollständige Anweisung zur Deutschen Orthographie, nebst einem kleinen Wörterbuch für die Aussprache, Orthographie, Biegung und Ableitung,* Johann Christoph Adelung, Curfürstl, Sächs. Hofrath und Ober-Bibliothecarius in Dresden (Leipzig: Weygandsche Buchhandlung, 1788). In the foreword, we read, "As little as we lack instruction in German orthography, so much the more have we felt the lack of a book of this sort in which the principles of writing are treated in a systematic way." Goethe ordered this dictionary to be used to achieve unity in the copies of his works, but as far as I know he never expressed an opinion on Adelung and his work.

21. Liselotte Bluementhal, *"Die Tasso—Handschriften,"* in *Goethe Jahrbuch,* 12 (1951), 89–125.

22. In the "correspondence" of March 1788 in the *Zweiten Römischen Aufenthalt,* Goethe reports on the first of the month, "First, the plan for *Faust* was made and I hope that the operation has been successful. Of course, it is quite a different matter writing the play now from what it was fifteen years ago, but I do not think it will lose anything in the process, especially as I think I have picked up the thread again. I also comfort myself about the tone of the whole thing; I have already worked out a new scene and if I blacken the paper a bit, I don't think anyone will discover that it comes from the old play. Since the long rest and absence have restored me completely to the level of my own existence, it is strange how like myself I am and how little my inner self has suffered as a result of time and circumstances. The old manuscript often gives me food for thought when I see it in front of me. It is still the first, the main scenes written without a plan, and now it is yellowed with age, dog-eared (the sheets were never stapled together), brittle and worn at the edges, so that it really looks like a fragment of an ancient codex, and as I transport myself by thought and conjecture into an earlier world, I have to transport myself into an earlier time that I have myself lived through."

23. Klaus Manger in his commentary on Christoph Martin Wieland, *Werke,* vol. 3, *Geschichte des Agathon,* ed. Klaus Manger (Frankfurt am Main, 1986), p. 915.

Chapter Three

1. Harald Keller, the great art historian and connoisseur of Italian art and literature, states: "The reader of the *Italienische Reise* cannot really grasp the fact that Goethe described the Roman Carnival, and he would be more surprised to learn that this description of the festival . . . was written in 1789, immediately after his return" (*Das Römische Carneval,* reduced photocopy of an uncut copy of the first edition [Dortmund: Anton und Katharina Kippenberg Stiftung, 1978], pp. 119f.): "the first thing about the 'Roman Carnival' is the miracle of its existence. Who managed to press the pen into the hand of the reluctant and bad-tempered writer?" On the

socio–utopian significance of the carnival, cf. Manfred Fuhrmann, *Fastnacht als Utopie. Vom Saturnalienfest im alten Rom,* in *Narrenfreiheit: Beiträge zur Fastnachtsforschung,* ed. H. Bausinger et al. (Tübingen, 1980), 29–42.

2. Isabella Kuhn, *Das römische Carneval,* ed. Isabella Kuhn (Frankfurt am Main, 1984).

3. Goethe diary entry, 24 September 1786.

4. Letter to Heyne, 24 July 1788.

5. See Ernst Beutler in his introduction to volume 11 of *Johann Wolfgang von Goethe. Gedenkausgabe der Werke, Briefe und Gespräche,* 24 vols., ed. Ernst Beutler (1st ed., Zürich 1948–54, and 3 supplementary volumes, Zürich and Stuttgart, 1960–71, cited here as *GA*): "Goethe's *Italienische Reise* is a work of sheer joy. There is scarcely another work in the whole of world literature that is its equal. It is the description of a chain of happily blissful days. If we see in the feeling of joy that we experience in it, the measure of the fulfillment of life, then the years in Rome were the peak of Goethe's existence. The melancholy that darkened his departure, the poet's confession that for the preceding weeks he had not been able to hold back his tears when he awoke in the morning, and his other statement that since he had left Rome he had never had a truly happy day only confirm the heights to which his sojourn in the south had raised him" (995). The *Italienische Reise* appeared in two volumes (without the "Second Italian Sojourn") as parts 4 and 5 (1816–17) of the autobiographical work *Aus meinem Leben* (From my Life) (Stuttgart and Tübingen: Cotta, 1811–22). The motto on the title pages of both volumes of the first edition was "I too was in Arcady." The motto was omitted in the final edition. It is a translation of the Latin *Et in Arcadia Ego,* a saying first found on a painting of Schidone's in Rome. It became more familiar through two paintings by Nicolas Poussin, in both of which shepherds are endeavoring to decipher an inscription chiselled into a sarcophagus. The saying was understood as an epitaph and was frequently quoted, as in J. G. Jacobi's *Winterreise:* "Whenever I come across a gravestone in the midst of beautiful fields with the inscription, 'I too was in Arcady', then I show the gravestone to my friends, we remain standing, give one another our hand and go on." Wieland and Herder use it in this sense. Herder says in his *Ideen zur Philosophie der Geschichte der Menschheit* (book 7, chapter 1), " 'I too was in Arcady' is the epitaph of all living people in a creation that is always changing and always being reborn." Bruno Snell has pointed out the origin of the transferred meaning of the name "Arcady." The scene of some of Virgil's *Eclogues* is "Arcadia." Snell sees it as a symbolic landscape, a symbol for peace, harmony, happiness: "I too was in Arcady, the land of happiness, I was happy, I was consciously here." Herbert von Einem translated: "I (death) too am at hand in Arcady." Goethe was admitted to the Society of Arcadians in Rome in 1787, a national academy founded in 1690; its founders nurtured the poetic forms of Pindar and Petrarch and their meetings took place *alfresco* in the Bosco Parrasio. It became the Accademia letteraria italiana dell' Arcadia, which still exists today.

6. Hecker, *Maximen: J. W. Goethe. Maximen und Reflexionen,* text edition of

1907 with notes and introduction by Max Hecker (Frankfurt am Main, 1976), p. 833. These words of Goethe were long understood as his acknowledgment of legalism, as a support of existing rules of governance. Maxims sounding like this were often cited: "It is better to be treated unjustly than for the world to be without laws; for this reason everyone should obey the law. It is better that injustices occur than that they should be set aside by unjust means." And, "The only thing that matters to the state is that property should be assured and safe: whether that property is justly acquired is of less importance to it." In his Goethe book, Hans Meyer states that it is only rarely that the occasion of this statement is mentioned. He therefore tries to put the "famous—notorious—statement" into the framework of Enlightenment thought; he sees here "bourgeois thinking" and not "abolutist legitimacy" (Hans Meyer, *Goethe* [Frankfurt am Main, 1973], 43).

7. Biedermann, *Unger* (Type foundry H. Berthold, Dept. of Privately Published Editions). In the imprint: "The nineteenth Berthold publication was manufactured by the L. C. Wittich court printing press in Darmstadt. 700 copies were printed." The book is indispensable for anyone doing research on Goethe's relationship to Unger. It is set in Unger *Fraktur* and also contains a few pictures of the title pages of Goethe's works, among them an English translation of *Iphigenie auf Tauris* that Unger published, or at least printed: "*Iphigenia in Tauris,* a Tragedy written originally in German by J. W. von Goethe. Berlin. Printed by J. F. Unger 1794."

8. *The Campaign in France* (*WA* I, 33, p.63). The head of the Centre Dramatique de Reims, Denis Genoun, wrote a five-act play, *La levée,* on the occasion of the 200th anniversary of the French Revolution and this was also produced. Goethe is the focus of attention, in the midst of the battlefield of Valmy he is writing his thoughts and his memories. In the fifth act, Goethe's dream of the "new epoch" is simulated in the form of a film.

9. Peter Demetz, *Goethes "Die Aufgeregten." Zur Frage der politischen Dichtung in Deutschland* (Hannoversch-Münden, 1952), p.9.

10. The earliest mention is in his diary, 16 February 1777, "I dictated some W. Meister in the garden."

11. I have already mentioned Blumenberg's *Epigonenwallfahrt.* Blumenberg takes this statement by Unger as the starting point for his essay on "Dissociation of Aura and Work." Although Blumenberg's sentences are couched in the conditional mood, he seems to want to identify with Immermann's and Gutzkow's point of view, that Goethe had not created a prevailing trend but merely given expression to one.

12. Friedrich Schlegel, *Athenäum Fragment,* 216.

13. Waltraud Hagen, *Goethes Werke auf dem Markt des deutschen Buchhandels. Eine Untersuchung über Auflagenhöhe und Absatz der zeitgenössischen Goethe Ausgaben* (*GJb,* 100, 1985).

14. Hans-Joachim Weitz has made a complete collection of Goethe's statements "about the Germans." The collection is astonishing in its quantity. Goethe simply did not like "the" Germans and spoke freely and frankly. He certainly saw many reasons why the Germans were reserved in their attitude towards him as well, as in

the reaction of certain circles towards *Götz* and *Werther* right at the beginning of his career; the hatred and scorn that he reaped for his way of life, his alleged lack of national consciousness, and for his presumed lack of markedly Christian feeling. Goethe was valued and praised; but he was seldom loved. And what must have affected him even more was that he was also little read by the Germans. He simply felt that they did not understand him. However, Weitz's collection also makes it clear that "the Germans" were a synonym for something that Goethe could not come to terms with, indeed something that he could not find—this "Germany": "Germany? But where is it? I do not know where to find the country / where scholarship starts, politics ends," we read in no. 122 of the *Xenien,* the distichs he wrote together with Schiller (July 1796); this distich is probably by Schiller, but Goethe's co-authorship means that he authorized it. In a conversation with Heinrich Lude, Goethe said in 1813: "I have a soft spot in my heart for Germany too. I have often felt bitter pain when thinking of the German people, that is so worthy of respect as individuals and so miserable as a whole" (*GA* 22, p. 713). One of the prosecutors in the war-crimes trials in Nuremberg wove Goethe's statement into his speech as though he were quoting an expert on the topic "The Germans," according to which the Germans "have faith in any ecstatic rascal who calls forth their worst qualities, strengthens them in their vices, and teaches them to understand nationality as isolation and crudeness." But he was guilty of a double falsehood by putting into Goethe's mouth what Thomas Mann had invented in his novel *Lotte in Weimar.* See *Goethe über die Deutschen,* (Frankfurt am Main, 1978), pp.107ff. Waitz's collection appeared, after its initial publication in a journal, in work published by the Südverlag (Constance, 1949). Thomas Mann and Karl Jaspers were moved by the topicality of Goethe's statements. Weitz showed that the statement quoted by the prosecutor in the Nuremberg trial in 1946, which allegedly came from the book that appeared from the Insel Verlag, *Aus Riemers Mitteilungen über Goethe,* was also a falsification. Weitz writes in the epilogue: "Goethe—citizen of the world and an inhabitant of Weimar—is the greatest German and could become at the same time a [*sic*] greatest European. To the extent that he was free, he has liberated himself from the qualities that ail the Germans. This too is an appeal with reference to our life among the peoples of the earth." The collection was revised and expanded in 1965 as volume 861 of the Insel Bücherei and enlarged once more in 1978 and published as an Insel pocketbook (325).

15. Ian C. Loram, "Goethe and the Publication of His Works" (Ph.D. diss., Yale University, 1949), p. 49.

16. 26 August 1797.

17. Letter to Körner, 28 October 1796.

18. Letter to Rahel Levin, 29 November 1796.

19. Liselotte Lohrer, *Cotta. Geschichte eines Verlags 1659—1959* (Stuttgart, 1959). Schiller's contracts with Michaelis have been preserved and appear in the appendix to *Schillers Werke. Nationalausgabe* (Weimar, 1943–). Forty-three volumes are planned (cited as *Schiller Nationalausgabe [SNA]*).

20. Letter to Cotta, 24 January 1808. Vieweg's 1825 edition bore the inscription, "For those who perished in the floods of the night of 4 to 5 February 1825."

Chapter Four

1. Theodor Heuss, *Von Ort zu Ort. Wanderungen mit Stift und Feder,* ed. Friedrich Kaufmann and Hermann Leins (Tübingen, 1959), p. 31.

2. Lohrer, *Cotta,* p. 55.

3. Kurt Wolff is an especially good example of the interaction between the founding of periodicals and relationships to authors. Periodicals are indicators, indicators too for dangerous competition. The *Weiße Blätter* proved to be this for S. Fischer. It polemicized against the S. Fischer publishing house and its authors and attacked the "arch-swine . . . Thomas Mann and Hauptmann who is now completely ga-ga." The program was pompously announced: "The *Weiße Blätter* is to be the organ of the younger generation of writers, as the *Neue Rundschau* is for the older." The *Weiße Blätter* appeared initially in his own publishing house. True, Ernst Rowohlt had intended to publish a periodical when the house was founded, but his attempts failed, as did the cooperative effort of Rowohlt and Kurt Wolff to found a periodical, *Fahnenmasten.* Franz Blei published *Loser Vogel* but it folded after twelve numbers, six of which were published by Kurt Wolff. Kurt Wolff had planned a high-grade periodical, *Arcadia,* but this too failed and he took over the radical biweekly *Pan 2.* But he gave up this plan as well as the periodical *Orion,* which was offered him by Kurt Tucholsky.

4. Cf. Manfred Fuhrmann, *Die vier Jahreszeiten bei den Griechen und Römern,* in *Die vier Jahreszeiten im 18. Jahrhundert* (Beiträge zur Geschichte der Literatur und Kunst im 18. Jahrhundert, 10), Heidelberg, 1986, pp. 9–17.

5. Letter to Duke Friedrich Christian, 9 January 1796.

6. In the introduction to the edition, Dorothea Kuhn writes an extensive "History of the Edition of the Correspondence": In 1875 and 1880, the Goethe scholars and editors Hermann Uhde (1845–79) and Wilhelm Arndt (1838–95) had proposed that the publisher bring out an edition of Goethe's letters to Cotta (because of the business nature of Cotta's letters to Goethe these could be dispensed with). The fact that the tone of Cotta's letters to Goethe was different from that of the friendly tone of his letters to Schiller, and that the situation of their being handed down was different, probably played a role in this decision. Cotta's replies to Schiller's letters were made available to the publisher by their owner, Schiller's daughter Emilie von Gleichen Rußwurm. Goethe's correspondence lay locked up with the rest of his unpublished posthumous works. When these were taken over in 1885 by the Grand Duchess Sophie of Saxe-Weimar—to whom they had been bequeathed by Goethe's grandchildren—she commissioned a complete edition of Goethe works, letters, and diaries in Weimar, the "Weimar Sophie-edition," the first volumes of which appeared in 1887. This probably revived the Cotta plan for an edition. Wilhelm Vollmer died in 1887 and the Cotta archives were left for two years without a keeper until Ludwig

Laistner (1845–96) entered the publishing house. Laistner, who, like Vollmer, was originally an editor, soon took up the project. When Goethe's working manuscripts were needed in Weimar for the "Sophie-edition" and especially when Goethe's letters to Cotta were asked for, they were to appear in volumes projected for 1893. Carl von Cotta used the opportunity to ask for an exchange of Cotta's letters to Goethe. Bernhard Suphan (1845–1911), the director of the Goethe-Schiller archives in Weimar, agreed to the Stuttgart plan for an edition in 1895; and Cotta's letters to Goethe were copied in Weimar for this purpose. In 1895, Laistner presented Carl von Cotta with a memoir in which he suggested that the correspondence between Goethe and Cotta should be published as soon as possible, so as to anticipate the complete edition of Goethe's letters in the Sophie-edition. What he had in mind was an edition of the correspondence, without notes, in the framework of a journal or an annual "From the Cotta Archives" in which other archival material should also appear. He must have realized that the wealth of materials for this correspondence, for the most part unpublished at the time, was an insurmountable hindrance to the speedy publication of it. Notes in his own handwriting that refer to material from the Cotta archives and from Goethe's posthumous works show that he had already been intensely busy with the edition both in Weimar and Stuttgart and knew how many materials there were. This work remained unfinished because of his early death in 1896. His successor in the archives, Otto Rommerl (1836–1909) was apparently only able to further it a little. On the other hand the copies of Goethe's letters that had been requested by Weimar (up to writings from the years 1808–10, which had been retained by Laistner and then apparently forgotten) had gone off to Weimar for the Sophie-edition: Goethe's letters to Cotta appeared there almost complete. In the notes to the later volumes some letters of Cotta to Goethe have been included by way of explanation, so that an edition of the correspondence gradually held less promise of containing hitherto unpublished material (*Goethe-Cotta* 3:1, pp.29ff.).

7. Among others: Ian C. Loram, "Goethe and the Publication of His Works" (Ph.D diss., Yale University, 1949); Karl Markert, "Goethe und der Verlag seiner Werke," in *Goethe Jahrbuch,* 12 (1950); Georg Witkowski, "Goethe und seine Verleger," Lecture in *Börsenblatt,* 72 (1906); Reinhard Wittmann, "Die Buchhändler sind alle des Teufels. Goethe und seine Verleger," in *Börsenblatt,* 27, 30 March 1982. The works of Herbert G. Göpfert were most helpful in guiding my footsteps through materials that were often impossible to survey. Of all the literary historians that have worked on the history of Goethe's books, as books, I am most indebted to him and I was always grateful for being able to rest on his shoulders. His latest work, *Von Breitkopf zu Cotta. Zur Druckgeschichte von Goethes Werken* (dedicated to the important compilation of *Quellen und Zeugnisse zur Druckgeschichte von Goethes Werken* [Berlin: Akademie Verlag, 1966–84], a work that was, of course, also a source for me) appeared too late for me to use it for the present work.

8. Just the work of deciphering Cotta's uncommonly complicated, almost impossible to read handwriting by the editor is stupendous. She must often have sighed like Jean Paul, who asked Cotta to reply but said, "May God grant you a readable ink!" The corpus of letters in volumes 1 and 2 consists of 269 letters by Goethe and 352 by Cotta.

This corpus of letters is one side of the edition's achievement. In volume 3, which is divided into two parts, there are over 700 pages of notes, explanations, commentary, and index. One has to work through these two volumes to appreciate the wealth and completeness of the whole apparatus. An introduction surveys the publishing relationship between the two. Every one of Goethe's and Cotta's letters is explained, there are archival materials relating to the correspondence, references to scholarly literature, surveys and tables about royalties, size of editions, free copies, individual copies of works that Goethe published with Cotta. A detailed chronological table lists dates not only relevant to Goethe and Cotta but to the history of the time, and there is an index of Goethe's works, of subjects, and an 87-page index of place and personal names.The reaction of contemporaries, the relationship of Goethe's works to contemporary literature, history, and politics, as well as to his own life—all of these are meticulously cross-referenced: it is seldom that an edition presents us with such a solid history of works and their effect, such a closely knit field of frequently unknown or unfamiliar and yet essential information. After Vollmer's macroview in the correspondence between Schiller and Cotta we are now given a microview. We now know what Goethe meant when he wrote to Cotta, before their first meeting, that he had often suffered in inns and was looking forward to a domestic circle—he was tortured by bedbugs. Now after expensive nights in hotels he was able to enjoy the publisher's hospitality that was free of charge—and of bedbugs; not a bad beginning for a relationship between a publisher and an author. Cotta wrote to Goethe on January 12, 1797, that he had not found a watch. We now know that Goethe, on the first night after his stay with Cotta in Tübingen, had left an enamel watch with double glass in the privy of the inn in Tübingen. Cotta tried to recover it via the mayor but had no success, and an advertisement in Cotta's newspaper did not bring the watch to light. These may be trifles but they are characteristic.

9. Robert K. Merton, in *On the Shoulders of Giants, A Shandean Postscript* (New York, 1965), gives the original version of this quotation: "A dwarf who is standing on the shoulders of a giant can see further than the giant himself." Cast in the form of a detective story, this book is one of the most amusing treatments of the problem of scientific progress. Newton's saying occurs in a letter to Robert Hooke in February 1675, but is traced back to a saying of Bernard of Chartres from around 1126. Merton derives a long genealogical tree for this aphorism that is so highly charged and revealing for the history of science that it leads down to Sigmund Freud in our own century, who offers a new variation on it. Freud had quarrelled with a student, Stekel, who had quite blatantly stated that his thoughts were superior to those of his master; and this was in reference to the Newton quotation, according to which the dwarf on the shoulders of the giant could see further than the giant. However, when the giant learned of this presumption he said angrily, "but not a louse on the head of an astronomer."

10. Bertolt Brecht wrote this letter when he was in exile on the Danish island of Skovbostrand in August 1938, on the occasion of Alfred Döblin's sixtieth birthday.

It is a typical Brecht letter: "Permit me on this your birthday, true to custom, to talk about myself." The letter ends: "With my most affectionate greeting in the darkest of times." (B. Brecht, *Briefe,* edited, with a commentary, by Günter Glaeser [Frankfurt am Main, 1981], p. 375.)

Chapter Five

1. Voss's son, who took over the task of watching at Goethe's sickbed, told the theologian A. H. Niemeyer on 12 August 1806, "Schiller was the first to recover, and scarcely was he allowed out than he went to visit his dear Goethe, after having me announce him. I was present at this reunion . . . they embraced one another and kissed one another with a long and loving kiss, before either of them uttered a word. Neither mentioned his nor the other's illness, but both enjoyed the unalloyed joy of being reunited in good spirits."

2. The history of the origin and the publication of Benjamin's famous essay *Goethes Wahlverwandtschaften* is as characteristic of Benjamin's existential situation as it is for Benjamin's influence or non-influence, his high reputation among writers, and his neglect by scholarship. In an unpublished letter to Adorno (18 March 1934) Benjamin wrote of the fate of his (and Adorno's) publications: "our productions are hard put to it . . . but do we not aim at apocalyptic effect? It is in this sense that I have—as you know—been happy to point to the fate that has been meted out to my things when they are published; whether it is a question of the copy of my dissertation that was burned or of Rowohlt's suggestion that you wrote me about: I recognize the same law." "Apocryphal effect": Rowohlt had offered to publish *The Elective Affinities* essay as a book; the edition never appeared. The first independent book edition appeared in 1964 from Insel Verlag. It was one of the first decisions I made after Insel Verlag had been taken over in Frankfurt, to publish Benjamin's essay in the Insel Bücherei (as volume 812) as a way of giving that traditional series a new topicality. The history of the origin and of the effect, which will some day be written, is unusual. There are hints by Benjamin about *The Elective Affinities* essay from 1917 onwards. It was begun definitively in the second half of 1919 and completed in the summer of 1922. Plans for the possible founding of periodicals were spun around a possible publication of the work; publishers were also involved. The publisher Richard Weißbach had to stop printing—it was already begun—Benjamin's projected periodical, *Angelus Novus.* Cassirer read the article and returned it after three months, but still offered Benjamin 15,000 marks for a further option on it, a tidy sum for the hard economic times of 1923. Benjamin then asked his friend Florens Christian Rang to intervene on his behalf with Hofmannsthal. He sent *The Elective Affinities* essay and the event then took place that hid the "apocryphal effect"; Hofmannsthal was enthusiastic about the "simply incomparable article." "I can only say that it marks an epoch in my inner life and that my thinking, to the extent that my own work does not require all my attention, has scarcely been able to tear itself away from it. . . . What seems wonderful to me—to talk of the apparently 'external'—is the great

beauty of the presentation in such an unparalleled penetration of the secret; this beauty stems from a completely sure and pure thought process of which I know few other examples. If this is a younger man, if he has my advantage in years, I would be totally taken aback by such maturity." Benjamin was twenty years younger. In spite of such a unique recommendation and the publication of the essay in three parts in Hofmannsthal's *Neue Deutsche Beiträge* (1924/1925), no publisher was to be found to publish it as a book.

Friedrich Podszuz, who was then a reader for Suhrkamp, drew my attention to Benjamin in 1953 by reading precisely this text aloud to me. From that moment, I have known Benjamin's sharp distinction between commentary and criticism: "Criticism seeks the truth content of a work of art, commentary its subject matter." The more time I devote to this essay and to Goethe's *The Elective Affinities,* the more I admire Benjamin's search for the "truth content" as an independent art-theoretical model; its subject matter however, always seemed to have more and more to do with Benjamin and his situation and less and less with Goethe's *The Elective Affinities.* It is only today with the edition of the *Gesammelte Schriften* that we know that Benjamin was really involved in a critique of Stefan George and his school: "In this work we find the judicial verdict on and the execution of Friedrich Gundolf." The *Neue Deutsche Beiträge* seemed to Benjamin just the right place for his "attack on the ideology of the George school." Benjamin develops—as a dialectical model—his own "organization" of *The Elective Affinities:* "The mythic as thesis," "Redemption as antithesis," "Hope as Synthesis." According to Benjamin, "the subject matter of the book is the mythic; the content appears as a mythic shadow-play in the costumes of Goethe's time." On the other hand, Benjamin cannot accept Goethe's claim to "be presenting social conditions and the conflicts within them symbolically" (cf. Walter Benjamin, *Gesammelte Schriften,* 1/3, edited Rolf Tiedemann (Frankfurt am Main, 1974), pp. 811ff.).

3. This is a pun in the original. "Vellum" is "Papier Velin" in the German, so we have the pun *papier velin/papier vilain.*

4. Albrecht Schöne, *Goethes Farbentheologie.* Mit einem Anhang "Goethes Gedichte zur Farbenlehre" (Munich 1987). Schöne takes Goethe's remark to Stieler in 1829 seriously: "I have busied myself with this matter for forty years and have written meticulously two octavo volumes, so it is only fair that people should give me a little time and pay me a little attention!" Schöne does this, and as a literary scholar he illuminates Goethe's *Theory of Color* as a *Theology of Color.* He maintains that Goethe did not talk of a possible technological disaster but of a definite "disaster caused by the new physics." "Who knows whether the epochal sickness that he thought he could diagnose in the symptom of Newton's divisible refractability of light and which he felt bound to attack, is not really a mortal disease for mankind?" (p. 135).

5. *FA,* I, 14, p. 486. Goethe says this in connection with an apparently live reading of his narrative, *Die neue Melusine:* he says that it has a great effect. He recalls that he had inherited from his father a certain didactic loquacity, and from his mother he had received the gift of "presenting in lively and forceful fashion everything that the imagination can bring forth and grasp, the gift of freshening up well-known

fairy stories and of inventing and narrating others." Doctor Gall (anatomist, phrenologist, founder of the controversial Gallean theory of the skull) is said to have asserted that he, Goethe, was "actually born to be a public speaker." Goethe shrank from this view. "For if there really were a basis for it, then everything else—because there is nothing to talk about in my nation—that I can undertake would unfortunately be an unsuccessful profession for me."

6. Friedrich von Müller/Marcel Reich-Ranicki, *Betrifft Goethe. Rede (1832) und Gegenrede (1982)* (Zürich and Munich, 1982), pp. 68ff.

7. It is a sign of true popularity that on 12 July 1988, that is, on the bicentennial, Christiane (Goethe's domestic sweetheart) was remembered in an essay by Eckhart Kleßmann.

8. To this extent, Herder's history of philosophy and *Sturm und Drang* aesthetics prepare the way for Goethe.

Chapter Six

1. In his *Tagebuch eines alten Schauspielers* (Leipzig, 1862), part 1, p. 247, the Weimar actor Eduard Genast gives an account of the Weimar production: "In the victory procession, Blücher appeared first with the Prussian army, then Schwarzenberg at the head of the Austrians, then Wittgenstein with the Russians, and Wellington brought up the rear with the English; each of these armies consisted of ten extras—so that the public could see what this struggle for the freedom of the fatherland had cost in human lives!" The chorus that was later set to music by Zelter, "Brothers arise! to free the world," referred with its refrain "At 'em, forward, at 'em" to Blücher, who was nicknamed "Marshal Forwards." Zelter gave Goethe an account of the performance on 8 November 1814 in the Berlin Academy of Singing at which Blücher was present; the old man was in tears, Zelter wrote to Goethe.

2. Boisserée, *Sulpiz Boisserée. Tagebücher, 1808–1854*, ed. Hans-Joachim Weitz, 4 vols. (Darmstadt, 1978), I, 314.

3. It should be remembered that it was during this time that Goethe wrote his essay *Sankt Rochus Fest zu Bingen*. In a letter to Sulpice Boisserée in September 1816 he characterizes this essay as "a cheerful representation that is at heart pious." And he had previously hoped that his essay would have a cheerful effect.

4. When Thomas Bernhard heard that I had been invited in 1978 to give a lecture on Hesse in Teheran, he spontaneously expressed the wish to accompany me. We had to go to Shiraz, to Hafiz's grave (without Hafiz, there would have been no *East-West Divan*). In Shiraz, as we were standing in front of Hafiz's grave that had been turned into a monument in 1939, Bernhard said that Hafiz was alive, and we found Goethe's words prophetic: "His memory is praised in the army of lovers, whenever the name Hafiz is mentioned in well-informed company."

5. In German the word for "lump" (*Klumpen*) and the word for "tankard" (*Humpen*) rhyme.

6. Annemarie Schimmel has something important to say on this question: "This characteristic is at the center of Islamic piety; for, as in Christianity, Mary had to be

a virgin, in order to conceive the uncreated word of God that was to be incarnate through her and given to the world, so the prophet had to be illiterate, so that the uncreated word that was to manifest itself through him as a book could be preserved in its purity. He was a vessel, unsullied by intellectual knowledge, so that he could pass on the word that was entrusted to him in total purity." Of the flight of the prophet, she writes, "Almost every great Persian epic contains a special chapter—after general praise of the prophet—in which the poet describes with the highest degree of imagination the heavenly journey that the prophet undertook on his elegant mount, Boraq, with its human face. The poets describe in ever-fresh images how Mahomet rides along the Milky Way through the spheres of the sun and the moon, talking to the prophets, surrounded by magnificently colored angels, until he reaches the divine presence, where Gabriel remains behind" (Annemarie Schimmel, *Mystische Dimensionen des Islam* [Aalen, 1979], p. 244).

7. In the *Tages und Jaheshefte* for 1817 we read, "for the sake of the Divan I continued my studies of oriental characteristics and spent a lot of time at them; but since the manuscript is so important in the Orient it is hardly strange that I devoted myself energetically to calligraphy, with little or no knowledge of the language, and for pleasure and profit I tried to imitate oriental manuscripts that I had seen before, even decorating them traditionally. The effect of these intellectual and technical efforts will not escape the attentive reader of the poems" (*WA*, I, 36, pp. 125f.).

8. Katharina Mommsen, *Goethe und die arabische Welt* (Frankfurt am Main, 1988). She quotes Goethe: "We find magnificent treasures among the Arabs . . . the most loyal devotion to family members, desire for honor, bravery, irreconcilable lust for revenge, softened by the sorrows of love, charity, sacrifice, all of them limitless." Mommsen points out with justification that in Fritz Strich's seminal work, *Goethe und die Weltliteratur,* Goethe's relationship to Arabian literature is not once mentioned. Now we have this overall treatment of Goethe's relationship to the Arabian world. From 1953 onwards Mommsen has treated the theme in numerous publications.

9. Goethe tells in his *Cipher* of "a different way" of communicating. It is "ingenious and affectionate" and at the same time "on an equal footing with the highest literature." The complete passage runs:

> But to get to our real purpose, let us recall a well-known but still secret way of communicating in code. If two people, who have agreed upon a book, fashion page and line numbers into a letter, they are certain that the recipient will work out the meaning without much trouble.
>
> The song that we call *Cipher* is about such an agreement. Lovers will agree to use Hafiz's poems as a tool for their exchange of feelings; they will indicate the page and the line that express their present state, and in this way poems will be created which are most beautifully expressive. Splendid scattered passages of the inestimable poet will be linked by passion and feeling; affection and choice lend an inner life to the whole, and those who are far apart find a comforting devotion, as they adorn their sorrow with pearls of his writings. (*WA,* I, 7, pp. 130f.)

10. Goethe's poem *Ginkgo biloba* is popular in Japan. The ginkgo leaf is the symbol of Tokyo and of the University of Tokyo. When I lectured there in November 1985 a German scholar jokingly drew my attention to the fact that a Japanese translator had once understood the word *Lieder* ("poems") as *Lippen* ("lips"). Did the translator answer the question as to whether Goethe wanted to make Marianne feel with his poems, his literary works, or with his lips, that he was "one and double"? Did he know, as Carmen Kahn-Wallerstein claims to have discovered, that on this 25 September, Goethe had given the thirty-one-year-old woman the one kiss in their relationship? (Carmen Kahn-Wallerstein, *Marianne von Willemer—Goethes Suleika* [Frankfurt am Main, 1984], p. 126).

11. Röte and Goethe rhyme.

12. For a long time the background to the *Divan* was a closed book to Goethe readers. Hermann Grimm, the son of Wilhelm and the nephew of Jacob Grimm researched the relationship of Marianne von Willemer to Goethe and the *Divan,* and by documenting the poetic exchange between the two assured her forever a place at Goethe's side among the pairs of lovers in world literature. Ten years after the death of Marianne von Willemer, Grimm discovered the carefully guarded secret and revealed Marianne as Goethe's "Suleika." Originally, in April 1868, Hermann Grimm turned to the publisher Harwitz with a plan to "write something about Marianne von Willemer that would be a suitable memorial to her memory." He wanted to show, what till then no one had known, "that she stood in a very special relationship to Goethe's *Divan* and that important poems in the *Divan* are by her." He wanted to add his extensive essay to an edition of the *Divan.* Apparently the publisher did not agree to the plan, and Grimm decided in 1869 to publish his article himself with the title *Goethe und Suleika.* The correspondence between Goethe and Marianne von Willemer was first published in 1877. In her correspondence with Hermann Grimm in her old age (*Im Namen Goethes. Der Briefwechsel Marianne von Willemer und Hermann Grimm,* ed. Hans-Joachim May [Frankfurt am Main, 1988]) Marianne describes her meeting with Goethe. But there was a leisurely quality about the correspondence. Marianne was seventy when the correspondence began, Hermann Grimm twenty-two and understandably totally enchanted with his "discovery." "Grandma" Marianne lived in the past and Grimm, who was later to write some great literary historical articles, made no effort to lead her into the present. In Martin Walser's words, both of them were "in Goethe's hand." This hand had once led Marianne but had then left her in the lurch: she made her contribution to Goethe's work and his life, both of which were for Goethe works of art; he did not lead her any further and she was no longer open to novelty, she could only reject the new spirit of Weimar with Liszt and Wagner, *Tannhäuser* and *Lohengrin.* Liszt and Wagner will, in her erroneous view, "be long extinguished with all their flames in the steam of time." (On the interpretation of the *Divan,* see also Christoph Perels, *Unmut, Übermut und Geheimnis* [Ortsvereinigung Hamburg der Goethe-Gesellschaft Weimar, Jahresgabe, 1987/88], pp. 4–23).

13. For Goethe there were "three sorts of translation." The first is "simply

prosaic," like Luther's Bible translation; the *Nibelungen,* in his opinion, should have been translated straight "into competent prose." The second sort of translation aims not only to assume control of the text in a foreign sense, but also to present it in its own sense. The final stage is that "where the translator would like to make the translation identical with the original, so that it will not be read instead of the other but will take its place. . . . A translation that strives to identify itself with the original comes close to an interlinear version and makes the understanding of the original much easier, and by this means we are led to the fundamental text, indeed we are driven towards it, and finally the whole circle is closed, in which the foreign and the native, the known and the unknown, approach each other" (*WA,* I, 7, pp. 237ff.).

14. Letter to Boiserée, 22 March 181, *WA,* IV, 48, p. 156.

15. "Young Germnay" (*Junges Deutschland*) was a social and literary reform movement in nineteenth-century Germany (ca. 1830–50). Largely inspired by the ideas of the French Revolution, it was opposed to the Romantic and Nationalist movements. See Georg Brandes, *Main Currents in 19th-Century German Literature,* vol. 6, *The Young Germany.*

16. Ludwig Börne, *Gesammelte Schriften* (Hamburg, 1819–34), vol. 8, pp. 119f.

17. Heinrich Heine, *Werke und Briefe,* ed. Hans Kaufmann (Berlin, 1961), vol. 5, *Die romantische Schule,* p. 58.

18. The famous quotation comes from the *Carmen heroicum* (line 1286 of his poem *De litteris, syllabis et metris Horatii*) by Tertianus Maurus, a Latin metricist living in the third century A.D. Just like the reader who takes them up, so books themselves have their own fate; that is, books have their fates according to the ability of the reader to understand them, his will to do so, and according to his cast of mind. The Börsenverein des Deutschen Buchhandels, founded in 1825, bears the quotation on its coat-of-arms. Goethe's translation, quoted here from *Maximen: J.W. Goethe. Maximen und Reflexionen,* Text der Ausgabe von 1907 mit den Erläuterungen und der Einleitung Max Heckers (Frankfurt am Main, 1976), p. 231.

19. Goethe was away when he was appointed minister. Two months later he asked for collaborators for his task. His memorandum documents what he regarded as Weimar's glorious position in the world and his own situation in it. "Weimar enjoys the fame of having spread scientific and artistic culture in Germany, indeed in the whole of Europe and, for this reason, it has become a tradition to seek good advice here in cases of doubt in scientific and artistic matters. Wieland, Herder, Schiller, and others awakened such trust that they often received such requests and they would often not honor them or would at least refuse politely. I, as the sole remaining person, have inherited these unremunerative legacies, even though I myself continually suffered from such demands and commissions."

20. A *Musenalmanach* was an annual anthology of verse, generally not previously unpublished, popular in the eighteenth and nineteenth centuries in Germany.

Chapter Seven

1. *Johann Wolfgang Goethe, "Elegie von Marienbad." Faksimile einer Urschrift, September 1823,* with a a volume of commentary by Christoph Michel and Jürgen Behrens in association with Wolf von Engelhardt, Renate Grumach, Rudolf Hirsch, Dorothea Kuhn. amd Ernst Zinn. Introduction by Arthur Henkel. Facsimile reprint of Goethe's *Schreib-calendar 1822* from the Goethe museum at the Deutsche Hochstift in Frankfurt. Unique and limited edition of 900 copies (Frankfurt am Main, 1983). Scholars could only surmise the genesis of the *Trilogy of Passion,* which included the *Marienbader Elegie.* The original manuscript of 1823 had long been missing. It reappeared in 1980 at an auction of original manuscripts in England, and the Frankfurt Hochstift succeeded in buying it. This original made it possible to determine the genesis of the poem. It was now possible to follow Goethe's idea that "works of art and of nature cannot be known when they are completed, they have to be seized upon while they are being created if we are to understand them in some degree" (to Zelter, August 1803). Goethe was "totally devoted to this half serious half playful genetic idea" (Arthur Henkel) although he tried to preserve the secret of the creation of his own works. In *Maxims and Reflections* he once more talks of the question of tradition: "The student of language and literature relies on the congruence of what is handed down in written form. The basis is a manuscript, but in it there are truly gaps, *lapsus calami* that cause a break in the sense and everything else that can be criticized in a manuscript. Then a second and a third copy turn up; the comparison of these copies means more and more that we are aware of what is comprehensible and reasonable in what is handed down. Indeed the scholar goes even further and demands of its inner meaning that it comprehend and present the congruence of what is being treated without external aids."

2. Goethe's poem *Du Schüler Howards,* that he dedicated to Ulrike von Levetzow is a nice example of the way in which he combines scholarship and literature. Luke Howard, an English meteorologist, wrote *The Climate of London* and an essay on the modification of clouds. Here Goethe found what interested him greatly and what he had been missing up till then, a classification of clouds. In 1821 Goethe wrote a poem to him, *To the Honor of Howard's Memory,* with the magnificent closing lines that sum up Howard's theory of clouds: "As a streak rises" (i.e stratus), "forms a ball" (cumulus), "flutters apart" (cirro-cumulus), "falls" (nimbus), "may the world remember you with thanks." Now Goethe is in the mood of the lover and he knows that the lover always turns up again as the "weather-watcher." This is the way the poem to Ulrike ends: "And if by silent twilight, / a most beloved faithful face / meets you on a tender threshold / do you know whether the weather is fine or it is raining?" But Goethe's situation at that time was unusual, at the beginning of his relationship with Ulrike, describing it so exactly: the verb *heitern* ("is it fine?") is striking: Goethe only uses it in one other place, and after him probably no one else uses it at all, but it keeps the poem in a state of tension (see commentary in *FA,* I, 25).

3. My teacher, Friedrich Beißner, only devoted a few lines to the poem in his

Geschichte der deutschen Elegie (Berlin, 1961). "The form of the poem is actually not elegiac, just as the conception of the experience is not purely elegiac, but is to a high degree tragic. It is not just a question of the attractive sorrow of a tender challenge and the actualizing of the past; in it the poet expresses himself in a tone of renunciation and a merciless harshness, saying that the gods have destroyed him. The 'reconciliation,' the main part of the trilogy that was written earlier, restores harmony almost exclusively for reasons of external artistic propriety.

"At the same time the verse form, even though it rhymes, is a happy choice for an elegy. It is related to the stanzas that Humboldt uses for his great elegy on Rome composed in the spirit of Schiller. The rhyming couplets that regularly fracture the cross rhyme also have something like an elegiac effect here."

Elizabeth Wilkinson wonders whether Goethe is probably not aiming, as in his other works, at protophenomena, prototypes, types; in titles like *Novelle,* ballad, idyll, elegy, at presenting in the *Trilogy of Passion* a prototype of tragic emotional structure. (Elizabeth M. Wilkinson, *Goethes Trilogie der Leidenschaft als Beitrag zur Frage der Katharsis* [Frankfurt am Main, 1957, p. 8]). In his genetic interpretation, Joachim Müller sticks to the "lyrical substance of this particular elegy and its prototypicality" in the genre question: "what is an elegy?" (Joachim Müller, "Goethes Trilogie der Leidenschaft—Lyrische Tragödie und Aussöhnende Abrundung," *Jahrbuch des Freien Deutschen Hochstifts* [1978] pp. 85–159).

4. The concept "main business" with regard to the final authorized edition appears first in a letter to Boisserée in December 1823; his "main business" that occupies him in his old age is to "secure his posthumous works and at least make a start on a complete edition of my works." With regard to the completion of *Faust,* Goethe uses the term "main business" in his diary entry on 11 February 1826 and frequently thereafter (*The Journeyman Years* are also referred to by this term).

5. The significance of Goethe's servants for his work has also been established in a scholarly monograph: Walter Schleif, *Goethes Diener* (Berlin and Weimar, 1965). Using every available source, the book treats the activity (as well as the lives) of the servants and clerks: Seidel, Sutor, Götze, Geist, Gensler, Eisfeld, Stadelmann, Schreiber, John, Färber, and Krause (a table lists chronologically all the other servants, members of the household, and secretaries). Schleif wants to emphasize Goethe's servants not as "anonymous shadows of their master," but in their roles as "noninterchangeable individuals" and also in their independence of the discriminating prejudices of the epoch—something of which Goethe's liberality was not entirely free.

6. Volume 1: engravings, woodcuts, drawings and paintings. Volume 2: carved stones, bronzes, medallions, coins, antique vases. Volume 3: mineralogical and other scientific collections (*Goethe's Kunstsammlungen,* 3 vols., ed. Christian Schuchardt [Jena, 1848–49; reprinted in one volume, Hildesheim and New York, 1976]).

7. The mention shows how few examples of his "school" the seventy-four-year-old can produce, if he has to mention authors like Schubart and Zauper who were not literary successes. Goethe talks of them in the *Tages-und Jahreshefte.* The works with which these authors "got close" to Goethe were: Karl Ernst Schubarth, *Zur*

Beurteilung Goethes mit Beziehung auf verwandte Literatur und Kunst (Breslau, 1818), and Josef Stanislaus Zauper, *Studien über Goethe. Als Nachtrag zur deutschen Poetik aus Goethe* (Vienna, 1822). Goethe included both books in his library.

8. Cotta acceded to Goethe's request and he had already received word of the manuscript from another source. Frommann, who prepared Eckermann in Jena for the world of Goethe after Eckermann had visited Goethe in Weimar, told Cotta in July 1823 of Goethe's great interest in the publication of this work. He (Frommann) knew Eckermann personally, valued him as an "honest, upright, original, and completely modest man"—a good characterization after so short an acquaintance! And he wrote, "I realize that there will not be much profit in publishing the work but in doing so you are doing a truly good work, which may in the future bear fruit in a quite different way" (*Goethe und Cotta, Briefwechsel, 1797–1832,* ed. Dorothea Kuhn, 3 vols. [Stuttgart, 1983], 3/2, p. 91). How right Frommann was, and yet publishing something as a favor is a difficult thing for a publisher to do. It is difficult and not infrequently delicate to use recommendations and suggestions of this sort from authors or advisers who are paid for that purpose, or even from well-wishers. On the one hand the publisher must reserve the right to accept or reject a manuscript according to his own criteria; on the other hand he must reckon with disappointment and annoyance on the part of the people doing the recommending and this is especially complicated when house authors are involved who set great store by a specific area of the house's publications. Even today a publisher can have the most remarkable experiences. A philosopher recommends a young author's manuscript to his publisher; the publisher reads it and takes a long time over his decision, but the philosopher to whom the manuscript is very important has already offered it to another publisher and, when the book is published by them, the philosopher reviews it as "the spearhead of a new tendency in contemporary German philosophy."

9. Martin Walser, *In Goethes Hand. Szenen aus dem 19. Jahrhundert* (Frankfurt am Main, 1984). Walser explains Eckermann's self-sacrificing devotion to Goethe's personality and work by the relationship of German classicism to German history.

Chapter Eight

1. As far as I am concerned, an irresponsible dedication. The whole text of Fichte's entry runs: "I saw you as a dear little boy, and loved you before you knew me. Perhaps I shall see you as a youth and as you grow to maturity. The nation has great demands of you, the only son of the unique man of our age. Count me then among those who will watch you with the greatest attention, to see whether you develop into someone worthy to fill your father's place, because I think I am among those who understand his worth most deeply and love him without envy. May this page serve as a warning, but also as a consolation" (in J. G. Fichte, *Gesamtausgabe der Bayerischen Akademie der Wissenschaften,* ed. Reinhard Lauth and Hans Gliwitzky, *Briefe,* volume 5, pp. 520f.). See also Walther Vulpius's statement: "Das Stammbuch von August von Goethe," in *Deutsche Rundschau,* vol. 68 (1891).

2. *Briefe: Goethe in vetraulichen Briefen seiner Zeitgenossen,* gesammelt von Wilhelm Bode, neu herausgegeben von Regine Otto und Paul-Gerhard Wenzlaff, 3 vols. (Munich, 1982; originally Boston and Weimar), vol. 3, p. 175.

3. The decree reads as follows:

> Both parties join together to fuse the correspondence between Schiller and Goethe. Goethe will take over the editing and intends to be as discreet as possible without doing damage to the interest of the contents; he will provide a clean manuscript which will form the basis for the printing. The manuscript can be delivered to the publisher in parts in order to facilitate printing. The book will be in royal octavo in accordance with the works of Schiller and Goethe; no volume shall exceed thirty signatures. There may be three or more volumes; this can only be determined on greater familiarity with the whole manuscript. The royalties for the volume would be two thousand Saxon Reichstaler, deadlines for payment to be determined when deadlines for delivery of the manuscript are agreed. Attention must be given to the length of time that the publisher shall hold the rights of publication and the conditions upon which future editions shall be produced. Thought might also be given to a smaller, less expensive edition, which recently seems to have become absolutely necessary. The income will be shared equally between both parties, partial payments will also be shared equally between the interested parties. This is without prejudice to the settlement of further details.
>
> Weimar 25 March 1824   Goethe
>
> (*Goethe-Cotta,* 2, pp. 112f.)

4. Naturally, Goethe had assumed that Cotta would be very interested in the originals; not only because Cotta could enrich his archives with such original manuscripts but because with Goethe as editor small differences existed between what was presented for printing and the originals. For this reason Goethe determined—and Frau von Schiller agreed—that the correspondence should remain sealed for twenty-five years and be placed in the hands of the Weimar government. It would only be completely edited after this period had expired. After the lapse of twenty-five years, Goethe's and Schiller's heirs were to be able to sell the whole batch. Cotta's grandson, Carl von Cotta, bought the whole lot and put it at the disposal of the Grand Duchess Sophie of Weimar for the Weimar edition. The originals are today in the Goethe-Schiller archives in Weimar.

5. Dorothea Kuhn managed to discover the following from the fragments of Georg von Cotta's diaries, that are now the private property of the Freiherr von Gemmingen-Guttenberg: "The burden of his indebtedness had become so great in 1826 that his children, Georg and Ida, had to take over guarantees to the sum of 250,000 gulden against the estates that they had inherited from their mother. Georg regarded this as a great sacrifice. He concludes his 1826 diary with the words: 'This year my father assumed the complete edition of Schiller's works for a period of twenty years at a cost of 70,000 thalers or 136,000 gulden, then Goethe's works for 60,000 thalers or about 108,000 gulden, finally Herder's and other works for nearly 60,000

gulden, then the purchase of this large town house [the Leuchtenberg Palais in Munich for 80,000 gulden], together a sum of nearly 400,000 gulden, or about 210,000 thalers. I can scarcely understand how he can justify all this. I enter the new year seriously and full of care, as always . . . ' " (from fragments of the diaries of Georg von Cotta, in *Goethe-Cotta,* 3/2, p.163).

6. Gervinus was the famous literary historian and politician, one of the "Göttingen Seven" (seven professors, among them the brothers Grimm, who were dismissed from the University of Göttingen for liberal political activity), honorary professor at Heidelberg, member of the Frankfurt National assembly, and later accused of high treason. He published his *Einleitung in die Geschichte des 19. Jahrhunderts* in 1853. He was convinced that the tendency of the century was bound to lead to democracy and freedom. The work caused a scandal. Gervinus was indicted for "urging high treason and incitement against the constitutional monarchy." The University of Heidelberg withdrew his right to teach. The verdict of two months' imprisonment was voided on appeal, but he was never formally declared "not guilty." The Insel Verlag published the documents in this case for the first time in 1967: *Der Hochverratsprozeß gegen Gervinus,* ed. Walter Boehlich.

7. See *Das Leben und Sterben der Kindermörderin Susanna Margaretha Brandt.* According to the records of the trial in the Free Imperial City of Frankfurt am Main, the *Criminalia, 1771,* presented by Siegfried Birkner, with contemporary illustrations (Frankfurt am Main 1989). The volume documents the criminal trial that lasted from August 1771 to January 1772, and through the individual case it gives us insights into the social structures of the time. Reproductions of drawings and engravings also give a vivid impression of Frankfurt in the second half of the eighteenth century.

8. *Neue Nürnbergische gelehrte Zeitung,* 30 July/3 August 1790.

9. Goethe has the Lord say that the devil may feel completely free, but that the true "sons of God" are to enjoy his creation. They stand in contrast to the fallen angels, with whom Mephistopheles belongs. In *Shakespeares Tag,* Goethe wrote, "what we call evil is only the obverse of good." Goethe always saw things in this light.

10. As told to the author in a letter from Waltraud Hagen.

11. As an example of its effect in the twentieth century we may mention the great treatise *Faust und Helena. Zu Goethes Auffassung vom Schönen und der Realität des Realen im Zweiten Teil des "Faust,"* by Wolfgang Schadewaldt (first published in the *Deutsche Vierteljahrschrift* 30 [1956]), now in *Spiegelungen: Goethe im 20. Jahrhundert. Spiegelungen und Deutungen,* ed. Hans Mayer, new edition (Frankfurt am Main, 1987). The classical scholar Schadewaldt aims to give the "elemental horizon" of the work; he is concerned with the figure of Helena, her being and effect as the ultimate beauty, and her connection with Faust through which Goethe wishes to show the meeting of classicism and romanticism, between Greece and the West as a reality—something that had so many consequences for modern Europe. Goethe, in Schadewaldt's judgment, shows "as a poet, in images and figures, *what* is and *how it is;* the exisiting in its own sort of double historicity, man in his tragic ambiguity; and

he does this in his advanced old age with the affirmative lack of illusion with which he had formerly looked gloomily at time and at man, while yet being able to utter the words: "No matter what it is like, life is good." *Ens est bonum* (p.450). See further, Wilhelm Emrich, *Die Symbolik von Faust II* (Berlin, 1943); Benno von Wiese in chapter 4 of his *Deutsche Tragödie von Lessing bis Hebbel* (Hamburg, 1948); Werner Milch, *Wandlungen der Faust-Deutung,* in *Zeitschrift für deutsche Philologie* (1951); Heinz Schlaffer, *Faust Zweiter Teil. Die Allegorie des 19. Jahrhunderts* (Stuttgart, 1981).

Index